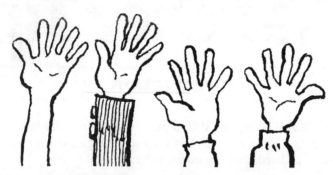

Learning Magazine's

SUPERBOOK
of Teacher Tips

Illustrated by Bob Walsh

Learning Magazine's
SUPERBOOK of Teacher Tips

Introduction

Within the pages of this book, you'll find more than 800 of the best tips, time-savers, and curriculum ideas published in *Learning* Magazine over 18 years. All have been revised, updated, and organized for easy use.

The ideas presented here are the ones teachers all across the country have found most effective in managing their classrooms and motivating students.

You'll find ideas for everything from welcoming students back to school to making an end-of-the-year memory book, from keeping track of lunch money to planning a Valentine's Day treasure hunt, from inspiring poetry writing to spotlighting a student to build self-esteem. Every area of the curriculum is covered. And there are chapters on thinking skills, class management, self-esteem, and more.

To use the book, just look in the table of contents for the general area you're interested in, then quickly scan for the specific subcategory that will meet your needs. Say, for example, you're teaching fractions and want to liven up the lesson. Go right to the Math chapter, Fractions section, and you'll find "Fraction walk," "Filling in wholes," "Fractions in a kit," and many more.

Or, if you're tired of the same old Halloween activities and want something new, go to the Holidays chapter, Halloween section, for plenty of spooky, sparky ideas such as "Cats on the prowl," "Creature cookout," and "Monstrous messages."

In the Language Arts chapter, you'll find more than 40 approaches just for writing.

Or, browse through the *SUPERBOOK.* You're sure to hit on lots of new ideas or creative variations on the ones you're already using. The class management ideas and general tips will work for any grade level. And many of the curriculum and art ideas can be adapted for use throughout the grades.

You'll refer to the *SUPERBOOK of Teacher Tips* again and again throughout the year—and for years to come.

Chapter 7 Social Studies

Chapter 8 Thinking Skills

Chapter 9 Art

Chapter 10 Holidays

Chapter 11 Potpourri

Chapter 12 End of Year

Project Director **Jeanette Moss**
Editor **Maureen Pross**
Assistant Editor **Rose Foltz**
Copy Editor **Nancy Papsin**
Teacher Consultant **Karen Hansen**
Production Manager **Katherine Murphy**
Production Designer **Donald Knauss**

Editorial Director **Charlene Gaynor**
Design Director **Edward Rosanio**
Director of Production **Bacil Guiley**

© 1991 by Springhouse Corporation

For information about Learning
Institute education seminars,
write: Springhouse Corporation,
1111 Bethlehem Pike, Springhouse, PA 19477-0908.

CHAPTER 1
BACK TO SCHOOL

First-day guidebook

An orientation guidebook for each student will ease the settling-in process.

The guidebook's cover—in addition to welcoming your students — could show the school's name, address, and phone number, and your name and room number.

Inside, you might include:

- a staff directory that introduces the principal, the secretary, the nurse, the custodian, and so on
- a simplified floor plan of the school (which could come in handy later during map study)
- listings of school calendar dates and events—holidays, conference days, vacations, even an occasional just-for-fun celebration
- a sample daily schedule
- a sneak preview of unit topics to be covered during the year
- a brief statement on classroom policy and procedures
- several blank pages for students to write the names and telephone numbers of classmates and record personal reminders and notes.—*Arlene Orensky, Taiwan, Republic of China*

First-day fun

Have a welcome packet of activities on each student's desk the first day of school. Early arrivers will have something interesting to do as you greet their classmates.

In a simple container, such as a Ziploc bag, include several activities. A typical packet for early graders might contain:

- a top sheet of paper with "Welcome to Second Grade" printed on it. Ask students to make as many words as they can from these letters. You can vary directions by requiring words of no less than three letters, no plurals, and so on.

- a questionnaire titled "All About Me." Ask questions about students' families; how they spend their free time; and what makes them happy, afraid, or sad. Have them list their favorite foods, games, and TV shows.

- puzzles made from magazine pictures or small posters. Instruct students to put the puzzles together, glue them to backing, then write a paragraph or story about them.

- a name tag for each child to decorate and prop up on his desk.

- a gift from you—such as a pencil, eraser, or small memo pad.—*Pam Engel, Wabash, Ind.*

Sliding by

Welcome your new class with a slide presentation featuring the special activities that the school year will bring.

Use photos of favorite projects from last year that you plan to repeat this year. Possibilities include slides of finished art projects, science experiments, social studies displays, learning centers, book jackets, and field trip sites.—*Jan Hoffman, Janesville, Wis.*

A beary good tour

Take early-grade students on this fun tour of an unfamiliar school, and grab the chance to teach them school rules as you go. To pull it off, you'll need to do advance planning with the school staff.

Tell your students that you were baking some gingerbread bears for a cookie treat, but the bears ran away toward the media center.

Of course students will want to look for the bears. At the media center, your students meet the librarian, who just found a note from the bears written in big, block letters. It explains library rules and directs the group to the next stop on the tour.

The hunt continues through the music room, gym, art room, lunchroom, restroom, and nurse's office—to all the rooms and staff students will need to know. In each location, a note from the bears explains the rules of that room. The final destination is the office, where your students meet the principal and find (and eat!) the cookies.—*Jacqueline McTaggart, Independence, Iowa*

Welcome aboard!

Help your students feel more at-home the first day of school by sending them a "welcome aboard" letter before school starts.

Make the hand-written note short and include a greeting, along with your name, the date and time that school opens, your room number, and what supplies to bring.

If you can't write to your students before school starts, you can still welcome them after the fact. These letters won't include the same orientation information; instead, you can refer to upcoming events. And because you've already met your students, you can personalize each note.—*Mamie E. Wiley, Bloomington, Ind.*

Cruising into the new year

Before school starts, send your students invitations to cruise into the new year with you.

Decorate the "ship" (classroom) with streamers, balloons, and a banner saying "Welcome Aboard the USS (your last name)."

Arrange the bulletin board to announce the scheduled stops (subjects), the daily schedule, the deck plan (seating chart), and the names of the captain and first mate (teacher and aide). Have the ship's pool (library area) tempt all to "Dive into a Good Book"; make sure tales of the sea and treasure hunts abound.

Plan a first-week-of-school bon voyage party. Have the principal come to see the ship off. And in the ship's galley (teacher's workroom), treat your students to a tray of cheese, crackers, fruit, and champagne (sparkling grape juice).

Hang cruise ship posters on the walls, set up games "on deck," and play calypso music for shipboard entertainment. At week's end, have your "passengers" write postcards about their cruise.—*Barbara Anderson, Waverly, Iowa*

Early greeting

Along with a short, personal note of greeting, send your new students a mini survey with questions about their summer vacations. For example:

- How have you helped around the house this summer?
- Write five things you've learned.
- Name some books you've read.
- List five things you've done.
- What do you remember most about the last school year?
- What are you looking forward to in the next school year?

Ask the students to bring their completed surveys on the first day of school. These can be the basis for a "getting-to-know-you" session.—*Julie Polak, Bucyrus, Ohio*

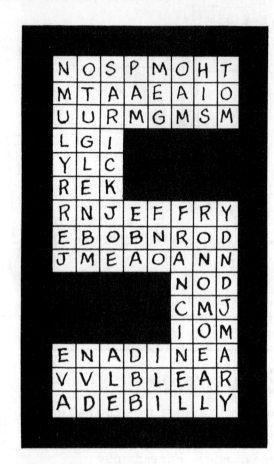

"Welcome" name search

On a sheet of paper, draw an outline of the numeral representing your grade level. Insert horizontal and vertical lines to form a grid within the numeral.

Using one letter per box, "hide" the first names of all your students and your own last name within a matrix of random letters. The names can read in any direction— vertically, horizontally, diagonally; forward or backward.

Include the following instructions, changing the specifics to refer to your own class: "Welcome to grade 5! Can you find the first names of your 30 classmates in this name grid? Can you also find my name?"

Put a copy on every desk before your students arrive on the first day of school.—*J. Royce Brunk, Hesston, Kan.*

You're invited

Dispel your new students' first-day anxiety—and perhaps even instill a little excitement—by sending them personal invitations to the big event.

A week or two before school starts, send each child an invitation (either homemade or store-bought) that notes all the relevant information—date, time, room number, and so on. Include a short personal comment, such as "Hope you can make it!"— *Cathy Toohey, Corona del Mar, Calif.*

Balloon notes

This surefire giggle starter makes for fun introductions.

In balloons put silly messages—one per balloon— such as, "Jump up and down three times" or "Do a somersault." Then, add a small gift and blow up the balloons.

On the first day of school, have your students introduce themselves. Then invite each child to pop a balloon and follow the silly instructions inside.—*Lorre Degani, Richardson, Tex.*

Happy New Year!

Create a festive welcome for your students by splashing "Happy New Year" in bold, colorful letters across the bulletin board and hanging streamers and balloons from the ceiling. Provide each student with party favors, such as pencils, folders, bookmarks, stickers, and erasers.—*Joni Becker, Litchfield, Ill.*

SUPER-DUPER BACK-TO-SCHOOL QUIZ

Directions: Check each question yes or no.

1. Did you visit any of the following places this summer? Yes ☐ No ☐
a. the moon
b. the Land of Oz
c. dreamland
d. the local supermarket
e. a park
f. any other place _____
_____

2. Did you travel by any of the following means? Yes ☐ No ☐
a. camel or ricksha
b. skateboard or skates
c. hang glider
d. roller coaster
e. foot
f. other _____
_____

3. Did you talk with any of the following? Yes ☐ No ☐
a. the president of the United States
b. Mickey Mouse
c. Santa Claus
d. a professional baseball player
e. a relative (uncle, aunt, cousin)
f. any other interesting person _____
_____

4. Did you build any of the following? Yes ☐ No ☐
a. a rocket ship
b. a sand castle
c. house of cards
d. a lemonade stand
e. a friendship
f. any other thing _____
_____

5. Did you catch any of the following? Yes ☐ No ☐
a. a butterfly
b. a thief
c. a cold
d. a ball
e. the wind
f. any other thing _____
_____

6. Did you get wet in any of the following ways? Yes ☐ No ☐
a. diving for treasure
b. riding river rapids
c. taking a bath or shower
d. playing with squirt guns
e. trying to find the end of a rainbow
f. other_____
_____

7. Did you see any of the following? Yes ☐ No ☐
a. a shooting star
b. a movie star
c. a flying saucer
d. a concert
e. an old friend
f. anything else _____
_____

8. Did you read any of the following? Yes ☐ No ☐
a. a friend's palm
b. a wonderful book
c. the newspaper
d. a street sign
e. a fortune cookie
f. anything else _____
_____

9. Did you lose any of the following? Yes ☐ No ☐
a. your memory
b. your allowance
c. your way (how did you get back?)
d. a fight

e. a game
f. a tooth
g. anything else _____
_____

10. Did you learn any of the following? Yes ☐ No ☐
a. how to become invisible
b. how to tie a knot
c. how to tell time
d. how to ride a bike
e. how to throw a curve-ball
f. how to cook an egg (or anything else)
g. how to do anything else
_____
_____

11. Did you do anything else you'd like to mention? Yes ☐ No ☐
a. Mention it here _____
_____

HOW TO SCORE YOUR QUIZ
Give yourself 10 points for each yes.

- If you got 0 to 30 points, you probably slept through most of the summer.
- If you got 40 to 60 points, sounds as if it was a so-so vacation.
- If you got 70 to 90 points, sounds as if things were cooking.
- If you got 100 points or more, sounds as if you had a good time—just as we'll be having this year.

Name games

These two card games can help students learn to know and read their classmates' names.

To prepare for the games, cut out twice as many oak tag playing cards as there are students in your class. Write each student's name on two cards—first name on one, last name on another. Then, invite your students to play Go Fish; a student's first and last name is a match.

For a whole-class game of Concentration, glue pockets on a large piece of poster board and place one name card backward in each pocket. Have students match first and last names.— *Bonnie Hughes, Ft. Wayne, Ind.*

Everyone has a story

Try these activities to show your students that even adults have stories to tell:

- Compile a loose-leaf chronicle of your life in photos from birth to the present, and share the portfolio with your students. As you show the pictures, relate anecdotes of your school days, vacations, wedding, family, pets, and some of the classes you've taught. Encourage your students to ask any questions they wish. Place your album in the class library, so parents, new students, and visitors can find out all about you too.

- Ask your students to bring in school-age photos of their parents. Then, invite them to guess who belongs to whom. Carefully mount parent and child photos side by side on the bulletin board.—*Susan Farley, Rochester, N.Y., and VaReane Heese, Springfield, Neb.*

How do you feel...?

Sharing thoughts and feelings about everyday experiences helps kids get to know each other and helps you get to know them. Suggest some of the "How do you feel?" situations below to get your new class acquainted, or invite students to talk about the items in pairs or small groups.

How do you feel when...
...it's late at night?
...you're reading a story in class?
...you're going to a party?
...someone else wins the game?
...you're on top of the slide?
...you're home alone?
...you don't know how to play a game?
...you earn some money?
...you walk in puddles?
...you see yourself in a mirror?
...you hear a siren?
...you're the first in line?
...you write your name?
...you're in a new place?
...someone asks to be your friend?
...you're eating an egg?
...you talk on the telephone?
...you see a big dog?
...you find money on the ground?

Encourage your students to go beyond simple "good," "bad," "scared," "proud" responses by having them tell a little about their experiences. Be sure to allow time for them to consider each situation before asking for reactions.— *Carolyn Bollenback, Rosemead, Calif.*

Paired interviews

To prepare your students for interviewing each other, ask them to think of questions that can't be answered with yes or no. Suggest they focus on questions beginning with "who," "what," "when," "where," or "why."

Now, pair your students, and give them 10 minutes to interview each other and to prepare brief statements about their partners.

When time is up, call the class into a circle. Invite each student to introduce his partner and relate one or two interesting facts about him.—*Roberta Gordon, Lincoln, Mass.*

Get-acquainted bingo

This personalized variation of bingo is a great icebreaker during the first weeks of school. Instead of numbers, information about your students fills the squares; children must ask each other questions to play the game.

To prepare the bingo card, draw a grid—five rows across, five down. (If you have more than 25 students, prepare a larger grid.) Next, fill each block with a few words that describe something unique to each student, such as "took a trip to Mexico this summer," "has red hair," "has five brothers and sisters." Be sure to include each student. If you have leftover blocks, you could make them free spaces or include facts about yourself.

Give a copy of the card to each student. Players must now find who fits the description in each block. When they find the boy with red hair or the girl who went to Mexico, they must ask their classmate to sign the appropriate block. The game ends when a student has all the squares of his card signed or when you call time.—*Kathy Klein, Dubuque, Iowa*

What's your bag?

Before the first day of school, send each student a letter and a small paper bag with the following instructions:

"Attached to this letter is a lunch bag. Please fill this bag with about 10 items that tell something about you, and bring it to school on the first day. Here are some ideas:

- something in your favorite color
- the wrapper from your favorite snack
- the best book you've read
- something you collect
- something that tells about your favorite sport. (Hint: Use a picture of a soccer ball instead of the real thing.)"

In class, have your students take turns introducing themselves by explaining the contents of their bags.— *Susan Hoffman, Vernon, Conn.*

Who's Who?

At the end of the first week of school, gather the class outdoors in a large circle. Give each student a pencil and piece of paper.

Have your students write their first names, then fill in the first names of their classmates in clockwise order around the circle. Tell your students to put question marks in place of names they don't know.

Encourage students to approach one another to learn the names of the "mystery persons" on their lists. Repeat the activity a week later, this time including last names.—*Dorothy Westwood, Obispo, Calif.*

Class composite

On a large piece of poster board, draw the grade level numeral of your class. Cut the numeral out and score it into as many puzzle pieces as there are children in the class. (Before cutting the pieces apart, number them in order so that re-assembling the numeral later won't be such a puzzle.)

Give each student a puzzle piece to decorate in a personal way. Encourage students to include a self-portrait, a drawing of a pet or favorite toy, symbols for hobbies, and the like.

When your students have completed their puzzle pieces, have them reassemble the numeral on a bulletin board. During the assembling process, encourage students to explain the significance of the pictures and symbols they used.—*Amy Ferraro, Endicott, N.Y.*

Trash tells all

Turn your students into archaeologists by having them examine getting-to-know-you trash.

Prepare a box of your personal trash for your students to scrutinize. Items you might include: a cryptic note, a parakeet feather, a cash register tape, tickets from a show or concert, a candy wrapper.

Allow some time for students to examine the trash, and then plan a follow-up session to give the archaeologists a chance to ask questions about the raw data. Try having them frame their questions in such a way that your answers will be only yes or no.

Have students collect some get-acquainted garbage of their own. Then arrange some student-to-student archaeology sessions.— *Grace Welton, Rancho Cordova, Calif.*

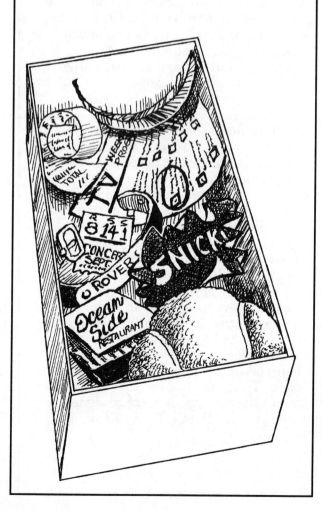

Spotlight on new students

Join with your co-workers to introduce the new students at your grade level to the whole school.

Invite student volunteers throughout the grade level to interview newcomers. After brainstorming a list of questions, have the volunteers conduct the interviews and create biographies of the newcomers. Display the biographies in a central school location.—*Frances Srulowitz and Maria Duggan, Wayland, Mass.*

Feet first

Prepare a "Start the Year on the Right Foot" bulletin board. To kick off the activity, pin up a labeled, decorated paper cutout of your right foot. As your students arrive the first day, invite them to make their own foot shapes to add to the display.—*Helen M. Lounsburg, East Berne, N.Y.*

Personal portraits

Start the new year off with an art project that introduces you to your students and your students to each other.

Make a collage, using words and pictures that depict your interests, talents, goals, hobbies, and family life. Ask your students to guess what they can about you from the clues.

Complete the activity by having your students make their own personality portraits, trading them with a classmate, and discussing each other's interests.—*Alysa Cummings, Audubon, N.J.*

Dear teacher

Use a first-day writing activity to get to know your students.

First, compose an introductory letter that describes you, your family, hobbies, and pets. Write the letter on the chalkboard or display it on an overhead projector.

Then, ask your students to write back. Have them tell you who they are, what they like or dislike, something about their families, and anything else they'd like you to know.— *Rebecca Webster Graves, Burlington, N.C.*

Postcard portraits

For a getting-to-know-you activity geared toward making the summer last, have your students make individual postcard packets spotlighting themselves instead of vacation locales.

Give each student a strip of paper 5½ x 24 inches. Measure and fold the strip accordian-style to make six postcard-sized panels. In the top panel, the child puts his name and photo (or crayoned self-portrait). In the other panels he writes or draws pictures of his hobbies, favorite foods, goals for the year, anything that describes him.

Make a display of the finished "postcards," and label it "Greetings from Me." When you dismantle the display, encourage students to send their "souvenir" packets to a grandparent or faraway friend.—*Elizabeth Dwyer, Bowie, Md.*

Mystery people

This activity puts each of your students in the spotlight and helps the class get acquainted at the same time.

Ask your students to prepare personal profile paragraphs, including such information as age, appearance, family size, best and worst school subjects, interests, and favorites. Have students sign their names lightly on the backs of their papers.

Over the next 2 weeks, whenever you have a bit of time, post a paragraph with the caption "Who's the Mystery Person?" Students read and ponder the paragraph, make their guesses on signed slips of paper, and deposit them in a box.

Close the guessing session after a reasonable time and distribute a sheet with 10 questions covering the various categories in the profile.

When students finish answering the questions, go over them together following this procedure: As the first question is answered, have all students fitting that description stand. As subsequent questions are answered, those still fitting the description remain standing; others sit down. Eventually, only the Mystery Person will be standing.—*Mildred J. Sims, Champaign, Ill.*

Friend for a day

This activity, spread over the first few weeks of the new school year, stresses writing and drawing skills while helping your students get acquainted.

Provide each child with a folder labeled "My Special Friends." Then prepare a name-draw box and every morning have each child draw a classmate's name. The person whose name is drawn becomes that child's "special friend" for the day. (Each child will be both the giver and receiver of special attention.)

Invite students to ask their new friends one or two questions. Next, have students write down the information the friends gave them, label it with the friend's name, and file it in their folders.

Then, have each student draw a picture for his special friend, depicting one of the favorite things or funny experiences revealed in the interview. The student should write his name at the bottom of the picture, and on the back he should write something he likes about his special friend.

Set aside a time for your students to deliver their drawings and share with the class information they learned in their interviews. —*Donna Anderson, Spencerport, N.Y.*

Helping new students fit in

The start of the school year is particularly tough for students new to the school. Here are eight ways you can help them feel more comfortable:

1. Ask *all* students to introduce themselves to the rest of the class and tell a little about themselves.

2. Appoint a temporary "buddy" for each new student.

3. Remind your class to include new students in recess and lunch activities.

4. Arrange for new students to tour the school building; include introductions to key staff members.

5. Don't give a new student too much attention—it could be embarrassing or make other students jealous and reluctant to be his friend.

6. Explain school rules to the entire class, even if most students know them. Suggest your PTA put together a book of school rules and schedules for new students' parents.

7. Explain special schoolwide or classroom events to new students.

8. New parents are nervous too. Call them at the end of the week and let them know how their child is adjusting to his new school.—*Brenda Johnson, Grand Forks, N.D.*

Easy name tags

Cut pencil shapes about 6 inches long from wood-grain, self-stick shelf paper. With a black permanent felt-tip pen draw on a few pencil details: a

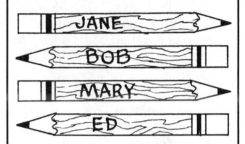

black point for the lead, a ragged edge where the sharpened end begins, two lines to indicate the eraser. Then, on each pencil print a student's first name in large, black letters.

To reuse the name tags, have students stick them to waxed paper at the end of the day.—*Laurie Carlson, Gilbert, Ariz.*

Who's (1,1)(4,1)(3, 2)?

Here's a get-acquainted activity with a mathematical twist.

On the chalkboard, draw a number grid with all the letters of the first names of your students where the gridlines intersect. (The one shown here can be used for at least 21 names.) On separate cards, write the first name of each student.

Review with your students the basic rule for reading coordinates: The first number indicates the number of intersections to be counted on the horizontal axis; the second number represents intersections on the vertical axis.

Practice with a few letter examples and then a name or two. Then have students take turns drawing a name card, writing the coordinates on the board, and calling on classmates to "decode" the name.—*June T. Page, Wilmington, Del.*

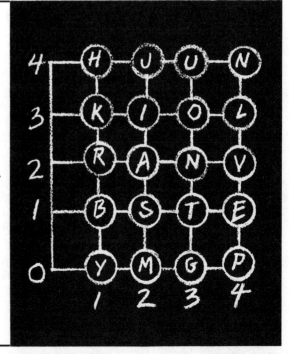

Name that food

To practice names, divide the class into groups of seven or less, and ask each child to think of a food that begins with the same letter as his name. Player One might say, "I'm Tina and I like taffy." Player Two says, "Tina likes taffy. I'm Matt and I like milk shakes." When one group is finished, start over with the next.—*Helen M. Lounsburg, East Berne, N.Y.*

Remember when...

This double-duty activity helps your students get to know one another and provides writing ideas.

Take a photo of each child and paste it onto a circular piece of paper or tagboard, representing a flower blossom. For the stem of the flower, use a strip of green construction paper, and on it write "I remember...."

Distribute three or four cutout paper leaves to each student. Invite the children to think about past experiences, events, and discoveries. Help your students compose brief endings to the sentence that hint at a story: "...when I got my cat, Snuffy," "...the time Grandma took me fishing." Have students write an ending on each leaf and attach it to their flower's stem.

Hold small-group question-and-answer sessions to help students use their idea leaves for writing. Invite children to read aloud other group members' leaves. Then have the members request further information.—*Marlene Keret, Albany, Calif.*

"Me" dolls

Reading, writing, getting acquainted, and building self-concepts—these six-page booklets in the shape of a doll can help with all four.

Use tagboard to make two cutout doll figures about 12 inches tall for each of your students. These will serve as front and back covers. (The shapes can be individualized to show a bit of dress or slacks, varying hair styles, and so on.) Next cut five copies of each shape from plain white paper for each doll. These will be the pages.

To dress each booklet's front cover doll, cut a tracing of the clothing pattern on colored or self-sticking paper. For the face, apply a disk of foil to create a mirror effect.

Assemble the booklets by stapling the covers and pages at the dolls' shoulders, leaving the lower edge free for turning pages. On the front cover write, "Read about Tanya" and Tony, and so on. Now your students can fill the pages of the booklets with information about themselves. The pages might go as follows:
Page 1. My name is _____
Page 2. I live at_____
Page 3. My phone number is _____
Page 4. My birthday is _____
       I am _____ years old
Page 5. I like _____
As an art project, invite your students to color their dolls' hair, skin, shoes.—*Mary Ellen Killelea, Worcester, Mass.*

Making new friends

Try to find a classmate who fits each of these descriptions, then ask that person to sign on the line. Even if you don't fill all the lines, see how many different names you can get—and how many new friends you can meet.

Find someone who...

1. is taller than you _____
2. is left-handed _____
3. walks to school _____
4. has curly hair _____
5. has no sisters or brothers _____
6. has initials that spell a word _____
7. was born in your town _____
8. is new to your school _____
9. went camping this summer _____
10. is the oldest child in the family _____
11. has an unusual pet _____
12. collects stamps _____
13. has blue eyes _____
14. was in your class last year _____
15. is on a sports team _____
16. has been to Disney World _____
17. has an eight-letter name _____
18. collects coins _____
19. has had a broken arm _____
20. has freckles _____
21. has a birthday this month _____
22. has traveled to five states _____
23. has long hair _____

24. was born in another country _____
25. lives in an apartment _____
26. wears glasses _____
27. takes music lessons _____
28. can whistle _____
29. just moved to a new home _____
30. has seen two oceans _____
31. is the youngest in the family _____
32. rides a bus to school _____
33. has been a hospital patient _____
34. loves to read _____
35. has red hair _____
36. has a tooth missing _____
37. has eaten a strange food _____
38. hasn't talked with you before _____

One-of-a-kind name tags

Invite your students to craft individual, collage-type name tags of whatever size or shape they choose.

Provide baskets of materials—felt-tip pens, pens, and paints; scraps of cloth, foil, and wrapping paper; pipe cleaners, wire, and string; glitter, sequins, plastic trinkets; and magazines full of pictures.

Each custom collage should reveal not only a name but something about the maker's likes, abilities, hopes, and feelings.

As an amusing follow-up, encourage your students to imagine what they'd be if transformed into an animal, a food, a color, or a piece of furniture. This is an offbeat but telling way for the kids to get to know one another.—*Shirley Russell, Lincoln, Calif.*

Class-y collages

Here's a first-day icebreaker. In the center of the bulletin board, create a portrait of yourself holding a "Welcome to School" sign. Cut the basic figure from oak tag or brown paper, and fashion fabric clothes, noodle hair, pipe-cleaner glasses, bottle cap earrings, clothespin tie clip, and the like.

Offer the same hodgepodge of supplies to your students, and invite them to create their own self-portraits to add to yours.—*Robin Shope, Lewisville, Tex.*

Personal place mats

Have pairs of students interview each other, finding out at least three things about their partners. Then, give each student a sheet of construction paper and tell him to design a place mat for his new friend, based on the interview. At lunchtime, each pair exchanges customized place mats, and they have plenty to talk about.—*Sister Margaret Ann, Martinsburg, W.Va.*

Signature bingo

You can help your students meet each other with this new twist to the old game of bingo.

Give each student a grid with as many blank squares as there are children in your class. Have students collect a signature from every student until each square on their bingo cards has a name on it. Then play the game, using students' names drawn from a container instead of numbers.—*Lorre Degani, Richardson, Tex.*

Silent "talk"

Hold a "discussion" that children join simply by raising their hands. Ask questions such as: How many rode the bus today? How many are excited about getting back to school? A little nervous? Sad to see vacation over? How many are new to this school?—*Helen M. Lounsburg, East Berne, N.Y.*

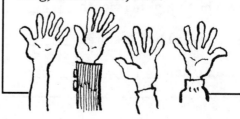

Summer sandwiches

For a change of pace, try this variation on the "Tales of My Summer Vacation" theme: Open a classroom deli, where students construct story "sandwiches" of their summer experiences.

Give each student five sheets of paper: Two light-colored sheets cut to the shape of bread slices (with "crusts" colored darker); one green sheet with torn edges, representing lettuce; one yellow sheet, with a scattering of holes, for cheese; one pink or brown sheet for meat.

Instruct your students to assemble their sandwich stories by using the first slice of bread for their name and story title. The rest of the sandwich shapes up as follows:

- Lettuce: How my summer began
- Cheese: Three things I did
- Meat: Two places I went
- Bread: How my summer ended

When the stories are finished, have the kids stack each sandwich and staple along the left edge. Provide time for students to share their books out loud in class.—*Paula Millender Goines, Baton Rouge, La.*

Looking for letters

Spark your young students' interest in letters by having them seek out the letters in their names.

Give your students scissors, paste, paper or tagboard, and an assortment of newspapers, magazines, and advertising flyers. Have children search for, cut out, and paste onto the paper, in order, the letters of their first names (last names too, if they're ready).

Accept a mixture of lowercase and capital letters at first, then ask that capital letters be used only where appropriate. Finally, have the children create a class poster with everyone's name on it.—*Marilyn Doner, Syracuse, N.Y.*

Dream vacation stories

Instead of the traditional "vacation reports," have your students create a story about their *ideal* summer vacation. Would they star in a movie? Become a swimming champion? Encourage them to stretch their imaginations.— *Julie S. Polak, Bucyrus, Ohio*

Somebody told me...

Put the accent on listening and speaking skills with this tales-of-summer activity.

Pair up students to talk over their doings of the past 2 months. After a set amount of time, have them switch partners and talk some more. When each student has had conversations with four or five others, have all students move into a big circle for a game.

Suggest that each student focus on one element from the preceding talks—something funny, something unusual. Then call on one student to relate such an incident, starting with "Somebody told me that...." Others have three chances to guess who the "somebody" is. Whoever guesses correctly can offer the next "Somebody told me" puzzle. (If no one guesses correctly, the "somebody" owns up and becomes the next speaker.)—*E. Schweitzer, Bolivar, Ohio*

Mark Twain's summer trip

Ask your students to write as if they were famous people (or animals, space beings, and so on) just back from a holiday.

Where would Mickey Mouse go for vacation? What mischief would Amelia Bedelia get into? Where would Neil Armstrong go for adventure? This approach might provide better clues to individual interests and writing abilities than would a description of the proverbial trip to Uncle John's.— *Kathleen Richko, Oak Ridge, N.J.*

I can read!

Frequently, 1st graders come to school expecting that they'll learn to read by the end of the first day. Satisfy that expectation by showing the children they're already readers.

Collect snapshots and magazine pictures of words on familiar signs and products—for example, Coke, STOP, and Corn Flakes. Then, display all the words in a slide show or on a bulletin board. The kids will be surprised at all the words they already know.—*Vera Milz, Bloomfield Hills, Mich., and Mary Lou Terko, Alburg, Vt.*

A class of characters

Your students can "try on" any number of achievements with these imaginative paper dolls. You'll need snapshots of your students and magazine pictures of people doing exciting things.

Invite your students to cut out the pictures they like and mount them on construction paper. Make copies of their photos sized to fit the magazine pictures, then have the students cut and paste their faces in place on the pictures. Arrange the portraits on the bulletin board.—*Donna Hubbard, Soquel, Calif.*

Preserving memories

This bulletin board project will help your students preserve their summer memories and share them with their new friends.

Begin with a discussion about the children's summer activities, making sure to describe some of your own. Ask if any of the children or their families grew a vegetable garden and, if so, what was done with the harvest. Talk about how food can be preserved and tell the children they're going to preserve some of their best summer memories.

Provide canning jar patterns that your students can trace onto white construction paper and cut out. Have them preserve their favorite summer experiences by drawing pictures or writing a few sentences about them. Paste a "lid"—a strip of paper with the child's name—on the top of each jar. Staple long strips of paper across a bulletin board and put the preserves on these "shelves" for all to savor.—*Louise Hoschak, Toledo, Ohio*

Message center

For a monumental "Welcome Back" message, convert a piece of white poster board into a giant loose-leaf page.

First, round the right-hand corners and cut three silver-dollar-sized holes along the left margin. Next, with a pink felt-tip pen, draw a vertical line a few inches from the left edge of the paper. Then, with a light-blue felt-tip pen, make horizontal lines about 1½ to 2 inches apart. Finally, laminate the board.

Post your notebook page and flank it with a giant pencil cutout. Write your welcoming words using grease pencil or dry felt-tip pen. But don't stop there. Use the giant page year-round for class schedules, proper headings for papers, vocabulary lists, extra-credit math problems, and more. To erase messages, simply wipe the board with a paper towel.—*Linda Rominger, Phoenix, Ariz.*

Howdy!

Make your students feel part of a special group by greeting them with this welcome acrostic:

When you

Enter this

Little room

Consider yourself

One of the special

Members of a group who

Enjoys working and learning together!

Then provide mirrors, oak tag, and a variety of art supplies so your students can draw, color, and cut out self-portraits. Then tack their cutouts around the acrostic. Beside each portrait, place an oak tag "balloon" with the student's name and birth date.—*Alma B. Sanderson, Albuquerque, N.M.*

Frankly, my dear...

Turn movie photos into a humorous bulletin board. Begin by clipping pictures (the bigger the better) of movie scenes from newspaper ads, old calendars, or movie catalogs. Staple them to the bulletin board, along with blank caption balloons, and number each picture.

Now ask your students to compose funny captions related to anything you're discussing, such as classroom procedures, social graces, safety rules, current events, or study topics. Vote for the captions that best fit the topic, and note the number of the picture they'll go with. Finally, add the captions to the board.—*John Lovering, Hampton, N.H.*

The color of friendship

Set the tone for a friendly year and introduce primary colors with this teaching display.

You'll need red, yellow, and blue cellophane or tissue paper, plus red, yellow, and blue balloons. Before you blow up the balloons, insert friendship messages such as, "Friends play together," "Friends laugh together," "Friends help each other." Then, decorate the board with the balloons, and use them to introduce your students to primary colors. At the day's end, send a balloon home with each student, with a reminder to pop the balloon and read the special message inside.

The next day, start a discussion of the messages and the special ways friends touch each other. Have your students trace their hands onto oak tag, then cut this pattern out of cellophane or tissue paper. Ask them to pin their hand shapes to the board with the fingertips overlapping—creating new colors to discuss.—*Rene Dernback, Portland, Ore.*

Compendium of class experts

To make the most of your students' talents, compile a classroom version of the Yellow Pages listing the students by their areas of expertise and interests.

To gather the information, distribute a questionnaire to each student. But first, to give students some ideas, discuss these specific possibilities:

- School subjects. In what subjects could you help your classmates? For instance, can you bisect angles with a compass? Demonstrate the uses of a lever?

- Sports, games. Could you help someone improve in a sport? Show how to serve a volleyball? Play a game of solitaire?

- Crafts. Are there crafts such as needlepoint or model building that you could help with?

- Other special interests or hobbies. Are you a drag-racing fan? Do you like to make up plays? Are you a singer? actor? tap dancer? Do you collect stamps or baseball cards?

Categorize the information from the questionnaires in a Yellow Pages format, cross-referencing where necessary. (Older students can take on this task.)

When your class resource is complete, encourage your students to seek help from classmates in their areas of expertise. And be sure to add on to the list as your students gain new skills.— *Mark Thomashow, Eugene, Ore.*

The year in preview

Knowing what's ahead of them will help your students be more active learners. Here are five ways you can get them excited about the coming year:

- Outline your end-of-the-year goals and identify the specific material you hope to cover.

- Encourage your students to examine their textbooks and familiarize themselves with materials in the room.

- Administer mock final exams featuring questions your students will be able to handle by June.

- Announce special scheduled days or programs your students can look forward to.

- Invite former students to review their year with you and answer questions.—*Denise Lee, Springhouse, Pa.*

Math matchups

Social interaction, automatic seat assignments, and the sweet satisfaction of success are the by-products of this activity, whose primary component is math computation.

In preparation, make two sets of cards, one with math problems your new students will recognize from last year's work; the other with their solutions. Make sure no two solutions are the same.

Before your students arrive, place an answer card on each desk, and set up a work area with scrap paper and pencils. As you greet your new students, hand each one a card with a problem and invite him to visit the work area.

At the work area, encourage students to help each other solve their problems and check their work. As students get answers, have them take the desk with the matching answer card.—*Jenifer Haler, Richland, Wash.*

Getting it home

During those first few days of school, recycle those plastic bags from supermarkets as classroom organizers and take-it-home totes for young students.

Stretch the handles of a bag over the back of each child's chair, then "bag" any notes to parents, reports, completed schoolwork, or students' personal belongings. At the end of the day, remind your students to take their coats and their bags.—*Darlene Pokorny, Evergreen, Colo.*

Match making

To pair your students for interviews or other get-acquainted activities, try these matchup techniques:

- Jigsaw puzzles. Cut half as many construction paper rectangles as you have students in your class. Then cut each rectangle in half in a different curving or zigzag pattern. Mix the pieces in a basket, and invite each student to choose one, then seek out its mate.— *Lori Diane Jurkiewicz, Erie, Pa.*

- Cartoons. Cut comic strips in half and have your students match them up.— *Maureen Hamilton, Hamden, Conn.*

"On this date..."

Start a classroom time line of events in September, and use it all year to help your students get a sense of the passage of time.

Begin by hanging a wire or string across one wall. From the string, hang the names of the months, written on 5 x 7- inch cards and equally spaced. Next, make autumn event cards by cutting out 4 x 4-inch squares of orange construction paper. You can use brown for winter, green for spring, and yellow for summer. Punch a hole in two corners of each card and hang it on the wire. (Hang each card by using opened paper clips— one end hooks the hole, the other hooks over the wire.)

On the first event card, you might write "The first day of school was September 9." Hang the card on the wire right after the September month marker. From that point on, write important class happenings, birthdays, coming events, and holidays on the cards and hang them on the time line.—*Pixie Holbrook, Higganum, Conn.*

Time...and time again

Invite your students to write personal "historical records." Seal these in a time capsule (an empty potato chip can) until the end of the school year.

For the most personal responses, assure your students that only they will read what they write. Encourage them to record such things as predictions for the coming year, what they'd like to accomplish, fears, and the person they most admire. —*Peggy Fowler, Kansas City, Mo.*

Pictures with class

Plan ahead to capture your students on film through the year. Bring a camera into the classroom early in the fall and start shooting. A field trip, an art project, or a ball game could provide many opportunities for catching your students in action or just being themselves.

At the end of the year, display the photos and have a nostalgia party. Then, use the pictures to compile a memory album for your class library.—*Dorothy Cole, San Jose, Calif.*

Early planning for year's end

Here's a new twist on the "Classmate of the Week" idea. At the start of the year, have each student fill out a questionnaire that asks such things as birthday, birthplace, favorites, special achievements, future plans. As you honor individual students, post their completed forms along with other recognitions and commendations.

Save the completed forms. Toward the end of the school year, put together a "Do You Remember..." quiz, using unusual items from each form. For example: *Alice in Wonderland* is _____'s favorite book. _____ is the only class member with four sisters.

Have the students take the quiz, just for fun, then go over the answers with them.—*Lana M. Holliday, Milford, N.H.*

All-year-long yearbook

Use the first day of school to start your class yearbook. Take lots of pictures, and encourage your students to record—with words or drawings—how they looked or felt when the "fateful" day arrived. Continue these photos and reflections throughout the year. And try these ideas:

• Have your students assemble the yearbook throughout the year, including selecting photos, writing captions for them, and writing profiles of themselves.

• Encourage students to include anecdotes and classroom inside jokes.

• Let your students take turns carrying the book home to share with their families. Display the growing yearbook at open house.—*Linda Putney, Bennington, Vt.; Darcy Stal, Portland, Ore.; and Margaret Noecker, Hastings, Neb.*

Counting the days

Here's a hands-on bulletin board that will get you through the whole year.

Cover a long board with a colorful, fadeless paper and border. Draw and cut out two large trees with bright, summer-green foliage and post one on each side. String a clothesline between the trees, add some clothespins, and you're ready for a hang-up display.

For primary children, you might use the display as a weekly calendar. Label the left-hand tree with the name of the month and the right-hand tree with the year. Print the days of the week individually on cutout shapes of clothing— shirts, pants, jackets—and numerals (for dates) on cutouts of socks. Children then share responsibility for hanging up the days and dates of each week.

To show the changing seasons, replace the green foliage on the trees with autumn-colored leaves, then with bare branches, and finally with spring buds.— *Mary Schmal, Watertown, S.D.*

Summer open house

Don't wait until opening day to establish a rapport with your new students and their parents. A week before school starts, telephone each student's family and invite them to drop by the classroom that week to get acquainted.

Take the opportunity to explain to parents what you have planned for the year. Give each student a suggested supply list and allow him to select a seat for the first day. —*Nancy Quinn-Simon, Canton, Ohio*

Parent postcards

During the summer, send a postcard to each student's parents asking them to write and introduce their child to you. What fun or interesting thing has the child done lately? What are his special interests or abilities? Request a recent photo of the child.

Then, on the first day of school, welcome your students with a "Getting to Know You" bulletin board. Include the photo and a few tidbits of information about each child culled from the parents' letters. Be sure to have an instant camera ready to snap newcomers or any child whose parent didn't respond.—*Lee Farnsworth, Troy, N.Y.*

Dear parents...

Get support from the home front early by writing a letter to the parents or guardians of each student in your new class. Introduce yourself and tell a little about your background. Let them know how you plan to organize the class. You might:

- tell about unusual projects or activities you've planned for the year.
- describe your grading system and homework policy.
- remind them of upcoming parent/teacher conferences and tell them you're looking forward to meeting them.
- invite them to visit the class during the school year.
- ask them to share their special talents with the class.
- give them a checklist of supplies students will need to bring to class the first week.—*Denise Lee, Springhouse, Pa.*

Parent night "portraits"

Right before parent night, ask your students to write a description of their parents' personalities and appearances. Post these portraits for parents to read on the big night.—*Barb Hoercher, Belleville, Ill.*

"You are here"

Show your students how they can help parents, newcomers, and visitors find their way around the school by posting "You Are Here" maps throughout your building.

Distribute school floor plans to teams of two or three students. Have each team select its own "You Are Here" site. Using yardsticks, measuring wheels, or tapes, they should figure out and list on the floor plan the distances to the nearest restroom, exit, or telephone, as well as the gym, office, library, and so on.

Make several copies of each floor plan and have students use felt-tip pens to highlight the best route to specific locations. Laminate the maps and place them on school walls.—*Karen L. Hansen, Doylestown, Pa.*

Gallery of graphs

Inform and impress your open house visitors with an array of schoolwide statistics presented through student-made graphs.

Identify prime topics by brainstorming with faculty, staff, and students. Categories might include:

- class enrollments (current and past)
- range of student heights by grade level
- library circulation data (most-used books by subject, for example)
- percentage of school day spent on various subjects at the different grade levels
- number of participants in specific sports
- costs of such items as textbooks, art supplies, food.

Have students collect the data and construct the graphs. Younger students might do picture graphs; older students, line or pie graphs.—*Mary E. Gerth, Ormond Beach, Fla.*

Picture power

On the first day of school, use a camera to take a formal and casual portrait of each student. Then, give the camera to the kids and let them take shots of each other.

Over the next month, catch your students as they study, read, think, or draw. For back-to-school night, assemble all the pictures into a slide show for parents.—*Suzanne Barchers, Denver*

Involve the parents

On parent night, involve parents in silent "dialogue" with their child at the child's desk. You'll strengthen communication between parent and child—and make time and space for yourself to talk with individual parents.

Ahead of time, brainstorm with your students some things they'd like their parents to see and do on parent night— such as meeting the classroom pets or trying musical instruments. Then ask each student to write a letter to his parents outlining his special requests.

Have your students decorate folders to hold the letters and samples of the good work they've done. They could also design a crossword puzzle, a fill-in-the-blank puzzle, or a typical class exercise for their parents to complete.

When the parents arrive, direct them to their child's desk. Ask them to go through their child's folder and then complete a letter you've enclosed, which begins, "I'm proud of you because...."— *Cynthia A. Slavish, Houston*

Taped tours

Provide your open house visitors with on-the-spot information and guidance through a taped tour.

With your students, list points of interest in your room— centers, displays, special equipment or materials. Then invite each student to select one stop and prepare a short summary about it for taping.

Precede each recorded speaker with an introduction. You also might consider numbering the various sites and having students announce the appropriate numbers on the tape for the convenience of your listeners.

You can end the taped tour with a short speech thanking your guests for coming, and perhaps asking them to sign a guest register.—*Lola R. Mapes, Des Moines, Iowa*

A great hanger-upper

As parent night approaches, consider having your early graders make easy gifts for parents: magnetized display cards for their refrigerator doors.

Each card is made of heavy tagboard, about 4 x 17 inches. You'll need a supply of clothespins (two for each child) and magnetic tape (enough for three 2-inch strips for each card).

Have the children print across their cards, "Look what I did at school!" Then have them decorate the card with a border or drawing. Cover each card with clear adhesive paper.

Glue two clothespins so that they open along the bottom edge of each card, spacing them to grab onto standard size paper. Finally, give each of your students three strips of magnetic tape and help the children space the strips evenly on the backs of their cards. Once the display cards are at home on the refrigerator, students can clip on new examples of their work all year.—*Pat Flanigan, Encino, Calif.*

A day in the life

Open house usually means sharing information about your daily program. The class can help by making a video about a typical day.

First, work on the narrative portion of the video. Divide the daily schedule among your students, and ask each one to write two or three sentences describing an activity. Be sure every student is included. (Don't forget such things as a trip to the nurse and students performing chores.)

When the script is refined to everyone's satisfaction, choose a narrator, and start filming your typical day.—*Connie Curtis, Ackley, Iowa*

And the winner is...

To increase attendance at your next open house, try giving a door prize.

Choose a prize that either a parent or child will enjoy, such as a stuffed animal or a small potted plant. A few days before the open house, show your students the prize and tell them only parents who attend can win.

As each parent enters the room, have him write his child's name on a piece of paper and put it in a basket. The next day, ask a student to draw a name from the basket.—*Denise Lee, Springhouse, Pa.*

Clone a great class

For your next open house, have life-size "clones" of your students "greet" parents as they enter your classroom.

Ask each child to bring to class a seldom-worn outfit from home. (Be sure they keep the reason a secret from parents.) In class, have students stuff the clothes with newspapers or rags, pin the garments together, and put rubber bands or string around the wrists and ankles. Real shoes will make the clones more authentic, but construction-paper footwear will work well too.

For the head, have your students stuff a paper bag (turned inside out so no printing shows), and draw in their features. Supply yarn for hair and construction paper for hands.

When the clones are complete, have students prop each one at his own desk.—*Linda Hanas, Mission Viejo, Calif.*

CHAPTER 2
CLASS MANAGEMENT

Getting organized

So that you're ready for every emergency, annoyance, and opportunity, *always* keep the following items in your classroom.

- screwdrivers—two sizes of the flat kind and one medium-size Phillips head
- a jar opener
- a first-aid kit
- a guide for removing stains
- an art gum eraser
- a sewing kit
- a ball of string
- masking tape
- a penknife
- rags—lots of them
- a hammer
- a laundry pen
- plastic bags—assorted sizes

- an ice bag
- household lubricating oil, plus graphite or some type of dry lubricant
- tweezers
- nail scissors and clippers
- a transistor radio—for following news events and weather emergencies
- a flashlight
- jars—assorted sizes, with lids
- slippers, heavy socks, smocks, and any other comfortable, protective clothing
- public transportation routes and schedules, maps of nearby landmarks and emergency buildings
- duplicate keys to your home, car, classroom, and so on.—*Denise Lee, Springhouse, Pa.*

Clothespin lunch count

Save yourself 10 to 15 minutes each morning with this quick way to take lunch count. You'll need some sturdy cord, plus a clothespin for each student in the class.

Attach four pieces of cord across a bulletin board near your desk. Label the cords "Home," "Brought lunch," "Sandwich lunch," and "Hot lunch." Display the month's lunch menu nearby.

Label each clothespin with a student's name and put it on the "Home" cord. When your students enter the classroom each morning, have them move their clothespin to the cord that shows what they'll have for lunch that day. Choose a student to complete the lunch form, based on the clothespins. (This student also moves the clothespins back to "Home" at the end of the day.)

Bonus: To take roll, simply check to see whose clothespin is still on "Home."
—*Pamela A. Halvorsen, San Antonio, Tex.*

Avoiding rest room relays

Here's an easy way to minimize interruptions and help your students feel more responsible.

Make two passes, one marked "REST ROOM" and the other "WATER," and place them in a colorful box. Put the box in a convenient spot and tell students they may use either pass when necessary without asking permission.

You'll want to stipulate that only one student may be out of the room at a time and set certain periods when the passes may *not* be used—such as when you're giving directions or discussing new material.—*Mary Modlin, Tarboro, N.C.*

While you were out...

Catching up after an absence will be easier on students—and on you—if you make absentee envelopes a part of your routine.

When you take attendance, set aside a large envelope for each absent student. As you progress through the day, write on the envelopes the text pages covered and the assignment given for each subject. Also note any upcoming special classes or events. Slip handouts inside.

When an absent student returns, he'll have a complete record of what he missed. Have him check off each task as he completes it, put his work inside the envelope, and hand the envelope in when he finishes all the assignments.—*Mary Glenn Haskins, Perrysburg, Ohio*

F.Y.I.

Does your desk overflow with take-home notes, makeup sheets, and so on? Clean up the clutter by creating a student message center.

Construct "mail pouches" from scraps of material (one for each student, plus a few extras). Attach a student's name to each pouch, then stitch the pouches in alphabetical order by name to a large piece of heavy fabric (unlabeled pouches at the end). Hang your "Message Center" in a convenient spot.

Put returned work, notices, and other handouts into the pouches. (You can even let students who've been absent know about missed assignments this way.) Use the extra slots for standard pick-up items such as book club order blanks and permission slips.

Appoint a daily mail carrier to fill the pouches. Each year, attach new labels.—*Sandra D. Baney, San Angelo, Tex.*

Classy lunch count

Frustrated by inaccurate lunch counts? Each week, appoint a class maitre d' and provide him with an official clipboard. Ask your students to make their lunch "reservations" with the maitre d' each day as they enter the room.

After the maitre d' tallies the reservations, he fills out the required form and takes it to the office.—*Jane Wagner, Lancaster, Tex.*

Absentee reminders

Try this "work-owed" approach to getting the word out on makeup assignments.

Set aside bulletin board space as a message center for absentees. Label it with the bumper sticker slogan: "I owe! I owe! So off to work I go." And stock up on 3 x 5 cards.

When a student is absent, write his name on one side of a card; on the other side, jot down the assignments missed (including any that are due that day). Then post the card on the bulletin board. If handouts were part of an assignment, post them with the card.

The returning student checks for a card with his name and hands in the card with the completed work.—*Bob Stremme, Norristown, Pa.*

STUDENT CHECK-IN				
NAMES	I'm here	I'm buying lunch	I'm buying milk	I'm buying nothing
Bill	✓		✓	
Karen	✓	✓		
Sam	✓			✓
Judy	✓		✓	

Student check-in

Avoid the time-consuming attendance and lunch-count routine by having your students check themselves in. Prepare a master chart with several column heads, such as "Name," "I'm here," "I'm buying lunch," "I'm buying milk," and "I'm buying nothing." Alter the column heads to fit your needs, and have a copy ready on your desk each morning.

As your students arrive, have them check the "I'm here" column and the appropriate lunch column. Have a pair of volunteers total the lunch count and take it to the cafeteria. Another student can read aloud the names of absent students as you fill in your attendance register.— *Sandy Bartlett, Erie, Pa.*

Lunch count with cups

Let your students take over the daily chore of keeping track of who's eating what.

Attach to a door or empty wall space three paper cups, each one decorated differently. Tack an envelope near the cups, and into it put Popsicle sticks each labeled with a child's name.

When your students arrive each morning, have them put their sticks in the appropriate cup—a red one, perhaps, for purchasing a hot lunch; a green one to indicate a lunch brought from home; a yellow one for going home for lunch.

Check the envelope for leftover sticks, and you have your attendance record for the day too.—*Delma Morton, Eureka, Calif.*

All well and accounted for

To simplify the frantic body count that goes along with fire drills, assign fire drill partners.

When the alarm sounds, children move quickly out of the building, as always. But when your class is outside, partners quietly find each other and stand together forming a double line. You can quickly note who's missing.—*Georgia Clark, Elton, Md.*

Attendance check

When you take daily attendance, use different colored pens to mark absent and tardy. When report-card time rolls around, the colors will stand out and be easier to count.— *Gaile Senette, Baton Rouge, La.*

Missed assignments

Are you an upper-grades teacher looking for a way to reduce the time you spend explaining assignments to absent or late students? Try using an assignment record book.

Each week, appoint a student to summarize the class lessons and homework assignments (with the date due) in a calendar notebook. Keep this book accessible for quick student reference.—*Sharon J. Burns, Philadelphia*

Group jobs

Delegating classroom jobs is a chore itself. Let your students take over—and learn to work together—by using a group job chart.

Divide your class into four groups. (The groups will take turns doing the classroom jobs for a week.) Have each group choose a color.

Then construct a job chart measuring 9 x 12 inches. On the chart, place the same number of pockets as the number of students in the groups. List all the classroom jobs on the front of the pockets, one or two to a pocket. Give each student an oak tag card that will fit in the pockets, and have them write their name across the top and draw a line below it in their group's color.

During their assigned weeks, group members will decide on their own method of choosing and accomplishing jobs. To keep track of who's doing what, each student places his oak tag card in the pocket of the job (or jobs) for which he's responsible.—*Judy White, Brewster, N.Y.*

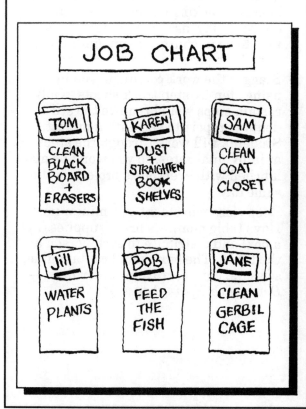

Cleanup lottery

Make cleanup time more enjoyable—and efficient—by injecting the element of chance.

Gather as many 3 x 5 cards as you have students in your class. Write each of your daily cleanup jobs on a card. On three cards, write the word "Supervisor." On the rest of the cards, write "Congratulations! No job today."

Each day, shuffle the cards and have each student choose one. Students who pick no-job or supervisor cards should get out of the way and let the others get to work.

As students complete their jobs, they take their cards to one of the three supervisors, who determines if the job was completed satisfactorily.—*Mark Thomashow, Eugene, Ore.*

Help wanted

Encourage students' feelings of responsibility and belonging by "employing" them to do necessary classroom tasks.

Start by creating a bulletin board that lists jobs for which your students can apply. Use the help-wanted section of the newspaper as a background and as a model for your listings: Under the heading "Help Wanted," divide the space into such categories as Monitors, Messengers, Caretakers, and so forth. Within these sections, post individual job descriptions and their requirements. Have students apply for openings that appeal to them by either filling out a form you supply or writing a short essay on why they'd be a good candidate for the job.—*Susan J. Kreibich, Winona, Minn.*

Attention grabber

To discipline students without interrupting the lesson, prepare an index card that says something such as "Please stop what you're doing and pay attention to the lesson. If you don't, I'll have to reprimand you in front of your classmates." Keep the card handy, and when a student is disruptive, simply drop it on his desk.—*John Lovering, Byfield, Mass.*

Bag it!

Are you constantly solving minor problems for your students? Here's a way to get them thinking up solutions for themselves.

Label a large bag "Bag Your Problems" and put it in a convenient spot. Have students anonymously write down problems they've had or observed in the classroom and put them in the bag. Typical problems include forgetting homework, losing supplies, or arguing with a friend.

Every so often, pull out a problem or two and brainstorm a solution. Before you know it, students will take the initiative to solve their own problems.—*Susan Paprocki, Elmhurst, Ill.*

Outnumbered

If your classes are getting larger and larger, and your headaches are getting stronger and stronger, relax. These ideas are designed for managing large numbers:

- If workbooks are "musts" in your school, let students check their own work in the teacher's edition. Set up a checkpoint area near your desk for easy monitoring. To help identify students who need reinforcement, put a message on each page, such as "See me if you have three or more errors." Form mini-groups of those who need extra help.
- Use the same procedure for work sheets by completing one yourself to use as the answer key.
- If a teacher's aide is available, have her sit at a "check-out" table. Students report to her to check work and get their next assignments. Have her list those having trouble with certain concepts.
- Have students assume more duties—taking lunch count, decorating bulletin boards, checking objective tests, and so on. Each day, assign a student assistant to be in charge of supplies and papers (both passing and collecting).
- Stagger the work coming to you by using step-by-step track sheets. Only certain steps would require the students to report to you with a project. Students will work through the steps at individual rates, so you won't be avalanched with everyone's project on the same day.
- Keep class movement to a minimum. Have table monitors bring supplies (in a box) and distribute to each person at the table. The box should contain glue, scissors, paints, crayons, and rulers.—*Denise Lee, Springhouse, Pa.*

Fair play

Is the same student always chosen last for a team? Are teams usually made up of the captain's friends? If so, try this approach.

Have the captains choose teams in the regular way. The twist, though, is that the captains aren't choosing their *own* teams. Tell everyone in advance that when the teams have been chosen, the captains will draw straws to decide which team is theirs.—*Paul Wangerin, Pompano Beach, Fla.*

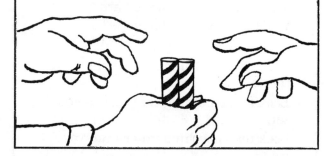

Attention, please

When your students can't seem to get into the task at hand, bring them to attention with tricks such as these:

- Don a party hat and blow a shrill whistle or a kazoo.
- Repeat "Good morning, class" until the class catches on and responds "Good morning, teacher."
- Relate an offbeat fact about the subject you're going to teach. For example, tell an anecdote about a famous writer, a historic figure, or an early mathematician.
- Have your students close their eyes and imagine themselves in a place you're going to discuss. Then ask them to describe what they see, feel, and hear.
- Bring in something visual that relates to your lesson.—*Alana Crews, London, Ky.*

Curtailing tattling

If you want to stem the tide of trivial complaints, try this technique.

When a child's complaint doesn't involve a physical injury or other emergency, ask for the facts in writing. Encourage your students to describe the situation and suggest a possible solution. For recurring problems, spend a class meeting discussing the solutions. Your students might even pick up some pointers on handling disagreements on their own.—*Marilyn Borden, Huletts Landing, N.Y.*

Time out!

To settle classroom disputes and help students take responsibility for their own behavior, try the "Time Out Corner."

In a quiet place in the classroom, arrange two chairs or put a small rug on the floor. When students argue, have them go to the "Time Out Corner." Tell them to sit facing each other. Each student should tell his side of the story without interruption, and both students must apologize. Neither student can leave the corner until both agree they've settled the argument.

At first, you'll have to direct the sessions. But as students become comfortable with the system, they'll learn to work out problems on their own.—*Annette N. Gibavic, Leverett, Mass.*

A real mood changer

To perk up yourself and your class, try assuming a new identity for a day. In the morning, write on the board, "(Your name) will not be here today. My name is Miss Pickleberry, and I will be your teacher."

Wait a few minutes for the students to notice and react. Then begin the class by announcing: "Your teacher called me last night to say that her class seemed a little gloomy lately, and she thought a change would do everyone good. So here I am. I'm sure we'll all get along well, and that you'll help me make sure everything runs smoothly."

For the rest of the day, conduct the class as the new teacher. Remember to stay in character and not to answer unless addressed by your new name.—*Beth A. Frank, Atlanta*

Hop to it

Bad weather doesn't have to dampen your students' spirits—or activity level. Use permanent felt-tip pens to draw a hopscotch pattern on a vinyl tablecloth or shower curtain liner. When your students are stuck indoors, push aside the desks, unfold the hopscotch board, and place it on the floor. Ask the players to take off their shoes, and use erasers as their markers.—*Pennye Pucheu, Lafayette, La.*

Window watchers

When your students' attention wanes, and your teaching goes out the window, run with it. Instead of drawing the drapes, help your students *really* see what's out there. Suggest a few guidelines for sorting out and listing some observations, and post these on the chalkboard. Because the possibilities in "look fors" are endless, you can change the list often. Encourage students to record their observations at random moments during the day. Here are some look-for starters:

- What can you see that's hard?
- What can you see that's red?
- Look for something beautiful.
- Look for something that begins with the "b" sound.
- Look for something that makes you sad.
- Look for something taller than you.
- What can you see that moves?
- What can you see that's round?

The look-fors might involve math, art, or critical thinking, depending on the level of the class and your current program.—*Deborah Saunders, Troy, Ohio*

Teach the teacher

For a change of pace everyone will enjoy, switch roles with your students. Divide the class into several groups, each of which will decide on a lesson to teach you. Possible lessons include demonstrating a craft, teaching a new song, or performing a magic trick.—*Debby Moyer, Sharon, Pa.*

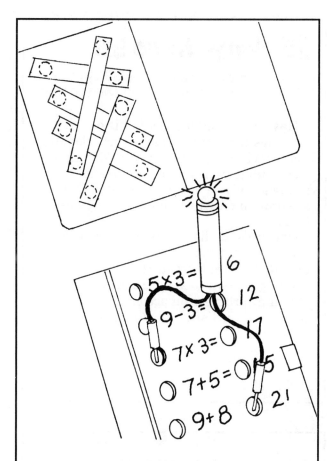

Electrifying idea

Brighten up routine pairing exercises by having your students make their matches with a circuit tester instead of a pencil.

You'll need a manila file folder, aluminum foil, masking tape, a hole punch, scissors, and an auto circuit tester that runs on penlight batteries (available at drugstores or hardware stores).

On the left side of the file folder's cover, write a list of questions; on the right side, write the answers in mixed-up order. Punch a hole in front of each question and each answer.

On the inside of the folder's front cover, lay a ½-inch wide strip of foil from the hole in front of each question to the hole in front of its corresponding answer. Cover the strip with masking tape, and tape the folder closed. The circuit tester will light up when a student matches a question with its correct answer.—*Barbara A. Palmer, Medina, Ohio*

Station break

To take the monotony out of the daily routine and provide activities for students with varying abilities, try introducing the station break.

Post, in two or three locations, copies of a sheet of paper on which you've listed each student's name along with an activity geared to his needs. Activities might include creative writing assignments, work with flash cards, listening center tasks, and the like.

Place any necessary materials near the activity lists. Whenever you announce "Station break," students should get to work on their assigned activities.—*Patricia Krivosh-Cheza, Masury, Ohio*

Take-a-break flash cards

On a set of large cards, draw simple stick figures in various postures. Show the cards to your students, one at a time, and have them imitate the figures' positions. Shuffle the cards for each flash-card break to keep the activity fresh.—*Thella Brock, Los Angeles*

Wonderful Wednesday

Here's how to set up an easy-to-plan day filled with new sights and surprising activities.

Start by enlisting three or four other teachers who'd like to be involved in a special class-exchange day. Ask each teacher to plan an activity she'll teach as groups rotate into her classroom.

Set up the day's schedule so each class spends about 45 minutes with each teacher. Give students a copy of the schedule for the day.—*Nancy Arber, Houston*

Friday free-for-all

Turn over an hour every Friday afternoon to the creative resources of your class. Prepare your students for this responsibility by asking them to think of activities, games, entertainment (native talent), demonstrations—whatever they'd like to see featured in a 1-hour slot on Friday afternoon.

Have the class vote on activity committee members—which should be changed periodically—to handle the initial screening of ideas. (Committee members are exempt from contributing ideas during their tenure.)

Each Monday, your students submit their activity ideas—written up in brief—depositing them in an idea box. The committee reviews the suggestions and announces about five finalists, which the class votes on toward the middle of the week. Depending on how you'd like the activity time administered, you may also ask the committee to handle bids for leadership and to assist in organizing the event.

Encourage students to seek out activity resource books and to brainstorm for ideas.—*Byron Pegram, Port Edwards, Wis.*

25-things-to-do list

This idea moves the responsibility of "What should I do now?" from you to the students.

Have each student create his own list of things to do in his spare time. Some items include reading a book, writing a story, implementing an art idea, memorizing a favorite poem—the possibilities are limited only by students' imaginations.

Of course, all lists must meet your approval—a fact students should be apprised of before they start listing. And you might want to keep track of students' progress on accomplishing the tasks on their lists.—*Greta Nagel, Belmont, Mass.*

Guinness guesses

The next time you're stuck with an extra 5 or 10 minutes, pull out a copy of the *Guinness Book of World Records*.

Choose an entry that involves counting or another form of measurement (you might want to flag some ahead of time). Read it aloud, but without telling the actual number (for example, "The oldest person in the world is ___ years old"). Give everyone a chance to make guesses, list them on the board, then divulge the answer.

You can expand on the questions to get your students thinking logically or exercising their math skills. For example, have your students make guesses to the question, "What is the largest number of coins ever stacked on the edge of a vertically standing coin?" (The answer is 205.) Then, tell them that a stack of 48 quarters is 3 inches tall; ask how the number of coins they guessed would measure up in inches.—*Caren Buffum, Philadelphia*

Loads of relays

To give your students a quick break, or to keep them warm during a chilly recess, try one of these relay races:

• Give each team an empty oatmeal box with both ends removed. With teams in a circle, have each starter slip the box over his right hand. He then passes the box to the left hand of the student on his right. That student transfers the box to his right hand then passes it to the left hand of the next player. The first starter to get the box back on his left hand raises it high.

• The props for this relay are brooms (or yardsticks)—one for each team. The first two players on each team mount their broomstick, ride pony-style to the goal line, and return. The partners then drop the broom and step aside to give the next pair their chance to ride.

• Collect an old book for each team, and have your students stand in a circle. The starter on each team balances the book on his head and proceeds as rapidly as he can around the outside of the circle. When he returns to his place, the student on his right sets out with the book. If the player drops the book, he must replace it and resume the race.

• Give each team a length of rope tied to form a circle and large enough for a student to slip through. Members of each team stand in a circle at arm's length from one another. Each starter passes the rope circle over his head and body, steps out of it, and hands the rope to the next player.—*Florence Rives, Selma, Ala.*

I want to know

With just a bit of preplanning, you can use spare moments to engage your students in thought-provoking discussions.

Ask your students to write on slips of paper questions about anything they want to know. The topics may be as broad as world peace and human relations, or as specific as how something works or why a particular event happened. You'll have the opportunity to read and edit all queries, so don't feel obliged to limit content.

Have students fold their slips of paper and place them in a box labeled "I want to know." (Tell them that they may add new questions to the box anytime.) Periodically review the slips on your own. Then, when an extra few minutes come up, choose a slip from among those you have prepared for and read the question aloud to the class for discussion.—*Jerre Repass, Brinkley, Ark.*

Odd moment fill-ins

Here's a collection of ideas to use whenever you have an extra 5 minutes here or 10 minutes there. Some require advance preparation; others will work on the spur-of-the-moment.

- Discuss the date's historic events or birthdays. (Check an almanac or special events calendar.)
- Ask for students' weather predictions, then check a newspaper's forecast. (This can be a natural lead-in for the next day's "waiting time" discussion about actual weather conditions.)
- Read a seasonal or topical poem. Listen to a piece of music together. Introduce a painting, along with highlights of the artist's life.
- Recommend new books available at the school library. Ask your students for their suggestions.
- Tidy up desks or activity areas.
- Run through the multiplication tables or problem spelling words.
- Read the headlines from the daily paper. Listen to radio news.
- Introduce a new word and use it in an amusing or memorable context.
- Invite the class to toss out as many thoughts as there's time for on topics such as ways to have fun without TV, ways to get to know people, ways to get smart without going to school.
- Following a typical talk-show format, interview a child (or have one child interview another) about background, hobbies, accomplishments, future plans.
- Do some stretching exercises.—*Denise Lee, Springhouse, Pa.*

Dramatic Simon Says

Turn the simple game of Simon Says into a dramatic script. Begin with Simon's usual commands: Pat your head; stand on one foot; bend your knees. Then, start a situation sequence. Here's an example: Simon says you're going on a trip to the moon.

- Simon says get into your space suit.
- Simon says put on your helmet.
- Simon says crawl into your space capsule.
- Simon says count down from 10.
- Simon says you are pressed back by thrust so that you can't move.
- Simon says you are suddenly afraid of heights.
- Jump out of your spaceship! (Would Simon really tell you to do that?)
- Simon says go on a walk in space.
- Simon says turn your rocket around and head for home. — *David B. Hakan, Fort Scott, Kan.*

Time well spent

Turn fire-drill "waiting time" into "learning time" with a standby supply bag.

Fill a shopping bag with paperback books, flash cards, children's magazines, newspapers, puzzles, pencils, and so on. The next time you have a fire drill, grab the bag as you head outside. After you take attendance, ask your students to sit in a circle, then distribute the materials. Before returning to the classroom, ask the students to put the materials back into the bag.—*Susan Doyle, Dallas*

Question the answer

Do a turnabout now and then when giving tests by providing students with answers and having them supply the questions for their exams.

For example, the question for the answer "Erie Canal" might be, "What was an important east-west waterway?" This backward reasoning is a useful problem-solving technique as well as a new approach for students who are too familiar with the usual test formats.—
Barbara A. Palmer, Medina, Ohio

Gone fishin'

Without interrupting the school calendar, you can give your students some "time off" to look forward to.

Choose a month, and write one student's name on each school day of the calendar. The day on which a student's name appears is his day off.

On a student's day off, he's free from whatever assignments you decide on. During that time, he may take a rest, do puzzles, play games, or daydream—anything but disturb the rest of the class.—
Sister Mary Jo, Santa Cruz, Calif.

Pick-me-ups

Perk up your students and ward off the blahs with these fun distractions. Try them all or pick a few favorites:

• Give your students a chance to get up and move about. Do exercises, play charades. Or for an even simpler change of pace, let your students change their seats for the day.

• Set aside a special time each week for your students to say what's on their minds. Let them voice complaints, give compliments, raise problems, ask questions, and make announcements.

• Once a week, take time out for laughter. Let everyone tell a favorite joke. Encourage your students to search the library during the week for riddles and jokes to share. Bring a few yourself.

• Set up a collection of puzzles—mazes, brainteasers, crossword puzzles, connect-the-dots, hidden pictures, anagrams, word searches. Let your students work in pairs to solve them. With the answer keys ready, circulate around the room, offering hints and encouragement.

• Choose a different song each week or let your students pick one. (Peppy show tunes and funny songs work best.) Begin teaching the words on Monday and continue singing throughout the week. By Friday, your students should know the song well enough to perform it for other classes.

• Prepare your students for this activity by talking about personal collections. What things do people collect and why? What makes a collection valuable? Bring in books about stamps, baseball cards, coins, dolls, and other things people collect. Have your students make a list of offbeat items to collect. Plan a Collection Day, when your students bring in their own collections for display and discussion. Invite other classes to come in, look, and ask questions.—*Evelyn Krieger, Watertown, Mass.*

Private eye

The Private Eye is an easy-to-make and fun-to-use tool for self-correction. To make your Private Eye, follow these directions:

1. From poster board cut two identical magnifying-glass shapes. Cut out a large viewing-area hole in both pieces.

2. Cut two pieces of red acetate a little larger than the center holes you've cut.

3. Tape both pieces of acetate tightly over the hole in one of the magnifying-glass shapes.

4. Glue the two shapes together with the acetate sandwiched in between.

5. To complete the Private Eye, cover all but the viewing area with clear self-sticking paper for greater durability.

Now, prepare an answer key that will work along with your Private Eye. First, write the correct answer with a light green felt-tip pen. Then, with red, orange, yellow, and pink pens write random words, numbers, and phrases directly over the green answer, until it looks like meaningless scribble.

When the Private Eye is applied, the green answer becomes readable, and the other colors disappear.—*Candace Purdom, Christopher, Ill.*

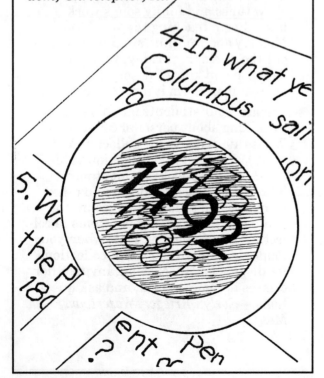

Can you believe this?

When your students come upon surprising information in class or out, have them record it as a filler in the class newspaper, on the bulletin board, or on a card in your Unusual Fact File.—*Helen I. Judy, Annandale, Va.*

Personalized permission

Join with the other teachers in your school or grade level to streamline hall-pass procedures. Have each teacher bring in something that reflects her personality or interests. (For example, an avid gardener could bring a pair of gardening gloves.) When a student leaves the room, he simply takes the personalized pass instead of a formal permission slip. Hall monitors can easily identify the passes— even from a distance.— *Grace Blanchard, Grants Pass, Ore.*

Late assignments

Here's an easy way to keep track of assignments that students hand in late. Use a colored pen to outline the empty square in your grade book where the mark eventually will be recorded. For example: John Doe: A C D □ B C □.— *Paulette Buck, Brainerd, Minn.*

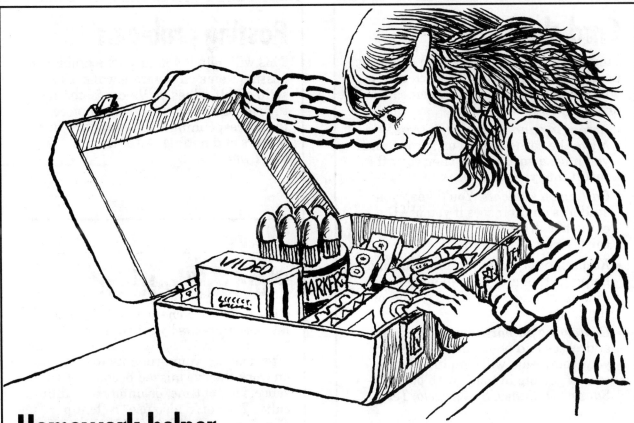

Homework helper

To introduce young students to homework, try an overnight suitcase filled with learning games, books, wipe-off felt-tip pens, paper, pencils, erasers, and other study tools.

Tell students about the suitcase and explain that they'll each get to take it home for 2 days during the school year. Include a laminated note to parents explaining that the suitcase is for reinforcing skills and concepts taught in class. The note should stress keeping everything intact for the next student and encourage parents to participate, but not to pressure kids to complete all or any of the activities.—*Linda Martin Mercer, Nashua, N.H.*

Homework tracker

To cure chronic cases of "homework amnesia," enlist parents' help by sending home an assignment checklist.

Prepare a form listing each subject followed by "yes" and "no." Leave space between subjects to write in assignments.

Issue a new checklist each day. If there's an assignment in a subject area, circle the "yes" and record the particulars; if not, circle the "no." Parents can check to be sure all work is completed.—*Rita Justice, Moses Lake, Wash.*

Take a number

Handle individual student's requests for help during times you're busy with this fair and orderly technique. Number a dozen 3 x 3-inch cards from 1 to 12; then punch a hole at the top of each card. Hang the cards in numerical order on a hook where your students can easily reach them. Students who need your help can take a card. Call the numbers as you're available.—*Amy Natiello, Hawthorne, N.J.*

Card shark

Simplify a variety of classroom chores by using a set of index cards—each card of which includes a student's name, address, and phone number.

- *Arranging and rearranging seats.* Move the cards around on a table until you have a good setup. Then copy the result into your plan book.
- *Calling on students.* You'll keep your students on their toes if you use the cards to call on them. (Shuffle the cards frequently.)
- *Keeping records.* As you move around helping students, you can make quick comments and even record grades on the cards.
- *Contacting parents.* Having students' addresses and phone numbers with your comments will simplify the process of getting in touch with parents.— *Sandra D. Baney, San Angelo, Tex.*

Posting problems

This will help if you have the problem of posting items on concrete walls. Place a strip of self-adhesive Velcro fastening tape along the wall, and small pieces of the corresponding Velcro tape on your posters and notices.—*Kathleen A. Welch, Old Lyme, Conn.*

Playing "ketchup"

Give students a chance to catch up on late assignments by scheduling "Ketchup Time." Set aside an occasional afternoon for your students to catch up on work they've missed because of absence, lack of time, or unforeseen difficulty. You could also use "Ketchup Time" to meet with individual students or small groups to review specific skills.—*Alyce Weiss, Sterling, Neb.*

An ounce of protection

Keep often-handled papers intact by encasing them in plastic. All you need is a roll of clear plastic and a can of spray glue.

Cut two pieces of plastic, each slightly larger than the paper you're protecting, and spray one side of each with glue. Lay one piece of plastic, glue side up, on a table and press the paper onto the piece. Then place the other piece of plastic, glue side down, on top. Rub lightly to force out air bubbles and to eliminate wrinkles. Let dry for 24 hours; trim off excess plastic.—*Opal Star, Las Vegas*

Catching early birds

Here's a host of ideas to keep your early arrivals busy before school starts:

- Invite students to use the typewriter, microscope, or other equipment.
- Allow students to take on projects from your "to-do" list—building a maze for the gerbil, constructing a model, creating a mural or map.
- Rotate favorite jobs among early arrivals: watering plants, feeding animals, decorating the bulletin board.
- Have a dictionary scavenger hunt. Post a few dictionary-dependent questions. For example: On what continent does an *aardvark* live? Are you a *native* of Boston? What would you do with a *busby?*
- Provide magnifying glasses and have students sketch their thumbprints or make detailed drawings of leaves.
- Draw two lines on the chalkboard. Invite students to copy the lines on paper and build a design or picture around them.
- Provide copies of a map—a mysterious island or an alien planet. Invite students to "bury" a treasure and write directions for finding it. Then have the students test their directions on a friend.
- Provide string and ask students to measure their ankles, knees, wrists, and necks in centimeters using the string and centimeter rulers.
- Provide a sealed mystery box that students can explore through sight, sound, smell. Ask students to record their observations and inferences. At the bell, reveal the contents.
- Play tapes of popular songs, and have students transcribe lyrics for a sing-along book.—*Doanne Marks Dunn, Brockton, Mass.*

What do you think?

Get good ideas for improving the classroom climate by asking what your students think. Here are some nonthreatening methods to use:

- Give each student an index card, and invite him to write a positive comment about the classroom on one side, a negative comment on the other.
- Once a week, ask students to write a list of questions, misunderstandings, and personal reactions—such as "What helped me the most."
- Put out a suggestion box for anonymous student contributions.—*Dr. Mary N. Lindholm, Fairfax, Va.*

Suggestion Box

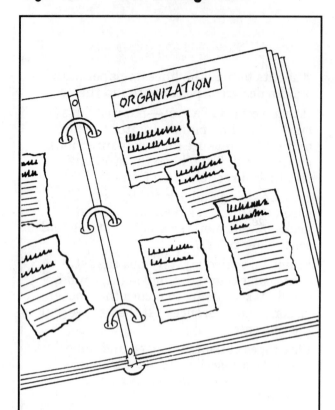

Great ideas book

Here's a surefire way to store and retrieve all the teaching ideas you get from colleagues and magazines.

Group the ideas under headings for specific subjects, classroom management and organization, games and fun, and other topics. Then write, paste, or staple them onto pages in a loose-leaf notebook or insert them into a photograph album with clear plastic pages.—*Diana Myers, Huntsville, Ohio*

Sticky solution

Write each student's name on a small gummed label, then arrange (and rearrange) the labels to your heart's content. When you have the perfect grouping, stick the labels onto paper. To make spot reorganizations, simply make new labels and stick them over the first ones.—*Shirley L. Russell, Lincoln, Calif.*

Pegboard possibilities

Pegboards are versatile, easy to use, and inexpensive. Here are just a few ways you can use them in your classroom:

- Write class jobs on pieces of tape positioned above several hooks. Hang the name of the student who's responsible for each job from the appropriate hook.
- Divide a large pegboard into sections that are assigned to individual students for their personal use. In their area, students may hang work or items of interest.
- Convert a pegboard into a learning center for practicing alphabetical order, sequential order, matching numbers, vocabulary words, or contractions.
- Wire the back of a pegboard and make an electrical answer board with a small battery-powered light bulb.—*Margaret McIntosh, Jefferson City, Mo.*

Great hang-ups

Here's an easy way to store posters, maps, bulletin board displays, and the like. Separate the various items into categories, such as months of the year, holidays, curriculum areas, or themes.

Put each group into a large plastic trash bag, and fold the bag over a wire hanger, securing it with clothespins. Label the bags, and hang them in a closet or storeroom.—*Barbara Vogel, Denver*

Student graders

Here are some new twists on pairing off students so they can correct each other's papers:

- Designate an "even" and "odd" partner in each pair. When you assign a work sheet, one partner does the even-numbered problems; the other does the odd. Students then swap completed papers and correct each other's work.

- Divide the tasks on the page into "expert" areas. For instance, one student will be the verb expert (finding all the verbs); the other will be the noun expert. They then correct each other's papers.

- Divide the pairs into two rows—movers and standers. On signal, the movers move to the corresponding standers and together they check their papers. If they agree on the answers, the stander stands, and the mover goes back to his seat. If they disagree, they stand together.—*Mary Avery, Ashville, N.Y.*

Flexible planning

To create a lesson plan "book" that maintains sequence but doesn't lock you into a specific time or day, you need a long file box, dividers, and a stack of index cards.

Write a brief description of each lesson on an index card, organizing your information according to such general categories as *Review, Introduce, Assign,* and *Comments.* Group the cards according to subject area, and insert them in sequence in a file box. Separate the disciplines with labeled dividers. After a lesson, throw the card away or save it for next year.

With this system, if you can't teach a particular lesson when planned, you don't have to disturb your sequence. The first lesson on file is always the next to be taught.—*Jack Giordano, Redwood, N.J.*

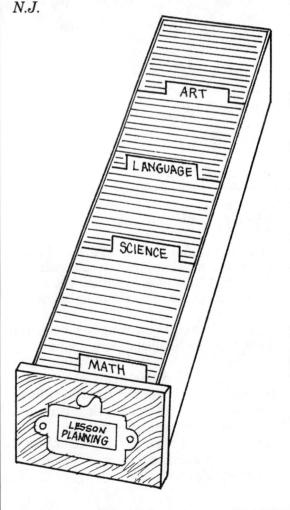

Nonemergency kit

To avoid unnecessary visits to the school nurse or the rest room, pack an "emergency" kit to keep in the classroom. Include such things as tissues, bandages, hand cream, emery boards, safety pins, nail clippers, and tweezers.—*Carolyn Backe, Westchester, Ill.*

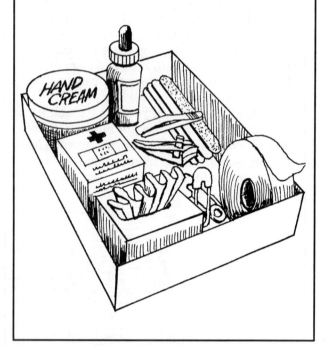

Wish list

Ask your students to write a wish list. The rules are simple: They can wish for anything that's possible in the classroom, except never working or having homework.

Schedule a class meeting to go over the most popular requests. (You might be surprised to discover that students just want simple dignities: being able to use the bathroom when they need to or having some input into class seating arrangements.) During the meeting, establish procedures for implementing the wishes worth granting.—*Suzanne Barchers, Arvada, Colo.*

Credit where credit's due

When a student answers a question correctly or makes a valuable comment, put a check mark by his name in your grade book or on a class list.

Explain to students that extra participation plays a part in their grades. To show them how they're doing, tally the checks and at the end of each marking period, distribute a voucher to each child showing how many he earned.— *Jacqueline P. Rogers, Collins, Miss.*

Call for help

Here's an easy, efficient, and fair way to help students doing similar independent seat work.

Have the students who need help list on the chalkboard their names and the numbers of the problems giving them trouble. Help students individually, or if several students are having trouble with the same question, call them together for instruction.

When these students understand the work, ask them to put check marks next to their names on the board. When a student asks for help with a question you've already explained, look at the board and assign as a tutor someone with a check mark for that problem.—*Wallace D. Campbell, Xenia, Ohio*

Mary 4
Bill 2
Sue 1
Jane 1

Positively excited

To keep a positive attitude in your classroom, declare a moratorium on groaning. With a smile, tell your students that they can think and feel a groan, but they can't express it. In fact, one audible groan could mean double homework. What's more, your students must act *excited*.

You might find that accentuating the positive gets positive results. Instead of complaining, "Do we *have* to?" you might hear your students crow, "We *get* to!"—*Carmen Ritter Hannah, Corunna, Mich.*

Code busters

Get your students settled as soon as they enter the room by turning them into "code busters."

Each day, before your students arrive, write on the chalkboard a letter/number code, such as C-4 or L-7. As soon as they come in, challenge your students to write down words that begin with the code letter and have the same number of letters as the code number.—*Krista Morehouse, Tulsa, Okla.*

Two-way street

Strengthen your homework program by trying the following approaches:

- Discuss the purpose of each assignment with your students. For example, "Doing this homework assignment should help you differentiate between fact and opinion."
- Be flexible. Students sometimes have legitimate commitments that conflict with homework assignments. Establish a specific number of times each grading period

that you will permit a student to turn in a late assignment without penalty.

- Give your students a list of homework assignments for the week, and make them responsible for establishing priorities and managing their time.
- Solicit student feedback. Ask them how long it took to complete certain assignments. Ask them what they liked or disliked about an assignment.—*Sandra Cunningham, Glen Ellyn, Ill.*

Circles in all sizes

You'll always have a circle pattern when you need one if you collect various sizes of plastic lids, punch holes in them, and slip them on a ring or ribbon.—*Isobel L. Livingstone, Rahway, N.J.*

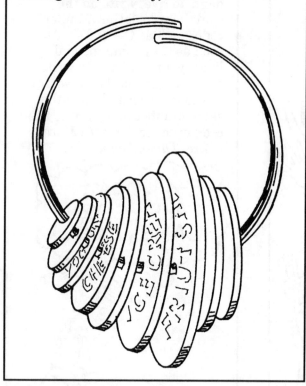

Test makers and takers

When students write their own test questions *and* provide the answers, everyone wins.

Tell your students to study certain material in a particular subject area as if they were studying for a test. Then have them create test questions. As part of the assignment, the students must also answer their own questions.

Review your students' questions to determine if they focused on the substance of the lesson and to spot any common misunderstandings. Select some of the questions to include on a real test and attribute the questions to their authors. — *Joan Mary Macey, Binghamton, N.Y.*

Getting steamed

Keep maps and posters from disintegrating by using this step-by-step procedure. You'll need Stitch Witchery (available in fabric stores), preshrunk cotton muslin or sheeting, and a steam iron.

First, completely cover the back of the map or poster with Stitch Witchery. Then cut out enough muslin to cover the Stitch Witchery completely.

With the iron on the wool setting, press muslin, holding the iron on each spot for 15 to 20 seconds. Let the fabric cool, then test adhesion by lifting one edge. If properly fused, the Stitch Witchery will lose its weblike appearance, and the muslin will be smooth. If necessary, press for another 5 to 10 seconds.— *James W. Tiller, Huntsville, Tex.*

Poster preservation

Prolong a poster's life by putting strips of masking tape on the back—in corners, along sides, and in the center. Use circles of tape to attach the poster to the wall, sticking the tape to the masking tape strips rather than to the poster.—*Kathy M. Peterson, Alpha, Ill.*

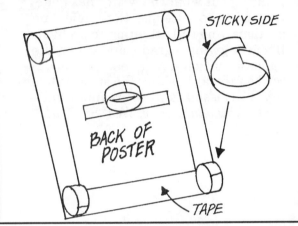

STICKY SIDE

BACK OF POSTER

TAPE

It's in the cards

Getting students and reference materials together can be quite painless with reference task cards—sets of cards, each card having one research task, each set progressively more difficult than the last. Distinguish each set (by Roman numeral or color) and number each card within each set.

Reference Skills Set I, for instance, might contain 10 numbered cards with simple assignments that send researchers to a dictionary or an encyclopedia. For example, a dictionary card might ask: "What is an ellipse? Draw one." Another set of reference cards might deal with using a specific atlas or map. More advanced sets would require students to select the most appropriate source, ranging from an almanac to a library book. Have students write set identification and card numbers on an answer sheet so you can keep track of their progress.—*Edith Lehman, Hamilton, Ohio*

Laminated "chalkboards"

When you're working with individual students or small groups, a laminated 12 x 14-inch piece of tagboard makes an ideal substitute for the chalkboard. You and your students can write on it with marking pens and erase it easily with a damp cloth.—*Ellen Athas, Tomah, Wis.*

Bandages for workbooks

Here's a solution for those workbook pages that tear after multiple erasures: white peel-and-stick labels from the stationery store. Cut to fit the spot, they provide a new writing surface that can even take another erasure or two.—*Myrna Gelsey, Miami*

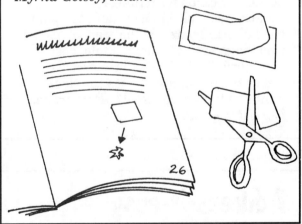

26

Instant transparencies

To create quick and inexpensive transparencies, set a roll of plastic wrap on one side of an overhead projector. Write on the plastic wrap with permanent felt-tip pens and pull the roll for clean writing space as you need it.—*Karen Verlinden, Adrian, Mich.*

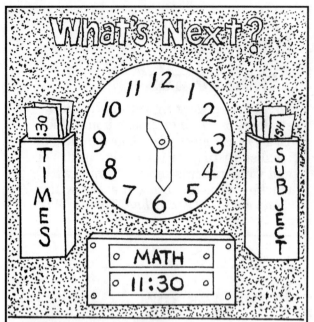

What's next?

Make a large clock with movable hands, post it on your bulletin board, and print *What's next?* above it. On the chalkboard, print your daily schedule. On one side of the clock, put up a pocket for cards with subject names; on the other, a pocket for cards with times.

Each week, assign a student to update the bulletin board: At the start of one period, he examines the schedule, posts the next period's subject and time cards under the clock, and moves the clock hands to the proper time.—*Phil Juska, Norristown, Pa.*

Address-it-easy

Here's a way to save time when completing all the papers that require someone to get back to you. Order inexpensive peel-and-stick address labels with your *school* address and telephone number. Among the many uses you'll find for them: book orders, school correspondence, notes to parents, loaned materials, teacher's manuals, classroom library books, and self-addressed envelopes.— *Shelly L. Fales, Standish, Mich.*

Tape your responses

You can have individual conferences with your students —even when time doesn't permit—by putting your comments and corrections on tape.

After reading a student's paper once, reread it, making comments into a cassette recorder as you go along. After pointing out what the writer has done well, go on to raise questions, offer suggestions, and call attention to problems. If you're giving a grade, mark it on the paper for privacy. After each review, record a message asking the student to notify the classmate whose review comes next.—*Pamela Lienke, West St. Paul, Minn.*

Grouping guidelines

Here are two quick and easy ways to form small groups for discussions and problem-solving tasks:

- Distribute playing cards to students, who can then caucus by suit or by face value.
- Distribute squares of colored paper or colored candies for grouping by color.

To help keep discussion groups on task, and to ensure that all members are involved, have each participant fill in an evaluation sheet that includes the following information:

- the assignment and the purpose of the grouping
- three positive and three negative features of the group and the grouping experience
- what they gained from the group
- any concerns they have about this experience.— *Sandra Bernstein, Woodlands, Tex.*

Creative lineups

Here's how to add a little variety to the routine task of forming a line:

- Encourage listening skills while discouraging racing by asking young students to line up on their tiptoes; with their hands on their hips, shoulders, or heads; with their arms folded across their chests; and so on.

- Review months by having your students line up according to their birthdays.—*Darlisa Ritter, Shelton, Conn., and Nancy L. Bauer, Iowa Park, Tex.*

End the classroom shuffle

Here's a way to collect and return papers in class with no fuss or break in the flow of your teaching.

For each group or row in the class, select a colored, two-pocket folder. Label the front of the folder with the class period and the group or row number. Pass out the folders as your students enter the room.

In the left-hand pocket of the folders, students find any graded papers, homework, and tests you're returning. (To avoid publicizing grades, fold papers lengthwise and write the students' names on the outside.) In the right-hand pocket, students put the work they're handing in.—*Susan G. Smith, Mason, Ohio*

Hands up

A sign in the shape of a hand can signal to you when a student needs your help.

To make a hand sign, have each student make two tracings of one of his hands on a piece of cardboard. Then have students cut out both tracings and glue them front to back onto the end of a Popsicle stick. When students need your help, they stick their signs in a lump of clay on their desks.—*K. Heather Harrison, Scarborough, Ontario, Canada*

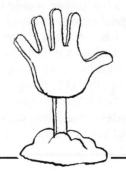

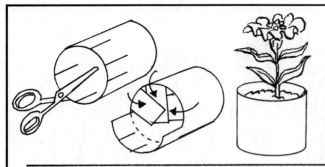
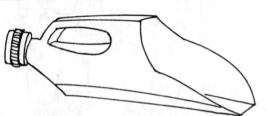
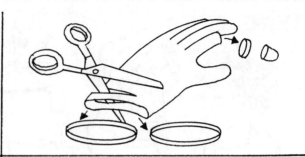
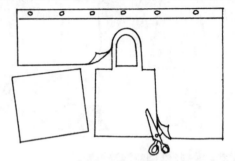

Practically perfect

Recycle common items easily for new life in the classroom. Even beginning recyclers can handle these conversions:

• **Plant pots.** Cut paper towel tubes into 4-inch sections. In one end of each section, cut four or more 1-inch slits. Fold in the resulting tabs to form a cup, secure them with masking tape, then fill the cups with soil and seeds. When grown, invite your students to take the seedlings home to plant, container and all.

• **Handy scoop/funnel.** On an angle, cut off the bottom of a plastic milk or liquid detergent jug that has a handle. Then, keep the cap on to scoop birdseed for the classroom bird feeder, dirt for plants, and beads and other loose items. Remove the cap, and the scoop becomes a funnel.

• **Rubber bands.** Convert worn out rubber gloves into a variety of sturdy rubber bands. From the cuff, cut heavy-duty bands. From the fingers, cut smaller bands—good for wrapping around pencils to keep young hands in proper writing position. Use the fingertips as rubber fingers for grasping papers.

• **Crafts apron.** Transform an old shower curtain or vinyl tablecloth into a bib apron for arts and crafts. Use another apron as a pattern, or measure yourself or your students for the dimensions. Cut strips from the reinforced border for the ties, or buy cloth tape, then pin, sew, or staple the ties at the waist. Attach patch pockets the same way.—*Beverly Maffei, E. Boston, Mass.*

Save a tree

To help solve the paper waste problem and to develop good conservation habits in your students, put a "tree box" in your classroom.

Call for volunteers to help you decorate a large cardboard box (use scraps of construction paper cut into tree shapes or an assortment of colorful autumn leaves). When the box is decorated and labeled, hold a class discussion about trees. Help your students see

that when they waste paper, they waste trees.

Then invite students to put their half-used papers into the tree box for others to use as scratch paper. Set an example by putting in extra work sheets and old memos.—*Gretchen Neilson, Marion, Ind.*

Extra, extra

Rather than filing extra work sheets or turning them into scrap paper, gather them in an "extras" box for your students' practice.

The work sheets will have many uses. You can recommend specific ones to students who need a review. Some students may appreciate a second try on a work sheet they struggled with the first time around. Others might like to take work sheets home as extra credit.—*Pamela Easley, Oklahoma City, Okla.*

'Tis the season – to recycle

The holidays offer a host of recycling ideas. Here are a couple to get you started:

- Save oversized cardboard tubes from holiday wrapping paper to use as storage containers for posters. Label the tubes by subject area, then list the posters included in each.
- Use the front of old Christmas and Hanukkah greeting cards to write thank-you notes to your students.—*Pat Forrester, Plano, Tex., and Diana Curtis, Albuquerque, N.M.*

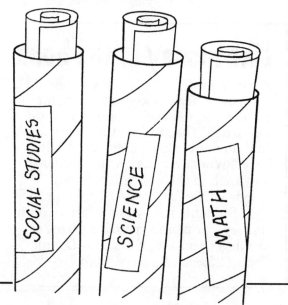

The 3 Rs—reduce, reuse, recycle

You can recycle "trash" into handy classroom supplies:

- Foam containers from supermarkets and fast-food restaurants make fine plates for class parties, "fibers" for weaving projects, glue pots, sorting trays for beads and other objects, and desk and shelf organizers.
- Plastic lids and foam trays make great stencils. With a utility knife, cut designs in the lids or trays. Then trace or paint in the opening.—*Beverly Maffei, E. Boston, Mass.*

Duplicating efforts

Don't throw out those old duplicating books! Instead, cover the pages with clear self-sticking paper and use them as work sheets. Have your students write their answers with felt-tip pens or grease pencils, so you can wipe off the writing with a damp cloth and reuse.—*Laura Wallace, Florence, Ala.*

Puzzling rewards

To get your students to work and play more successfully together, challenge them to earn a whole-class treat.

Cut out several seasonal shapes from 12 x 18-inch or 18 x 24-inch construction paper (for October, you might try ghosts, haunted houses, or witches' hats). On each shape write a reward—a popcorn party, an extra recess, a picnic in the room, a large pan of brownies, a game. Laminate the shapes. Then cut out a matching shape for each and mark it into puzzle pieces, varying the number of pieces from shape to shape. Cut apart the puzzle pieces, then reassemble them on top of the laminated originals. (Attach them with small loops of tape.) Post the shapes on a bulletin board.

Throughout the day, tally points for your class when students are working or playing well together. Then, at the end of the day, remove one puzzle piece for each tally mark. (Begin with the shape that has the fewest pieces.) When the shape is uncovered, the class earns that reward.—*Joan Rosche, Cedar Rapids, Iowa*

That's the ticket

To reward positive behavior, good deeds, or helpful gestures, hand out tickets from a strip like the ones used at amusement parks. Let your students know the kinds of privileges their tickets will "buy," such as an extra drink at the water fountain or a night of no homework. Periodically, you can also display items—such as stickers, pencils, or posters—that your students can buy with their tickets.—*Nancy L. Bauer, Iowa Park, Tex.*

Goodbye, gold stars

Cut out adjectives such as "awesome," "super," "wonderful," and "terrific" from newspapers and magazines and attach them to corrected work. The cutouts will get more attention than gold stars or rubber-stamped smiley faces, and students are more likely to take these papers home.—*Joan Mary Macey, Binghamton, N.Y.*

Phone home

Keep a list of your students' home phone numbers. Surprise them with a call when they've done an outstanding job on an assignment. Talk with parents too!—*Paulette Buck, Brainerd, Minn.*

Like money in the bank

Set up a system to give your students a "paycheck" for weekly achievements. Each week, tell each student how much he earned. The student then records that amount into a personal "checkbook." Whenever they want, students may cash in their earnings to buy "goods"—25¢ for candy, $1 for a privilege. Students may want to accumulate "money" for more expensive prizes or privileges you set prices on.—*Connie Cope, Colorado Springs, Colo.*

Chapter 3
SELF-ESTEEM

Photo comic strip creations

Lift your students' self-image while you stress language arts and creative thinking skills.

Divide the class into groups of three or four and invite each group to discuss something that evokes animated conversation—the best and worst food they've ever eaten, a close play in a game, how to keep your balance on a skateboard.

Take a series of instant photos of each group as the students are engrossed in their conversations. Together, explore the photos for cartoon-strip type stories. Imagine what the characters might be saying as you study their expressions. Does one shot suggest a punch line or surprise ending? Arrange and rearrange photos to discover an intriguing sequence.

Have each group mount its selected photos in final order on black poster board and put speech balloons in place.—*Alton F. Downer, North Colonie, N.Y.*

Vive la difference!

This activity will help your students see that the differences among people can be refreshing. From newsprint paper, cut out a chain of paper dolls. Staple these along the middle of your bulletin board. Attach a black beret on all but one of the dolls; on that doll, staple a different-colored beret. Title the board *Vive La Difference!*

   With the same pattern you used to make your chain, have each student trace and cut out his own doll. Then, have students write on their dolls something unusual about themselves. To make each doll even more unique, invite each student to design a construction paper hat for his doll. Finish off your bulletin board with these personal paper dolls.—*Sandra J. Frey, Lancaster, Pa.*

Vanity plates

Students practice saying a lot with few words when they make personalized construction-paper license plates. Have each student choose from one to three revealing words related to personal characteristics, a hobby, a nickname, or the like. The number of words will depend on the maximum number of letters that will fit on the piece of construction paper.

   Display the license plates, then have a match-the-plate-with-its-owner contest.—*Val Helmer, Sheboygan, Wis.*

Dictionary descriptors

Invite each student to write down 10 self-descriptive words. Review the lists, which more than likely will be quite ordinary. Now offer your students a collection of descriptive words, such as arrogant, jovial, benevolent, bashful, gullible, feisty, extravagant, eloquent, incredulous, negligent, skittish, effusive, diminutive, pessimistic, astute, and so on.

   Have plenty of dictionaries on hand, then invite students to add to their lists any words that apply to them. Encourage students to include words they might discover in the dictionary that weren't part of your list. Next, have students make a "Me Book" by writing each of their words on a single page and illustrating it with drawings, photos, or magazine cutouts.—*Carol Brownfield, Wichita, Kan.*

Give them space

Invite each of your students to claim a "spot on the wall" by drawing a self-portrait and hanging it up. That spot, plus enough space around it to fit several other displays, will be the child's own throughout the year. At the end of each day, your students may select samples of their work to hang; they also may display items brought from home.—*Irma Lynch, Elmira, N.Y.*

Be a star

Promote self-esteem by inviting each of your students to be a star. To reach stardom, each child draws four large stars, all the same size, on construction paper and cuts them out. On the first star, each student prints his name; on the remaining stars, he writes things he's good at doing. Each student joins his stars with string or yarn to make a mobile. Hang the mobiles from the ceiling for your students to share.—*Mary E. Brun, Mt. Clemens, Mich.*

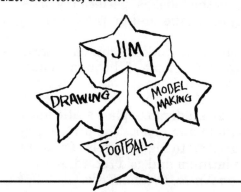

Creative collages

A Kleenex carnation, a clipping of baseball box scores, a drawing of a horse at full gallop, the foil from a chocolate kiss—a self-portrait of Mona.

Ask your students to collect magazine pictures, photographs, drawings, small objects, clippings, or other items that tell about themselves and things they enjoy. Then, have each student glue his collection—collage style—to a large piece of construction paper or tagboard. Encourage students to share with the class what the items represent.—*Marsha Adler, Royal Oak, Mich.*

Solid hits

Let the "top 30" in your class cut hit albums that boast about their accomplishments.

For each of your students, make a tagboard "phonograph record"—concentric circles defining five or six "bands" surrounding a center label. Separate the record into wedges and designate each section with a subject area.

Invite each student to mark the band separators with black and to put his name on the label as "performing artist." Then post the records on the bulletin board.

Whenever a student achieves a particular skill level in one of the areas named on the record, he may note the event on an appropriate band. When the record is filled, the student supplies a title and designs an album cover. The performer then goes on to higher levels of success with platinum and gold records.—*Kozette Van Natta, Orlando, Fla.*

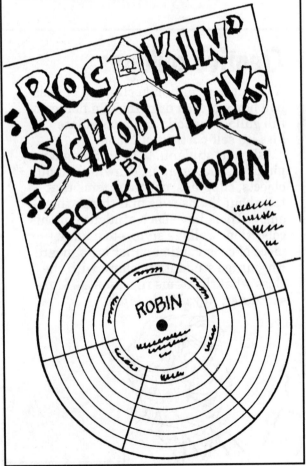

One for the books

Record your students' individual achievements in a class record book.

Design and duplicate a "This is to certify..." record sheet. Include space for the date, category, the record holder's name, your signature, and an explanation of the feat (for example, "can name six synonyms for *little*" or "scored 10 points in a basketball game").

Punch holes in the tops of the certificates so you can keep them in a three-ring binder. You might want to arrange them according to categories, such as academic, sports, personal, and so on.

When someone does "something for the books," fill out a card and add it to the binder.—*Ronald Burger, La Porte, Ind.*

Student spotlight

This activity allows each student to focus the spotlight on himself. Label a bulletin board "Student Spotlight," and post the year's spotlight schedule. Each week, encourage the spotlighted student to display photographs, hobby samples, a brief autobiography, artwork, handmade items—whatever tells his story.—*Sally Rubin, Burlington, Mass.*

Easy silhouettes

Each week choose a student at random to be featured in a silhouette drawing. Using a strong light source (opaque projector, slide projector), project the student's profile onto a large sheet of paper for tracing. Cut out the silhouette and mount it on a contrasting background. Have a classmate interview the featured student and write a personal profile paragraph to post with the silhouette.—*Mary R. Green, Elkhorn, Wis.*

Positive I.D.

This activity encourages students to come up with distinctive statements about their classmates—data from which others can identify the student.

Try the project on a group basis first. Select a person from the faculty or staff whom your students know well. Ask students to think about this person and contribute to a list of 10 unique and positive observations about him. You might suggest that students think of things that they personally find appealing about the person or of some specific instance when this person was kind or helpful to them. When your list is complete, invite students from another class to guess who your list is describing.

Now pair up your students and ask them to compose a 10-item list of positive thoughts about their partners. When the lists are complete, let the guessing begin.—*Nora Mitcham, Albuquerque, N.M.*

All boxed in

To spotlight one student at a time, turn an old refrigerator packing box into a TV. In the back of the box, cut a door large enough for a child to get through; in the front of the box cut a window in the shape of a TV screen. Invite your students to draw knobs and other features.

You can use your TV in a variety of ways, including game shows (with the emcee operating from outside the box), and interviews of historic or famous figures, workers in various occupations, visitors from countries you're studying (or from other planets).—*Joyce S. Reagin, Greenwood, S.C.*

THIS SIDE UP

Bragging bracelets

When a student does something that deserves being recognized at home, write what he did on a strip of construction paper and tape it around his wrist like a bracelet.—*Betty Ann Morris, Houston*

Picture this...

Cut apart a class composite photo into individual portraits and post the pictures on a bulletin board. Then prepare a collection of sentences about class members:

• She has the longest hair in the class.
• Who gets milk for us this week?
• He has a new puppy at home.

Write each sentence on a separate strip of paper, and post three or four sentences at a time on the bulletin board near the pictures. Invite students to claim sentences they think apply to them by placing their pictures next to those sentences. If more than one sentence applies to a student, he may choose which sentence to claim.—*Pat Flanigan, Los Angeles*

Everyone's a winner

Give each of your students a real boost by awarding a blue ribbon badge to everyone—just for being themselves.

To make the badge, cut out an oak tag circle for each student and staple two blue ribbons (pointing down diagonally, left and right) to the center back. On the front, cover the staple with a star or other plain sticker. Print "ME" on the sticker, and put a piece of double-sided tape on the back to make the award wearable.

When you award the ribbons, talk about how each person is different—but special. Your students may enjoy making their badges unique by decorating the circle around the sticker.— *Elsie Horvath, Greenville, N.Y.*

Reach out for pride

Help build self-esteem for your students through get–involved projects like these:

• Have your students put on a slide show, puppet play, or other program, and invite other classes to attend.
• Sponsor a contest, such as "Funniest Picture of the Year," and open the competition to the whole school. Your class can either enter or judge the competition.
• Suggest that your students organize a photo display focusing on their hobbies and interests. The theme might be "We Love to Roller Skate" or "Meet Our Unusual Pets."— *Kimberly Hannaway, Albany, Ore.*

Positive notes

Buy or create forms with headings such as "An Award to...," "A Special Note for...," and "A Thank You Telegram for...." On each form, mark places for the recipient's name, the sender's name, and the date. Then make copies.

Invite your students to use the forms to praise each other for sharing materials, being a peacemaker, offering to help, and so on. Emphasize writing only positive notes and not writing only to close friends. Read the notes aloud or post them on the bulletin board.—*Howard Meadoff, Hemet, Calif.*

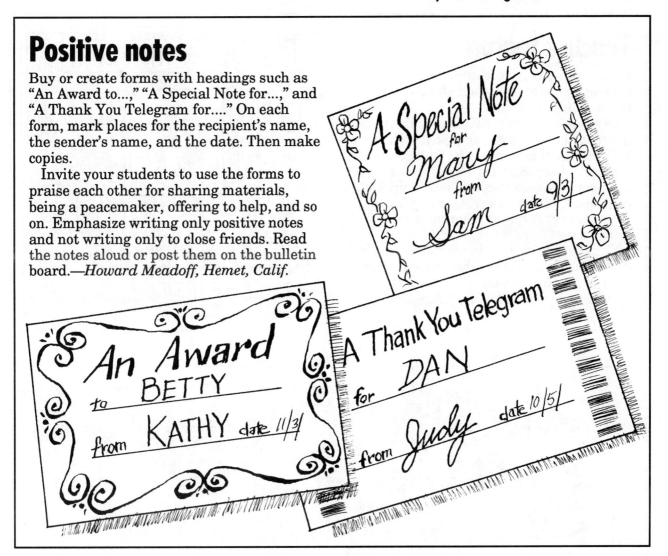

Surprise display

Help your Student of the Week (S.O.T.W.) feel extra special by getting the whole class involved in dishing out compliments.

1. Have the S.O.T.W. bring in a photo of himself or take one with an instant camera.

2. Have the S.O.T.W. go to the library while the rest of the class states things they like about him. Create a list of six to eight statements from these comments.

3. Before the student returns, post his name, picture, and list of good qualities on the bulletin board.—*Astrid Collins, San Jose, Calif.*

Compliments of the class

Ask your students to be quietly on the lookout for kind or thoughtful actions by their classmates. When they see one, have them write the person's name and a brief description of the action on paper and place it in a "Back Pats" box on your desk. You might want to submit a few "pats" yourself, just to make sure everybody gets one. Read the compliments during class meetings.—*Jane Nelson and Laura St. George, Sacramento, Calif.*

Teacher feature

Help youngsters get to know you and your colleagues better by establishing a teacher feature bulletin board.

Designate a highly visible area as the permanent display spot. Each month, choose a different staff member to be featured in the display, which includes whatever materials the person wishes to contribute: a brief autobiography, photos, awards, newspaper clippings, report cards, or other mementos from school days.

Enlist students to help assemble the displays and contribute to them by interviewing the featured person.—*Sister Corrine Dahlheimer, Coon Rapids, Minn.*

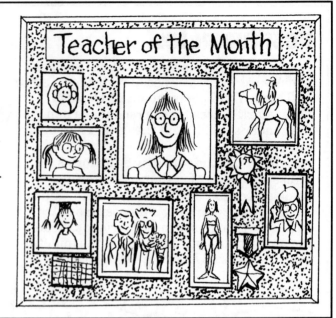

Yea, team!

Here are a few ways to help students feel as if they're important members of your classroom team.

1. Have each student design a class logo. Hold a contest to select a winner. Use the logo on T-shirts, on a rubber stamp for papers, and in other appropriate ways.

2. Have students select a class name—such as the "A-Team" or the "Star Makers."

3. Prepare a laminated personal ID card for each student, identifying him with your school and classroom.

4. Recognize one or more students every day. Celebrate a new brother or sister, new braces on teeth, sports accomplishments, creativity, and so on. Have the student stand after you recognize him so his classmates can applaud and offer congratulations.

5. Award students extra points toward a grade for sharing their out-of-school hobbies and interests with the class.— *Danny G. Fulks, Huntington, W.Va.*

Badge of accomplishment

"Can Do" shirts cover a wide range of accomplishments, including a lesson learned, a battle won, a skill acquired. Ask each student to bring a white T-shirt from home. Each time a student reaches a milestone, use a permanent felt-tip pen to draw on his T-shirt a "badge" representing the accomplishment—can ride a bike, can read a book, and so on. Throughout the year, add pictures symbolizing new accomplishments. And in May you might hold a Can Do party to remember good things about the year.—*Ellen W. Rich, Radnor, Pa.*

Keep your shirt on

This morale booster—for teachers!—comes in all sizes. Just outfit the staff in T-shirts (or sweatshirts) emblazoned with slogans such as:

• Can you read this? Thank a teacher.
• Teaching at (school name)—No sweat!
• Teach-Shirt

Or you may prefer specialty slogans:

• Science teachers have skeletons in their closets.
• English teachers have author-itis.
• Social studies teachers have all the dates.
• Math teachers have your number.
—*Shirley Ullom, Dodge City, Kan.*

Student—teacher dinners

During the course of the school year, arrange to have each of your students over for dinner, two at a time. Let the kids choose their dinner partners and also plan the meal.

Begin the festivities by having your guests stay after school to help with end-of-the-day chores. Once at home, let your guests pitch in with the meal preparation, setting the table, and cleaning up afterward. End the evening with a walk or a game.—*Sandra Bartlett, Erie, Pa.*

Easy does it

When you prepare a test, make half of it easy enough so that students who listen in class and briefly review the material will do well. Make the other half more challenging.

On the easy part of the test, your poorer students will do well enough to have more self-confidence and perhaps study harder the next time. From the more difficult section, you can tell who has a firm grasp of the material.—*Jerry Parker, Fordland, Mo.*

Special delivery pick-me-up

A great way to boost your students' spirits is by sending them a singing "messagegram." You might want to include all students in your grade level and split the cost with the other teachers, or even write and deliver the messages yourself.

Afterward, get students to think about people or occasions they might like to honor with this special kind of communication—birthdays, the last day of school, awards (Best Joke Teller, Most Helpful Bus Driver, or Favorite Custodian).

Have the class select several people or events, then give them a week to prepare lively messagegrams, either in groups or solo. Encourage them to jazz up their special deliveries with costumes, acrobatics, baton twirling, and the like.— *Carolyn Moriarty, Northampton, Mass.*

Chapter 4
LANGUAGE ARTS

One line at a time

Try this technique for helping fledgling writers learn to compose good sentences and paragraphs.

On a Monday, suggest an interesting topic—such as real or imaginary pets—to your students. Ask them to write one sentence naming the kind of animal they'll be telling about.

Collect the papers, and announce that Tuesday's sentence will tell the pet's name. On Wednesday have students tell about getting their pet; on Thursday, they tell about its most attractive feature, its likes and dislikes, or its most memorable moment.

Come Friday, return all four sentences to each student and have the students assemble them into a paragraph.

After a successful paragraph-building week, students may be ready for line-a-day essay building. Help them find topics that can be explored in three parts. Then, using the line-a-day procedure, students can build a paragraph about one subtopic each week. At the end of 3 weeks, each student will have a three-paragraph story to be proud of.—*Marinell Erven, Stockton, Mo.*

Rolling along

To help youngsters practice the curves of cursive, make rolling writers—roll-on deodorant bottles filled with free-flowing paint.

Enlist students and colleagues to supply the empty bottles. Using the tip of a blunt knife, pop the roller-ball assembly off a bottle. Wash the bottle and roller ball thoroughly, and fill the bottle with three parts tempera paint to one part water. Pop the assembly back onto the bottle and replace the cap.

Store the bottles upside down to keep the balls moist. Give each student large sheets of newspaper and a rolling writer. After shaking their bottles to mix the paint, your students are ready to roll.—*Irene Nowell, Garden City, N.Y.*

REMOVE ROLLER BALL WITH TIP OF BLUNT KNIFE

WASH BOTTLE AND ADD PAINT

PAINT

STORE UPSIDE DOWN

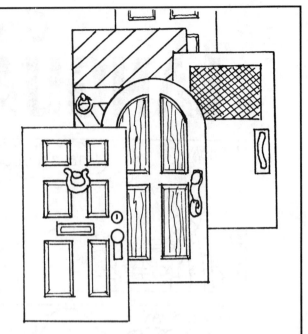

What's behind Door No. 2?

Here's a story starter idea to inspire either imaginative or factual writing. Ask your students to name as many different doors as they can think of. For example, their front door, the door to the school, the door to the ice cream shop, the door to a castle. Write their responses on the chalkboard, then discuss the different feelings a person might have as he went through each of the doors.

Now ask each student to create a door of his own, as down-to-earth or fantastic as he likes. Have students write adventure stories about their experiences after going through their doors.—*Jan Kurtz, Torrance, Calif.*

Please, please, please

To get your students to apply their letter-writing skills, ask each of them to write you a letter asking for a special privilege. The practice they get will be well worth the extra 5 minutes of recess or a night off from homework.— *Patric Murphy, McHenry, Ill.*

Getting off on the right foot

The red-letter treatment isn't the only way to point out a composition's strengths and weaknesses. Instead, have students reserve a wide margin at the bottom of each page. When you go through their papers, place a small number next to any item that needs correction or comment. Then key those numbers to comments at the bottom of the page, footnote style.—*Suzan Carns, Springhouse, Pa.*

Thanks a million

A $omewhat unu$ual me$$age can $park letter writing. Pass out to each of your students a sealed envelope containing a letter and a stack of fake money. The letter should explain that the writer is a millionaire who wishes to share his fortune with the student.

After the excitement dies down, the letter writing begins—in the form of thank-you notes. Encourage your students to include in their notes their plans for spending the money.—*Alyse Rynowecer, Chicago*

Writing to Ralph

Use an imaginary friend to entice your students into writing interesting letters and to help them practice punctuation. Mention that you have a friend who raises goats or collects baseball cards (or whatever). Give your friend a name—such as, Ralph—and tell your students that he loves to write letters. Suggest that they start corresponding with Ralph by sending him a class letter or individual letters.

Two weeks later, provide Ralph's reply. When you open the letter—what a shock! Ralph doesn't use any punctuation or capital letters.

Encourage your students to tactfully help Ralph with his problems as they carry on the correspondence. Produce letters from Ralph every 2 weeks or so, and pass out copies for everyone to read, enjoy—and correct. The next day, compose a reply. As the year progresses, so does Ralph's letter-writing expertise.— *Joseph T. Pawelski, Jamestown, N.Y.*

Writing for recipes

To begin a letter-writing lesson, ask students to scan magazines and food boxes at home for recipe offers. Have them copy complete ordering information onto 3 x 5 cards. When you have one recipe offer for each student, distribute the cards.

Each student then writes a letter requesting a class quantity of recipes. When you receive a good supply, have students clip pictures of luscious-looking foods from magazines and glue the pictures onto 12 x 18-inch sheets of heavy brown paper. Instruct students to fold up the bottom third of each sheet, then glue its two side edges together and fold the top third down to form an envelope.

Distribute the recipes for students to put into the envelopes. Have students tie the envelope closed with yarn or ribbon. The package is then ready to give to the student's favorite cook.— *Rosemary Stoelzel, El Paso, Tex.*

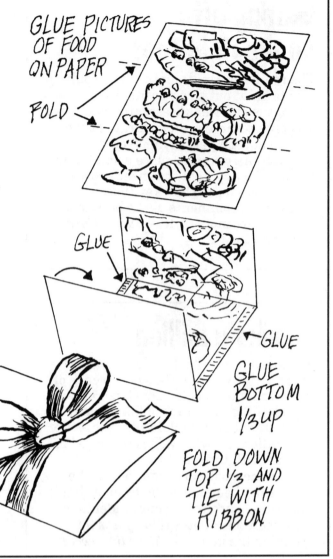

GLUE PICTURES OF FOOD ON PAPER

FOLD

GLUE

GLUE

GLUE BOTTOM 1/3 UP

FOLD DOWN TOP 1/3 AND TIE WITH RIBBON

You don't say!

To practice writing skills, schedule a write-in, a class period when everyone communicates only in writing.

When students enter the room, hand them each an instruction sheet, explaining that no one may talk during the period, that if anyone has a question, he should write it down and bring it to the teacher, and that if the teacher talks, everyone will enjoy 5 minutes of free time the next day.

The instruction sheet also gives students their assignment: to write a note to the person behind them. (The last person in each row writes to the first person.) The note should ask questions about the person's interests, experiences, and ideas. Students answer the questions in writing. Then they write to the next person in their row, trying not to duplicate their first questions.

When students finish corresponding with the kids in their rows, they should write a note to the teacher. They may write about themselves, the class, the assignment, anything they'd like the teacher to know.—*Jan Nielson, Coon Rapids, Minn.*

Double your ideas

You can multiply your creative writing ideas with a flip book. First invest in a spiral pad of unlined paper. Position the pad so that the wire spiral runs across the top. Then draw a vertical line down the center of the top page and cut the pad in half all the way through, so that each page has two parts that can be flipped over independently of each other.

Now browse through your creative writing ideas and adapt them to fit a two-part format: the first part suggesting a character or situation ("If I were an astronaut," "When Tiny was left stranded"), the second part being a phrase indicating time or place ("at the car wash," "about 2004 A.D."). Now, write the phrases in the flip book, the first set on the left section and the second set on the right.

Invite students to mix and match the pages to find a title that sparks writing ideas.—*Robert R. Saltzman, Imola, Calif.*

Message in a bottle

To get your students writing creatively, display an old bottle with a rolled-up paper inside. Then brainstorm about these questions:

- Where did the bottle come from?
- Where was it found?
- Who put the note in the bottle?
- Who found it?

Get lots of answers to each question; be sure the students include descriptive details. Choosing from all the ideas, each student writes answers to the four questions.

Let these story elements "brew" overnight, then have the students tie them together with a plot.—*Jan Coone, Wallace, Neb.*

Dessert hall of fame

Here's a surefire way to get kids' creative juices flowing. Have each child close his eyes and imagine a favorite dessert. Next, have him write down all the words he can think of to describe the dessert: *delicious, chocolaty, creamy, crunchy, sweet, scrumptious.*

Now, have students write paragraphs about their favorite desserts. Finally, have them draw colorful pictures of the desserts on large sheets of paper. Create a "Dessert Hall of Fame" display of paragraphs and drawings.—*Kathie Dewy, Salem, Ore.*

Friendly feedback

Encourage livelier papers by having students read and comment on their classmates' work. Attach a "reviewer's sheet" to each paper with instructions such as:

- Underline one sentence or phrase you especially like.
- Circle good action or descriptive words.
- Write a positive comment about the paper.
- Identify one part of the paper that seemed unclear.
- Suggest improvements.

Have the student-reviewer add any other constructive comments, then sign and date the sheet. Expand your students' audience further by inviting parents and students from other classes to be reviewers.—*Martin Tadlock, Ivins, Utah*

What Myrtle found

Use the tale of "Myrtle Matilda McGee" to start students writing lots of stories of their own. Tell them some of the strange things Myrtle, an offbeat custodian at your local arena, found while cleaning up after a crowd. For example, she discovered a curly red wig, an athletic bag stuffed wth money, and a goldfish bowl.

Invite students to write tall tales or descriptive paragraphs about:

- what Myrtle found
- her reaction
- why the item was left behind
- what Myrtle did with what she found.

To keep Myrtle's exploits ongoing, set up a writing center where students will find new items Myrtle found jotted on index cards. They can choose one and then write about it, or they can come up with their own "finds."—*Mary E. Modlin, Tarboro, N.C.*

Egg-citing ideas

You'll hatch several creative writing assignments when you encourage your students to think about what might pop out of an egg found in an unusual place. For starters, here are a few examples:

- on the dark side of the moon
- inside a great pyramid
- at the center of the earth
- inside an antique clock
- in a bank vault.—*Talis Byers, Opelousas, La.*

Letters that get results

Begin this stimulating letter-writing project by having students brainstorm for topics they'd like to know more about. When they've decided on their individual topics (for example, scuba diving, professional baseball, training programs for astronauts, ballet schools), send students to the library to obtain related association addresses.

Next, have students write to the organizations they've selected. They might ask for background information, news of upcoming plans and trends, posters, stickers, pamphlets, brochures, or other related items. They should have everything sent to the classroom so each student can share what he receives.—*Jule E. Marine, Jr., Salt Lake City*

Writers meeting writers

Research your community to discover resource people connected with writing—librarians, storytellers, authors, newspaper reporters, editors, illustrators. Find out if some of these specialists would be willing to share their expertise in an informal workshop setting.

The after-school conference might consist of two hour-long sessions with a choice of workshops for each hour. The workshops—open to students and parents—could focus on storytelling activities, poetry or newspaper writing, or specific writing techniques. Include plenty of hands-on participation rather than lectures or demonstrations.

Advertise your conference through an invitation/program that describes the classes, introduces the presenters, outlines the schedule, and includes a registration blank.

You might want to open the conference with a musical act or poetry reading, and end with a wrap-up or networking session.—*Joan Stommen, Ipswich, Mass.*

"Today's news is..."

Invite your students to produce a video news program to report school news. You'll need a video camera, index cards, and "news information sheets" (plain paper marked with the headings *who, what, where, when, why,* and *how*).

Divide your class into seven groups: reporters, producers, writers, sentence checkers, spelling checkers, punctuation and capitalization checkers, and newscasters.

The reporters each visit a classroom to gather the news and write it on a news information sheet. The producers, who oversee the project at every step, then attach to each of the information sheets an index card that members of the team will sign as they complete their jobs. The producers have the reporters sign the cards, then give the material to the writers.

The writers create stories from the information, sign the cards, then pass the stories to the sentence, spelling, punctuation, and capitalization checkers. The stories then go back to the writers for revisions. When the stories are in final form, the newscasters transfer them to cue cards, practice reading them, and appear before the camera for videotaping.—*Dean Phillips, Smithfield, Utah*

Getting personal

Here's a whole-class project for teaching personal letter writing.

Write each line of a personal letter on a 3-inch-wide strip of tagboard: The heading goes on three separate strips (one for the street address; one for the city, state, and zip code; one for the date); the greeting goes on a separate strip; each sentence of the body goes on a separate strip, and so on.

Then divide the class into five groups, and give each group the strips for one part of the letter—heading, greeting, body, closing, signature. Also, give each group several 3-inch squares that display commas, periods, and other punctuation marks.

Ask each group to arrange its strips in proper order, including any necessary punctuation. Then have each group tape its strips in order on the chalkboard. Invite the whole class to read the letter aloud to make sure they arranged it properly.—*Dorothy Seehusen, Hampton, Iowa*

Creative monsters

As part of a unit on paragraphing, read Maurice Sendak's *Where the Wild Things Are* (Harper and Row) to the class. After discussing the monster in the pictures and story line, give your students large white drawing paper and crayons. Ask each child to design his own monster.

In separate exercises, ask your students to write three paragraphs about their monsters:

- Paragraph 1: Describe the monster.
- Paragraph 2: Describe the monster's habitat.
- Paragraph 3: Describe the monster's personality.—*Sheryl S. Solow, Ottsville, Pa.*

True to form

To stress neatness, proper spelling, and capitalization, have your students fill in a variety of forms. You can make up a job application or ask students to bring in mail-order forms from cereal boxes and catalogs.— *Paula Moucka, Marion, Iowa*

Building a paragraph

To help your students better understand the construction of a paragraph, break it into its parts. Choose several short paragraphs and write the topic sentences of each, with plenty of space in between, on the chalkboard. Then, on strips of paper, print each of the remaining sentences and pass them out, one per student.

Have students read their sentences and decide to which topic sentence it relates. Then have them stand next to that topic sentence and decide with the other students gathered there the correct order of the sentences in the paragraph. When the groups are ready, have them read their completed paragraphs aloud.—*Jean Davis, Cincinnati*

A written "conversation"

Students will practice expressing themselves, and you'll get to know your students better with a once-a-week journal exchange. Each week, have each student write an entry in a notebook. He may tell something that happened at home or anything else he chooses. Collect the notebooks, respond to what each child has written, and perhaps introduce a new topic to keep the "conversation" going all year.—*Isobel L. Livingstone, Rahway, N.J.*

Window of opportunity

Students can improve their writing— and observation— skills by simply looking out the window. Have each student choose a window—either in your room or somewhere else in the building. Then, ask everyone to examine the view from his window, jotting down and describing what he observes.

Encourage students to add personal impressions about what they see. Then, have them organize and rewrite their notes in any form they choose—scientific reporting, poetry, or prose—and invite them to add illustrations.

After students have a chance to share their writings and artwork, file the papers. Then, a few months later, have students return to their windows to record changes they see. In all, have students visit their windows four times during the year. After the last visit, have students compile their writing into a booklet.—*Tana L. Lawson, Eugene, Ore.*

Creative cursive

The following activities combine drill with creative thinking to give students practice in cursive writing:

- **Thematic drill.** Choose a theme, such as "animals," and have your students practice writing particular letters by thinking of (and writing) animal names beginning with those letters: a*ardvark*, b*eagle*, *cat*, and so on. Other themes to try are "food," "household items," and "games."

- **Double duty.** If a student needs practice cursive writing a particular letter, ask him to write two words that go together beginning with that letter: *brown bear, sea serpent*. To add further challenge, ask students to write sentences in which every word begins with that letter: *Even elephants enjoy eating enchiladas.—Doris Cruze, Littleton, Colo.*

The great escape

Stage your classroom pet's escape to get your students writing creatively.

When your students are out of the classroom, take the animal from its cage and hide it someplace safe. Leave the cage door open and mark an escape route using "tracks" cut out of construction paper. The trail should provide rich possibilities for story development and descriptive writing. For example, the animal might cross certain desks, go in and out of an encyclopedia volume, climb the wall, linger over the bulletin board, explore the wastebasket, and so on. End the tracks mysteriously at a window.

When your students return, explain that you have the animal in a safe place. Then invite them to immerse themselves in the fantasy of the animal's adventure. Encourage them to speculate about why the animal visited various places.—*Rick Crosslin, Indianapolis*

Fun business directory

The next time you teach a unit on writing business letters, start by asking each student to consider a business he would like to run. Choices may be serious or humorous, real or imaginary.

After students have decided on their business identities, have them prepare entries for a class "business directory." Each entry should include the name of the firm (incorporating the student's name), a brief description of the products or services provided, and the address and phone number of the business. Each student gets a copy of the directory.

Ask each student to write to one business. The letters may request information, commend or complain about a product, order something, or apply for employment. Answers, of course, should be forthcoming.—*Nancy Nettesheim, Brodhead, Wis.*

Dear Susie...

To motivate writing, label a special section of a bulletin board "Message Center" and encourage your students to leave notes on it for each other. Post these rules to keep the message center running smoothly:

- Finish your assigned work before writing messages or visiting the message center.
- Don't write anything unkind or upsetting.
- Fold each message and write your name and the receiver's name on the outside.
- Say on the message whether it's private or okay to share.—*Rick Crosslin, Indianapolis*

Swapping stories

Divide your class into groups of four or five students. Have each group sit in a circle, and give each group member a sheet of paper and a picture from a magazine, book, postcard, or other source.

Ask the students to write the first three sentences of a story relating to their pictures. When you say, "Trade," the students pass their pictures and papers clockwise to the next member of their group, who adds three more sentences to the story.

Continue the activity until all group members have received their original stories and pictures; students then write endings for their stories.—*Christie Lehmann, Sterling Heights, Mich.*

Proofreading practice

Collect several short articles or ads, each of which contains one error in punctuation, spelling, or grammar. Number each one, make a copy of the set for each student in your class, and prepare an answer key.

Now have students number sheets of paper with as many numbers as there are articles. Each student proofreads the articles, writing the error in its corrected form next to the corresponding number on his answer sheet.—*Nancy Johnson, Ruckersville, Va.*

Practice makes perfect

Compile a list of common errors your students make and develop a work sheet for each. On the work sheet, put the rule to be followed, examples, and exercises demonstrating the rule. Assign a number to each sheet and organize the pages in a file.

When you read student compositions, rather than correcting each error, write the number of the violated rule next to the error. When students receive their papers, they pull out the rule sheets that correspond to the numbers on their papers, study them, and complete the exercises. They then correct the errors on their compositions.—*Susan Kaplan, Birmingham, Ala.*

Excuses, excuses

Propose a writing assignment that challenges students to come up with the most original, the most unlikely, the most fanciful, the most outrageous alibis for not turning in homework.

You might want to stipulate that excuses either take the form of one-liners (My brother developed a rare disease, and all he can eat is 4th grade homework.) or that they be paragraphs including the whole horrible story.

As a follow-up, ask your students to write excuses for fictional or historic characters who slipped up.—*Trudy Whitman, Brooklyn, N.Y.*

Easy as I, II, III

You can help students practice outlining with these personalized activities. Ask students to outline:

- a favorite story that has a distinctive "first, next, then, at last" pattern— "The Three Little Pigs" or "Goldilocks and the Three Bears," for example.
- the daily classroom schedule, as it is or as it might be on each student's idea of a perfect day.
- plans for an ideal vacation with three stops of their own choosing.—*Peggy Smith, Port Allen, La.*

Secret pen pals

On a Monday, write each student's name, and yours if you want, on a slip of paper and put the slips in a box. Everyone should draw a name but keep it secret. Tell students that they'll be the "secret pen pal" to that person for the week.

For homework each night, have students write anonymous letters to their pen pals. They can write about current interests, family events, favorite sports, books, and so on. They might even want to drop hints about their identity.

Each morning, have students put their letters in a class-made mailbox for distribution. On Friday, ask students to guess the identity of their secret pen pals.— *Karen Hansen, Doylestown, Pa.*

Funny business

The fictitious scenarios below give students a chance to write different kinds of business letters—and have fun in the process:

- **Smile-A-Plenty Modeling Agency.** This agency casts the actors in your favorite cereal commercial. Aren't you the best kid for the job? Wouldn't you be superb promoting this cereal? Write a letter to the manager of Smile-A-Plenty highlighting your best qualities and requesting an interview.

- **Go Anywhere Travel Agency.** You've inherited $25,000, and you want to take an exciting trip. Where will you go? A European city? An exotic island? Write a letter requesting information about tour packages to places you'd like to visit.

- **Purple Turtle Detergent Co.** You used this company's leading dishwashing liquid, Spotless. It not only cleaned food off the plates but also removed the pink rosebud pattern. Write a letter of complaint. How can the Purple Turtle Detergent Company satisfy you?

- **Marvo Shampoo Co.** You tried this company's new shampoo, Sunshine. Now all your friends envy your gorgeous hair. Write a letter to the manufacturer of Sunshine telling how much you like this new product.—*Karen Ehman, San Carlos, Calif.*

Kidnapping for kids

Encourage creative writing by inviting your students to write imaginary ransom notes.

First, have your students look for situations that afford an excuse for kidnapping, such as a problem that needs correcting.

The kidnapper might be the student, a well-known personality, or a character from literature. For instance, Scrooge, unhappy with his image in *A Christmas Carol*, might kidnap David Copperfield to pressure Charles Dickens into changing the story. Or a "Concerned Citizen" might kidnap the town's police force until the mayor agrees to clean up a polluted swimming hole.—*Gary K. Doi, Vancouver, B.C.*

Legitimate note writing

Set aside a specific time for note writing, and encourage students to write lots of friendly, positive notes to classmates. Any subject may be discussed, but be sure to stress the importance of *positive* notes. Have students design and create their own mailbags to tape to their desks to receive their notes.—*Ginny Diradour, Prince George, Va.*

Old stories never die

Keep work of past students available in a reading area or along a chalk tray so your students can read it for fun— and for ideas. Let your students know that their stories could be the inspiration for next year's students.—*June T. Page, Wilmington, Del.*

Telegram mania

Writing is fun when your message has the impact of a telegram. Get a telegram blank from Western Union and make a copy for each student. Before you distribute the blanks, discuss the kinds of messages that are sent by telegram. Write a few sample messages on the board using the conventional format.

As a first assignment, have your students send each other Feeling Good-a-Grams. To illustrate, send each student a telegram of this sort, such as "I FEEL GOOD WHEN YOU ARE ON TIME. STOP. YOUR TEACHER." Have the class draw names so each student gets a telegram.

Other assignments include a Riddle-Gram, in which the sender describes himself but signs off with "WHO AM I?," a Scary-Gram, bearing an anonymous warning, or a Fantasy-Gram congratulating a billion-dollar jackpot winner.—*Jule Marine, Salt Lake City*

A star is born

Legends about the constellations are great fodder for creative writing. Discuss with your students the stories of Cepheus, Orion, Cassiopeia, and other constellations. Then have each student draw a simple arrangement of stars on a piece of paper and write a story to mythologize its origin. Stars in the shape of a question mark could accompany a story about an inquisitive child; stars in the shape of a shamrock could inspire a story about leprechauns.

Cover a large wall with black or deep blue construction paper. Have each student set his constellation in the sky using foil star stickers. Put a small number next to each one, and put the same number on the corresponding legend. Post the legends at either end of the "sky."—*Lorraine Yadlon, Bayonne, N.J.*

A slideless slide show

To help students improve their descriptive writing skills have them write a script for a slideless slide show. To help the audience "see" the show, they'll have to make their descriptions vivid and complete.

First show a filmstrip. Then, have students think of ideas for good slide shows—for example, a sports event, a party, a class trip. Ask each student to jot down ideas for six or eight scenes and then write one-paragraph scripts for each.

A sample paragraph: "Here's the soccer team practicing before the big game. The field is sopping. The players' white uniforms hang on them, mud-spattered. The captain, on the sideline, looks tired. He's cradling a ball in his arms."

Have students present their "shows." Can everyone "see" each scene? Questions will prompt revisions.—*David E. Weber, Los Angeles*

Short takes

Old TV program listings can help teach students how to write short summaries. Have students study several viewing guides, noting the succinct style used in describing movies and programs. After discussing several examples of the summaries, show a short video or ask students to read a short story. Then invite your students to write, in viewing-guide style, about what they've seen or read.—*Cecil W. Morris, Roseville, Calif.*

My..., my...

This creative writing starter technique will encourage kids to relate their personal experiences from an unusual perspective.

Begin with: "My feet have been...." The students write sentences describing five or six places their feet have been, attempting to come up with examples no one else in class will duplicate—for example, "My feet have been on a 747 jet 40,000 feet in the air."

Have the students choose one of their sentences to expand into a short essay, continuing to write from the same perspective. Try other similar starters: "My hands have held...," "My eyes have seen...," "My laugh has been heard at...."—*Jule Marine, Salt Lake City*

Outline a lifetime

For a quick and easy outlining activity, have students look through newspapers for a week or so to find obituaries of people who led interesting lives or who were important to the community. Have students clip and bring in several obituaries.

Ask each student to choose a clipping, read it carefully, and outline it as if planning to write a report about that person's life. Most obituaries are organized into paragraphs dealing with where the person lived, his education, jobs he held, his community and professional affiliations, special accomplishments, and his family—each of which provides a natural topic heading.—*Ina Marantz, Livingston, N.J.*

You're invited

Use some *interesting* invitations to encourage good informational writing. All invitations tell when and where, but if the event is a river-raft trip or a bubble-gum-blowing contest, more details are required. Have your students think about the information needed in invitations to adventures such as:

• a surprise party
• a safari
• an archaeological dig
• a house-painting party
• an art exhibit.

Students should write invitations that include such details as the time the event begins and ends, what participants can expect to do, appropriate clothing, items to bring—whatever information is needed to prepare for taking part in activities. Have students read their finished invitations aloud, and ask the class to decide how informative they are.—*Sue F. Oldham, Oklahoma City*

Learning about the library

Send your class on a treasure hunt that can help them crack the code of the Dewey decimal system. Make several different master lists, each consisting of the call numbers and letters of several nonfiction books. Label the lists Hunt A, Hunt B, and so on. Write each catalog code, along with the hunt letter, on a separate index card. Insert each card—except the first from each hunt—in the book preceding it on the hunt list. During library period, give each student an index card with the first clue of a hunt on it.

Each student locates the book indicated on his clue card and finds that the jacket pocket of this book contains a card with the next clue on it. Students continue from book to book until they have found all clues, signaled by a "The End" card in the jacket pocket of a find.—*Kathleen Glassing, St. Paul*

Grocery guesses

To test your students' literal, interpretive, and creative reading abilities, set up reading packets based on grocery store flyers. Use a pocket folder with an ad page on one side and a list of questions or activities on the other. The questions can be divided into sets according to the level of the reading comprehension skills involved: Set A—literal, Set B—interpretive, Set C—creative/critical.

Set A questions could ask about listed prices, effective dates, and other specific material. Set B could ask for three phrases that give *facts* about products and three phrases that give *opinions*. Set C could ask why so many prices end with the digit 9.—*Lois Sonnenberg, Bowling Green, Ohio*

Talk to the animals

To encourage quiet (not silent) reading, stock a corner with books, pillows, a rug, and a small stuffed animal for each student in your class. When it's time for reading practice, invite each child to choose a book and read to an animal.—*Debra Ugalde, El Monte, Calif.*

The long-distance reader

You can raise money for charity or for a class outing—and spark interest in reading—by holding a daylong read-a-thon. Ask each participant to secure sponsors who'll pledge 10¢ or so for each hour the student spends in reading-related activities. Here are a few suggestions—beyond silent reading:

- a tour of the public library—focusing on the services and activities available
- a story-writing session—followed by a discussion of the masterpieces
- a word-game potpourri—play a variety of commercial and teacher-made games
- a treasure hunt—students fill in crossword puzzles, unscramble words, or solve riddles to get clues for finding the treasure
- a captioned silent movie—for a comic break in the day
- a rousing read-along, sing-along—display the words to favorite songs on an overhead projector.—*JoAnn Kraut, Bay City, Mich.*

Open the door to books

Spread the good word about favorite class books by decorating the doors of your classroom and library with oversized book jackets. Assign each book that the class has read to a design team. Have the group select and measure a door, then measure and cut butcher paper to cover it. Next, have the group design an intriguing "cover" that includes the book's title and author.— *Jodie Blassingame, Douglasville, Ga.*

It's in the cards

If your students bypass the library's card catalog, try a few rounds of card catalog trivia to change their habits. Prepare a form with a set of general tasks, such as:

- Find the title of one book that's written by _____ .
- Does the library have a multimedia kit on the subject of _____ ?
- Name three books the library has on the subject of _____ .

Make copies of the form. Then fill in the blanks, making each copy specific to a single card catalog drawer. After students have located all the required trivia, invite them to return to the card catalog to make up 10 original trivia items of their own—specific to a single drawer—for a trivia challenge with a friend.—*Carol Smallwood, Cheboygan, Mich.*

Spreading the news

Invite your colleagues to submit short, anecdotal accounts of two or three favorite children's books. Group the titles by author, subject, grade level, or teacher; list them in a booklet, *Books Your Teachers Read and Loved*, to keep in the library. Encourage students to compile their own "best books" lists.—*Marilynn Peterson, Troy, N.Y.*

The right expression

Dictate a few sentences—a portion of a story—to your students. On the chalkboard, write the excerpt along with several words or phrases that tell how the excerpt might be read: sadly, scarily, happily, angrily, teasingly, smugly, mysteriously, excitedly, sleepily.

Divide the class into two teams and whisper one of the words or phrases to each student. After each child reads the excerpt to convey the feeling you whispered to him, his team guesses which feeling he's performing. If the guess is wrong, the other team gets a chance.—*Nancy Glator, New London, Conn.*

Captivating book corner

Enliven your book corner with intriguing props and snappy signs. Here are some seasonal suggestions:

- *Props:* inflatable pool, swim ring. *Sign:* Dive into reading.
- *Props:* cornstalks, pumpkins, blanket. *Sign:* Fall in with good books.
- *Props:* cardboard carton fireplace, rug. *Sign:* Warm up with stories.
- *Props:* sleeping bag, pup tent. *Sign:* Camp out with a good book.
- *Props:* travel posters, duffle bag. *Sign:* See faraway places with books.
- *Props:* masking tape "baseball diamond" on the floor with a pillow for each "base." *Sign:* Catch the excitement—read!—*Karla A. Rhodeback, Elmwood Place, Ohio*

Read between the lines

To give your students practice in being aware of innuendos and hidden messages, give each child a copy of the following letter and read it aloud.

> Dear Jack:
> How are you enjoying school this year? My class is OK, but we spend a lot of time learning the times facts. I keep thinking how much I'd rather be with you at the ranch.
> You are really lucky to live on the ranch! There's always something fun to do. What are your plans for the summer? Please write and tell me everything.
> Your friend,
> Jason

Ask your students if they can find the hidden message in the letter. They'll easily see that Jason is angling for an invitation. Discuss hidden messages in general—why they're used in reading, writing, and conversation. Then ask your students to write letters, working in a hidden message.—*Faye Morrison, Palo Alto, Calif.*

Just joking around

Capitalize on the appeal of jokes to promote reading, listening, public speaking, and writing skills. Declare a once-a-week Joking-Around time. Anyone who wants to share a joke or riddle must write it out neatly and must be able to explain it if someone in the audience doesn't get it.

At the close of Joking-Around time, collect all jokes and riddles, so a student committee—whose members change throughout the year—can select several for publication in the class joke book. When you have about 10 selected jokes, copy them and staple them into booklets that students can take home and share with their families.—*Cynthia Stinton, Brush, Colo.*

Getting the best of a book

Your preplanning can help students get more from their reading. Here's how.

1. Read the book once for enjoyment only.

2. As you read it again, write comments and ideas for these three categories: quotations; style, theme, and content; and extended activities. For example, when a quotation appeals to you, write it in the quotation section. Put questions (comprehension, analysis, opinion) under category two. As you think of creative writing ideas, art projects, or other cross-curricular activities, jot them down under category three.

3. Review the material in each section, filling in gaps and making any changes.—*Rose Reissman, Brooklyn, N.Y.*

Character calling cards

Pass along readers' excitement about specific books with a character calling-card project. Have each student design a business card for a main character in a recently read book.

The card should identify the character and have an address suitable to the setting of the story. The card should also provide clues to the character's role in the story by listing his occupation or service he provides.

Have your students write the book title and author on the back of each card, then display the calling cards on a bulletin board.—*Daniel Meier, Brookline, Mass.*

Zip up that (book) jacket

Here's a new way to expose your students to books—and a new way to do book reports. Show your students the book jackets from some of their favorite books. Point out the eye-catching illustrations, character descriptions, plot summaries, and critical reviews often found on the jacket. Tell them that the next time they read a book independently, they'll create a *wearable* book jacket out of a large brown grocery bag.

Have your students write the book's title and author in a noticeable spot on the paperbag jacket, then use the rest of the space for written descriptions and illustrations of favorite characters, the most exciting scene, and so on. Invite other classes to a bookjacket fashion show, with your students describing the books they model.—*Pat Goldys, Baltimore*

5 Ws game

You can reinforce reading comprehension skills with this game that focuses on the news-story basics of the five Ws (who, what, when, where, and why). All you'll need are a die, a player token, and the game cards and game board described below.

To prepare:

- To make the game cards, clip 40 or so stories collected from newspapers or newsmagazines. The stories should be short, appealing, and include all five Ws. Mount each story on a 4 x 6-inch index card.

- To make the game board, use a sheet of oak tag or poster board. In the middle, draw a box and label it "Game Cards." Around it, draw five circles, each filled with a different color and labeled with one of the five "W" questions. Around the board make a border of boxes. Mark one box "Start." Color the boxes with the same colors used on the question circles and number them randomly from one to nine. Distribute both the colors and the numbers as evenly as possible.

To play:

- Player One draws the top game card and reads the story aloud.

- He then rolls the die and advances accordingly. The color of the box he lands on indicates the W question he must answer.

- If the group thinks his answer is correct, he gets the number of points shown on the box where he landed. If the group thinks his answer is incorrect, he gets no points. He puts the game card at the bottom of the stack.

- Play continues in this way until all players have returned to "Start," or until a time limit is reached. The highest score wins.—*E. Joan Abeles, Toronto*

Books on tape

Set up a cassette recorder in an out-of-the-way corner of the room and invite students to tape their impressions about books they've read. You might want to suggest a format for the reports to minimize long silent stretches on the tape.—*Emily L. Pierce, Lewisburg, Tenn.*

Booking get-togethers

Inject a social note into recreational reading by forming groups that will read the same book at the same time. Group your students by common interests and choose books that reflect those interests. Assign a portion of each group's book to be read by a specific date. Advise group members that when they get together again, they'll be discussing favorite chapters, reading passages aloud, and raising questions that they hope the book will answer as the reading continues.— *Margaret Goodwin, Chatham, Ill.*

Summaries to share

Devote a section of your bulletin board to book tips for students by students. First, discuss the writing of brief, lively book summaries designed to inform and intrigue prospective readers. (You might give some examples from book jackets.) Have your students follow that style as they write their own book summaries. Post these on the Book Tips bulletin board. In addition, ask each student to prepare three or four "book finder" cards with the title, author, and catalog number of the book. Place the cards in an envelope tacked below the appropriate summary. As the cards disappear, your students will know their classmates are following their recommendations.—*Bernita Brown Ford, Keyes, Okla.*

Handling interruptions

If your students frequently interrupt to comment or ask questions when you're reading to them, try reading the story twice. The first time, let the children ask as many questions as they want; the second time, don't allow any interruptions.—*Evelyn Witter, Milan, Ill.*

Extra, extra!

Instead of asking students to write individual book reports, invite groups of students who've read the same book to pool their ideas and prepare a single report using a variety of newspaper articles. Students write one kind of article to report on story happenings (standard news story), another to make critical evaluations of the book (editorial).

Other articles might feature:

- Weather. Was it a vital factor in the story? Were events or characters affected by the weather?
- Sports. Are any sports activities mentioned in the book? If not, can you imagine one of the characters involved in a particular sports event? Describe it.
- People. Who are the most important or most memorable characters in the book? Describe the traits that make them memorable.
- Advice. What advice might a character in the book ask of a newspaper columnist? What answer might he get?
- Classified ads. In view of the events in the story, what ads might characters in the book want to run: help wanted, employment wanted, lost and found?

When the reporting, writing, editing, and proofreading are completed, ask the groups to lay out their items in newspaper fashion, including enticing headlines. Display the reports on a bulletin board or compile them into a newspaper.—*Carolyn M. Wilhelm, Osseo, Minn.*

Plot lines

To help your students determine the proper sequence of events in a story, have them use a plot line—a 6-foot-long clothesline or piece of colored rope strung in a convenient part of the room. After you read them a story, help your students pick out five or six main events and print a brief statement about each on an index card. Then have students arrange the cards in sequence on the line, clipping them in place with clothespins.—*Jean Jenkins, Cranesville, Pa.*

"Cents-ible" reading material

This game, using supermarket coupons, is designed to generate reading interest among remedial readers. Collect a variety of "cents-off" coupons; make a list of the products for which you have coupons. Deal each player about 20 coupons, keeping a reserve for yourself.

Call out the name of a product from your list. All students who have that product in their collection turn in that coupon. If a student turns in a wrong coupon, return it— along with a coupon from your reserve. The player who gets rid of all coupons first is the winner.—*Dixie Parker, Cahokia, Ill.*

Books to borrow

If your students are willing to share their books after they've finished reading them, organize a separate classroom library for that purpose. All donations must have the owner's name written on the inside front cover. Ask for volunteers to be the librarians. Their job is to make a library card for each book by writing on an index card the title, author, lender's name, and original price of the book. The librarians place the cards inside the books and arrange them alphabetically on a bookshelf.

When a student wants to borrow a book, he signs the card and gives it to one of the librarians. Beside the borrower's name, the librarian writes the due date (2 weeks from the date the book's checked out) and files the card alphabetically in a card file box. If a book is damaged or lost, the borrower must pay the original purchase price so that the owner can replace it.—*Denise Lee, Springhouse, Pa.*

Classified clippings

Give your students a reason to read—
and reinforce their organizational
skills—by starting a newspaper clippings project. You'll need file folders,
scissors, a storage center, and a continuous supply of newspapers.

To begin, have your students browse
through the papers for a variety of story
and column categories: people, weather
and natural events, particular countries,
governments, sports, history, health, the
arts, and so on. Make file folders for
each category. Individually or in small
groups, your students choose a category
based on personal interest and check the
newspapers regularly for related articles. Then they clip, date, and label their
articles with the newspaper's name and
their own name, and file them in the appropriate category folder.

Your students can draw from the resource file for reports, story starters, independent reading, and bulletin
boards.—*Janice Whitaker, O'Fallon, Ill.*

Book report exchange

Team up with another teacher in your
grade level to give your students the opportunity for peer review. Give your students—class A—a book report
assignment. Explain that the reports
will be read and discussed (not graded)
by class B. Class B receives the same assignment.

Ask students not to put their names on
their papers. Instead, key each report
with a number matched to a master list.
As a group, Class A reads and discusses
class B's reports, and vice versa. A different student can read aloud each report
and write any comments on it.

With your colleague, establish ground
rules for the critiquing session. You
might ask students to consider what
they like about each report; what particularly good points the writer brings out;
and whether the writer tells enough
about a book for readers to decide if
they'd like to read it.—*Margaret J. Goodwin, Springfield, Ill.*

S-T-O-R-Y bingo

In this twist of the familiar game, students refresh their memories about stories you've read.

As soon as you've finished reading a book aloud to the class, invite students to brainstorm and list several questions about it—questions that involve characters and setting as well as plot. Each question should be phrased in such a way that the answer is the name of the book; for example: "What story has as its setting an art museum in New York City?"

Collect the questions from 9 or 10 books. Then create a five-by-five-square grid and distribute copies to your students, along with tokens. Have students randomly write in each square the title of one of the books you've read; some titles will appear more than once, but none should appear twice in the same column. When students have filled in their grids, have them head the five columns with the letters *S-T-O-R-Y*.

To play, read a question from your collection, introducing it with a column letter heading: "Under *T*: In which story would you find a dog who is given a violet-scented bubble bath?" Any student who has the title *Ribsy* in his *T* column should cover that square with a token. The game ends when someone covers five vertical, horizontal, or diagonal squares in a row and calls out "STORY!"—*Judy Divine, DeKalb, Ill.*

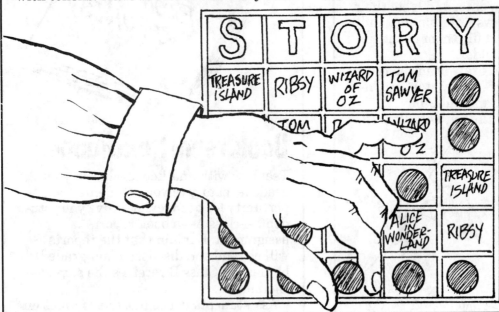

Reading smorgasbord

To stress the importance of reading, spread out a reading smorgasbord representing the myriad reading tasks a person performs each day. Display collected items—coupons, containers, bills, labels, ads, tickets—on tables around the room. To encourage investigation beyond browsing, provide a list of questions that students can answer by examining specific items. The questions might include:

- What's a child's dose of cough medicine?
- What three things does the electric company want you to check before you seal their return envelope?
- What choices do you have for TV viewing Tuesday at 8 p.m.?
- I contain corn syrup. What am I?
- Does Freddie's Pizza deliver?—*Nora Mitcham, Albuquerque, N.M.*

Winter wonderland

A personalized "winter (or fall, spring, or summer) scene" bulletin board can help your students practice their reading and artistic skills. Here's what to do:

- Cover a bulletin board with colored construction paper to create a simple winter scene (such as a frozen pond surrounded by snow-covered hills) as a background for student drawings.
- On small pieces of white construction paper, have your students draw themselves doing a wintertime activity. They should also draw a balloon above their heads and write what they're saying inside it.
- Have your students color their figures, cut them out, and tape them to the bulletin board.
- Now invite your class to read each other's work and discuss the various activities.—*Dorothy Zjawn, Jersey City, N.J.*

Madison Avenue mania

To practice alliteration, reading, and writing skills, have students invent fanciful products to display in a Madison Avenue campaign.

Ask each student to dream up an appealingly alliterative product name that contains his first or last name. For example: Helen's Heavenly Hazelnuts or Darrell's Dirt-Destroying Detergent.

When everyone has chosen a product name, invite students to design a package, including logo, and product information, such as weight, ingredients, manufacturer's name and address, guarantees, and so on.—*Jessie Hilton, Boca Raton, Fla.*

Comic comprehension

Here are a variety of ways to use comic strips to stress reading comprehension:

- Use comics to check comprehension on several levels. Ask questions calling for factual, inferential, or creative thinking.
- Use comics to study double meanings and puns.
- Use comics to teach students how to draw conclusions. Look for strips that invite discussion.
- Use cut-apart comic strips to help students practice sequencing. Make the task more challenging by putting separated frames from three episodes of the same strip into one envelope for sorting by story and by sequence within each story.—*Jill Kaiserman, Virginia Beach, Va.*

A wagon for a dragon

Capitalize on your students' fondness for silliness by introducing them to nonsense rhymes. All they have to do is connect two rhyming words in a phrase that projects an image: *fruit in a boot, a knight with a kite, a muff made of fluff, the gizzard of a wizard.* Have students illustrate their rhymes for an unusual display.—*Martha Snyder and Margaret Clayton, Reynoldsburg, Ohio*

Ad lit

Designed to stimulate the buyer, ad copy might prove an equally effective stimulator for your creative writers. Have students browse through magazines for ads with catchy phrases and interesting words. Each student should choose three favorites that become the word bank for some "found poetry." Students may begin word selection by choosing three exciting adjectives and three descriptive verbs. These words taken together may generate some images or conjure up some feelings that can help suggest a direction for the poetry. Of course, the product's name, uses, general reputation, or even the student's reaction to the product may suggest other ideas.—*Marilyn E. Miner, Orange, Calif.*

Letter-perfect poems

This poetry writing activity can show even reluctant poets how creative they are. Assign each student a letter of the alphabet. Ask each student to list nouns, verbs, adjectives, and adverbs that begin with the assigned letter. As students compile their lists, encourage them to say the words aloud, savoring the sounds and being alert for pleasing combinations. You might introduce the term *alliteration* while students are experiencing it. When each category contains 7 to 10 words, ask students to begin writing sentences and phrases to include in their poems. Here's an example:

> Proud as
> Peacocks, we
> People are.
> Perky,
> Polite,
> Patient, able to
> Plow through any
> Problem. Together
> Part of a
> Popular family.

After their poems are finished, ask each student to design a capital letter several inches high to introduce his poem. Next, have students tape or tack their letters and poems on a long sheet of shelf paper, in alphabetical order. Then let everyone enjoy an alliterative reading.—*Judy Ezop, Saginaw, Mich.*

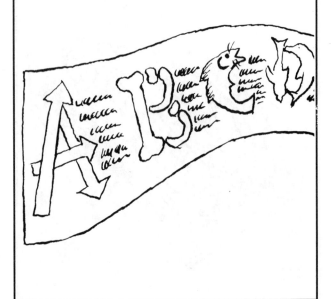

Grocery shopping for poems

To demystify poetry writing, have your students begin with something as mundane as a grocery list. Here's how. Divide the class into groups of three or four and ask each group to think of foods that might be on a grocery list. Then have them write the food names on scrap paper (one food item per piece of paper). You might want to give them supermarket flyers to spark ideas. After each group has generated 20 to 30 food names, encourage students to study and group the foods by moving them around like puzzle pieces. They might try grouping words that:

- begin with the same sound (alliteration).
- have the same vowel sound in the middle (assonance).
- end with the same sound (consonance).
- have the same number of syllables (rhythm).
- name green things, sour things, or strong-smelling things (sensory images).

When you've illustrated these familiar poetic elements, have your students use their words to create two- or four-line poems. Encourage them to add or eliminate words as they see fit. Appoint a secretary from each group to write the poems either in a notebook or on construction paper for display on a bulletin board.—*Joan Daniels Campbell, Ridgefield, Conn.*

Fill in the blanks

Here's a way to simplify the task of memorizing poetry and teach good enunciation skills in the process. Write a short poem on the chalkboard and discuss with your students its meaning, meter, and any unfamiliar words. Then ask students to read the poem aloud. Now erase one or two words, and have children repeat the poem, filling in the missing words. Continue erasing words and having children recite the poem until the entire poem has been erased—and memorized.—*Judith Groman, Lakewood, Ohio*

Triangular triplets

No matter how you look at it, a triangular triplet makes sense. It's a form of poetry that contains three rhyming lines, and the fun part is that the three lines can be read in any order. Have students glue together three Popsicle sticks to form a triangle. While the glue is drying, invite each student to look through old magazines or calendars for a picture—a nature scene, an animal, a cartoon—that sparks an idea for a poem. After selecting a picture, cutting it out, and gluing it within the Popsicle-stick triangle, the student writes three rhyming lines of poetry. Students copy their poems, one line per stick, onto the triangles.—*Lynne Ann Jones, Marietta, Ohio*

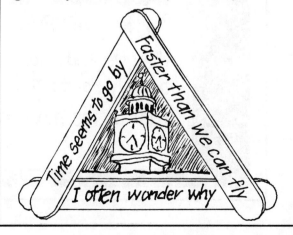

An illuminating project

Help your students understand imagery in poetry with a simple art form—"tissue on black." Each student will need two pieces of black construction paper, one piece of colored tissue paper, one index card, glue, scissors, pencil, and notebook paper. Read aloud a poem with lots of visual imagery—"Paul Revere's Ride," for example—and hand out copies of the poem. Then have students follow these directions:

• Choose a favorite passage and illustrate it with simple shapes on notebook paper.

• Shade in the parts you want to show in your picture, cut out the shaded parts, and discard them. Save the notebook page to use as a pattern.

• Place the notebook page on a piece of the black construction paper and outline the cut-out areas. Cut these out, and discard the cut-out black pieces and the notebook page.

• Use the cut-out sheet of construction paper to outline the design on the second sheet of construction paper. Again, cut out the shape and discard the pieces.

• Insert the tissue paper between the two pieces of construction paper and glue all three together.

• Write the title of the poem and the lines depicted on an index card, and glue it to the bottom of the illustration.

• Hang the finished artwork in the windows for a brilliant illustration of pictures in poetry.—*Scarlett Pirtle, St. Charles, Mo.*

Paul Revere's Ride

Then he said, "Good night!" and with muffled oar
Silently rowed to the Charlestown shore,
Just as the moon rose over the bay,
                    Scarlett Pirtle

Priming young poets

Inspiring poetry writing in youngsters is often a simple matter of coming up with the most appealing form. Here are several to choose from:

- **Personalized nursery rhymes.** If "Mary, Mary, quite contrary" becomes "Joanie, Joanie, tall and bony," will her garden grow differently? Invite students to put themselves into favorite nursery rhymes and let the situations develop as they may.

- **Sensory images.** A carnival, a holiday celebration, even a Saturday morning at home, all evoke images that relate to each of the five senses. Suggest a topic and ask your students to brainstorm sensory images, without using the words *see, hear, taste,* and so on. ("Bright singing and soft whispers/warm lights on family faces.") Stress the importance of starting each image briefly, making each word count. Be sure to stipulate that titles be brief (one or two words maximum) and that each line reflect only one sense.

- **Question-and-answer poems.**

  What is gray?
  A foggy bay
  On a cold, winter day.
  What is soft?
  A kitten's fur,
  A kitten's purr

- **Cumulative poems.** Students who liked "This Is the House That Jack Built" might be ready to work on "This Is the Stew That Lou Made" or "This Is the Car That Chris Fixed." Students should first map out exactly where the poem is headed—from largest to smallest elements or smallest to largest.—*Karen McGillivray, Salem, Ore.*

Haiku interlude

The brevity and simplicity of haiku make the 17-syllable form a creative writing staple. Add a little stage dramatics, and haiku writing can lead to an effective sharing time. Have students compose haiku on an agreed-upon theme, such as the seasons or colors in nature. Encourage each student to give plenty of thought to the poem's basic theme, and to the selecting of words to express the theme. When the poems are finished, view them on the overhead projector. Add appropriate music and invite students to read their poems aloud while they're being displayed.—*Helen Mills, North Plainfield, N.J.*

Digging out derivatives

Turn you students into industrious scribes (*scribere*—to write) by sending them on a unique word hunt.

First, prepare a list of about 10 Latin roots from which four or five familiar English words are derived. Then send your scribes to collect words based on those roots. Next, divide the class into four teams and have each team merge the word lists of its members, eliminating duplicates and verifying all words as true derivatives.

Finally, stage a "We Dig Derivatives" competition. Mark a section of the chalkboard into four columns—one for each team. In a box at the top of the board, write one of the roots. Working from their lists, the teams take turns coming to the blackboard to write one word at a time based on that root. Score one point for each valid contribution; deduct one point for repeated words.

When one team is stumped, others continue until all derivatives for that particular root have been transferred from team lists to the chalkboard. Then change the root, and have teams begin again.—*June Page, Wilmington, Del.*

In other words...

Students will build their vocabularies and practice dictionary skills when they play a guessing game with word equivalents. Explain the game by writing an example on the board and asking your students to guess its meaning. For example, "confidential optic" translates to "private eye." After students get the hang of it, invite them to make up their own. Here are more examples to get you started:

- infant jar—baby bottle
- solar spectacles—sunglasses
- molar bristles—toothbrush
- replete habitation—full house.—*Bill Gilson, Villa Park, Calif.*

Lifesaving list

Instead of waiting for kids to learn cautionary words the hard way, introduce a lifesaving vocabulary list. Include such words as *caution, emergency, flammable, physician, toxic, voltage, yield,* and so on. Post the list on a bulletin board and discuss how and where the words are commonly used.—*Sandra Frey, Lancaster, Pa.*

WOW! (Words of the Week)

Give students time each day to read from newspapers and magazines. Ask them to choose three unfamiliar words, underline them, and cut them out in context—a paragraph, a caption with its picture. Students paste the clippings into their WOW notebooks, then look up the underlined words and write the meanings next to the appropriate clippings.—*Elizabeth Maniaci, Cedar Grove, N.J.*

Banished vowels

Give your students a chance to fool around with words—and learn something about synonyms too—by banishing the vowel of your choice for a day. First let children with that vowel in their names choose a new name for the day. Then ask students to do the following—without using the forbidden letter:

- Plan a nutritious meal.
- Describe what they're wearing.
- Rewrite a nursery rhyme, substituting synonyms for words containing the banned letter.—*Shirley Russell, Lincoln, Calif.*

Vocabulary varieties

Here are three ways to reinforce vocabulary words:

- **Wall of words.** When a student finds a new word, encourage him to investigate its meaning and usage then copy it onto a construction paper "brick." Add the word to a cumulative vocabulary wall above the chalkboard or bulletin board and have its sponsor introduce it to the class.
- **Creative cartoons.** Have each student choose a word from the vocabulary list and draw a cartoon that conveys its meaning. Then have students caption their drawings with the words.
- **Symbiotic synonyms.** Ask each student to write a vocabulary word in large letters across the center of a piece of paper. Then, using a dictionary or thesaurus, have him look for synonyms to attach to the word, crossword-puzzle style.—*Lola Mapes, Des Moines, Iowa; and Donna H. Gibson, Germantown, Tenn.*

Words, words, words

Using unfamiliar words in intriguing contexts encourages kids to probe for meaning. These ideas use pictures to expose students to new words:

- Post a word like *idyllic* on the bulletin board. Beneath it place some pictures—a peaceful valley, a battle scene, someone mopping floors, for example. Then ask which of the pictures is the *idyllic* scene.

- Display an action picture of two people and ask: Is one person trying to *hoodwink, throttle, solemnize,* or *indemnify* the other?

- Show a picture suggesting strong personality traits and ask students to choose among *genial, naive, malevolent,* and *coquettish.—Lucy Fuchs, Brandon, Fla.*

Top 10

Stimulate creative thinking by having your students develop individual "Top 10" word lists in these categories:

- the most beautiful words
- the most ugly words
- the most delicious words
- the most scary words
- the most comforting words
- the most boring words.—*Jule Marine, Salt Lake City*

Poster pinups

This get-involved activity is designed to reinforce your students' reading vocabulary.

At children's eye level, display a large poster showing several separate picture elements that are easy to identify—for example, a zoo animal, a story character. Make a set of small tagboard word cards that describe the items on the poster.

Each day, have several students pick cards and attach them to the appropriate picture elements on the poster. Discuss the different words they might use to identify one picture. For example, cards labeled *puppy, dog,* and *beagle* could all describe the same animal. Continue the activity until all the cards have been used.—*Judy Shellabarger, Finn Rock, Ore.*

Setting "word" records

To prepare students for this activity, introduce them to the *Guinness Book of World Records*. Then challenge students to set their own records, by finding as many specific types of words as they can. Possibilities are endless; here are a few to get you started:

- In 15 minutes, find the most words that begin with the prefix *pro*.
- For homework, find the most living things beginning with the letter *s*.
- During this period, find the most homophone pairs— blue, blew; seen, scene; and so on.

Stretch long banners of colored paper around the room for posting final results and the names of current record holders.—*Sue Kreibich, Winona, Minn.*

Purfle the peplum, please

Challenge your students to dig into their dictionaries and come up with a collection of offbeat words. You might suggest a goal of 10 words per digger; no proper nouns, no foreign words, no abbreviations, no archaic words. Have students record the meaning of each word, its pronunciation, and its part of speech. Then have them use each word in a sentence.—*Robert E. Rubinstein, Eugene, Ore.*

Word search

Create a word montage board by clipping familiar words from magazines and newspapers and mounting them randomly on tagboard. Then invite your students to use the board for a variety of tasks, including:

- Find and write down as many nouns as you can. Do the same for verbs.
- Look for contractions and record any you find. Write the words the contractions stand for.
- Find six adjectives. Put them in pairs any way you like, and use each pair to describe something in the room.
- Choose a partner and take turns reading words aloud, going in alphabetical order. Are there any letters you can't find words for?—*Tana Lawson, Elmira, Ore.*

Concentration—with a twist

This game, "Concentration on Yourself", requires careful listening.

Prepare about 60 statements that apply to one or more of your students. Think of things the kids do, wear, like, and dislike; of their appearance, family, neighborhood, and friends. The statements can be general ("I wear jeans.") or specific ("I collect old coins."). Number the statements.

Read to your students the first five statements, with their numbers. Each student should try to remember the statements that apply to him. When you say "Write," the students write each applicable statement and its number. Both number and statement must be accurate.

Read the five statements again so students can check what they wrote. If, on the second reading, they recognize a new applicable statement, they can't write it down. Instead, they put a stroke mark on their paper. Then you proceed to the next group of five statements, and so on until you're finished.

Students tally the statements and the stroke marks. This gives them their actual and potential scores. The goal, as you play the game more, is for the two scores to come closer and closer.—*June Cavarretta, East Dundee, Ill.*

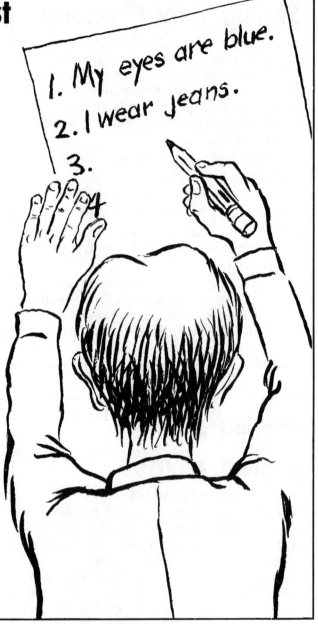

A search for clones

This activity combines listening skills, sequencing, and public speaking into one fun practice session. Prepare about 10 designs for your students to duplicate *solely* by your oral instructions. Some designs can be recognizable, such as a smiling face; others can be abstract.

Begin by reviewing such concepts as *first, second, next, right hand corner, zigzag,* and *curve.* Hand out blank paper and give students directions for duplicating your design. Then have students compare their designs with your original. Encourage them to comment on whether your directions were clear or vague. Invite students to create a design and direct the class to duplicate it.—*Gail Rosenfeld, Spring Valley, N.Y.*

The three little "oinks!"

Strengthen listening skills by inviting your students to provide sound effects as you read them a story. Choose a story with a lot of action. Underline the characters' names along with a selection of nouns and action verbs. Ask your students to improvise a sound for each of the underlined words—for example, *water* might be sounded as "swishhhh."

Read the story aloud. Whenever you come to an underlined word, the students should respond with their rehearsed sounds. You can have the class respond in unison, or you can assign a different word to each child or small group.— *Judith Spitzberg, Brookline, Mass.*

Eggs-tra sensory perception

Help your students refine their sense of hearing by shaking up some sound. You'll need a dozen plastic eggs and a large basket to hold them.

Choose a number of items to put in the eggs that'll make distinctive sounds when you shake them—for example, rice, sand, paper clips, dried beans, and so on. Put the same amount of each item into two eggs. Now mix all the eggs together in the basket.

Have your students take turns picking two eggs, shaking each one, and listening to decide whether or not they sound alike. Give each student three tries. If he thinks he has a match, he keeps it; if not, the eggs go back in the basket.

When all the eggs are paired, have the class listen as the six children with the pairs shake each of their eggs. If everyone agrees that the sounds match, have them guess what's inside and check their perceptions by opening the eggs.— *Linda Oggenfuss, Maywood, N.J.*

Personally speaking

A classroom collection of personalized riddles will flatter your students into practicing listening and a host of other skills.

Compose simple riddles that incorporate the children's names. Print the riddles on the board and read them aloud. Then ask the students to copy the riddles and to answer them in writing. For example:

- Joe brings it to school every day, but it's always gone by the time he goes home. What is it? (his lunch)
- Terry has some that are black, and she has some that are brown. They always come in pairs. What are they? (shoes)
- Lynn sees better with them. She drinks from them. What are they? (glasses).—*Beth Ann Black, Beeville, Tex.*

Tuning in to news

Help students become alert, aware, and involved listeners by scheduling a weekly news spot and "debriefing" sessions.

Tape a radio newscast and develop 10 questions about it for students to answer. Start out with factual-recall questions that have short answers. As students learn to listen better, include opinion questions.—*La Trobe Barnitz, Landisville, Pa.*

Today there was a 3-alarm fire at a clothing store on Market Street. There were no injuries and damage was small.

Thoughtful listening

Choose a textbook selection. First talk about how to ask good questions, then divide the class into groups of four or five. Select a student in each group to read a section aloud from the text while the others listen. Remind the reader that he should be thinking of one or two questions to ask the listeners when his time's up. Circulate among the groups as they answer and discuss the questions. When they've finished, have a new reader continue in the same fashion. Have the groups write up questions for a class review after they finish each textbook selection.—*Susanne F. O'Brien, Concord, N.H.*

"Did you follow directions?"

Challenge each of your students to create a test requiring classmates to follow directions. Ask a volunteer to prepare and dictate a 10-item test, which can call for written or oral responses. Here are some sample items:

- On the first line of your paper, print your full name in capital letters.
- Turn your paper over and on the back draw a large circle.
- Divide the front of your paper into four sections using a vertical and horizontal line that cross in the middle.—*Patricia A. Cianni, West Deptford, N.J.*

Listen closely

Sharpen your students' listening skills by inviting them to play the game of "Categories." Have each player contribute a word to a stated category, such as mammals or things found in a fast-food restaurant.

Announce the topic and set a time limit for giving answers— perhaps 5 seconds. Also decide on a signal your students can give when they hear a wrong or repeated answer. To play, have your students stand beside their desks; they'll sit down if they give a wrong answer, repeat an answer, or can't think of an answer. Play continues until one student remains standing.—*Theresa Pennington, Ashland, Ky.*

A chorus line

Stretch attention spans during spelling review by getting your students actively involved. Identify physical characteristics that several of your students have in common—wearing sneakers, having black hair, wearing earrings. Call out the characteristics one by one and ask everyone fitting that description to stand up and spell in unison one of the review words.—*Joyce McShara, Putnam Valley, N.Y.*

In sight, in mind

Help your students remember their spelling words by offering a variety of ways to write and review them. For example, your students can:

- write words in the middle of long paper strips then staple or tape them into a chain to wear or display.
- write words on folded paper hats or on cut-out oak tag visors.
- write words "rainbow" style with each letter in a different color, or make all vowels one color and all consonants another.
- make a simple map on plain paper and use spelling words to name all of its features—"Top Street," "Best Park," "Turtle River."—*Debbie Lerner and Helen Nash, Kansas City, Mo.*

Help with homophones

Help your students learn to spell troublesome sound-alikes by working together to create picture clue sketches. For example, use a crown for *prince* and two or three footprints for *prints*. On their study lists, your students can draw their picture clues next to each homophone to help them remember and link the words' meanings to their spellings.—*Nancy Stempek, Salem, Ore.*

Spelling survey

Have students collect and analyze their spelling errors over a period of weeks. By studying the various misspellings, students might be able to discover some patterns—doubling letters, dropping letters, and so on.

Next, devise a survey sheet with questions such as:

- What words do you find difficult to spell?
- Why do you think these words give you trouble?
- Do you have any tricks to help you spell words (not just the words you've mentioned)?
- Why do you think people misspell words?

Have each student interview three people over the age of 16— siblings, parents, neighbors. Compile a master list of difficult words, including a frequency-of-response tally for each word. Students may select words from this list to add to their own.

Compare the survey's "reasons for misspellings" with your students' reasons; determine if the tricks people use for remembering spellings yield any valuable ideas to adopt.—*Lola R. Mapes, Des Moines, Iowa*

An international flavor

Wake up your students by including useful and interesting non-English words on spelling lists. If you have students from various cultural backgrounds, use this built-in resource for bonus words such as *amigo, shalom, salaam, maestro, chapeau.* If your class has no bilingual students, use non-English words that tie into social studies or geography units.—*Paula Steinback Hamilton, Alamogordo, N.M.*

Spelling puzzle

Invite students to use their spelling list to create word puzzles for classmates to decipher. Choose about 20 words and draw a grid that will hold all the letters of the words plus several extra. Copy the grid and give one to each child. Have students write in each of the required words, either vertically, horizontally, or diagonally, and fill in the remaining spaces with any letters they choose. Then have students write their names on the backs of their papers and pass their grids to their neighbors for deciphering.—*Fred J. Philip, Combined Locks, Wis.*

Teacher plays too

In this spelling game, the teacher participates by supplying all consonants; students supply the vowels. First, assign a
small group of students to each vowel.
Then announce a word and, if it begins
with a consonant, say the first letter.
Continue calling the consonants until a
vowel is required. The students who represent the proper vowel should say it;
the back-and-forth exchange continues
until the word is correctly spelled.—
Brenda Logan, Boise, Idaho

Open book spelling

At the conclusion of some spelling tests,
give students a few minutes to look up
words they want to correct or confirm.
The exercise will help students recognize
incorrect words and give them practice
using the dictionary.—*Jane S. Hancock,
Glendale, Calif.*

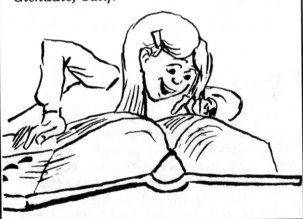

But can you spell it?

For personalized tests, include students'
names on your spelling lists. You can either include several names over a period
of weeks or you can focus one week's
spelling assignment on just names.—
Glenn Fisher, Berkeley, Calif.

Roll and spell

Give the traditional spelling bee a new
twist by turning it into a roll-it-and-spell-
it game. To begin, write several spelling
words on large blank cards, one to a
card. On the flip side of each card, write
the number of letters in the word. Place
the cards, number side up, on the chalk
tray.

Now take a blank die and mark it with
the numbers found on the backs of the
word cards. Divide the class into teams.
The first player from the first team rolls
the die, picks a card whose number
matches that shown on the die, and
gives the card to the scorekeeper. The
scorekeeper turns over the card, and
asks the player to spell the word. If the
player spells it correctly, he wins for his
team the number of points on the back of
the card. If he spells the word incorrectly, he receives no points. Players
from both teams alternate turns. The
winning team is the one with the most
points after a designated time period.—
Esther Bovest, Canton, Ohio

Quotation station

To stress writing dialogue correctly, provide at a learning station the following activities:

- On a work sheet, write phrases snatched from conversations. Write all statements in lowercase and leave them unpunctuated. Students supply capital letters and punctuation marks.

- Glue Sunday newspaper cartoons to paper and cut them apart by frames. Have your students arrange the cartoons sequentially, then have them write down the dialogue, crediting the speaker and adding punctuation.

- Supply a tape recorder and have students tape interviews with other students or adults in the school. Students then write as direct quotations both the interviewer's questions and the responses.—*Nancy Ludwig, Manhein, Pa.*

Pop-up punctuation

To teach ending punctuation marks, assign various students the roles of periods, question marks, and exclamation points. Then give each student a sheet of poster board on which to draw his assigned mark. Now read aloud some sentences. The student whose punctuation mark is appropriate for each sentence should quickly stand and hold up his sign.—*Brenda Harger, Kuna, Idaho*

Quote collectors

Inject some life into practicing dialogue punctuation by sending your students on a 1-day mission of quotation collecting. Ask students to discreetly jot down interesting conversation they hear in the classroom, the hallways, lunchroom, playground, gym, bus, and so on. Encourage them to collect a variety of sentence types.

Set up a quotation collecting box for deposits throughout the day. Later, select a number of quotations from the box to write on the chalkboard. After everyone's had a chance to read and enjoy them, use the quotations for demonstrating and practicing the mechanics of quotation punctuation.—*Shirley T. Shratter, Pittsburgh*

New twist on an old mark

To liven up punctuation study and spur creative thinking, ask students, "What is an apostrophe and who invented it?" But before they turn to a reference book, explain that you want the answers to come from their imaginations. Here are two actual student responses:

- The person who invented the apostrophe was probably an old man with an aching back, all bent over so that he looked like an apostrophe himself. His name was William Apostrophe.

- An apostrophe was invented when a smart person's pen slipped, and she kept on writing.—*Shirley Russell, Lincoln, Calif.*

When? Now!

Put some punch into punctuation practice—and help your students speak expressively—with this quick sentence-making game.

First, prepare a set of word cards. On each card, write one word and an end-of-sentence punctuation mark. Pass out the cards, then ask each student to use the word in the kind of sentence the punctuation dictates. Invite volunteers to read their sentences with appropriate expression.—*Ellen Sheer, Teaneck, N.J.*

"No shoving!" squawked the squash

To get students to write imaginative—and accurately punctuated—dialogue, suggest they "listen in" to conversations taking place among groceries in a shopping bag.

Distribute supermarket advertising circulars to give students ideas about grocery products. Ask them which ones might be especially talkative, excitable, pushy, and so on. List the ones they choose on the outside of a brown shopping bag, and post it for reference on the bulletin board. Now give each student several blank speech balloons. Ask them to write on their speech balloons complaints, observations, quips, and repartee that might be coming from inside the bag.

Now have students convert the speech balloons into written quotations complete with proper punctuation and speaker identification. Some examples:

- "Lettuce out of here!" shrieked Mrs. Iceberg.

- "The tide is high," hummed the detergent.—*Elaine LaFleur, Mattapoisett, Mass.*

Personal figures of speech

Help your students see themselves in a different light by reviewing simile and metaphor. Get your students to think about themselves with questions such as: "How would you describe the way you look?" "What are some of your personal goals?" "How do you go about solving a problem?" "What makes you feel disappointed?"

Ask them to use these personal profiles to find unusual match-mates—a plant or animal, a game or toy, something used around the house or at school, a food, a season or holiday, and so on. Next, have your students list common characteristics of themselves and their chosen match-mates. Using these comparisons, your students can now write personal poems, with their names as the titles:

Molly
Brightly blooming (prickly, too),
A rose bush twines and climbs,
Stretching
To see the world beyond the fence.
—*Hope Crescione, New Haven, Conn.*

Understanding idioms

Although idioms add color and expression to language, they can hamper reading comprehension. Here's an exercise that can help children better understand idioms. Begin by mentioning several idioms:

- Hold your head up high.
- It's raining cats and dogs.
- This car's a lemon.

Next, list several idioms on the board. Have each student select one, write it across the top of his paper, and draw a picture to accompany it. Across the bottom of his paper, have him write the real meaning of the idiom. Encourage students to share their work—*Dr. Elizabeth K. Liddicoat, Allentown, Pa.*

The classroom speaks

For a creative writing idea that combines personification and poetry, ask your students to imagine that all classroom items—textbooks, pencils, erasers, chalk—can talk. What would they say? To get your students thinking, write these questions on the chalkboard: What does the object do? What does it see? How is it treated? What are its wishes?

Choose an object by group vote, and have your students answer the questions about it. List their answers on the board, one under the other. When you have several ideas, read them aloud, then together, revise, reorganize, and edit the list to create a poem. Now, invite your students to choose an object and try the exercise on their own.— *Sally Krause, Penn Valley, Calif.*

Multiple meanings

Make a list of 20 words that have more than one meaning. As a class, create a dialogue that includes all the words on the list. The conversation should use only one meaning of each listed word. Then revise and rewrite the dialogue so that the speakers use a different meaning of each word on the list.

Compare the two dialogues for similarities and differences. Discuss how the context of each conversation made the speakers' meanings clear.—*Mary K. Simpson, Woodbridge, Va.*

Whooo's a night owl?

With the class, brainstorm a list of metaphoric situations in which animal characteristics are attributed to humans, and vice versa. For example:

- The squirrel is a miser storing nuts for the winter.
- Mary Ellen is a night owl, working until dawn.
- Grandpa is a bear in the morning.

Have students write a story based on one of the metaphors listed during the brainstorming session. Then, have students rewrite the story reversing the roles of the human and the animal, changing the subject for instance from a miserly squirrel to a squirrelly miser.—*Mary K. Simpson, Woodbridge, Va.*

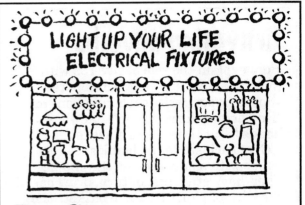

Pun City

Tap into pun appeal by inviting your class to design and create Pun City—a place where every business has a pun for a name.

Have your students list businesses that might be found in Pun City. Next, to get into a punny state of mind, your students might:

- list for each business its daily tasks, the equipment and materials it uses, the kinds of people it serves; then select from that list the words that have more than one meaning. For example, a bakery has flour (flower), and two words connected with money—"bread" and "dough."
- think of pun-filled expressions that could be connected with a business ("upper crust," "chicken feed," "top dog," "time on my hands," and "hair-raising").
- list homophones (pair, pear; rein, reign) and words with multiple meanings (right, bill), then try working one of these double-meaning words into the name of a business.

Mix any of these tactics, with your creative punsters' sense of humor and watch Pun City businesses come to life: Holy Heaven Doughnut Shop, Light Up Your Life Electrical Fixtures, and Shampoodle Dog Grooming. Top off the fun by having your students draw pictures of their stores with the pun names prominently featured. When the stores are cut out, line them up on a Pun City bulletin board.—*Sandra J. Frey, Lancaster, Pa.*

Activating adverbs

Help explain the role of adverbs with this charades-like game. On separate slips of paper, write such directions as "Hop across the room" or "Clap your hands." Put the slips in a basket.

Give each student a blank sheet of paper with a crease down the middle. Then have students, in turn, draw one of the slips of paper from the basket. The first student reads the direction to himself and performs the action; the other students write on one side of their paper *what* the child did, and on the other side *how* he did it.

For example, after a student claps her hands, a classmate might write "clapped her hands" on one side on the paper; on the other, he might write "loudly." When everyone has had a chance to perform, compile a list of the adverbs used.— *Alida Ciampa, Fairbanks, Alaska*

Complements: the object of the game

This activity turns an ordinary deck of cards into a grammar-practice aid.

Separate the deck into suits and assemble four different-colored permanent felt-tip pens. With one pen write on each heart card a noun or pronoun suitable for the subject of a sentence. With another pen, write on each diamond a complement: predicate adjectives, predicate nouns, predicate pronouns. On each spade write a verb, with about half being forms of "to be" and other linking verbs. The clubs are objects—both nouns and pronouns. The fact that the subjects and complements appear on suits of the same color helps to establish an association between these sentence elements.

Deal the entire deck to two, three, or four players. The first player lays down a subject; the second, a verb. The next player can either declare the sentence finished (for four points) or add an object or complement, depending on the verb. The next player starts a new sentence.

Each player receives the face value of the cards he plays, writing the score as soon as cards are played. If a player doesn't hold a playable card and cannot declare the sentence complete, play passes to the left. Play continues until all possible plays have been made. The highest score wins.— *Patricia Randall, Newton, Kan.*

Where there's a will...

Writing wills full of such sentences as, "I leave Burt, my best friend, my entire teddy bear collection," can make learning indirect objects easy—and fun.

Begin by writing a few sample sentences on the board—*Tami wills eighth-grade cheerleaders her worn-out poms-poms,* for example. Then ask students to prepare their wills. Encourage them to have fun with the assignment; the wills needn't be serious.—*Shirley Ullom, Dodge City, Kan.*

Noun and verb on rye

Here's a way to illustrate how the parts of speech fit together to make a sentence. Out of construction paper, cut out items to resemble slices of bread, pieces of cheese or meat, a jar of mayonnaise, and a salt shaker. Label the bread "noun," the cheese "verb," the mayonnaise "adjective," and the salt "adverb."

First, make the simplest kind of sentence sandwich by putting a piece of cheese or meat on a slice of bread. Ask your students to supply examples of this kind of sentence, such as "Cows eat" or "Children skip." Add another noun by adding another slice of bread: "Cows eat grass"; "Children skip rope." Add some mayonnaise to put an adjective in your sentences: "Big cows eat grass"; "Young children skip rope." Add salt and your sentences become: "Big cows eat grass lazily"; "Young children skip rope happily."—*Denise Lee, Springhouse, Pa.*

The odd couple

This activity, which teaches subjects and predicates, produces amusing as well as reinforcing results.

On individual squares of construction paper write a collection of sentence subjects. Make half as many sentence parts as you have students in the class. Do the same for sentence predicates, using different colored construction paper. The two sentence parts shouldn't be coordinated; in fact, the more incongruous, the better. Here are some examples:

- **Subjects.** The monkey, seven silly snakes, the bragging bunny, the old rusty car, eight falling stars
- **Predicates.** Tripped over the ball, called for help, jumped rope, got stuck in the locker, cried

Give each student a square, and ask him to choose a partner with a different colored square. Have the partners read aloud their sentences.—*Kelly Macaulay, Homer, Alaska*

Language land

This activity is bound to keep your students interested in learning parts of speech.

Draw a follow-the-path game track with sections large enough to accommodate word cutouts. Give a copy of the game sheet to each student. Invite students to cut out of magazines small pictures of objects or people and glue one next to each empty section on his sheet. Then have students label each picture with an appropriate noun.

Have students exchange game sheets. Each player grabs a magazine and begins the race toward the end of the track. To get there, he must cut out an adjective to accurately describe each noun—in sequence—and paste it in the empty section next to the noun.—*Sandra Frey, Lancaster, Pa.*

thick · (ABC) book · slimy · octopus

broken · shiny · diamond

car · FINISH

rotten · sharp · knife

apple · smelly · pipe

smiling · girl · delicious · pie

small · house

angry · fat · cowboy

dog · START

Grammar graphics

Learning the parts of speech can be fun when you invite your students to make illustrated grammar charts. You'll need magazines and catalogs, scissors, glue, and several sheets of paper for each child. Give your students the following directions for noun, adjective, verb, and adverb charts:

- **Nouns.** Hold a piece of paper horizontally and fold it into three vertical columns. Cut out several pictures of people and places and glue these to the center column. Next, identify each picture by writing a common noun in the left-hand column and a proper noun in the right-hand column.

- **Adjectives.** Cut out a few pictures of people, places, and things and glue them randomly on a piece of paper. Near each picture, write words that could describe it. Circle each adjective and draw a line from it to the picture.

- **Verbs.** Hold a piece of paper vertically and fold it into six horizontal rows. Paste a picture of someone or something at the beginning of each row. Then write words telling different actions that the pictured people or things might do.

- **Adverbs.** Glue several pictures of activities to a piece of paper. Above each picture, write a verb describing the action being shown; below the picture, write a word telling how the action is being performed.—*Lucinda L. Klevay, Millersburg, Ohio*

Having a ball

You can help your class appreciate modifiers with this poster-making project. Each poster will focus on a general category—balls for instance—that have many subsets.

Have students work in small groups, each concentrating on a specific kind of ball: beach ball, football, cotton ball. Each group brainstorms to list words that describe its ball— its size, surface, weight, action, and so on.

Then, a poster-making committee uses illustrations of various balls (drawings or pictures clipped from catalogs) as the centerpiece of a display about balls. The committee then fills the surrounding space with modifiers from the group lists.—*M. Louise Meyer, Hanover, Pa.*

It's in the cards

This variation of gin rummy is a handy way to teach noun and verb agreement and to familiarize students with what makes a complete sentence.

Ask each student to make up five descriptive sentences using as many single adjectives, adverbs, and prepositional phrases as they wish. Have students write each of the subject parts of the sentences and each of the predicate parts on separate index cards.

Appoint a dealer to shuffle the cards and deal out six to each player; place extra cards facedown in the center of the playing area. Each player combines as many subject and predicate cards as he can to form complete sentences and displays the sentences on the playing area. Then the first player draws from the facedown pile, tries to complete another sentence, and then discards. The next player may draw either the discard or a card from the pile. Play continues until a student has formed all his cards into complete sentences and calls out "Sentence Rummy."

Each complete sentence is worth five points; subtract one point for each card left in a player's hand after a certain number of rounds.—*Marshall Levy, Milton, Mass.*

May I take your order?

The Short Vowel Restaurant, complete with real food, will help kids recognize short vowel sounds.

At the beginning of the week, write the five short vowels on the chalkboard and ask your students to think of food names with those sounds. Review the sounds with the students and have them add to the list throughout the week.

Midweek, invite students to bring in foods from the list for the Short Vowel Restaurant on Friday. Prepare menus, including food prices (one smile, two claps, one hug). Ask school staff members to come eat at the restaurant.

On Friday, have the children push their desks together and arrange their foods by short vowel sounds. As they serve, have them say the name of the food and short vowel sound it contains.—*Mary Fran Wagner, Stevens Point, Wis.*

Bag, beg, big, bog, bug

Here's an easy way to help students who are having trouble hearing and pronouncing short vowel sounds: Put the letter *b* in front of each vowel and the letter *g* behind it. For example, when you add *b* and *g* to *e*, you get *beg.* Hearing each short vowel sound as part of a word helps children identify and remember the sound more easily.—*Cynthia Wise, Newnan, Ga.*

Jailing the rule breakers

Phonetic rules are helpful, but let's face it, there are a lot of exceptions. Rather than let those exceptions become a problem, why not put them in "jail." A shoe box with windows cut in the sides and fitted with pipe-cleaner bars will provide maximum security for the most phonetically undisciplined.

When you present new words, let your students be the jury, deciding which go to jail and which roam free. When a word is found guilty of rule breaking, send it to jail by writing it on a slip of paper and tossing it in the shoe box. Students may visit the rule-breakers to review and study them. You can set the jailbirds free when your students have mastered them.—*Michele Delperuto, Camillus, N.Y.*

Mind your ABCs

For this game, designed to teach alphabetizing, you'll need two sets of letters-of-the-alphabet cards and a box. Organize two teams and have each player draw a letter from the box. Allow 2 minutes' thinking time during which each player thinks of three words beginning with his or her letter and puts the words in alphabetical order.

Alternating teams, randomly call on players to give their words. If their order is correct, the team gets a point. If not, a team member must correct it before play goes on.—*Elizabeth Markstahler, Broadlands, Ill.*

ABC items

Take stock of your room with an alphabetical eye— abacus, books, crayons, dictionaries, and so on. Make up several boxes of alphabetize-the-items collections for students to put in order. Point out the possibility of alternative orders based on variations in naming items— notebook instead of binder, pen instead of ballpoint.— *Barbara Conrady, Los Angeles*

Handling problem letters

Here's a trick to help students remember the difference between *b* and *d*. Have each child make fists and face them toward his body with thumbs extending up. The configuration of the left hand forms a lower case *b;* the right hand, a *d.* As a bonus, the letters appear in the same order as they do in the alphabet when viewed left to right.— *Christine Filipski, Altmar, N.Y.*

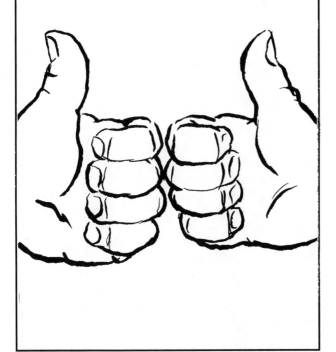

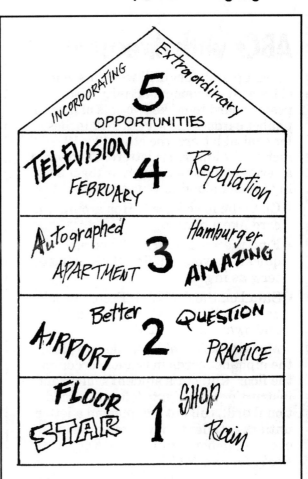

Syllable house

This activity will help your students develop pronunciation skills and learn how to group words according to syllables.

On the chalkboard, draw the outline of a five-story house. Ask your students to tell you words to put into the house— one-syllable words on the first floor, two-syllable words on the second floor, and so on.

Using poster board, you can also make a syllable house self-checking activity for a learning center. Invite students to make game cards by cutting out words from newspapers and magazines. Working in groups, have students mount the words on index cards, marking the number of syllables on the backs of the cards as a self-check. Then students or groups can work independently to place cards on the proper floors of the house and reinforce their knowledge.—*Linda H. Bair, Spring, Tex.*

ABCs with direction

Liven up alphabet drill with this whole-class body-movement activity. Use poster board to make two sets of large alphabet cards—one set (12 x 12 inches) for capital letters, the other (9 x 12 inches) for lowercase letters. Then write a series of directions such as the following to read aloud to your students:

- Go to the lowercase *b*. Hop around the card like a bunny.
- Find the small letter *q*. Then as quickly as you can, find the small letter *g* as in *go*.
- Stand on the capital *A*. Pretend you're an acorn that grows into a great oak and sways in the wind.

Move desks or tables aside and place the alphabet cards in random order on the floor. Call out a student's name and instructions for him to follow. For additional drill, call out a name and a letter until the students have brought you every alphabet card.—*Jessie Knight, Rocky Mount, N.C.*

Contraction crossover

This version of musical chairs will help students associate contractions with their root words. You'll need word cards—some with contractions, some with their corresponding root words.

Have all your students, except one, place their chairs in a circle. The remaining student stands in the center. Give each seated player a word card, instructing him to note what's on his card then to hold it out in front of himself. Call out a contraction. The student holding that contraction quickly changes places with the student holding its corresponding two-word combination. Meanwhile, the student who's standing scrambles for one of the vacated chairs. Whoever is left standing gets to be in the center.

Vary the game by calling out the two-word combinations instead of the contractions. After several plays, have students pass their cards to the left.—*Judy Montgomery, Fountain Valley, Calif.*

Chapter 5
MATH

Wacky word problems

These word problems are light on words, heavy on analyzing. Students must interpret the problem, determine the operation, and discount irrelevant data. Consider the following:

3 cats	*4 dogs*
1 car	*4 boys*
How many pets?	

6 girls	*2 cats*
3 boy	*0 bike*
How many cats' eyes?	

4 cars	*2 cats*
3 birds	*7 bikes*
How many wheels?	
How many legs?	

Wacky word problems are especially useful where reading skills are limited. But you might want to try them as a group activity first, to help kids get used to the format and style.—*Rich McKenzie, Battle Creek, Mich.*

Roman numeral puzzle

Plotting points on a graph that's also a puzzle adds interest when kids learn about Roman numerals. Use the following activity as a model for you and your students to make up similar examples of your own.

Draw a 7 x 6-inch grid, making the lines 1 inch apart. Label each line with a different Roman numeral. Choose the numerals at random and don't put them in order. Above the grid, write coordinates of points chosen on the grid, but use Arabic rather than Roman numerals. In this example, these points are chosen:

1. (33, 611)	7. (1900, 16)
2. (105, 2070)	8. (500, 19)
3. (90, 14)	9. (90, 16)
4. (500, 40)	10. (105, 80)
5. (1900, 9)	11. (90, 9)
6. (1006, 80)	12. (500, 40)

Each of these numbers is the same as one of the Roman numerals on the grid.

Have students first write the equivalent Arabic numerals next to each Roman numeral. Then have them plot the points in the coordinates given and connect them in the order in which they were plotted. If they can't find a coordinate, they know they've made a mistake in converting one of the numerals.— *Sandra J. Frey, Lancaster, Pa.*

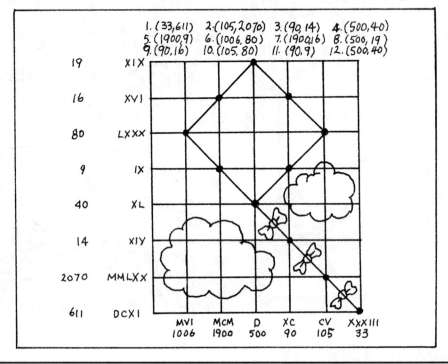

Hanging around

To encourage your students to think mathematically, post a standard multiplication table and invite them to investigate it.

Your students will discover lots of interesting patterns and observations. For example, what do they notice when they study a diagonal or four adjacent cells. Ask them what they get when they multiply, add, or subtract the diagonals. Just because a math expert documented a relationship ages ago doesn't make the discovery any less valid for your students.—*Paul Shechtman, Media, Pa.*

Cereal that counts

Students get to eat their totals during this counting game designed for four to six players.

Fill a bowl with cereal, choosing one with small but not minuscule pieces. Tell your students that the object of the game is to accumulate exactly 10 pieces of cereal (25 or more for advanced players). The players take turns rolling a die and taking the number of pieces indicated on the die.

As a player comes close to the required total, he's in danger of rolling too high a number. If this happens, he must refrain from taking any cereal and wait until the next turn to try again for the exact number he needs. When he throws the right number, he eats his pile of cereal and starts over to accumulate another 10 pieces.—*Helen L. Miller, Granite City, Ill.*

Handy math

Ask each child to trace an outline of his hand, cut it out, label it with his name, then write any five numbers from one to nine on the fingers. Now ask students to try the following activities, then exchange hands with a partner to check answers:

- Add a given number (which you've written on the board) to the number on each finger.
- Find the sum of all the numbers on the hand.

You'll think of lots of other ways to use this hands-on idea.—*Sister Margaret Ann Wooden, Martinsburg, W.Va.*

Hull Gull, instead

Play the old game of Hull Gull—revised with subtraction in mind—as an alternative to traditional drill and practice. For each player, you'll need a small plastic bottle, such as a medicine vial, filled with 20 dried beans.

Pair up your students and instruct Player One to hide a few beans in his hand, then say, "Hull gull." Player Two asks, "Fistful?" to which Player One responds, "Guess." If Player Two happens to guess the right number, Player One must hand over the hidden beans. If the guess is wrong, Player One tells the correct number; Player Two calculates the difference between his guess and the right number and surrenders that many beans from his collection. Now it's Player Two's turn to hide some beans and Player One's turn to guess.

After 15 minutes or so, the player with the most beans is the winner; the loser calculates how many beans the winner has to give back to him to put 20 beans in both vials.—*Josephine Isenhoff, Caledonia, Mich.*

Playing with place value

This game will help provide practice in regrouping. You'll need paper strips representing ones and tens and a deck of message cards. The cards should instruct players to give out or collect ones—"Your gerbil is out of food. Pay the player to your left 2 ones for sunflower seeds." "You've won a pie-eating contest. Collect 4 ones from the bank." For five players, you'll need 35 to 40 message cards. Include among the message cards six or seven "Free From Jail" cards.

Two to five players plus a banker may play the game. To begin, the banker gives each player 9 ones and 5 tens. He then places the message cards in the center of the group. Players take turns drawing a card, reading the message to the group, following the instructions, and then discarding the card. (A "Free From Jail" card may be kept until needed.) If a player runs out of ones, a ten may be converted at the bank.

When a player's supply of ones reaches 10 or more, he must— before drawing a card on his next turn—turn in to the bank those 10 ones for a ten. Failure to do so sends the player to jail. Prisoners draw cards in their turns but cannot transact regular business until they acquire a "Free From Jail" card. (A player holding such a card may sell it to a prisoner.)

When all cards have been played, the players calculate the total value of their holdings; the one with the highest total wins.—*Sherrill Sensensey, Ocracoke, N.C.*

Picking apples, practicing facts

Give your students a fresh alternative to flash cards with this game of picking apples. First, trace and cut out red construction paper circles (apples) about the size of a quarter. Using a felt-tip pen, write a math problem without the answer on each circle.

On poster board, draw a large tree with a basket sitting on each side of the trunk. Trace quarter-size circles on the branches and, in each circle, write the answer to an "apple" problem. Attach the red paper problem apples to their tree-circle answers with loops of masking tape or Velcro dots.

Students can play the game individually or in small groups. A picker chooses a problem on the tree, answers it aloud, and then "picks" the apple to check his answer. If the answer is correct, the picker sticks the apple on one of the baskets.

After all the apples have been picked, students can return the apples to the tree by playing another version of the game. They read the math problem on the front of each apple and find the correct answer on the tree.—*Mary Frances Lucas, Mingo Junction, Ohio*

Rolling more—or less

Try this simple dice game for extra practice with the concepts of "more" and "less." You'll need two blank cubes. Label the faces of one cube with the words "more" and "less," one word to a side. Label the other cube with the numbers "100" and "1,000" in the same way. (If you want to add a challenge, slip in a "10" or a "10,000.")

Each player starts with a score of 12,345 written on his score pad. The first player rolls the dice and figures 100 or 1,000 more or less than the 12,345—according to what the dice dictate.

Players may do the math mentally but should keep a running total on their score sheets. The winner is the player who has the highest—or lowest—score after a specified number of rolls.—*Cheryl Dodd, Watervliet, Mich.*

Spill and add

As a quiet alternative to addition games that use dice, try "Spill and Add."

Trace 10 circles about the size of a quarter on poster board and cut them out. Lay the disks in a row and write a numeral on each, from 0 to 9. Then turn the disks over and write the numerals 9 to 0. Put them in a container that has a cover— such as a potato chip canister or a hinged fast-food box.

Two to four students can play. In turn, players shake the container, dump out the 10 disks, and figure out the sum of the numbers shown. Each sum is a player's score for one turn. If a player guesses incorrectly, he receives no points. The game continues for a set number of turns or for a specified length of time. The player with the highest score wins.—*Rebecca W. Graves, Burlington, N.C.*

Human numerals

Give your students a chance to really put themselves into the "I"s, "V"s, and "X"s of Roman numerals.

Using gym mats as a work surface, call on students to become "human numerals." For example, one person lying with hands at sides and feet together becomes a Roman numeral I. Two students lying with feet touching and bodies angling outward form a Roman numeral V. For a figure X, have two students lie back to back and with torsos and legs angling outward.

Students who aren't forming numerals learn by observing. Later they might remember the configurations by recalling which friends lay where.—*Jane Wagner, Lancaster, Tex.*

Greater than, less than

You can use an ordinary deck of cards to help primary students learn number value and number relationships. Assign number cards their face value. The joker is 0; the ace, 1; and if you're working with numbers through 13, the jack, queen, and king are 11, 12, and 13.

Two to four students can play at a time. To start, lay a shuffled deck of cards face-down in the center of the playing area. The first player draws a card and, concealing it from the other players, announces, "My card is two greater than 4." (Or "My card is one less than 7.") The next player must name the card being held. If the answer is correct, that player wins the card, places it faceup in front of him, and draws a card from the deck. If the answer is incorrect, the first player keeps the card for his faceup pile.

When all the cards in the deck have been drawn, the game is over. The player with the largest pile of faceup cards wins.—*Sister Bernadette Keller, Menomonee Falls, Wis.*

Math mat

Invite your students to put their money where their math is—on a math mat you've designed.

Mark off the back of a piece of carpet in a grid. Inside each box put a problem featuring a process you're working with—such as the multiplication of mixed numbers. Also prepare a stack of game sheets, blank grids that look just like the math mat but with the boxes empty. (Use one of these sheets to make up an answer key.)

Give each player a game sheet. Then, from a standing-on-a-chair position with hands at waist level, have each player drop 10 pennies onto the math mat. When a penny lands in a box, the student takes the game sheet and writes down the problem, putting it in the box corresponding to the location on the math mat. Coins falling on the lines or off the mat have no value and cannot be re-played.

Players then work out the problems they've collected, check their answers, and copy each correct answer into a column for easy totaling. Totals on the game sheets are compared, and the player with the largest total wins.

You can also set up a contest at a math station with a running score sheet near the mat. A student would record a total if it topped the previously recorded high.—*Dorean C. Kimball, Penacook, N.H.*

A more-or-less number search

This game will help your students work out "greater-than (>)," "less-than (<)," and "equal-to (=)" relationships and signs. You'll need a large 10 x 10 100-square grid marked with the numerals 1 to 100 in consecutive order. (Begin in the upper left corner.) Cover the grid with clear self-sticking paper.

To open the game, the first round's leader chooses a number secretly, writes in on a scrap of paper, and gives it to you for safekeeping. The leader now stands ready to accept and respond to yes-or-no questions concerning the size of the secret number. Write each question on the board, using the appropriate greater-than, less-than sign. After answering the question, the leader uses a crayon to cross out numbers eliminated by each greater-than/less-than designation.

At first, students might take wild guesses at the number, but they'll quickly realize the greater-than, less-than strategy works best.—*Linda Oggenfuss, South Dartmouth, Mass.*

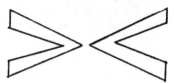

Division delineator

This long-division aid is designed to help students work through the step-by-step process of a format that can be confusing. Make copies of the format shown here and distribute it, along with various problems using it, to your students. The guide can help students see each step more clearly and remind them to use and correctly position zeros.—*Peggy L. Griffin, Globe, Ariz.*

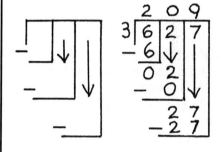

Finger multiplication

If your students have mastered multiplication tables 1 through 5 but are struggling with tables 6 through 9, try a solution that's right at their fingertips. They should enjoy the visual and tactile feedback they'll get by following these steps:

- Turn palms upward with the fingers pointing toward each other.
- Label the fingers according to this diagram.

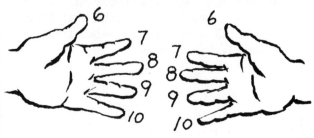

- To solve a problem, such as 9 x 7, touch the factor fingers together as shown in this diagram.

- Count the touching fingers, plus all the fingers above them, as 10 each (60). Of the remaining fingers (the ones below the touching fingers) multiply those of one hand by those of the other (1 x 3 = 3). Now add the two figures (60 + 3 = 63).—*Dennis Dietrich, Kutztown, Pa.*

J+O+A+N = 34

This math grid will have your students searching for things to help them practice addition.

You'll need a large sheet of poster board to use with the entire class or smaller cards for individual use. Draw a "bingo-card" grid of 30 squares, five columns across and six columns down. Using the top row, write random numbers as headings for the columns. Write the letters of the alphabet randomly in the other 25 squares. (Y and Z can share a square.)

Give each player the names of five students, including his own. Then ask him to determine the value of each name, using the following steps:

- Find the first letter of the name in the grid.
- Find the number at the top of the column that has that letter. Write down the number.
- Do the same for the other letters in the name.
- Find the total value of the name by adding the letter values. (Double letters in a name invite multiplication practice.)

Students also can figure out the value of items in their lunches, names of sports teams, animals, even spelling words. Offer new challenges by rearranging letters or renumbering the cards.— *Mary Kay Allberry, Adrian, Mich.*

1	13	2	5	7
A	N	E	H	T
L	W	P	R	J
B	D	F	YZ	U
M	O	Q	I	K
C	X	G	S	V

Pea-and-bean computer

For some basic experiences with place value and regrouping, try setting up a pea-and-bean computer.

Line up three half-pint milk cartons side by side and staple them together. Cover the outside with self-sticking paper. Label the cartons, or bins, "ones," "tens," and "hundreds"—right to left. Affix a dried green pea to the outside of the "ones" bin, a dried chick-pea to the outside of the "tens" bin, and a large white bean to the outside of the "hundreds" bin.

Now explain to your students that this computer cannot hold any more than nine seeds in any one bin. To put a number into the computer, first collect the number in ones—16 green peas, for example. When you've put nine green peas into the "ones" bin, it's time to do some trading. Trade 10 green peas (the 7 left over and 3 from the "ones" bin) for one chick-pea. Put the chick-pea into the "tens" bin. The remaining six green peas stay in the "ones" bin.

Now have students use their pea-and-bean computer to practice regrouping. To add two numbers, first convert both into appropriate seeds, and put one number into the computer. Begin to add in the second number, starting with the ones. Trade in 10 ones for a single ten (or 10 tens for a hundred) whenever it becomes necessary.

The computer can handle subtraction to 0. Try 31 minus 16, for example. Put the 31 into the computer (3 "tens" and 1 "one"), and start to take 16 out. Since there aren't enough ones in the bin to take six away, convert a ten into ones, lining them up outside the computer. Take six away from that group and put the four "leftovers" into the ones bin (now there are 5 "ones" in the bin). Now go on to subtract the tens.—*Barbara Masley, Webster, Mass.*

Defining numbers

Get students to think more about the numbers they hear every day by asking them to describe numbers in different ways. For example, 12 can be the number of objects in a dozen, inches in a foot, and months in a year. Five can be the number of fingers on a hand and school days in a week. Have students define 60, 7, 90, 25, 11, 100, 4, and others.—*Charlotte Jaffe, Clementon, N.J.*

Blockbuster numerals

Help young students see the connection between specific quantities and the numerals that represent them by introducing a simple blocks-and-numerals activity. You'll need a supply of small blocks (or other counters) and sets of numeral cards (0 through 9) in a large size (8 x 8-inch cards are ideal).

Have a student identify the numeral shown on a card, then count out the number of blocks it represents. Next, ask him to place the blocks directly on the numeral, following its configuration (see illustration). While students are in the early stages of numeral recognition, you might want to mark each numeral with pieces of tape corresponding to the number of blocks; later, remove the tape.— *Lynne Strautz, Fort Wayne, Ind.*

The price is right

You can build excitement into math practice by offering motorcycles, jewelry, refrigerators, and Caribbean cruises as incentives.

Set up a game patterned after the TV show "The Price is Right," complete with fantastic prizes—represented by travel posters, magazine ads, and other props.

Invite four contestants to "come on down." Describe the prize they're trying for and explain the rules: The price tag for each prize is contained in a division problem—one in which the dividend cannot be divided by the divisor evenly (for example, 17 ÷ 3). Ask each player to estimate the "whole number" part of the quotient. (In other words, what number x 3 comes closest to 17 without going over?)

Award duplicate prizes in case of ties. After four or five contestants have had turns, winners try for the "Grand Showcase." This involves several items with "prices" that must be estimated without going over.—*Patricia Dubie and William Kane, Dorchester, Mass.*

Math mural

For this math work sheet with a difference, students contribute problems for their classmates to solve.

Tack to the areas beneath chalkboards and bulletin boards a generous length of bulletin board backing paper or shelf paper. Label it "The World's Longest Math Sheet." Now, have each student create a logo—a personal symbol with which he'll sign his mural contributions. Collect these logos and compile a "logo key" to post.

During odd moments, encourage students to sit on the floor and contribute unanswered, signed problems involving whatever process the class is working on. They should start at one end and work around the room. Contributors then make copies of their problems and carry out the work to provide an answer key.

As soon as a supply of math problems is available, invite everyone to choose someone else's problem to solve on the world's longest math sheet. He marks near his answer his initials. The designer of the problem then checks the answer. If it's correct, he puts a small check mark by the answer. If it's incorrect, the designer helps the solver correct the error. As students fill the mural with problems, they'll be creating a record of math growth.—*Ellen Schwartz, Houston*

Decade + duet = dozen

For word problems with a twist, try this activity that links words with numbers. Make a sheet of words that describe a quantity (quartet, decade, score, triangle, octagon, gross, triplet, aught, millennium, duo, pentagon). Have your students look up words they don't know and supply the number associated with each word.

Use words from the list to create math problems. For example, students studying fractions could try this problem: solo/duet x millennium = _____. Invite your students to add number words to the list and to challenge you and their classmates with problems they make up.—*Beatrice Bachrach Perri, Chicago*

Review to go

Create math-review homework with special appeal by packaging it in popular take-out food containers, such as pizza boxes, fast-food containers, or recycled cereal boxes.

The materials you prepare for "take-out" might include games, puzzles, workbook sheets (with separate answer sheets), or sets of homemade manipulatives with directions for use. Give each container a different theme, so your students can review a variety of skill areas—place value, math acts, word problems, using money, and so on.

Stock each take-out package with six or eight tasks and a letter to parents explaining the guidelines. A math-to-go box might, for example, be carried home on a Monday for return on Friday. The borrower would be expected to complete a specified number of activities each night, with parents checking the work.—*Joyce Hopkins, Marietta, Ga.*

What's my number?

This activity will help students understand that numbers are all around them. Give each student a card with a number on it and tell him to write on the back a question whose answer is that number. For example, here are some possible questions for the number 3:

- "How many bears were in the famous story?"
- "What is the sum of 1 + 2?"
- "How many letters are in the word *cat*?"
- "What's half of a half dozen?"

Collect the cards and read the questions aloud, challenging the class to come up with the correct number answers. Then post the cards—question side up—under the title, "What's My Number?"—*Isobel Livingstone, Rahway, N.J.*

Bird feeder math

If you're able to put a bird feeder outside your classroom window, you'll have the makings of a fascinating math tool. Ask younger students to count birds on the feeder, birds on the ground, birds on the wing. Have them classify birds according to size, color, kind.

Older students can tackle more complex calculations, such as how much seed is eaten on an average day; how many days a bag of seed should last; and how much the seed costs per ounce, per daily ration.—*Earl Hoffmann, De Kalb, Ill.*

Computations to freedom

Add spark to the math work sheet by turning it into a "Get Out of School" escape plan.

Draw a floor plan of an imaginary school. Fill it full of dangers and terrible places to pass through: "Mr. Grouch's Room," "Cafeteria of Man-Eating Creepers," "Monster-Filled Hallway to Freedom." Then draw in the escape route, sending it through the various danger spots, with math problems along the way. In order to reach safety, students must answer the problems.—*Patric Murphy, Gary, Ill.*

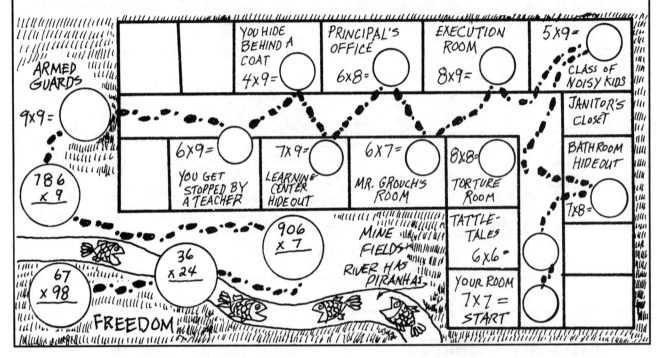

I have your number

The phone book's listing of area codes provides a novel source of three-digit addition, subtraction, and multiplication practice. It also promotes map-reading skills and knowledge of U.S. geography.

Using the phone book's area code map as a model, prepare a map of the United States with the area codes on it. Then prepare a set of math problems based on the area codes:

- Western Nebraska plus Missouri equals?
- Eastern North Carolina minus Colorado equals?
- Northern Minnesota times Arizona equals?—*Carol Luritzen, Kansas City, Mo.*

Math vocabulary

To help your students keep track of the math terms and symbols they're learning, have them develop a glossary in a small notebook. Instead of lengthy technical definitions, encourage them to use examples to *illustrate* meaning. A typical entry might be: *Factor: 3 x 4 = 12* (with the three and four circled to identify them as factors). Students can refer to their glossaries as needed, plus use them for regular review.—*Linda Butler, Johnson City, Tex.*

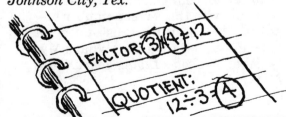

Right on the money!

Try introducing the game "Counting Coins" to students who are learning how to count money. You'll need:

- 100 cards, made from 5 x 8-inch index cards cut into fourths. On one side of each card, write "Counting Coins." On the other, write an amount from 1¢ to $1.

- play money: 10 ten-dollar bills, 10 five-dollar bills, 80 one-dollar bills, 2 half-dollars, 4 quarters, 10 dimes, 10 nickels, and 10 pennies.

The game works best with two to four players and a banker—a student who's good at counting coins. The banker gives 10 one-dollar bills to each player and keeps the remaining bills. He stacks the coins within the players' reach.

In turn, each player takes a Counting Coins card, reads the figure aloud, and selects any combination of coins that equals that figure. The banker checks for accuracy. If the amount is correct, he gives the player a dollar. If it's incorrect, the player must pay the bank a dollar. After his turn, the player returns the coins to the stacks. He can cash in dollar bills for five-dollar or ten-dollar bills at anytime.

The game continues until the card deck is exhausted; a player is bankrupt; or time is called. The player with the most money wins. Elements of chance can keep the game lively. For example, give a bonus dollar or extra turn to a player who draws a card with an amount over 86¢—and he counts out the coins correctly. Or have a player who draws a 6¢ or lower card skip his next turn.—*Eleanor Robins, Loganville, Ga.*

Numbers and numerals

Here's an idea you can walk away with: Help children understand number-numeral relationships with pairs of footprints. First, ask students to trace both of their shoes on construction paper. Then have them cut out the pair. They can decorate the cutouts with borders if they want to, but be sure they save the center space for number work.

As you introduce the number and numeral 1, have students mark the left footprint with one dot and the right with the numeral 1. Students can make new footprint pairs to illustrate new numbers they learn. If you like, have your students make a pair for zero—blank space on the left foot, the numeral 0 on the right.

When each child has a complete set of pairs, you'll have materials for matching games and addition and counting activities.—*Mary Jean Hellenack, Herkimer, N.Y.* **(5A77)**

Egg carton calculator

You can reinforce multiplication facts through 12 with an egg carton and 144 sunflower seeds. Mark the numerals 1 to 12 in order inside the egg cups. Put the seeds in the carton lid.

Introduce problems with stories to help students understand the concepts. For example, suggest that the cups represent birds that eat the seeds. When using the egg carton for multiplication, begin with simple problems, such as: "You want to feed three birds. If you give each bird two seeds, how many seeds will you use altogether?" Have the student distribute the seeds to find the answer. After the problem is solved, write it with numerals and symbols: 3 x 2 = 6.

For division, suggest problems such as: "You have eight seeds. If you want to give two seeds to each bird, how many birds can you feed?" This student can put two seeds each into four cups to show 8 ÷ 2 = 4.

To help students use the egg carton independently at a learning center, make up activity cards. Write a problem on each one, and on the back draw a picture of egg cups with seeds in them to show the answer.—*Dot Ransom, Cumberland, Va.*

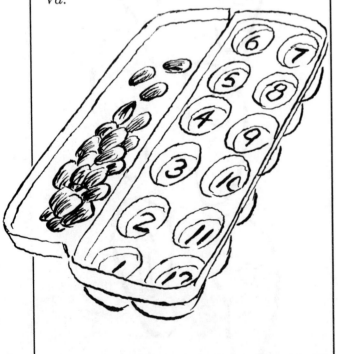

Early grade skills

All you need to help your students practice matching, sequencing, and comparing is an old deck of cards. Using the cards with the numbers 2 through 9, cut each card into three sections so that the center pieces contain only the suit, and the side sections each contain a numeral. Mix together the center sections and half of the side sections. Invite your students to match numerals and symbols. You can also use the center sections to practice sequencing and the concepts of more, most, less, and least.—*Candy Connery, Philadelphia*

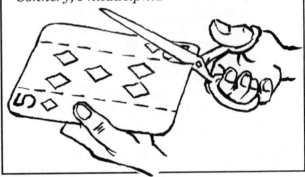

Computation tapes

For an inexpensive computation tool, start a class-wide campaign to collect cash register tapes from the supermarket, drug store, and variety store. You can pick and choose the lengths and numerical ranges that fit the present computational capabilities of your students.

Cut apart each tape between the listed costs and the total. Mount both sections on construction paper or index cards, if you like. Then put the sections with the listed costs into one shoe box; the sections with the totals into another.

Challenge your students to find and match the pairs of separated tapes and put them back together. You might want to code the parts for an answer key or create a pattern-matching device so the activity will be self-checking.—*Carolyn Lamoreaux, Saratoga Springs, N.Y.*

Code calculations

Add a new twist to computation by relying on the telephone. Tell your students their names are really a number, and they have to use the telephone dial (or buttons) to decode it. (Use zero for Z and 1 for A.)

Use these decoded names as addends or multiplication factors. Or challenge students to write an equation using their name-numerals to come as close as possible to a designated value. For example, if the value is 3, a student named Jim could use his numbers this way: $(5 + 4) - 6$. After your students find the numbers for their own names, get them to decode other names, such as those of famous people.—*Paula Millender Goines, Baton Rouge, La.*

Highs and lows with dominoes

A domino can act as a two-digit number, or even two two-digit numbers, depending on how the domino is turned. Consider:

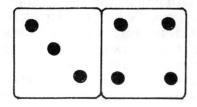

It can be 34 or (turned around) 43. Now, try adding a 5/6 domino to the 3/4 domino.

Possible combinations include:

$$\begin{array}{cccc} 4 & 43 & 34 & 43 \\ +6 & -63 & +65 & +56 \end{array}$$

Or turned another way:

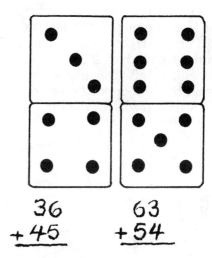

$$\begin{array}{cc} 36 & 63 \\ +45 & +54 \end{array}$$

Have students experiment with dominoes in this way, then pair off the class to try a game of "Highest Sum."

Player One draws two dominoes and arranges them to make the highest possible sum. That player records his calculations along with the sum, then Player Two draws, following the same procedure. After a specified number of rounds, the player with the highest total wins.

Now try "Lowest Answer." This time the two dominoes are used to make subtraction problems with the smallest answers possible. (Answers must be zero or greater.) Students will find that in this game, the arrangement of the two dominoes isn't as obvious as in "Highest Sum."—*Joan Akers, El Cajon, Calif.*

Slide rule arithmetic

Make adding and subtracting visible and concrete for your students by having them calculate on a king-size homemade slide rule. To construct one, you'll need two sticks about 36 inches long. (Yardsticks painted white work well.) On each stick, print the numbers from 1 to 100, evenly spaced.

Place the sticks side by side and demonstrate addition and subtraction problems. To add 25 and 50, for example, slide the stick on the right until the zero on it is aligned with the 25 on the left stick. Locate the 50 on the right stick, then look at the number directly across on the left stick—the sum, 75.

Do subtraction problems by sliding the sticks so that the number being subtracted is on the right and is opposite the number from which it's being subtracted—on the left. The answer is the number on the left, opposite the zero on the right stick.—*Mark C. Fleming, Columbus, Ohio*

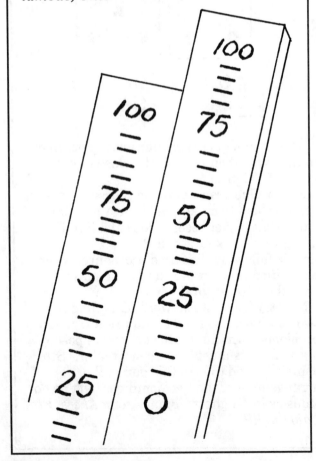

Fishin' for number sentences

An old card game, Fish, can bring new life to math practice. For this version of the game, remove kings and queens from the deck. Have students collect three cards that can work in a number sentence such as "3 plus 4 equals 7," or "7 minus 3 equals 4." (An ace is worth 1; a jack is worth 0; other cards are worth their face value.)

Remind students to think of cards they need and ask other players for them. They should "fish" from the draw pile when those cards aren't available. When a player has a sentence, he shows it and "reads" it. The players with the most card sets, or number sentences, wins.—*Eileen J. Nowicki, Sayreville, N.J.*

Paper trick

To keep numbers in neat columns, have your students turn their ruled paper horizontally. The technique works for addition, subtraction, multiplication, and long division as well as for place value.—*Joyce K. McShara, Putnam Valley, N.Y.*

Multiplication practice

This game, "Second Chance Multiplication," can enliven the task of memorizing multiplication facts.

To play, students will need to make individual product cards. First they figure out all the possible products (be sure each student comes up with the correct 18) that could result from multiplying together the numbers 1 through 6, each number with all the other numbers. Then they write the 18 products on a piece of tagboard. Laminate the cards for write-and-erase use.

Assemble playing groups of two or three students, each of whom has a product card, and provide each group with a pair of dice. The first player rolls the dice and states the product of the two numbers thrown. If the other players agree that the stated product is correct, the player crosses out that number on his product card. If the player gives an incorrect answer, another player should help him out, but no number is crossed out that turn.

If a player rolls two numbers whose product has already been crossed out, he simply states the product, and play moves to the next player. Be sure to emphasize that students who give an incorrect answer should note the correct product; they'll most likely roll those numbers again, therefore getting a "Second Chance."

The game continues until one player has a completely crossed-out product card—or until a time limit is reached. In the case of the latter, the player with the most crossed-out numbers wins.—*Sandra J. Frey, Lancaster, Pa.*

Oral drills

Get your math class off to a fast start with fact-filled warm-up problems on the board or overhead projector. For example:

- Start with the number of years in a century.
- Add the number of blind mice.
- Subtract the number of seconds in a minute.
- Multiply by James Bond's number.
- Add the number of players on a football team.
- Subtract the number of singers in a quartet.
- Subtract the number of centimeters in a meter.
- Add the anniversary celebrated with gold.
- Add the number of days in a leap year.
- Divide by ½ dozen.
- The answer is today's date (10-4 [October 4]).

As an out-of-the-ordinary homework assignment, ask your students to make up their own drills.—*Albina Cannavaciola, Hamden, Conn.*

Touchdown!

Kids will eagerly review math facts if the format involves a good game of football.

Draw an outline of a football field on the chalkboard. Use colored chalk to make it decorative. Include 10-, 20-, 30-, and 40-yard line markers and goalposts, a 50-yard-line decoration, and a scoreboard. Draw two solid lines down the length of the field where the two sets of hash marks are located.

Divide the class into two teams, and position them on opposite sides of the room. Explain the following rules:

- Members on the offensive team take turns answering questions. For each correct answer, the team advances its ball—a chalk mark—10 yards toward the opponent's goal.

- If a team member fails to answer the question correctly, the next player on the same team tries to answer it.

- If all three players cannot provide the right answer, you provide it. Then roll a die with the following results: If you throw a 1, the team kicks a 50-yard punt; a 2 means a 40-yard punt; a 3 means a 30-yard punt; a 4 means a 20-yard punt; a 5 means the defensive team blocks the punt and recovers the ball; a 6 means a fumble with the defensive team recovering the ball and running with it. Another throw of the die indicates how far the defensive team advances with the fumbled ball—each number representing that many times 10 yards from the point of the punt.

When one team reaches its goal line, it scores 6 points and has the option of attempting a 1-point conversion. Any player on the team may answer either conversion question. The ball then goes back to the opponent on the 50-yard line. Someone keeps the score on the scoreboard up-to-date.—*Thomas Best, Monmouth, Ill.*

Keeping things in line

To help students learn to keep numerical columns straight, give them quarter-inch-gauge graph paper on which to work their two- and three-digit math problems. Students fill in one square per digit.—*Julie Dudek, Fort Collins, Colo.*

FACT-O

Review factors and products with this easy-to-set-up game.

Copy onto index cards products your students should be able to factor (1, 2, 3, 4, 5, 6, 7, 8, 9, 10, 12, 14, 15, 16, 18, 20, 21, 24, 25, 27, 28, and so on). Cut scraps of construction paper into ½-inch squares for use as markers. Then make a set of FACT-O cards (arranged like bingo cards) with 24 possible factors and a free space in the middle.

F	A	C	T	-O
1	4	5	7	▨
0	6	10	16	2
9	17	FREE	20	21
3	15	25	▨	12
14	28	11	8	18

Distribute the FACT-O cards. Pull a product card from the pile, read it out loud, and have your students use the paper scraps to cover the factors on their FACT-O cards. (For example, if 24 is pulled, a student could cover 2 and 12, 3 and 8, or 4 and 6.) Instruct the students to cover only two factors for each product you call. Keep a master list of factors.

The first child covering any vertical, horizontal, or diagonal row calls out "FACT-O," then reads the factors covered. If your records agree, he wins and the next game begins.—*Patricia Scaturra, Glendale, N.Y.*

Topping large numbers

Here's a game that lets students build numbers while practicing what they've learned about place value.

To set up the game, cut and mark tagboard in 54 1-inch-wide strips of varying lengths: nine each of 6-inch-long strips, 5- inch-long strips, 4-inch-long strips, and so on down to 1-inch-long strips. On each 6-inch strip, write a 6-digit round numeral—100,000 to 900,000. On each 5-inch strip, write a 5-digit round numeral—10,000 to 90,000. Continue in

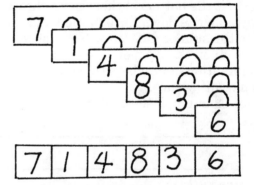

this manner with thousands, hundreds, tens, and ones, using a different color felt-tip pen for each length of tagboard.

To begin play, the dealer shuffles the strips and deals five to each player. Starting with the person on the dealer's left, the first player with a 6-digit strip lays one on the table. The player on his left lays down a 5-digit strip—or the next largest number value in his hand—on top of the first strip. Each player who lays down a strip must read the number it creates—for example, the first player might read "200,000"; the second player might add 20,000 and read "220,000"; and so on.

If a player reads a number incorrectly, he must take back the strip he played, and the game moves on to the next player. Play continues until a 1-digit strip is played and read, completing the number and the round. The next player to the left who has a 6-digit strip starts a new round. The winner is the first person to use up all his strips or who has the fewest strips when time is called.—*Gretchen Pelletier, Webster, Mass.*

Dealing with math

Kids get practice in adding and subtracting when they play this calculation card game in pairs or small groups. Each group will need a deck of cards, and each player writes the numbers 0 through 20 in a row on a piece of paper.

Players take turns being the dealer. The dealer announces whether the players should add or subtract in that round and then turns the top two cards faceup. Counting aces as 1, jacks as 11, queens as 12, and kings as 13, the dealer says the equation out loud. At the bottom of their game sheets, players write down the equation and compute the sum or difference. Then players cross off on their papers the number or any combination of numbers that equals the sum or difference.

For example, if the dealer indicates addition and turns over a 9 and a 5, the dealer says, "Nine plus five." Players write $9 + 5 = 14$ on their game sheets, and cross out 14 or a combination of numbers that equal it, such as 2 (+) 12, 6 (+) 3 (+) 5, or 16 (−) 2. Players must write out under the original equation the number or the combination they crossed off. Players cannot use a crossed-off number again.

If a player has used all the possible numbers that might be combined for one particular round, he waits for better luck in the next round. A player who crosses off all 20 numbers must read off all the equations listed at the bottom of his game sheet. If the sums and differences are correct and no numbers are duplicated, he takes over as dealer and starts a new round.—*Becky Rosten, Houston*

Burger and fries to go

By setting up a facsimile fast food center, you can pique students' interest as you reinforce math skills.

You'll need a supply of paper bags and cups, along with containers (or pretend containers) for burgers and fries. You can make the containers from fabric scraps, cardboard, or Styrofoam. Next, make a menu, basing prices on your students' skill level. Then prepare tape-recorded "orders," each with an identifying number for the "customer." Again, vary the complexity of the orders according to your students' skill level.

When you're ready for business, have a student listen to the tape and fill the bags with the orders. When he's completed several orders, have another student—the "manager"—check for accuracy. You might want to have students complete the sales by collecting play money and returning change. Other students may figure the price of each order from the menu.— *Sheryl Block, Louisville*

Brown bagging it

These activities will help students become wise consumers while improving their math skills. You'll need brown paper lunch bags, felt-tip pens, glue, colorful grocery advertisements and coupons, index cards, tagboard, and clear self-sticking paper.

Label one bag "Shopping Spree." Measure a piece of tagboard 5½ inches by 12 inches. Cut out 5 to 10 pictures of grocery items and glue them to the upper quarter of the tagboard. Then list each item with its price below the collage of products.

On an index card, write a series of problems for students to answer. Ask questions such as:

- How much would it cost to buy the five most expensive items?

- Which costs more: three cans of soup or two bottles of dressing?

- If you buy one of each item, how much will you have to pay? How much change will you get if you pay with a $20 bill?

Use another index card for an answer key. Cover both index cards and the price list with the self-sticking paper and put them into the "Shopping Spree" bag. The colorful product photos will show above the bag opening.

Make a series of these bags for students to use at learning centers. You could title one "Coupon Capers" and include pictures of products, a price list, and discount coupons for the listed items. Problems would revolve around the coupons and the discounts they offer. Another bag called "To Market to Market" could have problems involving items sold by the pound or dozen.—*Pamela Amick Klawitter, Mount Nebo, W.Va.*

Meat market math

To beef up your math curriculum, have students bring in meat ads from market circulars and newspapers. Ads should include the name of the cut, the price per pound, and a picture of the meat, if possible. Label ads by market if you wish, and mount them on cards or on a chart categorized by kind of meat, cut, or market.

The mathematics of meat may take several forms. Younger students might practice reading the dollars-and-cents prices. They might also compare prices—*more than* and *less than*. If ability allows, ask them to compute the specific differences. Discuss with your students the meaning of pricing "per pound." List other items sold by weight.

Older students might compute the cost of a 3-pound pork roast at Ed's Supermarket, or the cost of a 4-ounce (before cooking) serving of hamburger at $2.49 a pound. Students may want to watch the prices of several particular cuts over a period of time, calculating the amount of change and the percentage of change—perhaps graphing the data. Or they might want to compare cuts from market to market.

You can expand on the activity by asking students to clip articles relating to meat prices or inviting a butcher to discuss various cuts and explain why their prices differ.—*Dolores Allen, Quantico, Va.*

Big number bingo

Here's a game that helps students get the upper hand on monstrous figures, and work with place value.

Prepare game cards that are five rows deep and that have as many columns as there are digits in the largest number your students are ready to tackle. Label the columns; then randomly write in one-digit numerals—including a few "free" spots—to fill all the cells on the game card grids.

Prepare a set of number cards with random numbers, ranging from the thousands to the highest place value you've established—289,736 for example. Provide each player with a game card and markers as in bingo, and determine what the winning configuration will be—for example, four corners, five diagonal cells, or one vertical column. Begin play by drawing a number card and reading its number. Then write it on the board. Give players time to cover the appropriate cells in the various columns. For 289,736, for example, a student might cover a 2 in the 100 thousands column, 8 in the 10 thousands column, and so on.

Check winning claims against the chalkboard by having the student read aloud the numerals—and their respective place value positions.—*Dennis Duncan, Port Angeles, Wash.*

100 MILLIONS	10 MILLIONS	MILLIONS	100 THOUSANDS	10 THOUSANDS	THOUSANDS	HUNDREDS	TENS	ONES
6	1	5	2	5	3	4	8	6
3	7	0	8	7	9	0	3	1
3	4	2	0	5	FREE	6	7	9
5	9	4	9	8	1	4	4	5
9	6	FREE	1	3	2	7	9	2

Practice in a flash

Reinforce addition and subtraction fact "families" using triangular flash cards. Here's how to make them:

- Cut out oak tag triangles with sides about 3 inches long.
- In the right corner of each triangle, write a sum; in the other corners, write the addends that yield that sum.
- On the side of the triangle between the two addends, put a plus sign; on the other sides, put minus signs.

Partners can use these three-cornered flash cards to quiz each other. One student covers one of the three numerals; the other figures the hidden value by adding or subtracting as the signs direct. (To avoid negative answers, advise your students to subtract the smaller number from the larger one.)

For individual practice, a student holds the stack of cards by a corner so one numeral of the top card is covered. He calculates the answer to the problem shown, then slides the top card out to check his answer, revealing two numerals of the next card.—*Larene J. Wolfe, Arvada, Colo.*

	2	3	4	5	6	7
4	8					
5						
6						
7						
8						
9						

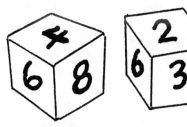

Fact practice fun

Here's an engaging fact reinforcer for groups of two to four young players.

Shuffle a deck of cards and deal six to each player. Deal six more faceup in a line in the center, and stack the remaining cards facedown in a draw pile.

Tell your students that the six faceup cards represent six answers. From the cards in their hands, they try to find two cards whose sum or difference matches an answer card. (The ace is worth 1 point; jack, 11; queen, 12; and king, 13.)

If the first player has a match, he announces the equation he's made. Next, he picks up the answer card and stacks it faceup on top of his two cards in a bundle at his playing spot. Then, he draws two new cards from the draw pile.

If he's not holding a match, he puts one card from his hand faceup with the answer cards, then draws a replacement from the draw pile.

When their turns come, the other players have two options: to match any of the answer cards, or to steal any of the other players' bundles by making an equation that matches a bundle's top card. (The bundle's other two cards become part of the player's hand.)

Continue until cards run out or no one can produce an equation. To calculate their scores, players count up the number of cards in their bundles and then subtract the number of cards still in their hands (or they can use the point value of both).—*Eileen M. Streib, Woodhaven, N.Y.*

Times-table relay

Put a little zest into multiplication drill by making it into a fill-in-the-grid dice game for the entire class.

The game requires a pair of customized dice, which you can make by covering the faces of regular dice with blank labels. Then mark one die with the numbers 2 through 7; the other, 4 through 9. Next, prepare two identical game boards, each consisting of a 36-cell 6 x 6 grid. Number the columns 2 through 7; number the rows 4 through 9.

Divide the class into two teams, and give each team a game board. Team A's first player rolls the dice, determines the product of the two numbers he rolls, and on his team's gameboard writes the answer in the cell in which the two numbers intersect. (For example, if the player rolls a 2 and a 4, he writes an 8 where column 2 and row 4 intersect.) For some combinations, there will be a choice of cells in which to write the answer.

If a player's answer is incorrect, the turn is lost and the other team gets an extra turn. If a cell has already been filled in, play passes to the other team. The first team to fill in its grid wins.—*Paula Schuler, Madison, N.C.*

Food for thought

A cooperative cafeteria staff can be a gold mine of information for some interesting math exercises. Take advantage of this resource by arranging for students to spend a period in the cafeteria.

Assign groups of students to gather statistical information from the cafeteria staff or through observation. Ask for statistics such as:

- the number of pounds of spaghetti the cafeteria serves on a given day; the weight of a pound of uncooked spaghetti; the estimated number of uncooked pieces in a pound; the length of a single piece of spaghetti
- the number of half-pint cartons of milk sold on a given day
- the number of straws used each day; the length of each straw.

The next day, list the information on the chalkboard or distribute it on handouts. Then ask students to use the information to figure out problems such as these:

- If individual pieces of spaghetti were placed end to end, how many *miles* of spaghetti would the cafeteria have served on a given day?
- How many gallons of milk were sold in the cafeteria on a given day? How much will have been sold at the end of the school year?
- How many feet or yards of straws will be used during the school year?—*Sandra J. Frey, Lancaster, Pa.*

What's your sign?

By *being* a plus, minus, multiplication, or division sign, kids can have fun practicing the four fundamental operations.

Divide the class into groups of four. For each group prepare four large cards, each one displaying a different operation sign. Punch holes in the top corners of each card and attach string or yarn so each student can wear a card around his neck. Then, make a game sheet consisting of a list of numbers, each preceded by an operation sign: x3, –57, +12, and so on. Give each group a copy of the game sheet.

Announce the "game number"; for example, 124. Each group writes that number at the top of its game sheet, and play begins. If the first listing on the game sheet is x3, the person wearing the multiplication sign gets the game sheet. After he completes the computation and writes the answer, the sheet moves to the next sign, as indicated by the next listing.

The first group to finish—with all correct answers—wins. After each round, rotate the signs.—*Barbara Homan, Oxnard, Calif.*

Taking an educated guess

Help your students make the leap from "guesstimating" to calculating with this old contest standby: Fill a large jar with jellybeans and invite your students to tell you how many beans are in the jar. Make sure your students know the size of the jar and let them measure a jellybean. Then encourage them to use their knowledge of estimation, volume, and multiplication to come up with guesses. If you like, offer a prize to the student whose guess comes closest.

Challenge your students with other contests such as the number of soft-drink cans in the recycling bin on a given day or the amount of paper in the copy machine.— *Henry Gettenberg, Madison, Conn.*

Can you spare a dime?

Show your students what it *means* to "borrow" 10 by using a manipulative they can readily relate to: money. Here's how to set up subtraction problems using pennies and dimes for ones and tens:

- Place two clear plastic cups side by side. Put two dimes in the left-hand cup and three pennies in the right-hand cup. Ask your students to tell you the total value, then write 23¢ on the chalkboard.

- Now, pose a subtraction problem: 23¢ – 5¢, for example. Children can see that the right-hand cup doesn't have enough pennies in it to take away five. To fix that, suggest moving a dime from the left cup into the right cup, showing that the value remains the same: 20¢ and 3¢ is the same as 10¢ and 13¢.

- Next, get students to tell you that the dime in the right cup equals 10 pennies. Replace the dime with pennies. With 13 pennies now in the right cup, students will have enough to subtract the 5¢. After they do, they'll *see* that they now have one dime remaining in the left cup and eight pennies in the right one and that they have the answer.—*Marien McGuire, New Brunswick, Canada*

Clip-on addition

All you'll need for this math-reinforcing activity are tagboard and spring-type clothespins.

Cut a stack of 4½-inch squares from tagboard and mark each with a grid that divides the square into nine 1½-inch boxes. Leave the row of boxes along the bottom of the card and the row down the right-hand side blank. (These are the answer boxes.) In each of the remaining four boxes, write a numeral. The numerals you choose—which can be added both horizontally and vertically—will depend upon the combinations your students need to practice.

Mark each clothespin—front and back—with the answers. The students will clip the appropriate pins in the answer boxes. (You'll need plenty of duplicate answer pins so that finding an answer is no problem.)

To make the cards self-checking, put the answers on the backs, positioning them where the tips of the four clothespins will be. You can adapt this device to other processes, too, such as comparing sizes of two numbers and finding a common denominator.—*Sister Marie Therese Kaufman, Sigel, Ill.*

Art that adds up

Give your students added math practice while they challenge their friends with pictures that incorporate numbers. Suggest, for example, that numbers can become features on a face, parts of a flower, shingles on a roof, or can be worked into the design of a sports car or strange invention.

After they've drawn their pictures, have your students calculate the sum of the numbers they've used. Then ask them to compose a challenge but to keep the sum a secret until others have found the answer.

The challenge for a picture of a face might be: "This is Ed. Find the hidden numbers to equal his age." For a sports car picture, the challenge might be finding numbers to equal the car's top speed. Another type of challenge might be: "Find all the threes in the picture and calculate their sum." When a number appears more than once in a picture, encourage students to use multiplication facts to arrive at the answer.—*Charlotte Jaffe, Cherry Hill, N.J.*

Be a number

When you give youngsters their own personal numbers, math operations and relationships involving that number might be easier to remember.

Prepare for a number draw, using several sets of the numerals 0 through 9. Have each child copy his number onto a 4 x 6-inch card and attach it to a Popsicle stick. Then proceed through the following tasks:

- Assemble students into groups of 0 through 9. Ask one student to choose two numerals. The two children representing those numerals come forward and decide on an equation they'd like to form with the help of a third numeral in their group. Repeat the task with other children and then with other groups.

- Divide the class into groups of six or eight. Have half of each group face the other half. Ask each facing pair to tell the sum and then the difference of their two numbers. Have the children rotate positions and calculate sums and differences with new partners.

- Divide the class into groups of three or four. Have each group arrange itself to make the highest possible number, then the lowest possible number. To extend this activity, have all the groups arrange themselves in order, first by highest three- or four-digit number, then by lowest.—*Becky Alchin, Farmington, Mich.*

Fraction walk

Take your class on a fraction walk to demonstrate how much a part of our environment fractions are. The first stop might be a house with three windows facing the street. Each window is one-third of the whole set of windows. How many windows have blue curtains? What fraction of the whole is that?

Continue on your walk, encouraging students to notice parts in a whole—the panels of a door, the posts of a fence, the cars in a lot. When you return to the classroom, help students recall their observations, then draw representations of them.—*Janice Druga, Amelia, Ohio*

Rhythm review

(Slap, slap; clap, clap; snap, snap)..."½."
(Slap, slap; clap, clap; snap, snap)..."³⁄₆."

To play this old favorite, announce a category such as, "fraction equivalents." All players in the group then perform in unison this rhythmic pattern: slap lap twice, clap hands twice, snap fingers twice. On the snapping of fingers the player whose turn it is must give a contribution to the announced category. Play proceeds around the group with players listening carefully to each other. If a student gives a repeat answer or a wrong answer, all players who detect it freeze, remaining motionless until the player supplies a correct answer or passes. Then the rhythm rolls on.—*Sarah Riace, Galveston, Tex.*

Worming your way into fractions

Introduce your students to fraction basics with this worms-and-apples matching game.

Cut several apple shapes from red construction paper and divide them into equal pie-shaped parts. Then cut away several of the parts from each apple to represent various fractions. The cutout parts represent the numerator of the fraction.

Now cut out some brown construction paper worms. On each worm, print a fraction that corresponds with a cutout apple fraction. As a group or individual activity, display an apple and then ask a student to choose the corresponding worm from all the available worms. Introduce new fractions by asking students how much of each apple is left for the worms to eat.—*Patricia Zell, Wabash, Ind.*

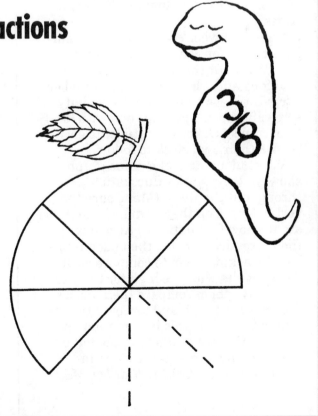

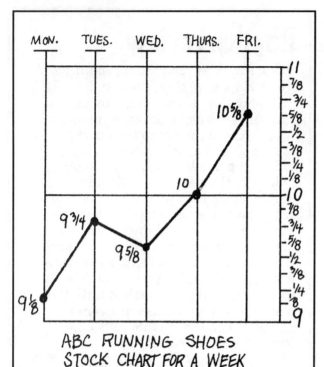

ABC RUNNING SHOES
STOCK CHART FOR A WEEK

Get "bullish" on fractions

Discover hidden dividends for your math students in the newspaper's financial pages.

Bring in a week's worth of stock-market listings for your students to examine. Point out that stock listings use fractions and whole and mixed numbers. Have the class chart a week's activity of a specific stock—perhaps one with local importance. Or let your students each choose their own stock to follow.

Ask students to make a line graph showing their stock's fluctuations throughout the week. (Make sure the vertical scale on their graphs is appropriate to show fluctuations.) Also, have them practice working the mixed numbers by asking them to compare each day's results with the high for the week. Then have them compare their week's high with the high and low over the preceding 52 weeks (this information appears in the two columns to the left of the company name on the stock tables).—*Bennett Downes, Riddley, Md.*

Filling in wholes

Review and reinforce fractions with a parts-of-the-whole game for your students' free time.

To make the game, prepare a master game sheet with 10 circles, squares, or rectangles. Leave the first shape unmarked to represent a whole. Divide the second into halves, the third into thirds, and so on. Then, make enough copies for a class set. You'll also need different colored crayons or felt-tip pens, plus a deck of playing cards with picture cards removed.

Player One draws two cards from the top of the pile—for example, 2 and 7. He uses the cards as the numerator and denominator of a proper fraction (2/7). After announcing the fraction, the player uses a felt-tip pen to fill in two sections of the figure that's divided into sevenths on the answer sheet, and writes 2/7 below the figure. Then, he places the two cards in a discard pile. If he later draws a 4 and a 7, he can use a different colored felt-tip pen to fill in four more sections on the sevenths figure.

Play continues this way, with players striving to fill every section of the figures on their playing sheets—including the "whole" shape, which they may use as a backup if they get fractions that won't fit into the other figures. To make the game trickier, let players convert fractions to equivalents (for example, 2/8 instead of 1/4).

When all cards have been drawn, players reshuffle the deck and continue playing.—*Jane Fletcher, Genesee, N.Y.*

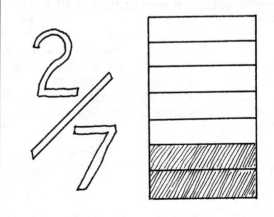

Living fractions

This activity will help make fractions come alive for your students. To begin, have 12 children come to the front of the room. Ask them to group themselves to show halves. Now ask them to think of some unique ways to demonstrate the fraction one-half. (Six students might stand while six sit; six might laugh while six cry; six might face the class while six turn their backs.)

Choose a student from the class to write a statement on the chalkboard describing what's being shown. Then ask the "living fractions" to group themselves into thirds. Again ask them to think of creative ways to demonstrate the fraction. Repeat the activity with fourths and sixths.

Pick a new group of 10 students and go through the process again, this time using halves, fifths, and tenths.—*Isobel L. Livingstone, Rahway, N.J.*

Fractions in a kit

Students will benefit from having their own set of fraction "tiles," which they can handle, compare, and fit together. Here's how they can make their kits.

Give each student five 4-inch squares of construction paper in different colors. Then have students arrange their squares as follows: purple square, leave whole; orange square, fold then cut in halves; yellow square, fold then cut in quarters; blue square, fold then cut in eighths; red square, fold then cut in sixteenths. (Provide plastic sandwich bags for storing kits.)

Now, invite students to manipulate and compare their fraction pieces. Encourage them to establish equivalencies and other relationships between pieces or groups of pieces. Have them record their findings using color references, for example:

- 2 yellows = 1 orange, therefore 2 fourths = 1 half ($\frac{2}{4} = \frac{1}{2}$)
- 1 yellow is larger than 3 reds, therefore 1 fourth is larger than 3 sixteenths ($\frac{1}{4} > \frac{3}{16}$)

Challenge students to mix the pieces to create "combination wholes," which they can package in individual sandwich bags as puzzles to be solved, tangram style.— *Mary Jo Hanlon, Hayward, Calif.*

Denominator strips

Here's a way to help students find the common denominator when they're adding or subtracting fractions.

On a piece of 1-inch square graph paper, have students make a times table chart for the numbers from 1 through 10, and then cut these charts into strips so that they have one number and its multiples on each strip.

Encourage students to use the strips to solve problems. If they're adding ⅔ and ⅘, for example, have them lay the 3 strip and the 5 strip next to each other. They'll readily see that 15 is the lowest denominator common to both.

If the denominator is larger than 10 (⅛ + ²⁄₁₆, for example), point out that both 8 and 16 are on the same strip, which means that both denominators can be 16.—*Margaret Reschetz, Decatur, Ill.*

4	8	12	16	20	24
8	16	24	32	40	48

Molding fractions

Help your students dig into fractions by setting up a center that uses clay. Direct students to form clay into imaginary foods such as an apple, a piece of cheese, a banana, and a cookie. Then have them divide the shapes (using plastic knives) into equal parts—enough for four people, six people, and so on. Student gourmets may make large disk pizzas and cut them into sixths, eighths, or twelfths. For an added challenge, ask them how they'd divide the "foods" into thirds or sevenths.

Don't forget to include fraction facts when distributing classroom materials or announcing activities. For example, ask students how you can give 12 stickers fairly to four students, or announce that one math group can use ⅓ of the chalkboard.—*Melody Davis, Oklahoma City*

A perfect match

Fractions and equivalents are perfect fodder for matching activities. Create interlocking halves and your matching activity gives immediate reinforcement.

Cut sturdy stock into uniform rectangles of a size best suited to the age of your students. Mark a free-form center divider line on each and then mark the card with its pair of symbols. Cut along the divider line and you have puzzle pieces ready to use.

If a student is sure of a match, he quickly puts the pieces together. If he isn't, the contour of the dividing edge acts as an aid. For older students, make the contour less pronounced to provide more challenge.—*Kevin J. Swick and Dormalee Lindberg, Carbondale, Ill.*

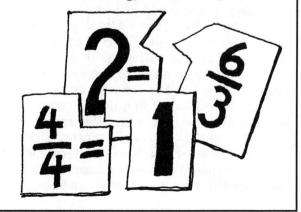

The great race

This game provides lively practice with the addition and subtraction of fractions as well as dealing with fraction equivalents.

On tagboard make a winding, segmented worm. The segments should be equal in size and each marked with $\frac{1}{18}$ (or $\frac{1}{12}$ if you prefer). Display on the game board an equivalency chart, as shown. This chart can help students see the relationships in the fraction family being used and might help in the process of determining common denominators.

Make up a stack of problem cards, such as $\frac{1}{3}+\frac{1}{3}=?$ or $\frac{1}{2}+\frac{1}{6}=?$ if your students are ready for unlike fractions. A player draws a card and solves the problem, following the procedure of finding the lowest common denominator and later reducing the answer to lowest terms. Then comes the player's chance to move on the board. The player converts his answer to its equivalent in eighteenths and moves the indicated number of spaces. Players continue to draw cards, solve problems, and move in turn until one player reaches the goal.—*Harriet DeLouise, Albuquerque, N.M.*

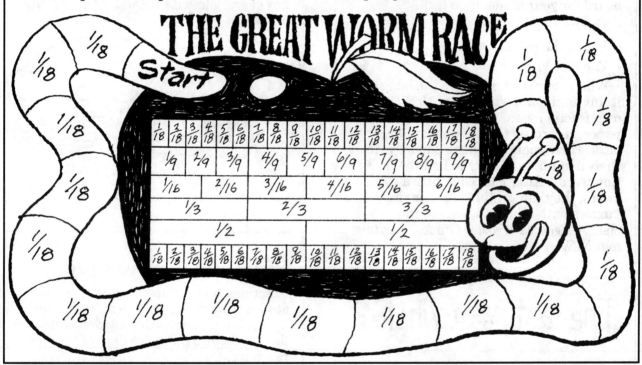

Mystery fractions

For a bit of math fun, think of a fraction and then ask students to identify it from clues you give them. All clues must be true, though all may not be equally helpful in uncovering the mystery fraction. Encourage students to take notes to aid in narrowing down the possibilities. Ask them to signal you when they can identify the fraction.

Here are examples of the kinds of clues you can give:

1. The denominator of this fraction is a prime number.
2. Its numerator is an even number.
3. Its denominator is greater than 10.
4. Its numerator is less than 10.
5. Its numerator is a multiple of 3.
6. The fraction is equivalent to $\frac{36}{66}$.
(The correct answer is $\frac{6}{11}$.)—*Sandra J. Frey, Lancaster, Pa.*

Fractured words

Kids will have a better idea of what the numerators and denominators of simple fractions represent after they make up word puzzles for each other to solve.

Present a "fraction word" by writing this example on the chalkboard: "The first ⅖ of dough = do." Then explain that the denominator shows how many letters are in the whole word, and the numerator shows how many letters are in the fraction word. The position is designated by "first," "middle," or "last."

Put a few more puzzles on the chalkboard for your students to try:

• The first ⅗ of piece = ?
• The middle 2/4 of math = ?
• The last ¾ of what = ?

When your students have the hang of it, invite them to create 5 or 10 of their own fraction word puzzles on a sheet of paper, recording the answers on the back. Have them exchange papers with their neighbors and try to find the fraction words. After checking their answers, they can continue exchanging puzzles with other students in the class.—*Rebecca Webster Graves, Burlington, N.C.*

The last ¾ of what=?

Fraction festival

Focus on fractions in a party atmosphere with this project.

Set aside a lunch period for an in-class party. Ask student volunteers to supply the food—in fraction form. For example, ¾ of a pound of macaroni salad, 7/12 of a bag of rolls, 25/38 of a bag of pretzel sticks, 5/12 of a dozen cupcakes, ⅔ of a sheetcake, ⅚ of a six-pack of fruit punch, ⅘ of a pan of lasagna, and so on. After eating, play your favorite game, but with prizes such as ⅙ of a set of felt-tip pens, ¼ of a pack of stickers, ⅛ of a box of granola bars.—*Denise Lee, Springhouse, Pa.*

Combine and conquer

Fractions take on new meaning when students work together to build wholes by combining parts. Cut 12 identical discs—about 6 inches in diameter—from tagboard. Cut six of the discs into fractions—halves, thirds, fourths, fifths, sixths, and eighths (with younger students, stick to halves, fourths, and eighths). Label each fraction piece with its appropriate number name.

Give a whole disc to six students, who will serve as fraction collectors. Then distribute the fraction pieces to the other students. Invite students holding fraction pieces to put together wholes among themselves. Finally, have students assigned to whole discs collect the put-together fraction pieces, making sure they exactly cover their discs.—*Andy Klee, Superior, Wy.*

Greeting card cut-up

Used greeting cards can help your class understand halves, fourths, eighths, and sixteenths. Ask students to bring in a few old cards from home. Then give each student the front panel of a card, scissors, a pencil, and a small envelope. Next, guide them step by step:

1. Write your name on your envelope and on the back of your picture.

2. Fold your picture carefully in half. Then open it up and cut on the fold. How many pieces do you have?

3. Put the pieces of your picture together.

4. Fold and cut each half of the picture in half. Now how many pieces do you have? Put the picture back together. Is the job harder or easier than before?

5. Fold and cut each picture piece in half again. How many pieces do you have? How many pieces will you have after you cut the pieces in half again? Write that number on your envelope.

6. Now cut the pieces in half and count them. Did you guess correctly?

7. Put the picture back together. Is it easier or harder to do than the last time?

8. Put your picture pieces inside your envelope. Trade envelopes with someone near you and put that person's picture together. Does your neighbor's picture have the same number of pieces as the puzzle you made? Are the pieces in the same shapes as yours?

As they cut the cards, tell students they've created halves, fourths, eighths, and sixteenths.—*Helen L. Miller, Granite City, Ill.*

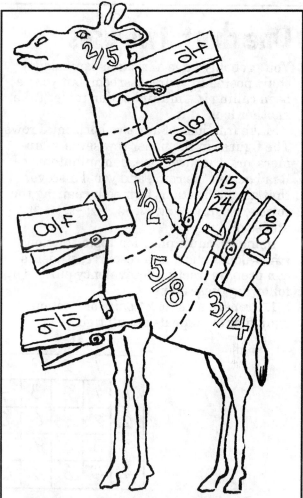

Clothespin computing

Here's a way to pin down the idea of reducing fractions to their lowest terms. Cut out of tagboard a large animal and divide it into four unequal sections. In each section write a lowest-term fraction such as $\frac{1}{2}$, $\frac{2}{5}$, $\frac{3}{4}$, and $\frac{5}{8}$.

On clip-on clothespins, write fractions that can be reduced but whose lowest term is written on the animal. For example, if $\frac{3}{4}$ is on the animal, write $\frac{6}{8}$ on a clothespin. Prepare 12 to 20 clothespins.

Have students clip the clothespins onto the correct sections of the animal. You can check their work or provide an answer key for self-checking. Pairs of students can work together, turning the activity into a game. A third student can use the answer key for reference.

For a greater challenge, include a few clothespins that don't belong on the animal.—*Denise Lee, Springhouse, Pa.*

One chart, two uses

You probably have a fraction equivalency chart posted in your classroom, but you've been calling it a multiplication table. Take another look at it.

Make fractions of any two horizontal rows: The figures in the upper row serve as numerators; the lower one, denominators. Read across the rows, and you'll discover that all the fractions formed by pairing the rows are equivalent: ¼, ²⁄₈, ³⁄₁₂; ²⁄₃, ⁴⁄₆, ⁶⁄₉, and so on.

Using the multiplication table-fraction equivalency chart as a resource, students can prepare fraction equivalency puzzles by following these steps:

1. Prepare a list of 24 pairs of fraction equivalents. Repeats are all right.

2. Fold a sheet of paper into 16 equal parts by folding it in half four times.

3. To keep puzzle pieces from getting mixed up with someone else's, mark each of the 16 boxes with a "trademark" design. Then turn the paper over.

4. There are 24 fold lines separating the boxes. Place one fraction of a fraction pair to the left of a fold and the other on the right, or one fraction above a fold and the other below.

5. Cut the boxes apart along the fold lines. (Have an envelope ready in which to store the pieces.)

6. Challenge a friend to put the pieces of your fraction equivalency puzzle back together.—*Isobel L. Livingstone, Rahway, N.J.*

X	1	2	3	4	5	6	7	8	9
1	1	2	3	4	5	6	7	8	9
2	2	4	6	8	10	12	14	16	18
3	3	6	9	12	15	18	21	24	27
4	4	8	12	16	20	24	28	32	36

Now you're cooking

Tempt your students' math appetites with a project that yields properly reduced fractions—and a batch of delicious snacks.

Take a favorite cookie, snack, or no-bake recipe and alter it by changing all the measurements to equivalent fractions needing reduction. For example, change "¼ tea-spoon ginger" to "⁹⁄₃₆ teaspoon ginger."

Distribute copies of the strange-looking recipe for fraction reduction. When your students have correctly reduced all measurements to lowest terms, they can prepare—and enjoy—their fraction-action treats.—*Susan Mobley, Prineville, Ore.*

Keeping tabs on toothpaste

With a little help from your students, you can combine a dental health campaign with an introduction to graphing. As you and your students discuss good dental care, suggest that each child bring in a toothpaste box from home. Cut a panel from each box, trying to maintain some consistency in width, and return the panels to your students.

Tally the number of brands represented and prepare a chart with a column for each one. Label each column with the toothpaste brand, and run numbers up the vertical axis of the graph. Have students tape their panels in the appropriate columns.

Now, discuss the data. According to the chart how many people use brand X? Brand Y? How many more people use brand W than brand Z? Which brand is the most popular?—*Mary Neff and Cheri Saffro, Lincolnwood, Ill.*

Cooperative coordinates

This sophisticated version of connect-the-dots helps students reinforce graphing skills.

First, give each student a pencil, a straightedge, and a sheet of graph paper on which the x and y axes are marked. On an overhead projector, project a coordinate plane on a screen, and tell students that as a class they're going to create a picture of a dog (or a house or a flower). Start the action by placing one point on the overhead graph. Tell the students the coordinates—for example (7, 3)—and what part of the picture you're beginning, such as the dog's nose.

Then randomly invite students to help construct the dog by choosing pairs of coordinates. As a student calls out coordinates, everyone marks the spot on their graphs and connects it to the previous coordinates. You follow along on the overhead projector.

Later, students can embellish their pictures, adding color and background, and display them on a bulletin board.— *Virginia Boyd, Morgantown, Pa.*

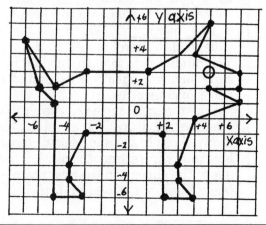

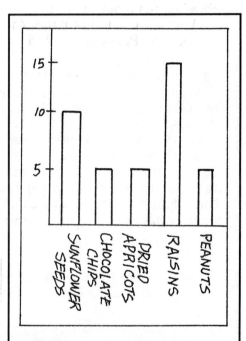

Delicious data

In this activity students get to eat the fruits of their labor. Give each student a paper cup containing an assortment of snacks—15 raisins, 5 peanuts, 10 sunflower seeds, 5 dried apricots, 5 chocolate chips. Ask students to make a line or bar graph of their snacks—then allow them to sample the data.—*Kelly Macaulay, Homer, Alaska*

What's in a name?

This name-graphing activity involves whole-class participation and helps children become familiar with the letters in their first names.

Make a large grid with 1-inch squares. Include a row for each student, and make sure the grid is wide enough to accommodate the longest first name in the class. Next, collect a large supply of 1-inch cubes or blocks. Finally, prepare a tagboard strip for each student and a supply of cutout letters for students to use in making individual name cards.

Have each student glue onto a tagboard strip cutout letters to spell his name. Then have each child count the letters in his name and collect that many 1-inch cubes. Ask each student to arrange the cubes in a row and then to transfer that image to the graphing grid by coloring in the appropriate number of squares.

Post the graph and, next to each student's colored-in row, hang his name tag. Using yarn, connect each name to its corresponding row of colored squares. Then challenge students to decipher the name graph by asking questions such as:

- Whose name has the fewest letters? Whose name has the most?

- How many names have fewer than five letters? How many have more than five?

- Which number of letters do you find more often than any other?

- How many classmates' names have the same number of letters as your name?

As a follow-up activity, invite students to graph their last names.—*Helen L. Miller, Granite City, Ill.*

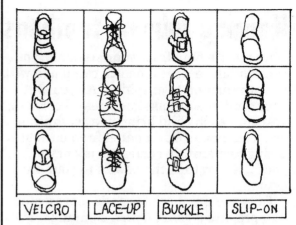

| VELCRO | LACE-UP | BUCKLE | SLIP-ON |

Graphing is a shoe-in

When teaching young students about making comparisons and using graphs, real objects and a reusable, oversize graph mat make the difference. You can easily make your own mat by marking a vinyl window shade with an indelible felt-tip pen.

Invite your students to sit in a circle on the floor. Have each one take off a shoe and place it in the center. Can students tell from looking at the pile how many shoes have laces and how many are slip-ons? Are there any with buckles or Velcro?

Begin placing the shoes on the graph mat by type: lace-up, slip-on, buckle, Velcro, and so on. As they watch, students will discover graph "rules" for themselves. Now ask volunteers to put the rest of the shoes where they belong.

When all the shoes are in place, ask students to name the rows—lace-up shoes, slip-ons, and the like. Then ask questions they can answer by studying the graph. For example, "How many shoes are in the lace-up row? How many in the Velcro row? Which row has more shoes? How many more?" and so on. You might want to place labeled index cards beneath each row to remind students of categories.

Ask students to use the graph to make other comparisons. For example, how many shoes have fancy sole designs, and how many have smooth soles? What else about the shoes can they compare?—*Patricia Flanigan, Tarzana, Calif.*

Birthday graph

To help young students understand bar graphs, make a class "birthday graph"—one that shows how many students have birthdays in each month of the year.

Total the number of birthdays in each month. Then draw a large bar graph with the months of the year written along the horizontal axis and the number of birthdays in each month depicted on the vertical axis.

Expand the activity by challenging students to make a birthday graph for another class or for school staff, such as the nurse, custodian, principal, and so on.—*Barbara Lassman, Morristown, N.J.*

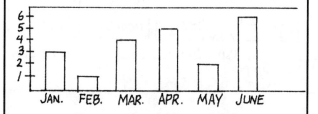

TV grid math

Help your students learn how to follow the weekly television program grids—which are actually horizontal bar graphs—while reviewing computation skills.

First, ask your students to bring last week's program guide to class (or photocopy a few different pages from your own). Have them identify the local channel numbers, then make up some problems to go with various programs listed in the guide. For example: Add the channel number that shows *Winnie the Pooh* to the channel number that shows *Wheel of Fortune.* Or: If you watched *Growing Pains, The Cosby Show,* and the local news, how much time did you spend in front of the TV? Encourage your students to make up problems to challenge their classmates.—*Alan Klayminc, Brooklyn, N.Y.*

Get the picture?

Math and art overlap as students plot missing multiplication factors on a chart to reveal a color graphic.

Duplicate a grid with 10 columns and 10 horizontal rows for each student. Write the numbers 0 through 9 in the first column from top to bottom and label the column "Given Numbers." In the top row, write the numbers 0 through 9 from left to right and label the row "Missing Numbers."

On a master grid, plot a simple picture, using various colors of crayons or felt-tip pens. Next, set up multiplication problems with missing factors. Each equation corresponds to one of the colored boxes on the master grid. The students must figure out the missing factor to find the box that they're supposed to color.

List the problems on the chalkboard or include them on the master with the blank grid, noting in parentheses the color that the students should use to fill in the appropriate box. For example, in the problem 3 x ? = 12 (black), the box where the Given Number column (3) and the Missing Number row (4) intersect should be colored black.

Arrange the problems so that the picture isn't revealed until the last few boxes are colored in.—*Sandra J. Frey, Lancaster, Pa.*

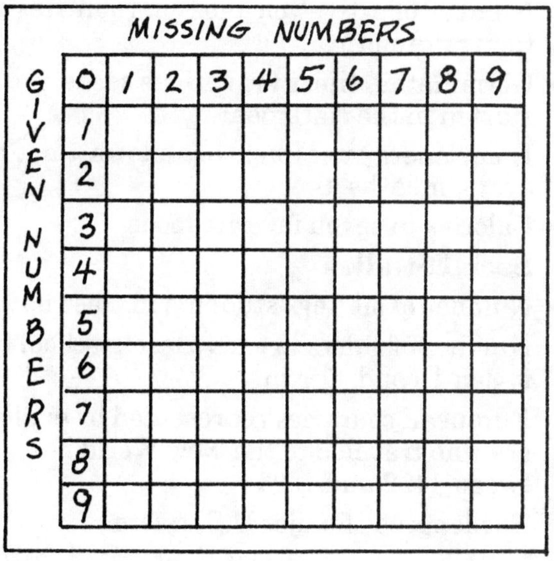

MISSING NUMBERS	0	1	2	3	4	5	6	7	8	9
1										
2										
3										
4										
5										
6										
7										
8										
9										

(GIVEN NUMBERS label on left axis)

Spelling-word graphs

Here's a way for your students to get practice making bar graphs, while you spark some interest in spelling.

Make a vertical axis for a bar graph out of oak tag. After each spelling test, have a "spelling statistician" write on separate strips of oak tag each word the class misspelled. Have him place the strips side by side across the bottom of the graph to form the horizontal axis. To form the graph, have the statistician tally the number of times each word was misspelled, then use different colored construction paper strips to show those numbers on the vertical axis.

Start over with a new list each week, including last week's most misspelled words, if you like.—*Gail Guida, Alexandria, Va.*

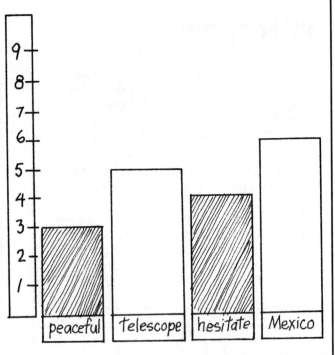

Graphing across the curriculum

To incorporate graphs into all subject areas, challenge your students to graph the following:

Science

- Number of sunny days each week for a month
- Average number of eggs laid by a robin, a penguin, a pigeon, a wild turkey
- Number of active volcanoes in countries of Central America
- Germination times for various seeds started in the classroom
- Home energy use (monthly kilowatt-hour) over 4 months' time
- Calories in seven favorite foods

Social Studies

- Number of siblings students in class have
- Number of riders in cars passing school between 10 and 11 a.m.
- European countries represented by explorers who traveled to the New World between 1492 and 1693
- The lengths of major U.S. rivers
- The number of children of U.S. presidents
- Public school enrollment from 1900 to 1980

Math

- Numbers between 2 and 100 evenly divisible by 2, 3, 4, 5, 6, and 7
- Proportion of objects on one wall of the classroom that are square, rectangular, circular, or triangular
- Performance of a chosen stock for 10 days
- Class sales of popcorn for 1 week

Language Arts

- Students' six favorite book topics
- Number of words on a textbook page that belong to one of seven word families. Divide the class into seven groups and assign one phonogram— -and, -ill, -ot, and so on, to each.
- The occurrence of specified figures of speech in a collection of poems
- The number of times each vowel appears in one newspaper article.—*Denise Lee, Springhouse, Pa.*

Graphing bottles

This activity provides practice in graphing, with an emphasis on metric. You'll need a collection of bottles in a variety of distinctive shapes—ones with angles, curves, and bulges; a measuring cup—calibrated in milliliters—with a pouring lip; a 30-centimeter ruler; 2 or 3 liters of water colored with food coloring; and graph paper and lined paper.

To begin, set up a bottle-graphing center with instructions similar to these for your students to follow:

1. Choose a bottle to graph and make a rough sketch of it.

2. Prepare a chart with two columns: one headed "milliliter"; the other, "height in centimeters."

3. Fill the measuring cup with colored water to the 30-milliliter mark and empty it into the bottle.

4. Measure the height of the water level and record the data on your chart.

5. Continue steps 3 and 4 until the bottle is filled.

At this point, challenge your students with a discussion of what they've seen so far: When the water reaches a place where the sides of the bottle bulge out, does the water level rise more quickly or more slowly than where the sides are straight? Where the sides curve inward, does this affect the way the water rises? How?

6. On your graph paper, draw axes and plot milliliters along the horizontal axis, centimeters along the vertical axis.

7. Take the data from your chart and plot points for your graph. Connect the points.

8. Compare the sketch of the bottle's shape with your finished graph. What does the graph curve look like when the bottle is straight sided? When it's skinny? Look around at other graphs. Can you spot one with a pattern similar to yours? Is its bottle a similar shape too? What about the size of the other bottle compared with yours?

As a follow-up activity, use completed graphs to set up a matching game. Label each graphed bottle with a letter; number each graph. See if students can match the graphs and bottles.—*Randall J. Souviney, San Diego, Calif.*

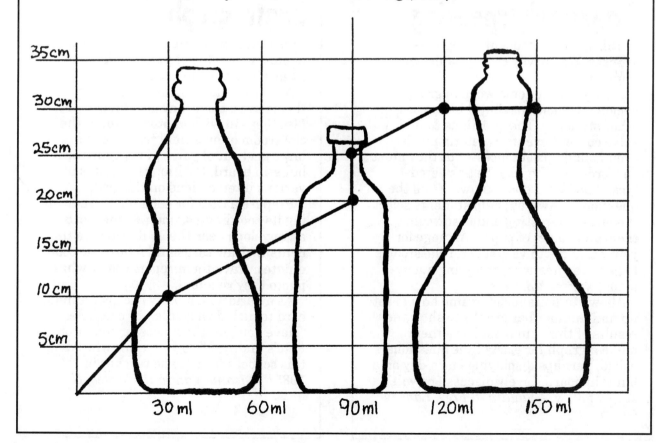

"X" marks the spot

Students will find "Tic-Tac-Graph" an easy and fun way to learn to graph ordered pairs. You'll need graph paper for half the number of students in your class. On each sheet, draw lines and numbers as shown.

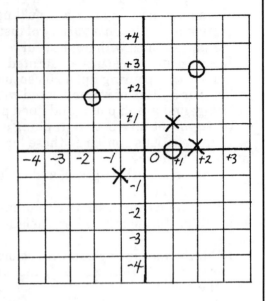

Pair students and give each set of partners a graph sheet and a supply of 1-inch construction paper squares. Have students number each square with one numeral, from the lowest negative number to the highest positive number (including 0) on both axes.

Partners decide who'll be X and who'll be O. One player shuffles the number squares and places them facedown. Each player draws two number squares. The first number drawn indicates the number of spaces the player will move along the horizontal axis; the second, the number he'll move along the vertical axis. The player places his mark where the two numbers intersect. The first player to place three Xs or three Os on the same line wins.—*Sue Harvell, Greensboro, Ala.*

Graphically speaking

In this activity, students graph responses to a survey they organize and conduct.

Have your students work in groups to decide on questions they'd like to ask other students. The questions could involve current events, cafeteria meals, even fashion preferences—but they must be worded so they can be answered "yes," "no," or "I don't know." From the questions drawn up, help students select the most interesting and then write them on a sheet of paper. Arrange for your students to visit several classrooms to ask the questions, accepting anonymous, written answers.

Allow students to determine how to set up and number bar graphs to show the results of their surveys. Have them make a graph for each of the questions asked, perhaps displaying one a day on a bulletin board. Lively discussions will surely follow.—*Sandra J. Frey, Lancaster, Pa.*

Photo-graph

This graph, made up of class-contributed photos, will help get your students excited about plotting coordinates.

Ask students to bring in photos of themselves, their families, their pets. Mix these in with photos taken in the classroom or on a field trip. Make a large grid out of yarn on pegboard or a bulletin board. Position the photos at various intersections on the grid.

Prepare a card for each photo, indicating its coordinates, and put the cards in an envelope near the grid. Invite students to draw cards and follow the coordinates. Have them report orally what photo they've found.

As a variation, modify each coordinate card to include a riddle, for example, "Have you met the newest member of Pete's family?" "Do you know who was this school's first-grade teacher in 1985?"—*Jeanie Vance, Rochester, N.Y.*

My toe is fatter than your toe

Enlist the imaginations and competitive spirits of your students to help them learn the metric system. Designate an area of the chalkboard as the Challenge Board, where students may write their claims to fame. The only requirement is that entries must pertain to something measurable. For example, the fattest big toe, the longest lunch box, the heaviest tennis shoes.

Up to two other students may challenge a claim to fame, proving their cases by measuring with the appropriate metric unit. Compile a class record book, allotting a page to each winner.—*Shirley Schultz, Richardson, Tex.*

"Metric pass"

Try this activity to help your students grasp the concept of grams and kilograms. Bring in food cans and packages with metric labels. Invite students to lift and compare the items to develop a sense of what a variety of weights feels like. Then have your students play "Metric Pass," a game for four or five players.

You'll need cards labeled "Trade for low total," "Trade for high total," "Lowest," and "Highest." Make about five cards for each category. Distribute the food packages equally among the players so that collections have comparable weights. Each player calculates and records in grams the actual weight of his "groceries."

To start the game, Player One draws a card and reads it aloud. If the card reads, "Trade for low total," each player passes his heaviest item to the left. Then players sub-tract from their totals the weight of the item given away; they add the weight of the item just passed to them. Each player reports the total weight of his groceries; the player with the lowest amount scores a point.

If the card reads, "Trade for high total," players pass their lightest items, subtracting that weight from their totals and adding the weight of the item they received. This time, the student with the highest total weight scores a point.

If the card reads, "Highest," the player with the highest total at that moment scores a point; if the card reads, "Lowest," the player with the lowest total gets a point.

You might try a variation in which students choose what to pass by lifting each item and estimating what is heaviest or lightest without checking the weight figures.—*Lori Abbott, Ithaca, N.Y.*

Sliding into metrics

For a seat-of-the-pants activity designed to reinforce metric knowledge, turn to the playground slide. Here are several suggestions for compiling a mountain of data:

- Have students figure out how long it'd take to slide the equivalent of the distance between two cities, such as Portland and Salem, Oregon (61.5 kilometers).
- Take estimates on the amount of time it'd take to accomplish 10,000 slides.
- Compute individual performance distance. For example, Peter slid down the slide (6 meters, 15 centimeters long) 48 times. How far did he slide?
- Compute class distances.
- Compute average speeds of sliders.
- Convert distances into the English measurement system.—*Homer Clark, Portland, Ore.*

Minding your P(ints)s and Q(uart)s

A desk-size chart can help kids remember that it's 4—not 2 or 6—quarts to a gallon, and so on. On a sheet of construction paper, have each student draw a large *G* for "gallon." Inside the *G*, he puts four *Q*s for "quarts"; inside each *Q*, he puts two *P*s for "pints"; inside each *P*, he puts two *C*s for "cups." Encourage students to refer to their charts until the equivalents become familiar.—*Elsie Miller Johnston, Hudson, Ohio*

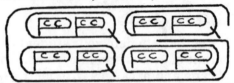

Trading pints and quarts

Try a supermarket approach to learning liquid measurements. Set up a store area stocked with plastic gallon, quart, pint, and cup containers of colored water, bearing labels such as "dinosaur bubble bath—1 gallon." Prepare a master list of measurement equivalents to post at the store.

Next, make a set of cards, each marked with a liquid measurement such as 8 ounces, 3 cups, 1 pint, 2 quarts. Make enough duplicates so that each "shopper" can have five cards to exchange for merchandise.

At the store, shoppers present combinations of cards that match the volume of items they want to buy (unless you plan to have them figure "change"). For example, one 1-pint card and two 1-cup cards will buy 1 quart of "pink piano polish." Shoppers may also trade with each other to get the cards they need.

Appoint a storekeeper to approve purchases and to help shoppers make another selection when they don't hold the right cards for the item they want.—*Tena Cheatham, Mt. Judea, Ark.*

Peanut power

To explore the concept of volume, you can rely on the simple peanut.

Divide your students into groups of four or so and give each group a large cardboard carton, a liter container (a box 10 centimeters long on each edge—kids can make their own), a metric ruler, and enough peanuts to fill the liter box. You'll also need a scale.

Tell each group they'll be figuring out how many peanuts it'll take to fill the large carton and how much the carton of peanuts will weigh. Then encourage students to puzzle and speculate their way toward the idea of volume. After students have recorded their findings and weighed their boxes, discuss the results of the experiment.

As a follow-up activity, give each group a jar of peanuts and ask them to estimate how many peanuts the jar contains. Then have the groups count the peanuts and compare the two figures. When all is said and done, have a peanut-eating party.—*Douglas A. Gilberts, Stevens Point, Wis.*

Pour a liter

This game provides metric manipulation and practice in the second language of measurement. You'll need:

- one die
- four plastic gallon-size milk containers
- a metric measuring container
- a large bucket
- 4 liters of colored water
- self-stick labels
- clear adhesive paper
- razor-blade knife.

Cut six self-stick labels to fit the faces of the die and mark them as follows: 60 ml, 80 ml, 125 ml, 160 ml, 180 ml, 250 ml. Stick one label on each die face and cover with clear adhesive paper.

Cut off the tops of the milk containers at a level at least 10 cm from the base, turning the containers into square "bowls." Pour a liter of the colored water into each bowl; on all four sides of each bowl stick a label where the water comes and mark on the label the exact water line and "1 liter." Cover the labels with clear adhesive paper for waterproofing. Empty the bowls into a bucket and place it in the center of playing groups.

To play, give each of two to four players an empty bowl. Player One rolls the die and, measuring from the bucket, pours into the bowl whatever amount of water is indicated. Play moves to the left following the same procedure. The first player whose water level reaches the liter mark wins.

As a variation, have each player record the amount of water used in each turn, keeping a running total.—*Ginger Manchester, Oxford, Miss.*

Metric detectives

To get your students thinking in metrics, suggest they sneak a peek into their family pantries for metric labels. Ask students to start collecting labels from used packages— those showing metric units of capacity, mass, and length as well as English units. Encourage students to search out variety in kinds of products and in package sizes, and have them save the whole label, rather than a cutout portion. That way the label will reveal something about the size of the container—how tall, for instance, a 1.36-liter (46 ounce) can of tomato juice might be.

When students have a sizable number of labels, have them paste them into scrapbooks. Challenge them to analyze their collection and decide on a system for classification. As their collections grow, try asking students to estimate an item's mass or length—just to see how the metric thinking is coming along.— *Kathleen Ann Kutie, East Chicago, Ind.*

Centimeter rulers

A good way to introduce youngsters to metrics is to have them make their own metric rulers. You'll need several 8-foot lengths of lath (purchased at a lumberyard), sandpaper, glue, and felt-tip pens.

Cut the lath strips into 20-cm lengths, one for each student in the class. Give the laths to students along with strips of paper on which you've marked the centimeter spaces. Have students use small squares of sandpaper to smooth the ends of their wood pieces. Then have them glue the paper strips onto their wood pieces and complete their rulers by numbering the spaces from 1 to 20.

Invite students to use their rulers to measure various objects in the room to get an idea of what a centimeter is.— *Charlene Siewert, Norristown, Pa.*

Converting within metric

Here's an easy way for your students to keep track of the decimal point when they convert from one metric unit to another.

Have them write the unit equivalencies above the problem. (For example, 1 m = 100 cm.) Then, ask them to draw an arrow pointing to the larger number in the equivalency. The arrow will show them which way to move the decimal point, and the number of zeros will tell them how many places to move it.—*Patricia Swisher, St. Joseph, Mich.*

$$1m \qquad \xrightarrow{} = 100\,cm$$
$$48.9\,cm \qquad = \underline{}\,cm$$
$$48.90\,m \qquad = 4{,}890\,cm$$
$$1{,}000\,g \qquad \xleftarrow{} = 1\,kg$$
$$6{,}400\,g \qquad = \underline{}\,kg$$
$$6{,}400\,g \qquad = 6.400\,kg$$

Metric monsters

Here are a variety of activities that encourage kids to use their imaginations as well as their knowledge of metrics. To get started, set up a center with instruction cards such as the following:

- Draw a geometric shape that has a perimeter of (state number) centimeters. Add to this shape—any way you'd like—to make the most monstrous monster you can imagine.

- Create a monster with straight-line segments, measuring and recording lengths as you go. Keep all measurements in even centimeters (no extra millimeters). Challenge others to estimate the length of the segments and/or the perimeter of your monster. Estimators can check by measuring.

- Draw a metric monster with straight-line segments and, without measuring, try to come as close as you can to (state number) centimeters for its perimeter. Check by measuring.— *Kari Yokas, Arcadia, Calif.*

One gallon wins

This game is designed to help your students master the relationships between cups, pints, quarts, and gallons. To prepare, cut from a 12 x 16-inch piece of tagboard the following measurement cards:

- 30 "cups" (1 x 1 inch)
- 20 "pints" (1 x 2 inches)
- 15 "quarts" (2 x 2 inches)
- 1 "gallon" (4 x 4 inches)

Then make a cardboard spinner disk, about 6 inches in diameter. Divide the spinner into 10 equal sections and write in each section a direction, such as "Take 1 quart," "Take 1 pint and 1 cup," and "Take 3 cups." Attach a cardboard arrow to the spinner, using a paper fastener.

Stack the measurement cards in separate piles. Players (two to four) take turns spinning the arrow and following the directions, taking from the stacks of cards the amounts indicated. Players should trade smaller denominations for their larger equivalents, for example, 2 cups for 1 pint. The winner is the player who exchanges 4 quarts for the only gallon.

Students can check equivalencies by superimposing the pieces: 2 pints exactly cover a quart, and so on. For more advanced students, you might want to include half-gallons or use directions such as "Give back 1 cup."—*Amanda Donovan, Cambridge, Mass.*

Grasping the geometric

This hands-on activity gives young students a feel for geometric shapes.

Hand each student a whole graham cracker (two squares), which has been left out overnight to soften; a plastic knife; and a square of waxed paper to use as a work surface.

Let students try recognizing and making different geometric shapes by asking them questions such as: What shape is your graham cracker? What shapes do you have when you cut your cracker in half? Can you cut one of your squares into two triangles? Can you make two smaller triangles out of your big triangle? Can you nibble around your other square until it changes into a circle?—*Patricia Flanigan, Thousand Oaks, Calif.*

Milk-carton math

Pint-size milk cartons, cleaned and dried, can provide a basis for investigating congruent figures, right angles, parallel lines, perimeter, volume, and the relationship of two- and three-dimensional figures. Supply the following list of tasks to guide early explorations:

1. Measure the edges of the bottom of the carton. Use these measurements to find the perimeter of the bottom of the carton.

2. Cut off the slanted top of the carton as evenly as possible. Cut a 1-inch square out of the piece you've cut off. Use this template to find the number of square inches in the bottom of the carton.

3. What measurements will you need to find the volume of the carton (without its top)? Make these measurements; then find the volume.

4. Make the carton lie flat by cutting along the creases. What is the area of the surface you've made? Flatten another carton, cutting along different creases to make a flat carton of another shape. Is the area the same?

5. Trace a flattened carton. Mark all the right angles in red.

6. Cut apart a flattened carton by cutting along all creases. How many pieces do you have? Do any pieces exactly match in size and shape?

As a follow-up activity, have students collect different-size cartons—two of each size. Ask them to flatten one carton of each pair and to paint all the cartons the same color. Prepare a work area where students can match three-dimensional cartons with their two-dimensional counterparts.—*Sandra J. Frey, Lancaster, Pa.*

Toothpick geometry

In this challenging activity, toothpicks serve as both the framework for geometric structures and the standard for measuring them.

Divide your students into groups of three or four. Give each group a pile of round-tipped toothpicks and a chunk of plasticine or clay. The first challenge is to design and build any kind of geometric structure—the more unusual and complex the better. Then have students complete the following tasks:

- Measure a toothpick to the nearest centimeter. Use this as the basis for all your measurements.
- What is the height of your structure? (Use the highest point.)
- What is the perimeter of your structure? (Measure the greatest distance around.)
- What is the area? (Use the greatest length and width.)—*Ruth Landmann, Copenhagen, Denmark*

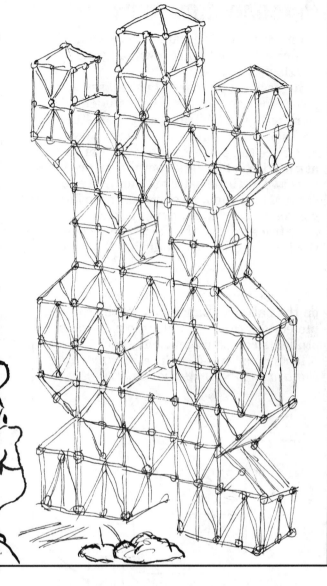

Square surgery

A square is just a square—until you draw two perpendicular lines through it. Then one square becomes four squares. Add two more lines, crisscross fashion, and get a set of eight right triangles. Experiment with this sort of square surgery to develop a collection of slice-a-square challenges that suit the math abilities of your class. Then provide students with pencils, rulers, and a supply of 8-inch squares, along with a collection of slice-a-square challenges. Here are a few samples:

- Make 4 congruent squares.
- Make 16 congruent squares.
- Make 2 congruent triangles.
- Make 3 triangles of different sizes.
- Make 4 congruent triangles and 1 square.

Some challenges might have more than one correct solution. Encourage students to seek alternatives and to devise their own challenges for others to solve. For a striking display, have students color in their geometric patterns.—*Deanna Bettis, Kent, Wash.*

Personal tangrams

After exploring tangrams, invite your students to create their own tangram puzzles.

Suggest students try to use all seven pieces to form pictures. Have students work with the tangrams on paper—the backs of extra handouts—so that they can trace the patterns they like. Later, ask students to select from their tracings two or three patterns they'd like to share. Have them reconstruct these favorites on colored art paper and carefully trace around the pieces, going over the lines in crayon so that they'll be easy to see.

Invite students to compose a sentence or phrase about each picture and write it on the pattern's paper. Collect the completed tangram originals into a packet so students can share and solve each other's puzzles.—*Charlene Harames and Sandra Rich, San Mateo, Calif.*

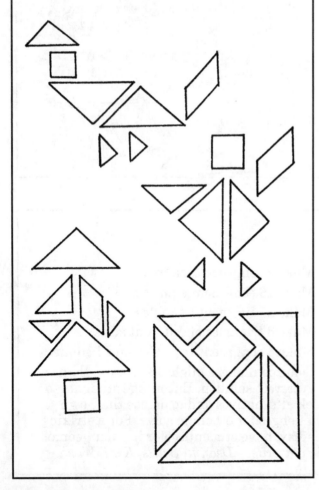

Pac-Man geometry

Resurrect Pac-Man, the video-game character, to add appeal to the study of angles. For drills about the difference between acute, obtuse, and right angles, make handouts on which students must identify the kind of angle formed by Pac-Man's mouth.—*Hayward Adams, Beverly Farms, Mass.*

Alphabet angles

To help your students grasp the concepts of right angles, acute angles, and obtuse angles, turn to the alphabet.

Have students sort out all the straight-line letters (A, E, F, H, and so on) and copy them on graph paper. Suggest they use a color-code system to mark the angles they find—for instance, red for right angles, orange for obtuse, blue for acute. Invite angle spotters to experiment with letter formations to achieve different combinations of angles. They might, for example, try making an X with lines crossing to form right angles, then make an X with two acute and two obtuse angles. Here are other challenges to pose:

- Which letters have acute and obtuse angles in them?
- Can you write a word that has eight right angles in it?
- What letters can you make with three acute angles?— *David Baer, Berry Creek, Calif.*

Easy as pi

This activity helps students explore pi in a concrete way. Assemble a collection of circular objects in a variety of sizes. Review the terms *circumference* and *diameter*. Discuss and demonstrate the concept of relationship: One item is twice as large as another, or three times as fast, or half as tall.

Have students choose a method for measuring circumference. (A string or measuring tape works well, and using the metric system avoids fractions.) Prepare a record sheet with columns for object, circumference, diameter, circumference/diameter.

Invite students to measure the items and record the data. Have them start with the circumference. Then, to measure the diameter, have students place a metric ruler on a point of the circumference and pivot the rule back and forth to find the longest measurement across the circle. Now ask the following questions: Which is the longer measurement, the circumference or the diameter? How many diameters could fit around the circumference?

Have students make a diameter length with string and use this unit to measure the circumference. Does the answer come out even? Students can find the actual number of diameters in a circumference by using the process indicated by the fourth heading on the record sheet— that is, by dividing the circumference by the diameter. The resulting number, of course, is pi.

After students repeat the process for several circles, have them compare the results they've gotten. How much does the value of pi vary? Why is this so? As a follow-up, have students figure out the circumference of an object when only the diameter is given and vice versa.—*John Newton, Onondaga Nation, N.Y.*

How long is a song?

To get students interested in calculating distances, switch the focus of your problems from trains and planes to audiocassette tapes.

Your students already know the time factor: A 60-minute tape plays for 30 minutes on each side. Supply the rate factor by explaining that during play a tape advances $1\frac{7}{8}$ inches per second (industry standard). Now ask, "Is the tape longer or shorter than a 100-yard football field?"

Challenge students to apply the D = r x t formula to find out. Here's how they might proceed:

• Convert the one-side tape time to seconds.

• Multiply the time in seconds by the $1\frac{7}{8}$ inches-per-second rate to find the tape's length in inches.

• Convert the inches to feet and the feet to yards, then compare with the 100-yard football field.

Your students might enjoy checking their calculations by unwinding an old 60-minute tape down a football field, if possible, or a pre-measured hallway.— *Anne Mele, Brooklyn, N.Y.*

Car-fact percentages

Capitalize on most kids' fascination with cars to get them involved with percentages. Visit the school's parking lot or a larger one nearby at a low-traffic time. Divide students into pairs and provide them with survey sheets. The sheets might ask for the number of:

- in-state license plates
- out-of-state license plates
- personalized license plates
- cars that are blue or red (or other colors)
- Fords, Chevrolets, Toyotas
- cars with bumper stickers
- cars with AAA stickers.

Finally, ask students to count the total number of cars. Back in the classroom, have them calculate what percentage of the cars have in-state license plates, out-of-state license plates, and so on. Students can make bar graphs or pie charts to illustrate the information.—*Timothy Hornberger, Trenton, N.J.*

On a roll

This game, "Plot Four," is designed to help students cope with positive and negative numbers while giving them practice with plotting graph coordinates.

To create "Plot Four," make a game board—a 12 x 12 grid divided into quadrants by vertical and horizontal axes. Mark the intersection of the axes with a zero, and number the other axis/grid-line intersections from 1 to 6—positive numbers above and to the right of the zero, negative numbers below and to the left of the zero.

You'll also need two sets of dice in two different colors (one set for positive numbers and one for negative numbers). For markers, give each of two players a collection of dried beans (a different type for each player).

The first player rolls the two sets of dice, chooses *any* two of the four numbers to plot, and places a marker at the appropriate coordinate point. (Players may pick which die comes first in the coordinate pair.) The second player follows the same procedure. The goal is to "take" four points in a row in any direction.

As the board fills with markers, a player might be unable to work out a combination that correlates to an open intersection. When that happens, the player loses his turn. If players reach a stalemate before anyone has achieved four in a row, the player with the most markers on the board wins.— *Marianne Armstrong, Urbana, Ill.*

5½ pencils high

Rulers aren't the only tools that can provide measurements. Even the common pencil can be used for measuring, as this activity demonstrates.

Begin by establishing the length of an unsharpened pencil with an eraser (usually 7½ inches). Then have your students stand with their backs to a wall and make marks level with the tops of their heads. Have each child use an unsharpened pencil to measure his height. Then ask students to convert their "pencil heights" into inches.—*Owen J. Kilbane, Lucasville, Ohio*

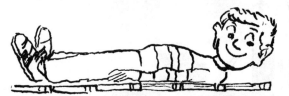

Divided we stand

Put a little action into division practice by calling on students to assemble themselves as stand-in divisors and dividends. First, give your students an 8½ x 11-inch piece of paper. Ask them to use a crayon or felt-tip pen to write a large, easy-to-read 1-digit number. Next, draw a supersize division bracket on the chalkboard, placing the top line slightly above the height of your tallest student. Then, recruit a division problem by calling on students by birth months, color of clothing, number of siblings, and so on. Place two students—holding their numbers high—beneath the division bracket, the others to the left of it. Those remaining in their seats can solve the problem and get ready for the next call-up.—*Mark Hughes, Cairo, Egypt*

Ratios of colors

Offer your students a colorful and tasty approach to ratios, using M&M's chocolate candies or something similar. For each student, make a set of 10 candies in assorted colors, and store the set in a plastic bag.

Have your students dump out the candies, count them, and sort them by color into subsets. Encourage them to arrange the color subsets in parallel rows, graph-fashion, to make comparisons easier—and to help fix the mental image of a ratio. Guide the students' exploration with questions such as these:

- How many candies do you have altogether?
- How many orange? yellow? brown? red?
- What's the ratio of the number of brown to the number of orange?
- What's the ratio of the number of yellow to the total number?

With 10 candies per bag, your students can also figure percentages. At lesson's end, suggest a taste test—if the students haven't already thought of this.—*Sally A. Kievert, Lafayette, Ind.*

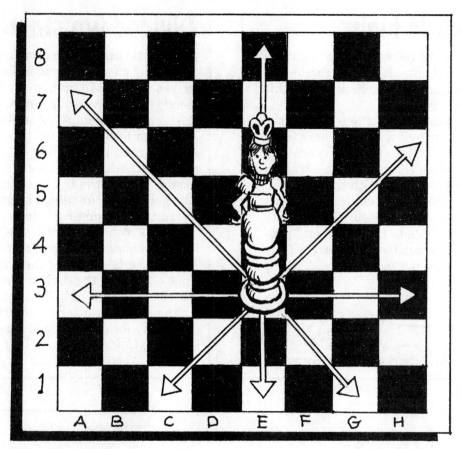

Chessboard math

If you have a chess set, you have all the makings of a math lesson stressing coordinates, percentages, fractions, and fun.

Mark a chessboard (or checkerboard) with location referents. Mark a letter below each square in the bottom horizontal row and label the left-hand side column of squares with numbers so that each square on the board can be identified by coordinates. Help students practice finding specific squares, such as (D,6) or (G,2).

Prepare task cards large enough to accommodate a mini-chessboard illustration alongside the directions. And, although you'll probably need to post a chart of rules for the movement of each chess piece, you may also want to repeat pertinent information on the cards. For example: The queen may move in a straight line—forward or backward—any number of spaces vertically, horizontally, or diagonally. Task cards for the queen might include the following questions:

1. If the queen is on (E,7), how many squares can she move to, that is control? What fraction of the squares on the board is this? What percentage of the board do these squares represent?

2. On which square or squares would the queen control the greatest percentage of the board?

Other tasks might ask students to carry out specified moves for various pieces under conditions described or to calculate moves to take pieces.

Younger students may enjoy chessboard tasks that involve the colors and shapes on the board.

1. Trace around a rectangle that has the same number of black squares and red squares.

2. Trace a rectangle that has more blacks than reds.

3. Trace a set of touching squares that has four reds and one black.—*John Noel, Visalia, Calif.*

Assembly-line division

When students solve long-division problems in assembly-line fashion, each student learns his step thoroughly before being rotated to the next job.

To begin, divide your class into about five groups and write that many long-division problems on the chalkboard. Then tell the first student in each group that he's the "set-up" person on the job; he must estimate how many times the divider will go into the first number of his group's problem. Have him write the estimate over the number; for example, if he were dividing 751 by 5, he'd put a 1 over the 7.

The next student in each group works the multiplication step — in this case 5 x 1. The third student subtracts 5 from 7 and writes in the answer. The fourth student in each group checks all the steps for mistakes. If he finds an error, the student who worked that part of the problem makes the correction. (Any worker who sees a mistake the inspector misses can also point it out.) After the inspector OKs the work on the first digit, he brings down the next number in the problem for division.

Work continues in step-by-step fashion until the problem is solved and checked. As each group finishes a problem, write another on the chalkboard. Every few problems, have group members change jobs so that each has a chance to work with every step.—*Ann Tabone, Detroit*

The power of exponents

Have calculators handy for this activity about exponents. Begin by telling your students the following tall tale about a salary negotiation: A worker agreed to a starting salary of 2¢ a day, provided the boss agreed to keep the worker for 30 days and to increase his salary by one power each day. This meant that on Day 2 he'd receive 2¢ squared, or 4¢; Day 3, 2¢ cubed, or 8¢; and so on. The boss thought he'd made a great deal.

Next, draw a calendar grid on the chalkboard and ask your students' help in filling in the salary day by day. They'll quickly realize that the worker was a shrewd negotiator. By Day 26, his salary has become 2¢ to the 26th power, or $671,088.64 a day.—*Victoria Freire, Brooklyn, N.Y.*

Math in the great outdoors

To spark your students' interest in math, try conducting a class or two outdoors. Here are a few projects to get you started:

- **Using bases.** Survey the school and environment for things that can be counted: cars in a row, windows on the building or side of the building, fence posts, paving blocks, and so on. Assign each student a countable and a base to count it in. Later, have the class convert all findings to base 10.
- **Area and perimeter.** Let students choose their own units (meters, yards, jump ropes) to measure and compute perimeters and areas for playing fields, parking lots, and game areas.
- **Percentages.** The basketball court is the site for this activity. Invite each student to make 10 tries at making a basket. Have students record the number of makes and misses and then compute the percentages.

Take a look around and see what other outdoor math projects await you. Encourage your students to make suggestions too.—*Robert A. Zaske, Circle Pines, Minn.*

Budgeting for a vacation

Students can use their math skills and learn about budgeting by planning imaginary vacations. Have them gather brochures, magazines, transportation fares, and sample menus.

Tell them to plan a weekend vacation and find out how much it'll cost. They need to consider travel (bus, train, or airplane), lodging, and food, as well as any "extras" they'd like—such as camera film and movie tickets. Have the travelers list their expenses and figure out the total cost of their trips. Combine this with a writing or oral exercise by asking students to describe their travel plans.

After students complete this project, find the average cost of the vacations. Give students a figure below the average, and tell them that's their travel budget. Ask them to plan another vacation that meets that budget.—*Denise Lee, Springhouse, Pa.*

Money mania

Bring a sense of wonder and curiosity to math investigations with these facts about paper money:

- Thickness: 0.0043 inch
- Length: 6.14 inches
- Width: 2.61 inches
- Weight: 0.033 ounces

Challenge your students to figure out how many bills it would take to reach across their desks, the playground, their state. How many would it take to cover a student's desk? The classroom floor? The school parking lot? A baseball diamond? How many bills would it take in a stack to reach the height of a parking meter? The Sears Tower? Could a bank robber carry 1 million bills in a suitcase? Why or why not? How much would 1 million bills weigh? Encourage your students to make up their own problems.—*Carole E. Greenes, Boston*

The square foot

The idea of the square foot may be hard for students to understand—until they complete their own square-foot mats. The resulting creative designs will make beautiful bulletin board displays.

You'll need rulers, scissors, glue, and construction paper in many colors. After a lesson on the square foot, explain that each student is going to make his own by measuring and cutting out 144 squares (1 inch by 1 inch) from construction paper and pasting them carefully on a base mat (a sheet of construction paper that's 12 inches by 12 inches).

Encourage students to work together—trading squares for new color combinations and helping with designs. They'll soon see the value of planning their designs before cutting out and pasting squares.—*Lee Mann, Lowell, Ore.*

Everybody wins!

This contest gives kids practice in a variety of operations—while it releases some pent-up energy.

Tell your students a contest is about to begin, but that you won't tell them what it takes to win. Appoint a record keeper and move outdoors to one corner of the school building or playing field. Have students run to the next corner, keeping track of how many steps they take. Take turns so that only two students are running at the same time. After running, each contestant reports his number of steps to the record keeper.

Then, move back inside where the record keeper lists the numbers of steps—arranged in sequence from lowest to highest—on the board. With your students, discuss the range, find the median, and compute the average.

Finally, announce the winners, making up categories to include everyone. Class One winners might be those whose numbers fall nearest the median. Class Two might be the prime numbers. The following classes could include numbers above the average, numbers that can be evenly divided by three, all even numbers, and so on. Encourage students to come up with their own categories.

After the contest, have students deal with more concrete considerations: measuring the actual distance run and figuring the length of each person's running step; estimating the number of steps required to cover the distance at a walk; pacing off the distance and figuring the length of one's pace to use as a portable measuring tool.—*Pauline Davies, Aberdeen, S.D.*

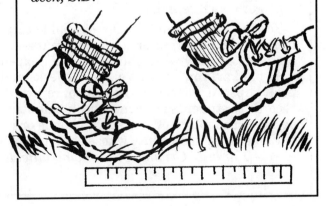

Tic-tac-toe to the third power

Four to the third power will sound less obscure to your students after a few rounds of this specialized tac-tac-toe game.

You'll need one ordinary die and one smaller cube, which you customize by putting the numerals 1, 2, and 3 on the faces, using each numeral twice.

Almost any number of students can play. Each needs paper and pencil, and all must first draw their own tic-tac-toe grids.

Have students prepare a list of numbers they'll be using in this game: the powers of 1, 2, 3, 4, 5, and 6 through the third power— 1, 2, 3, 4, 5, 6, 8, 9, 16, 25, 27, 36, 64, 125, 216.

Each player chooses nine of the above numbers to fill his grid. A leader rolls both dice and reads the results, giving first the base number on the large die and then telling the exponent shown on the smaller die. The leader computes and records the answer. Each player computes the answer and puts an X through it if it appears on his grid. Three Xs in a row wins.

Two players might share a grid in true tic-tac-toe style. The first roll of the dice is for Player One, who puts an X through the answer if it appears on the grid; the second roll is for Player Two, who puts a circle around his answers. The first player to mark three numbers in a row wins.—*Lois Barson, Oreland, Pa.*

Checkbook math

Turn a checkbook over to each of your students and watch them put its power to work—to improve their math skills.

Have each student make a starter checkbook kit, complete with deposit slips and a transaction records sheet. Start the students with initial deposits of $50. Subsequent deposits will depend on homework turned in ($15.36 for a week's work); quiz scores (assign a set amount or make each point worth $1); and other earnings you and the class agree on.

Students must write checks to cover regular expenses such as:

- weekly desk rental, $21.39
- missing assignments, $7.65
- unsigned note or test, $9.14
- pen or pencil rental, $5.50.

You might also want to offer special luxury items— privileges, entertainment, treats—that students can buy when they meet their expenses.

As banker, you'll collect all used checks and deposit slips. At the end of the month, return these records to students for a checkbook-balancing session. You might offer a special bonus or nonnegotiable treat to students whose checkbooks balance.—*Karen L. Grimm, South Somerville, N.Y.*

Mental math

Get your students to do mental computations with this game, called "Sorry!"

Before starting, you'll need to prepare three times as many math problems as there are students in your class, with all problems having a different answer. Copy each answer onto a small piece of paper, fold the papers in half, then give each student three. Now display one problem at a time. Here are some samples:

- Which is larger: 0.25 or 0.6?
- Subtract 0.6 from 3.
- What's 1% of 225?
- Triple 5⅓.
- Find the perimeter of a triangle if its sides are 0.8, 1.2, and 0.75.

Each student will need to complete the mental calculation and check his papers to see if he holds the correct answer. If he does, he selects a wrapped gift. (Each time you play, have four or five wrapped items, such as pencils, erasers, pens, a homework pass.) Instruct "winners" not to open their gifts.

After all the prizes have been taken, any student with a correct answer takes a prize from a former winner, and says, "Sorry!" Play continues until all the problems have been read. Students who hold prizes at the end of the game get to open and keep them.—*Diane Julian, Walkersville, Md.*

Picturing percentages

Help reinforce the concept of percentage with this artistic assignment. Distribute sheets of graph paper with enough squares to outline 20 10 x 10 grids. Have your students leave a little space between each grid.

Ask them to fill in 25 percent of one of the grids, creating any pattern or design they like. (They can use felt-tip pens, colored pencils, or crayons.) Suggest other percentages, such as 5, 50, and 90 to fill in their other grids. Have them write *5%, 50%,* and so on under the corresponding grids.

The practice helps students see what percentages really are—for example, that 5 percent isn't very much, but 90 percent is. Encourage students to choose other percentages and come up with interesting ways to picture them.—*Judy Roxborough, Foxborough, Mass.*

In my estimation...

To give students practice at making "good" guesses, start each week with a Monday Morning Estimation Contest. Plan tasks that involve quantity and have elements students can use to qualify their estimates (rather than just wild guesses). Here are a few challenges just for starters:

- If the pieces of licorice in this package were laid end to end, how far would the licorice extend—in centimeters? You may measure one piece.

- How many grams does this bag of marshmallows weigh? Here's a marshmallow to weigh.

- How many inches will this plant grow in 2 weeks? You may take measurements twice during the first week.

- How many pounds will our class weigh all together? You may weigh one person besides yourself.

- How many seconds will it take you to run around the school building twice? You may measure the distance and try a 10-second test.

Have students graph their guesses, then go through the various processes for checking out the challenge and getting the correct answer.—*Craig Yaker, Los Alamos, N.M.*

Cash calculations

To capitalize on the real-world appeal that money holds for kids, set up a money math center.

Collect a variety of ads from newspapers, store circulars, and sale catalogs. Then cut out prices—from 29¢ to $299.99—composed of whatever numbers and symbols your students are prepared to work with. Mount each price on colored oak tag.

Store all price tags—the larger the collection the better—in a box or envelope at the math center. Invite students to draw tags from this bank to complete work sheets with activities such as the following:

1. Choose eight prices and put them in order from smallest to largest.

2. See how many sets of two prices that are exactly 1¢ apart you can make.

3. How many sets of two prices that are exactly $1 apart can you make?

4. Choose any five prices under $100 and add them.

5. Choose four prices and write what you think they would buy. (Example: $1.98—a puzzle.) Check a catalog to see how good your guesses were.—*Barbara McMahon, Mount Morris, Pa.*

Chapter 6
SCIENCE

Flowers through the year

Make flowers regular classroom visitors for learning and enjoyment. Over the year, bring in a variety of favorites to study, such as local wildflowers, chrysanthemums, African violets, poinsettias, and daffodils.

If you don't have access to a garden, a single stem in a place of honor can be quite effective. If loads of flowers are available to you, bring in one for each student to study.

Aside from the obvious art projects that flowers inspire, have your students record sight and scent observations; encourage them to research facts about a plant's origin, range, varieties, and so on. Ask students to write to local agriculture and horticulture agencies to find out what plants are native to your area. Cultivate seeds and bulbs, timed so that one is blooming while the next is growing. Have groups of students alternate in taking care of the developing plants, recording growth data, and noting other changes.

Have students share the responsibility of keeping a class notebook of the year's flowers, including pressed blooms, leaf rubbings, and facts they learned during their research. At year's end, review the booklet for a fond reminder of the flowers you got to know.—*Elizabeth B. Huband, Wilmington, N.C.*

Sprout and eat

For an easy—and tasty—science lesson, try sprouting seeds in your classroom. For each batch, you'll need water; a large, wide-mouthed jar; cheesecloth; and a rubber band. Look in your local health-food store for seeds or beans; alfalfa seeds are the most familiar, but you can also use cabbage seeds, mung beans, or others. Follow these directions:

1. Put 2 tablespoons of seeds in the jar. Cover the jar with a double layer of cheesecloth and secure with the rubber band.

2. Fill half the jar with water. Let stand overnight.

3. Pour out the water through the cheesecloth. Then turn the jar several times to spread the moist seeds over its inner surface. Rinse the seeds with water through the cheesecloth two or three times a day. Then respread the seeds. (They need to be moist but not wet.)

4. After about 4 days, your class can discard the cheesecloth and eat the sprouts.

Try starting several batches a half day or 1 day apart. Then have students taste all the sprouts on the same day. Do 3-day-old sprouts look and taste different from 5-day-old sprouts? Students will enjoy the delicious, nutritious comparisons.—*Denise Lee, Springhouse, Pa.*

Mystery animals

Develop your students' observation skills and their attention to detail with this project.

After they've studied animal groups, ask your students to secretly select one animal. Encourage them to find pictures of that animal, read about it, then select one of its most unusual or interesting features. (For a porcupine, it might be the quills; for a bush baby, the big eyes.)

Give every student two sheets of white drawing paper, which they staple together across the top. On the first sheet, have them write a question to go with the unusual feature they selected. (Whose beautiful beak? Whose watchful eye? Whose furry tail?) Then ask them to draw a scene that depicts only that feature (for example a tree with a tiger's paw showing at its base). On the inside paper, have your students draw the entire animal and label it.—*Gail Walters, New Haven, Conn.*

Animal experts

Teach your students about pet care by turning each child into an expert on a specific animal.

Begin by making a long list of pets. Include many types of birds, dogs, cats, guinea pigs, and other animals so you can give students plenty of choice. As you compile the list, discuss the reasons for excluding wild animals.

After selecting a pet, each student should gather data on feeding and housing the animal, caring for its special needs, and so on. Students might enjoy writing their reports in advice-column form. (Examples of pet-care columns from newspapers will help students stylize their work.) They can share their columns with the entire class and perhaps through a school-wide publication as well.—*Florence Rives, Selma, Ala.*

Tagalong nature trail

For this trail-tagging activity, you'll need a supply of blank baggage tags and one of the following: ample school grounds, access to a vacant lot, or an outdoor education site.

You'll need to visit your chosen trail several times. The first visit is one of true exploration. Depending upon background and experience, your explorers might discover habitats, a variety of plants, signs of animal life, evidence of the action of sun and water, and evidence of interactions between living things and their environments. Encourage students to take notes.

Back in the classroom, discuss what you found. You might want to enlist the aid of a recorder—human or tape. Take down at least enough trail "features" for one per student.

Now to the baggage tags. Describe on each tag one trail feature from the list. For example, "This is a plant that can't make its own food"; "This is a home for a social insect." Before the second visit to the trail, give each student a trail tag to study and speculate about. (Descriptions may fit more than one situation.)

The group should probably stick together on the second visit to the site in order to consult and share information. When the group comes across something fitting a tag description, the student holding that tag reads it aloud, if possible identifies the feature more specifically on the back of the tag, and ties the tag in place at that location (bring some sticks or stakes). At the end of the walk, the group can discuss left-over tags and place them by consensus.

You may leave tags at their locations as temporary markers, or you may collect, laminate, and replace them for a more permanent nature trail. Invite other classes to retrace your steps and study the markers on the tagalong trail.—*Lib Roller, Nashville, Tenn.*

Featured creatures contest

Take advantage of your students' fascination with exotic animals by holding a Featured Creatures Contest—an event that inspires scientific research. Prepare by clipping several pictures of unusual animals from nature magazines. Mark each with a code letter and write a separate research question for it. For instance, you might ask, *Where do lemurs live?* or *What is unusual about the bowerbird's nest?*

Next, make "official" entry forms with spaces for a student's name, one animal's name and code letter, the answer to the research question, plus an extra fact the student researched.

At a Featured Creatures Contest display, post the animal pictures, with code letters underneath and research questions alongside. Have entry forms close by, along with a box for completed ones. Give students who want to enter the contest 1 week to research the animals and complete their entry forms. To discourage wild guesses (and promote trips to the library), limit students to one entry per animal.

When the contest is over, use the facts on the entry forms for class discussion.—*Kathy Loch Klein, Dubuque, Iowa*

Claim a plant and name it

The next time you schedule a field trip to a meadow, forest, or seashore, ask each student to pick out a plant he likes—preferably one not selected by someone else. In the process of avoiding plants already claimed, students must observe carefully, making comparisons to determine whether they've chosen the same, or merely similar species, as a classmate.

When a student has claimed his plant, invite him to name it. Names could refer to the plant's appearance: "hairy carrot," "green arrow"; to its location: "dune topper," "swamp beauty"; or to the plant-finder himself: "Brandt plant."

Take an instant photo of each student's plant. (Don't pick or dig up wild plants.) Back in the classroom, have students mount their photos on poster board, identifying the plants with both their newly created and common names. (A little research may be in order.)—*Larry Guthrie, Gary, Ind.*

BILLY'S SUNSHINE
DAISY

TRUM
RHO

GREEN CRAWLER
ENGLISH IVY

Planting seeds of learning

Bring several seed catalogs into your classroom, and you'll also be bringing a host of learning opportunities. Here are a few ideas to get you started:

1. *Vegetable and fruit study.* Invite each student to name a favorite fruit or vegetable and then look for it in the catalog. Why are some not listed? What varieties are listed? How are the varieties different? Have students make a reference chart or booklet with names and pictures of fruits and vegetables.

2. *Seed growing.* Order seeds for a plant that will grow well in the classroom. (What information does the catalog give about growing season, soil, light needs, watering?) Have your students help complete and check the order. How long is it supposed to take for the seeds to come? Mark the date on the calendar.

3. *Word study.* Have students look through the catalog for words they'd like to know about: annual, perennial, mulch, cultivate, for example.

4. *Plant lore.* Have students investigate plants' needs. Which plants grow well in shade? Which need lots of room? Which plants grow slowly?

5. *Bug study.* Ask your students to find out what the catalog says about insect pests. Then have them do further research on garden insects.

When you've exhausted all the science-related activities from your seed catalogs, invite students to cut them up for art projects.—*Jo Fredell Higgins, Aurora, Ill.*

Birds as builders

This winter, collect several abandoned or fallen bird nests for your students to study. Before you begin your investigation, photograph the nests or have students make detailed drawings. The nests will never be intact again.

Divide students into groups and give each group a nest. Ask students to observe the structure, shape, and size of their nest. What kinds of materials did the birds use? How do the parts fit together? Are the materials at the bottom of the nest different from those at the top? How? Why? How is their nest different from the others?

Next, explain that twigs and sticks are commonly found in bird nests. Every stick represents a flight to the nest. Ask students to estimate the number of stick-carrying trips. Then have them tally the sticks as they carefully dismantle their nest. They'll be surprised at how many trips the bird took— one class dismantled a nest that had 1,700 sticks!

Students also will discover an assortment of other materials such as string, feathers, hair, and grasses. Have students separate these into categories and count them.

When finished, groups can create displays showing the nest materials, original photographs and drawings, and statistics of pieces collected.—*M.J. Laird, Tucson, Ariz.*

Who saw our Whozzi-saurus?

Even classes with no dinosaur background should enjoy a dinosaur hunt.

Divide the class into teams of about six. Invite each team to design and draw a prehistoric creature. Authenticity could be a ground rule if this is to be a review; otherwise, kids can be free to consider a wider range of forms—animals past, present, future, or fanciful.

Have team artists sketch the "dinosaur" on light-colored construction paper—a different color for each team. The artists then draw lines to partition the creature, jigsaw style, into 12 sections, which are numbered 1 to 12. Later, students will cut apart the sections to become "fossil" pieces.

While artists are working, other team members collaborate in writing a short history of their team's creature, providing data on its habitat, food-getting behavior, predators, and so on, as well as the probable cause of its extinction. You might suggest that even if the dinosaur is imaginary, a little science vocabulary can add an authentic tone to the description. The history should also include a small sketch of the creature—based on the large drawing—and of course its name.

Students now cut apart fossil pieces and hide them—one team working at a time—within a specified area inside the building or out on the school grounds. Students should establish rules for hiding the pieces. For example, some part of each "hidden" piece must remain visible.

Now, the hunt begins. Team members work together to collect another team's dinosaur in bits and pieces. The first team assembling all 12 pieces of a dinosaur wins. When all the dinosaurs have been put together, have each team read aloud its own dinosaur's history. This will enable dinosaur hunters to identify the wondrous creatures they've managed to unearth.—*Michele L. Brill, Cherry Hill, N.J.*

Underground surveillance

Leaves stretching toward the sun and blossoms unfolding are only part of the plant-growth picture. Important action is going on out of sight below the ground. To spy on this interesting activity, build a root view box.

Building the box is easy—you might want to make six or seven; they'll come in handy for controlled experiments. For each one, you'll need a plastic beverage jug (or cardboard carton); a utility knife or sharp scissors; heavy acetate or other stiff, clear plastic; rubber bands; masking tape; ruler; seeds; and soil.

To make a box:

- Cut the top off the jug.
- On one side of the jug, draw a rectangular window measuring about 2½ x 4 inches.
- Cut across the top and down both sides of the window to make a flap that's still attached at the bottom.
- Working inside the jug, cover the window area with clear acetate and tape the ace-

tate in place.

Now fill the root view box with soil. When you plant the seeds, be sure some are close to the window side of the jug. Keep the window flap closed and secured with a rubber band most of the time because the roots will tend to grow away from light. Also tilt the box toward its window side so that gravity will encourage the roots to grow where they can be seen easily.

You might use root view boxes to explore a number of plant behaviors. Conduct experiments to discover how roots develop in various soils (potting mix; potting soil with fertilizer; schoolyard soil; schoolyard soil with fertilizer; schoolyard soil with other additives, such as peat moss, perlite, sand, potting soil, and so on). Use the boxes to investigate how water moves through various soils. Think of ways to find out how roots respond to light and gravity.—*James E. Abbott, Los Angeles*

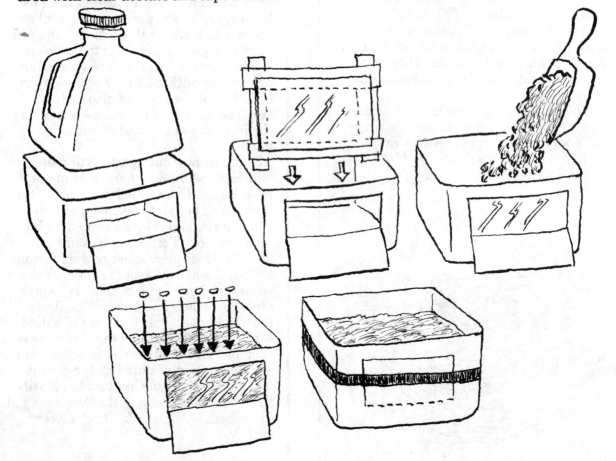

Tree diaries

Give your students the opportunity to make scientific observations and to develop an appreciation for one of our most valuable resources by having them keep tree diaries. The project is especially effective during a season change or during a season with dramatic weather conditions.

Have each student select a tree to observe over a set period. Provide students with notebooks in which to record their observations every 3 days or so. They might also want to add drawings, photos, or leaves to their diaries. At the end of the project, invite students to report what they've learned to the class.—*Louise Romero, Glencoe, Minn.*

Protozoan progeny

Add appeal to the study of protozoa by having students track the number of descendants that Ami the Amoeba produces in a 24-hour period.

Provide a roll of shelf paper, sheets of graph paper, and a calculator. Remind researchers that the amoeba reproduces by splitting in two, and suggest that for this project students should count on a split every 20 minutes.

You might begin the project as an illustrated time line, starting with Ami-nucleus, protoplasm and all—at high noon. At 12:20 p.m., Ami becomes two animals; by 1 p.m., eight places are needed at the Amoeba dinner table. Before long, your students might have to resort to tallies, then numerals. Sometime during the evening generations, even the calculator will run out of display area.

After they've calculated Ami's daily progeny, students might wish to check the procreation process of more moderate creatures— such as a pair of mice— over a 6-month period.—*Holly C. Van Scoy and Joan Porter Smith, Austin, Tex.*

Environmental scavenger hunt

Combine research and environmental awareness with this activity.

Make a list of about 20 items for your students to identify. For example:

- a deciduous tree
- a coniferous tree
- a metamorphic rock
- a wild mammal
- an example of erosion
- a seed not dispersed by the wind
- a perennial plant
- an annual plant

Split your class into groups of five or six and have them research any terms they're unsure of. For the hunt, groups won't need to collect actual examples; instead, have them make sketches or get an adult's verification. (If possible, have a parent assigned to each group.) Try the hunt at different seasons of the year. Consider using it during upcoming field trips to locations that might include different environments: a swamp, field, forest, city, farm, construction site, landfill, stream.— *Raymond Bottom, Monroe, Mich.*

Classification safari

Lighten up animal classification tasks with your own classification labels and artwork. Prepare a collection of strange and wonderful creatures according to a system of characteristics. For instance, you might start with the kingdom Animalia, phylum Teetopsum. These animals would have T's on their heads. Within the Teetopsum phylum there might be two classes: Springzata and Spikezata. These groups would be recognized by their springs and spikes.

Depending upon the skills of your students, you might move on to more detailed classifications: order, family, genus, and species. And for those who are ready for real adventure, provide a silly safari on which students search for the animal that has the following classification:

- Kingdom: *Animalia*
- Phylum: *Teetopsum*
- Class: *Springzata*
- Order: *Zigzagtia*
- Family: *Noseocirculisee*
- Genus: *Trinoseocirculisee*
- Species: *Trinoseocirculisee leafola*

Can the hunters find the *Trinoseocirculisee leafola* among the animals pictured in the illustration? To track the animal down, hunters must separate animals with T tops from those without; T-topped animals with springs from those without, and so forth. The animal they seek has a T top, springs, zigzags, a circular nose—three circular noses—and leaves. Who else but the poozie?

When students become adept at analyzing word clues to animal characteristics, they might want to invent new classes, orders, families, and so on, and draw animals based on their descriptive nomenclature.—*Bob Hauch, Chicago*

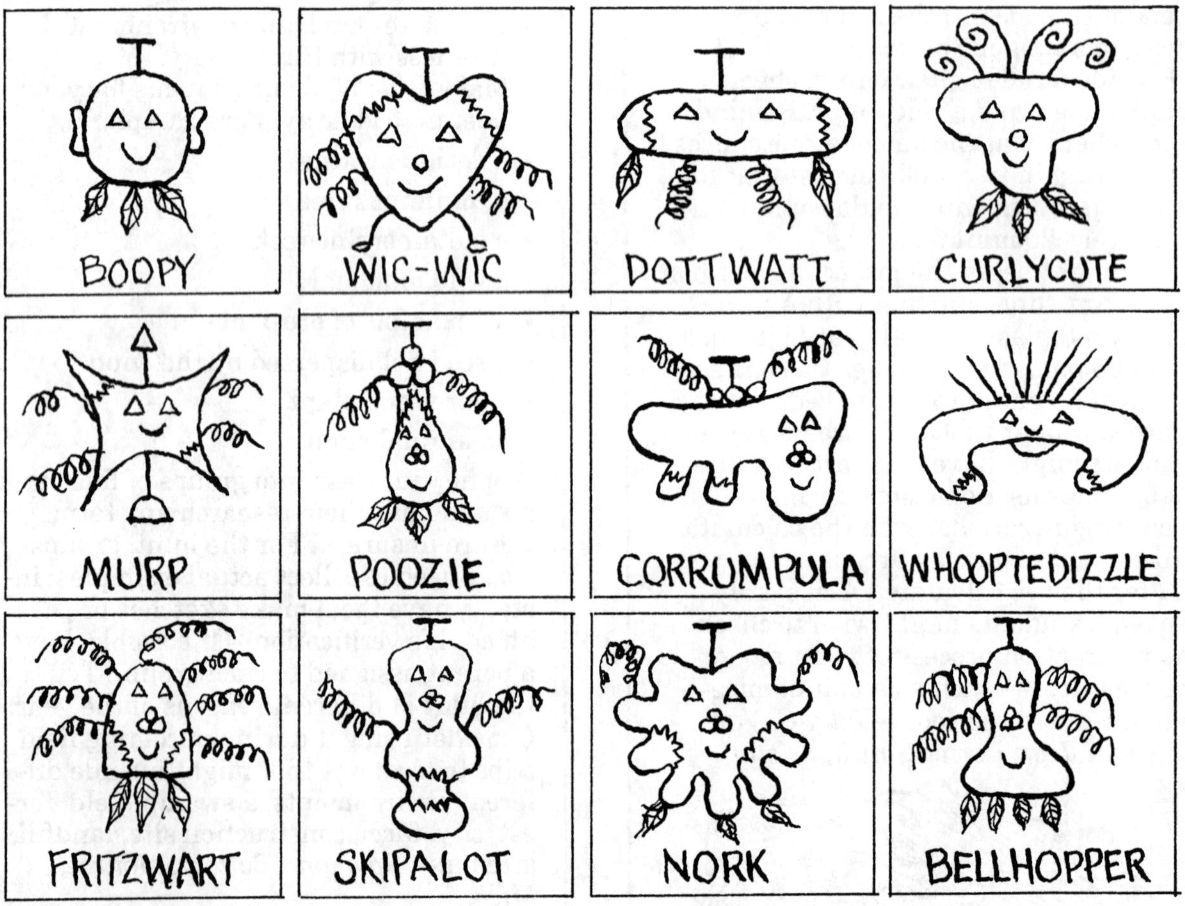

BOOPY · WIC-WIC · DOTTWATT · CURLYCUTE

MURP · POOZIE · CORRUMPULA · WHOOPTEDIZZLE

FRITZWART · SKIPALOT · NORK · BELLHOPPER

Increase your Fly-Q

The next time a fly lands in your classroom, instead of swatting it, use it as a springboard to an unusual science lesson.

Start the lesson by giving your students the following Fly-Q test. Tell them it's just a pretest, and encourage them to guess if they don't know an answer.

1. What is a fly? (An insect with a single pair of wings)
2. What are the three main parts of a fly? (Head, thorax, abdomen)
3. How does a fly breathe? (Through openings, called spiracles, in its thorax and abdomen)
4. How long does a fly live? (About 30 days in summer, longer in winter)
5. How does a fly see? (Through compound eyes that can't move or focus. Each eye has about 4,000 lenses)
6. How fast does a fly fly? (About 4½ miles per hour)
7. How many times per second does a fly beat its wings? (About 200)
8. How does a fly stabilize its flight? (By using tiny, modified wings called halteres)
9. How does a fly eat? (By dripping saliva on solid food to liquefy it, then sucking it)
10. What positive things does a fly do? (Pollinates flowers, eats other insects, provides a food source for other animals)

Instead of giving the answers, list some of your students' answers on the board and discuss them. Then divide your students into small groups and challenge them to research the answers. Have them present their findings to the class. Afterward, have them retake the test to see how much they've learned.—*Robert S. Young, Eugene, Ore.*

Plant exchange

Add a new twist to your unit on plants with this culminating activity.

Ask your students to bring to class a houseplant they'd be willing to trade. Tell them they'll need to prepare a plant-care card, which should include the plant's name, suggestions about watering and light, and other important information. (Ask your librarian to set aside some appropriate books.) On the day of the exchange, invite a local florist to class to talk about indoor plants. Then, arrange the adoptable plants and their care cards on a table, and have your students draw a number to determine the order of selection. Some students might want to keep their new plants in school.—*Alysa Cummings, Audubon, N.J.*

Dynamite dinosaur

Let students' enthusiasm for dinosaurs fuel an activity that gives them practice measuring and drawing to actual size.

Have the class choose a particular dinosaur, research its appearance, and find out its measurements (height and length). Students will also want to take note of data about various parts of the dinosaur's body: the length of its tail, legs, and neck; size of its feet; and so on. If measurements are given in feet, have students convert them to yards.

Take your group onto the playground with yardsticks and colored chalk. On the pavement, ask students to measure off the dinosaur's height and length. Then have students draw the dinosaur as they expect it would have looked thousands of years ago.

Invite other classes to see the life-size dinosaur and to hear a short presentation about it.—*Virginia L. Cowan, Pinellas Park, Fla.*

Reaping harvest facts

Take advantage of the fall harvest time to teach your students basic facts about the planting, growing, and harvesting of various fruits and vegetables.

Collect an assortment of resource materials—books, charts, pamphlets, seed packets—that provide information about gardening and plant life. Then enlist your students' help in bringing to class a variety of fresh fruits and vegetables. Have the children examine each piece of produce carefully— the leaves, skin, pulp, seeds—and discuss observations. Use the resource materials to answer questions, explain concepts, and provide "fact finds" about the various plants.

Following the class exploration, give students a chance to review and reinforce their newfound horticultural knowledge by setting up a "roadside stand" simulation. To make the stand, remove one side of a large cardboard carton and cut a window in the opposite side. Set the carton on a table on which baskets of fruit and vegetables are displayed. Have students take turns acting out the roles of farmer and buyer. Each customer asks the farmer one question relating to some aspect of planting, growing, or harvesting. If the farmer can't answer the question, decide whether outside consultation or additional research is in order.

To culminate the harvest-time activity, dice the fruit and vegetables and invite the class to enjoy a nutritious snack.—*Norma H. Keller, Mineola, N.Y.*

Dissecting a daffodil

For a hands-on approach to horticulture, plan your unit on flowers to culminate when daffodils are blooming—in early spring. Then give each student a daffodil and a labeled diagram of a flower. Have available several hand lenses and a microscope.

Tasks and investigation questions such as the following can guide the dissecting process and flower study:

1. Make five observations about the flower using four of your senses. (DO NOT TASTE.)

2. Describe the stem.

3. List some of the important things the stem does.

4. Describe the area between the end of the stem and the beginning of the flower.

5. According to the flower diagram, what's inside this part and what develops there?

6. Open this part and describe what you see.

7. Observe the inside of the flower with a hand lens and describe it.

8. Rub your finger in the middle of the flower and describe what you see on your fingers. What is this substance?

9. Observe this material through the microscope and write a description of what you see.

10. How does this substance get from one flower to another?

11. How do you think it gets to people who are allergic to it?

12. Remove the outer petals and, using a hand lens, describe how the petals are attached.

13. What is the purpose of the brown leaves you see below the flowers? Use the diagram to find and name the parts of the flower.

14. Using the diagram and the flower leaf, explain the development of buds in the flower.

Your budding botanists should enjoy this activity, especially because every student gets to operate on his own specimen.—*Joan P. Martin and Anna P. Mote, Wilmington, Del.*

Captive critters spark curriculum

For a lesson in almost every area of the curriculum, take your students to the local pet shop.

As your students watch the fish, snakes, lizards, birds, gerbils, and other pets, have them think of ways to classify the species by body covering, structure, respiration, locomotion, food needs, and so on. Encourage students to note the way various animal needs are met in captivity, then do research to discover how animals meet those needs in their natural habitats.

Start a class discussion on the factors involved in selecting appropriate pets, preparing the home, and caring for pets. During physical education, invite students to explore animal locomotion—hopping, ambling, wriggling, creeping, slithering, stalking, fluttering, soaring. The varieties of birds observed can become the focus of art projects, including fashioning masks for a parade of the birds. And of course don't miss the opportunity to send animal researchers hunting through the library for fiction and nonfiction follow-ups on their discoveries.—*Denise Lee, Springhouse, Pa.*

Fast flowers

For a lesson in botany your students won't soon forget, try growing an amaryllis in your classroom. Its dramatic growth and spectacular blooms make it an ideal plant for young students to study.

In February or March, plant your bulb in a fairly small pot that allows 1 inch of soil between the bulb and the pot. Two-thirds of the bulb should be below the level of the soil; one-third, above. Growth will be best in a south-facing window, but an eastern or western exposure will work.

When the flower stalk begins to appear, stand back. Growth is rapid enough that students can make daily recordings (great for graphing). The time of flowering and the time the blossom holds greatly depend on room temperature, with cooler temperatures slowing both. The flower parts are easy to see—the better to diagram and label.

You can try pollinating your amaryllis by hand to allow seeds to develop. When the stigma turns upward and becomes sticky, the amaryllis is ready for pollination. Have your students use cotton swabs to carry pollen from the anthers to the stigma.

The blossom will die and the ovary will grow as the seeds mature. Eventually the ovary will dry and crack open so that students can gather the seeds. Some budding botanists might want to try planting these, but you should warn them that hybrid plants rarely grow well from their own seeds. And that once a plant is started, it won't flower for 3 years.—*Sally Laird, Muskegan, Mich.*

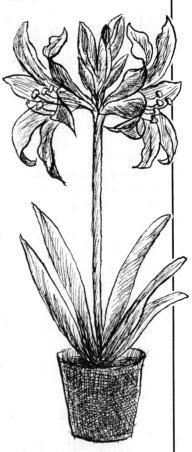

Collection, classification, and then some

When good weather beckons everyone outside, go on a collection walk.

Although the destination may vary—a park or nearby woods, a meadow or the schoolyard—the project is the same: Have each student collect 10 natural items that will fit into a small plastic bag. Wide variety in kinds of items is not necessary; you might even suggest that students "specialize," collecting 10 pebbles, 10 leaves, and so on.

Back in the classroom distribute large sheets of paper and have each student spread out his collection. Invite students to study their items and try to separate them into several categories. Next, have students study these primary categories for further sorting possibilities. They'll be looking for likenesses and differences in color, texture, shape, size, pattern, weight, and so on. On their papers, students may draw boxes or circles in which to house the various groups. They then give each set of items a descriptive label. A student whose collection is of leaves might organize the specimens into long leaves, roundish leaves, and big leaves.

Before students get too technical in their sorting, call a sharing session. Discuss and record some of the vocabulary they've been using in the grouping process: *same, different, group, set, match.* Were some items "left over" or in a set of one? Were any of the items they found *exactly* alike? What would it be like to try to put all of the students in the class into sets in the same way the children had classified their leaf and stone collections?

Help students see that although grouping things is often useful for study purposes, uniqueness and diversity are important.—*Connie Zane, Azusa, Calif.*

Tom Thumb visits the park

This activity combines science with creative thinking and writing—all in an outdoor setting.

Prepare the class by asking students to activate their senses and then to think low—about 2 inches above the ground. Each student is to select a spot—an area no larger than can be encircled with the arms—as a park site for the use of persons 2 inches tall. The park planners then explore from the vantage point of 2-inch-tall park visitors by getting down to ground level and using hand lenses to check out the landscape.

Suggest that students jot down "landmarks" that enhance their parks. As they list features, they should try to imagine how these sights might appear to tiny people: Twigs might seem like fallen trees; pebbles might loom as if they were boulders; and one might come face to face with an ant the size of a dog!

In describing their parks, students may include what a visitor might see as well as the visitor's reactions, feelings, and experiences. Students might try writing about "A Walk Through the Park"—an account by a diminutive park visitor who describes scenic spots along a particular footpath.

If you start the project early enough in the year, you can sponsor park tours in the fall, winter, and spring, with students noting seasonal changes—as viewed from 2 inches above the ground.—*Don Englert, Woodstock, Ill.*

Branching out

The leaves, bark, seeds, and fruit of trees can be the basis of innumerable studies throughout the year. Here are a few ideas to get you started.

In fall, photograph and identify the trees in your schoolyard or neighborhood. Have your students carefully collect a few leaves. Invite students to dip the leaves in paraffin to preserve them for a scrapbook or continued study; draw their outlines on paper; make crayon rubbings; make sun prints (place the leaves on photosensitive paper in a sunny window); or make ink prints on paper to use as stationery or gifts. (Leaf study might also lead to the study of circulation in humans.)

In spring, collect seeds and fruit from trees. Students can use their finds to make ornaments and to decorate cigar boxes, salt or oatmeal boxes, or juice cans by spray-painting seed cases, twigs, and so on, or leaving them in their natural state.

At any time of the year, students can study a tree's bark. Have your students make bark rubbings using crayons and paper. Note and compare textures, as well as scars, growths, and evidence of disease. You can also do a year-round study of particular trees. Take photos of them at various times of the year. Then discuss how longer and shorter days and changes in temperature and weather patterns affect plant life.— *Sharon Silberman, Brooklyn, N.Y.*

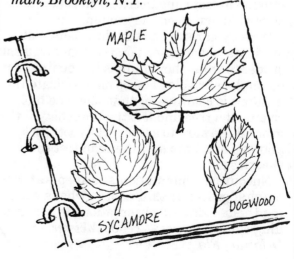

Houseplant "roots"

For easy-care living things in the classroom, you can't beat hardy houseplants. But even the sturdiest of these have several basic needs, and fulfilling those needs calls for a little research.

Quick-reference books about houseplant care provide the fundamental how-to's, but you and the class might also look into the native habitats of plants—places in which the environment (including soil, sun, water, climate, interrelationships with other living things) meets the plants' needs naturally.

Have students start with encyclopedias to research the more common houseplants. Then check with a librarian for plant-origin resources. Help students prepare a map showing regions where various houseplants are native and attach pictures of the plants in appropriate spots. You might have students indicate rainfall and temperature range on the map.

While they're researching, encourage students to list family connections among plants. This material could be the basis of a report—or a plant family tree.—*Patricia E. Paden, Needham Heights, Mass.*

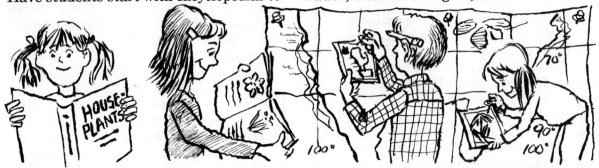

As nature changes

This school-yard activity will help kids notice and understand changes in their surroundings.

As you "tour" the school grounds, ask students to watch for indications that changes are taking place. You may need to get them started by pointing to cracks in concrete or shriveled leaves on the ground.

When you return to the classroom, list students' observations on the board and ask students what they think is happening. For example, shriveled leaves may indicate that autumn is coming—or that someone has trimmed a tree and left the branches on the ground. Be sure to accept all hypotheses, and ask students how they can test their theories.

Encourage your students to keep watching for changes—and think about what's causing them. Add new observations to a continuing classroom list.—*Teddy Meister, Orlando, Fla.*

Class rock collections

The next time you teach about rocks and fossils, set up a "Rock Swap" table in your classroom. For each rock a student wants to trade, ask him to provide background information, such as type of rock, approximate age, geologic era, where it was found, distinguishing features such as fossil prints or trace elements, and so on. Get ready for some knowledgeable wheeling and dealing—and a renewed interest in geology.—*Rick Crosslin, Indianapolis*

Rock watching, anyone?

Here's an interesting way to teach scientific observation, comparison, and classification. Ask your students to bring in small rocks they find.

Give each student a small plastic bag containing five rocks. (With younger students, start with only one or two rocks.) Encourage them to come up with different ways to observe and classify rocks— by size, shape, color, texture, and so on. Ask them to look at their rocks carefully and notice what makes them different or similar. Then have them write descriptions and draw pictures.

Next, have students meet in groups, combine their rocks, and find ways to classify them. Then ask each student to use his written descriptions and drawings to pick out his own rocks.

Have the class talk about what words they used to classify their rocks. Discuss how the meanings of words such as *heavy* or *light* can change, depending on what's being compared. Introduce similies at this point: as small as a pea, as big as a baseball.—*Chris Benz, Cucamonga, Calif.*

Rock records

If each student brings in just one rock that he likes, the whole class can practice observing, describing, drawing, and writing.

First, have your students briefly explain why they chose their particular rocks. Then, have them each draw a picture that closely matches their rock's size, shape, color, and markings. Next, ask them to write detailed descriptions of their rocks. Tell them they should write so precisely that a reader could pick out their rock from all the others.

Your students can also create histories of their rocks. They might write realistic narratives or imaginary tales. For example, a student could tell how his rock killed Goliath, was stepped on by a dinosaur, or came from another planet.

Finally, have your students compile all their rock records into individual booklets for presentation and display.—*Nancy Banks, Raleigh, N.C.*

Sun fun

Have students research interesting facts comparing the sun and the earth. For example, if the earth weighed 1 ounce, the sun would weigh 10 tons. It would take 100 earths to stretch along the diameter of the sun. If the sun were hollow, 1.3 million earths could fit in it. A person weighing 160 pounds on earth would weigh 2¾ tons on the sun. The sun is 332,946 times heavier than the earth.—*Karen L. Hansen, Doylestown, Pa.*

Rotate vs. revolve

Here's how to help younger students understand the earth-action terms *rotate* and *revolve.*

First, point out that *rotate* has the letter "a" near its center. Then explain how the earth rotates on its axis and ask your students to associate "a" with *axis.* For emphasis, write *rotate* and *axis* as shown.

You could also ask your students to link "a" with *day* because a full rotation takes 1 day.

Next, write *revolve* on the chalkboard as shown. The lines radiating from the "o" represent the sun. Explain that the sun is at the center of our solar system and that the planets (represented by the other letters) revolve around it. Post these two word-picture clues for easy reference.—*Nancy Veenendaal, Sun Prairie, Wis.*

The long and short of it

This activity is designed to get your students thinking about shadows. First, have each student pick a shadow to get to know for a day. It can be his own shadow or one cast by an inanimate object. Ask him to measure and record its length and width three times during the day. Then, discuss these questions:

- How are shadows alike? How are they different?
- Why do shadows exist?
- How does your shadow change from one time of the day to another?
- Why does it change?
- Do you think all shadows change the same amount throughout the day?
- Do you think shadows change the same way throughout the state? The country? The world? How would you find out?

Use this activity as a springboard to more student observation and research.—*Michael Hartoonian, Madison, Wis.*

Moon jumpers

The fact that the moon's gravitational pull is one-sixth that of the earth's can lead to activities that promote physical, math, and writing skills. The first step is to have students suppose that they're suddenly empowered to make moon jumps—to leap six times as far as they can usually jump.

With the help of the physical education instructor, find out what everyone's actual jumping record is. When students have measured and recorded their earth-jumping abilities, have them multiply their scores by six to determine their moon-jumping prowess. Even students with less-than-fantastic athletic skills will feel a sense of accomplishment when they realize they could leap close to 30 feet on the moon.

But just how far is 30 feet? Let students see for themselves their impressive jumping records by designating an area along a wall or on the floor for students to measure and label their moon jumps.

While students' imaginations are still leaping, ask them to consider how their moon-jumping skills—if they really possessed them—could be put to use on earth. Have students write up tales of fantastic jumping feats, perhaps with illustrations. Display these on a bulletin board, surrounded by moon facts.—*Johanna Weinstein, Rowe, Mass.*

Old constellations, new names

Following a study of constellations, your students might enjoy taking the role of ancient astronomers and renaming some star patterns. What pictures—animals, birds, people (even machines or TV characters)—might modern-day children see in the stars?

Prepare a constellation configuration sheet (using gummed stars) for each student. (Older students could do their own.) Ask students to look at the patterns and imagine pictures in the stars. Then have them draw and label the pictures with their new names for the constellations. Encourage students to make up myths about how the star groups got their new names.—*Wilhelmina Lucille Lewis, Harleysville, Pa.*

The daily round

This activity will help demonstrate to students how slowly the earth rotates. Tilt a globe (preferably 23.5 degrees from the perpendicular) and turn it very slowly from west to east (counterclockwise if you're looking down on the North Pole). No matter how slowly you turn the globe, it won't be slowly enough; the earth turns only 15 degrees of longitude per hour. Have kids locate a city that's 15 degrees of longitude from your area to illustrate an hour's earth trek.

You might turn the globe so that Philadelphia is at center front. Then, once each hour, turn the globe 15 degrees. By the end of a 6-hour school day, you'll still be seeing the U. S. (Nome, Alaska).

Have students research the length of a day on various planets in our solar system. Which are longer than the earth's? Which are shorter? Invite students to construct a bar graph to illustrate the differences.—*Robert N. Saveland, Athens, Ga.*

Shadows on the move

On your next sunny outing, have your students investigate their shadows as you suggest these movements:

- How tall can you make your shadow?

- How short can you scrunch it?

- Can your shadow stand on one leg?

- Can you make your shadow's arms disappear?

- Can you put your shadow in back of you?

- Try to move around quickly without bumping into anyone else's shadow.

- Can you put your own foot on your shadow's head?

- Put your shadow on a wall.

- Get together with three others and make the biggest shadow you can.

After some shadow manipulation, suggest that students play shadow tag. Choose a few students to be shadow chasers. Rather than trying to tag others, the shadow chasers try to stand in or on someone's shadow. You might want to vary the game with these suggestions:

- Designate an area in which any player is "safe."

- Declare a player safe unless a chaser has both feet in the player's shadow.

- Decide whether a tagged player becomes a chaser or sits out, counts to 50, and then reenters the game.—*Kathy Patak, Pittsburgh*

Solar walk

Dramatize the vastness of space for your students by inviting them to pace out the distance between planets.

First, prepare large signs for the sun and each of the planets. Then, appoint one student to hold each of the signs; other class members will be "distance pacers." Move out to the schoolyard; have the student holding the "sun" sign stand at the farthest point.

Invite the first distance pacer to begin moving away from the sun using baby steps. Explain that each step represents 1 million miles. After 36 baby steps, the pacer holds his position, and the student assigned to Mercury steps into place. Continue setting up the planets in this fashion, using the chart below as a guide.

Distances from the Sun in Millions of Miles	
Mercury	36
Venus	67
Earth	93
Mars	141
Jupiter	484
Saturn	887
Uranus	1,780
Neptune	2,794
Pluto	3,658

At Mars, you might wish to speed the process along by switching to the "giant step" mode, with each step representing 10 million miles.

The vastness of space will become more real as students pausing on Saturn find themselves nearly 90 giant steps from neighboring Uranus.—*Beverly J. Anderson, Concord, Calif.*

Weather graph

This activity encourages your students to keep track of weather patterns. Display a large calendar for the month. Have students cut out a bunch of yellow suns, blue raindrops, gray clouds, and white snowflakes, if appropriate for your area. Each day, ask a student to describe the weather and record conditions by pinning an appropriate symbol on the calendar grid. At the end of the month, have students count up the sunny, rainy, cloudy, and snowy days. As a class, make a large bar graph, coloring in units to represent the symbols on the calendar.—*Sandra D. Rich, Atlanta*

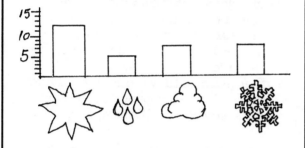

Making predictions

Help your students learn about weather and develop listening and forecasting skills by challenging them to make their own weather predictions.

Videotape a weather report from a local news program. Then, in class, play the background part of the weather report—the maps, satellite data, and instrument readings. (You might want to interrupt the tape to review important weather terms, such as *barometric pressure* or *humidity*.) Before the reporter gives the full forecast, stop the tape and invite your students to write their own predictions based on the information they've heard. When they're done, finish playing the tape and let students compare their forecasts with the professionally prepared one.—*John Lovering, Hampton, N.H.*

The Beaufort Wind Scale				
Beaufort Scale Number	Wind Description	Miles Per Hour	Wind Effect	Beaufort Symbol Used on Weather Maps
0	calm	0-1	Smoke goes straight up	○
1	light air	2-3	Smoke drifts in Wind direction	
2	slight breeze	4-7	Weather Vanes turn; flags flutter, leaves move	
3	gentle breeze	8-12	flags blow out; small branches	

The wayward wind

Your students can explore the ABCs of wind speed in a learning center that also provides practice in map reading and perhaps writing too.

First, make a chart of the Beaufort Wind Scale, which can be found in children's weather books and some science texts. Next, run off copies of a U.S. map with states outlined but not named.

Use postcards as the center's task cards. Write them as if they were sent from various places in the United States. You might prepare a set of cards with appropriate pictures—cars for Detroit, the Maine seacoast—or shop around for some that depict seasonal changes.

On each card, write a message describing the weather:

> Dear Tina:
> I'm having a great time in Texas. It's hot, but there's a gentle breeze (8 to 12 miles per hour) today. See you soon.
> Your friend,
> Jay

To use the center, a student takes a postcard and a map, reads the message, selects the correct wind symbol from the Beaufort Scale chart, and draws the symbol on the state from which the postcard was "sent."

Encourage students to add postcards to the collection, until the wayward wind blows through all 50 states.—*Deborah Beaucaire, Bridgewater, Mass.*

Storm warning!

Make use of nature's unfriendly forces—especially those common to your area—to stimulate dramatic discussions and research projects. For example, if you've decided to study tornadoes, these activities will make your students experts:

- Use last year's almanac to find dates and locations of tornadoes. Mark the locations on a map.
- Contact your local weather bureau for information on how tornadoes are traced and studied.
- Invite weather reporters from a local radio or TV station to visit your class and explain how they gather and report information about tornadoes.
- Write to relief agencies to find out about emergency preparedness procedures and costs. Compile a list of public and private sources of emergency aid.
- Research the role of the National Guard in natural disaster emergencies.—*Florence Rives, Selma, Ala.*

Today's weather is...

Here's a simple way to help younger students see how weather patterns affect not just their lives but their town and the rest of the country.

Make a large U.S. map out of felt and post it on a bulletin board. Using newspaper weather symbols as guides, cut felt pieces into suns, raindrops, clouds, high- and low-pressure systems, and so on. Put these in small plastic bags.

Each day, bring in the weather map from the newspaper and select two students to be class "meteorologists." They can look at the weather map and put the symbols on the felt map for that day. The class can watch and discuss the movement of weather fronts, high- and low-pressure systems, and temperature changes. After a while, students will be good at predicting the next day's weather because they'll understand how weather patterns move across the country.—*Marsha Baker, Wichita, Kan.*

Forecast charting

Blow some fresh air into your study of weather with an activity that exercises your students' charting skills: comparing local weather reports for accuracy.

Divide your class into three groups and assign each group a network TV channel. Tell students to watch the local weather segment of the evening news and note the forecast for the following day's high and low temperatures and sky conditions.

In class, provide large sheets of oak tag, and have your students chart each network's predictions, plus the actual weather statistics as reprinted later in the local newspaper.

For each day's forecast, select the network with the most accurate prediction. Keep the tally for 3 or 4 weeks to see which network had the best record.
—*Gary Monterosso, Bridgeton, N.J.*

Watch your pulse

Usually you *feel* a pulse, but with this activity, you can *watch* it. For each student, you'll need a short wooden matchstick and a small ball of clay. Invite students to put the ball of clay over the pulse point on their wrists. Have them flatten the bottom of the ball slightly and stick the matchstick into it. Then have them rest their arms on a table. Each student can watch his pulse, counting how many times the matchstick moves in a set time period.—*Denise Lee, Springhouse, Pa.*

Compliments of the chef

This activity gives kids a chance to be creative while getting practice planning nutritious meals.

Suggest that each student is about to become owner and head chef of a new restaurant. Students will need to create a name for their restaurants and an impressive menu of mouth-watering meals.

The emphasis for these restaurants will be on serving the ultimate in nutrition. Using the four basic food groups, invite each chef to come up with two or three breakfasts, lunches, and dinners—nutritious meals with variety and good taste.

To add more challenge, have students price meals or encourage them to establish their restaurants around a theme. Students who want to offer food with a foreign flair should do plenty of research to ensure authenticity.—*Elise Wolcott, Marina Del Rey, Calif.*

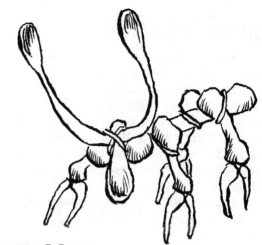

Wishbone connected to the...

For this activity, which is part science and part art, your students will need to bring in bones from their dinners at home—chicken, lamb, ham, steak, rabbit—the greater the variety, the better.

Ask students to wash bones thoroughly, using a plastic or nylon-mesh scrubber. Then have them boil the bones in vinegar water and allow them to dry before bringing them to school. As students bring in bones, find out what kind of animal and from what part of the body they came. Observe the sizes and shapes of the various bones; compare chicken bones with ham bones, for instance.

Students then deposit their contributions in the class "boneyard," a large open box, where the bones can become completely dry. The collection of bones should be large enough for each child to select several.

After devising an equitable mode of distribution—some bones will undoubtedly be more popular than others—see that each student has a bone pile to work with. From the bones, the children construct their own creatures—dinosaurs, more than likely.

Have rubber cement, white glue, wire, masking tape, and modeling clay ready to connect the bones. Display their work, labeled with mock scientific names.—*Drenda Underwood, St. Louis*

Round the table

Four lively board games teach students about the four basic food groups, while they give a lesson on table-setting.

To prepare for the games, you'll need to collect a large assortment of pictures showing foods from each of the four food groups. Mount about half the pictures from each group onto index cards and label each food with its name and its food group. On the back of each card write "food pack". The remaining pictures will be used on the game boards.

Prepare another set of cards with table-setting items: placemat, napkin, plate, glass, knife, salad fork, dinner fork, spoon. On the back of each card write "table setting."

Now for the game boards—one for each of the four food groups. Each board resembles a Monopoly board, with blocks marked off along the edge. In the center, put a drawing of a place setting with each item in its correct position. Also in the center write the name of the food group being featured.

Fill in the gameboard blocks with labeled food pictures—some from the food group of the board's title and some not. On several blocks write directions to make additional moves ("Go back one space"), to lose a turn, or to draw a card from either the food pack or the table-setting pack.

To play, students will need a spinner with the numbers 1 to 4. Player One moves the number of spaces indicated. If he lands on a food picture, he must tell whether that food belongs to the board's group. A correct answer earns him the right to draw and keep a card from the food pack.

When a player draws a table-setting card, he must place the card over the appropriate item on the drawing in the center of the gameboard. The game is over when each item in the drawing has been covered. The player with the most food cards wins.—*Marilyn Gruen, Los Angeles*

The dangers of smoking

Try this demonstration with your students to drive home the effects of smoking. You'll need rubber bands, 5-gallon plastic bags, and plastic liter bottles.

Cut off the top 3 inches of the plastic bottles and discard the rest of the bottles. Gather the bags around the bottle tops and hold them in place with tightly wrapped rubber bands.

Arrange for volunteer adult smokers and nonsmokers (about the same size and age if possible) to report to your classroom at a specific time. Distribute a lung tester to each volunteer and ask him to take a deep breath, blow into the plastic mouthpiece, then twist the bag in front of the mouthpiece with his hand to keep the air from leaking. Ask your students to compare the results. (Generally, adults who smoke have less lung volume that those who don't.)—*Michael Brownstein, Chicago*

Food folk

For a lesson on nutrition, collect magazines with food-focused advertising and have your students cut out as many food pictures as they can. Have the kids separate the pictures into food groups.

Now invite students to use the pictures to create food folk—characters composed of food pictures that represent a food group or a special nutritional problem, such as junk food. Students might decide to create a Sweet-tooth Sam or a Debbie Dairy, a meat muncher, or fruit-and-vegetable twins.

To create their food folk, have students draw outlines of characters on tagboard and then fill in the outlines with food pictures, arranging, trimming, and rearranging for the best effect. Allow students to add features in black felt-tip pen or construction paper if they like.

When the figures are finished, encourage students to add captions for their food-fashioned characters. The captions, which reinforce nutritional messages and describe personality traits, could be direct quotations or dialogue.—*Donna Anderson, Churchville, N.Y.*

A sound idea

Try this activity to help students grasp the speed-of-sound concept. Explain that the approximate speed of sound is 1,125 feet per second. Then divide the class into several groups, one for each major hallway in your school. Give each group a yardstick and ask the group to measure the length of its assigned hallway. Then, have each group calculate how long it takes sound to travel the length of its hallway. Your students will be surprised to find that sound whizzes down the hallways in a fraction of a second. They might wish to share this news with the rest of the school by posting the traveling times in the various hallways.—*Karen Boetcher, Arlington Heights, Ill.*

The world's greatest pump

For an "ears-on" introduction to the heart, have students listen to each other's heartbeats. Make a simple stethoscope by using an 18-inch piece of rubber tubing and two kitchen funnels. Fit the ends of the tubing over the narrow ends of the funnels. One student can put a funnel to his ear, while placing the other funnel on another student's chest. The "lub-dub" noise is the sound of blood rushing through the heart, and the heart's doors—or valves—closing behind the blood.—*Denise Lee, Springhouse, Pa.*

Sight simulators

This activity will allow students to *see* how certain eye diseases affect vision.

You'll need four pairs of paper cups for each set of simulators. Students look through one or both cups at a time to see what the world would look like if the condition were present in one or both eyes.

For the first pair, cut three slits in the bottom of each cup. Looking through the cups will produce a dotted effect, representing conditions in which tears in the retina create patchy vision.

For the second pair, cut the bottom off each cup and tape waxed paper over the openings. The cloudy images seen through the paper represent the eyesight of cataract sufferers.

To represent the loss of peripheral vision, cut a dime-size hole in the center of the bottom of two cups.

To represent peripheral vision, or loss of central vision, cut the bottoms off two cups, cover with clear plastic wrap, and place a dime-size circle of white correction fluid in the center of each.—*Laura J. Gray, St. Louis*

Apples, bacteria, and skin

Have your students do this simple experiment to help them understand how our skin protects us from infection.

Divide students into groups of four or five. For each group, you'll need toothpicks and two good apples. You'll also need one rotten apple for the entire class.

Have students use the toothpicks to tear the skin of one apple. Give each group a small piece of the rotten apple and have them put some of it on the exposed apple and some on the skin of the intact one. Label the apples and put them aside.

After 5 or 6 days, the results will be dramatic. You'll find that the torn apple has begun to decompose, and the other apple still is healthy.

Explain that our skin is similar to an apple's in that it protects us from infection. What happened to the torn apple is similar to what happens to us if we get a cut and allow bacteria to invade it.— *Mary Ghisolfo, San Francisco*

What's that I hear?

This outdoor activity is designed to get your students thinking about sound. Bring some noisemakers, such as a kazoo, whistle, bongo drum, or rattle, and ask student volunteers to demonstrate. Tell the rest of the class to think about how the noise was started, what vibrated, how the noise can be made loud or soft, and how the pitch can be changed. Then ask your students to bring in something that makes a sound and describe the "hows" and "whats" of their noisemakers. Be prepared to see— and hear—a variety of musical instruments, toys, and things quite strange and fun.—*Linda Freeman and Phyllis Strayer, Centerville, Ohio*

Build a body

Take advantage of the Halloween skeleton decorating your classroom to give young students a science lesson.

Prepare six cards, one for each of six body parts: head, arm, hand, leg, foot, body. Tack the skeleton on a bulletin board and attach the labels. (Another game could be created around a jack-o'-lantern, using the labels head, eyes, nose, mouth, teeth, and ears.)

Print the body vocabulary words on a wooden cube, one word to a side. The cube serves as a die. Or put the six words on a spinner.

Divide your students into groups of four to six, and make sure each player has a piece of paper and a pencil or crayon. The object of the game is for each student to draw a body, part by part, as the words come up on the die. Here are the rules:

1. A specific sequence is required. A player can't start drawing until he gets a "head." Then other parts must be attached to a part already drawn. You can't draw a hand without getting an arm first.

2. Only the person who rolls the die may read the word. The labeled skeleton serves as a reference.

3. The student finishing a body first is the winner.— *Julie Kleinberger, Bradford, Pa.*

Shape up, skeletons

If you want to avoid a dry-as-bones approach to the study of the human skeleton, try this activity.

Assign your students (in teams of two) a human bone. Each team should carefully research the bone, then make an enlarged, accurate drawing of it on butcher paper or 18 x 24-inch drawing paper. Have the students tape another sheet of paper to the back of the original, then cut out the drawing so they have two copies. Next, they should fit the edges of both cutouts together and staple, leaving an opening about 3 inches wide. Have them use a ruler or yardstick to stuff crumbled tissue or newspaper through the opening to make a puffy bone.

Place the completed three-dimensional bones in a large box. Call on students to grab one, name it, and mime an action showing that bone in use. Challenge some students to put on a blindfold and try to identify the bone by touch alone.— *Barbara Stroup, Gettysburg, Pa.*

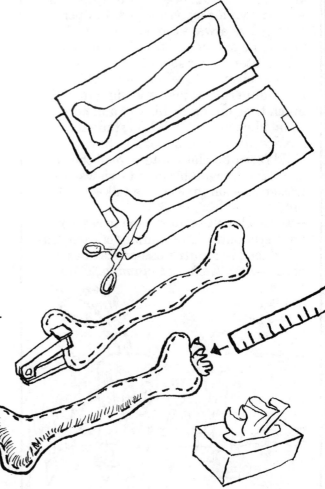

Conversations with a carrot

Staging a personal interview with a self-important carrot, a rowdy radish, or an athletic green bean might be just the whimsical touch needed to spice up a nutrition lesson. Invite each student to research a fruit or vegetable—plain or exotic. Suggest that students focus their research on the following areas:

· description of fruit or vegetable

· its food value

· history of its development and use

· where and how it's grown.

The students then use this information to prepare—in writing—people-to-fruit/vegetable interviews. Encourage students to invest their subjects with distinctive characteristics, which will be revealed in their answers: "Naturally, I'm well known for my vitamin A, but personally I've always considered crunchiness to be my most attractive feature."

The interviewer should try to steer their subjects into telling about their food value rather than spending too much time on family history and personal idiosyncracies. When students have written their dialogues, have each child recruit a classmate to read the part of the fruit/vegetable as interviews are presented—on tape or in a talk-show format.

To conclude the interviewing session, have students share samples of their featured food in a nutritious-snack smorgasbord.—*Judy Nichols, Columbus, Ohio*

Two broccoli burgers, please

For a fun exercise in nutrition, have your students imagine that meat—and meat-serving fast-food restaurants— are a thing of the past. Working in small groups, have your students design a new fast-foods empire, focusing on vegetables. Students should create new names for restaurants—Karrot King, Kentucky Fried Beet—and new menus—spinach shakes, grilled zucchini sandwiches, cornburgers. Encourage students to include recipes and tummy-tempting menu descriptions for their new concoctions.—*Denise Lee, Springhouse, Pa.*

Menu monitoring

Each day, take a few minutes before lunch to help your students learn about nutrition.

Begin by making a bulletin board of the four food groups and asking your students to cut pictures from magazines to illustrate the groups. Then, before lunch, read the day's menu and have your students identify the proper group for each food.

You can carry this activity one step further by gathering menus from local restaurants, hospitals, and other institutions, and noting how the four food groups are represented.—*Ojetta Pearson, Dublin, Pa.*

Haven't we grown?

Children don't realize they're growing and changing on a daily basis. To demonstrate how they've changed, ask each student to bring a baby picture to class. Have them keep their pictures private until all pictures are ready for posting; then they can have the fun of playing "Name the Baby."

Have students register their speculations about who's who and encourage discussion about criteria for guesses. Students might find that their decisions were made on the basis of "things that haven't changed": Jerry's brown eyes and dark skin, Kim's curly hair, Shannon's dimples.

List on the chalkboard those characteristics that haven't changed; then discuss and list things that *have* changed. Compare the lists. Hair color, for example, sometimes changes and sometimes doesn't.

Copy selected samples of students' change/no change comments and add them to the bulletin board display of pictures. Finally, add the name below each picture and the approximate age at which the picture was taken. You might add up-to-date photos for "Haven't We Grown?" contrast. For contrast of another sort, prepare a companion display showing the development of a butterfly or a frog.—*Holly C. Van Scoy and Joan Porter Smith, Austin, Tex.*

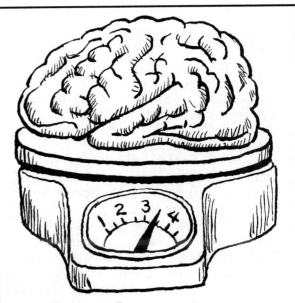

Body books

Students will discover all kinds of fascinating facts with this creative anatomy project. Have the class choose a body part to study—the brain, for instance. Each student draws a picture of the brain—on both sides of a piece of heavy white paper—with as many details as the student cares to include. Ask students to leave space on each side for writing.

On one side of the brain drawing, the student writes a fact (or two) about the brain, something he has learned in class or through individual research. For example: "The average human brain weighs between 3 and 4 pounds." On the other side, the student writes a brief description of some remarkable accomplishment of the brain. The anecdote can be factual or imaginative: "My brain stores the directions to at least a hundred different places—the homes of friends, stores, picnic spots, fast-food restaurants, classrooms...."

Collect the "brain facts" papers and bind them into a "Book About the Brain" for the class library. Encourage students to read and enjoy their classmates' anatomic fact finds. Repeat the same activity for other body parts. At the end of the year, take the book apart and give each student his pages to save for reference.—*Myron Flindt, Paradise, Calif.*

"Yum Rummy"

This game, which is based on the basic four food groups and the 4-4-3-2 helping formula, adds up to balanced nutrition. You'll need 52 cards for your "Yum Rummy" deck (index cards work well). You'll also need a collection of food pictures cut to fit the cards: 16 pictures from the fruits and vegetables group, 16 from bread and cereals, 12 from dairy foods, and 8 from the protein group.

Paste one food on each card and write the name of the food group below it. This reminds a player that peanuts are in the protein group while rice is in the bread and cereals group. Two to four students may play the game, which follows the rules of rummy. Each player receives seven cards. The rest of the cards become a draw deck that's placed in the center of the game area. The top card is turned over and laid faceup to start a discard pile.

Player One picks a card from the draw deck or discard pile. He may then lay down any of the following sets he holds: four cards from the fruits and vegetables group, four cards from the bread and cereals group, three cards from the dairy group, two cards from the protein group. Player One then discards, and play passes to the left.

The winner is the first player to lay down a set from each food group—balanced nutrition for a day. (Discarding on the winning play isn't necessary.)—*Deborah Beaucaire, East Bridgewater, Mass.*

Going shopping

To add realism to your next nutrition lesson, package pictures of food items in plastic foam meat and fish trays for the kids to sort.

Cut out pictures of food from magazines, cover them with clear self-sticking paper, and trim them. Mount each picture on a plastic foam tray and store the trays in a grocery bag. Write out the names of the four basic food groups on large strips of paper. Include an extra strip labeled Junk Food. Lay the strips on the floor. Invite students to remove the food trays from the bag and sort them under the correct headings on the floor. Then have students take turns selecting foods from each group to make a balanced meal.—*Carol Rondeau, San Diego*

Food swap

You can help young children learn what makes a nutritious meal with an activity that involves movement, trading, and thinking.

Collect pictures representing major food groups: grains, fruits and vegetables, milk and milk products, and protein foods. Fold each picture two or three times and place it in a shoe box.

Bring together a small group of students (or the whole class if you have enough cutouts). Invite each student to pull four pictures from the box. Next, have students open their pictures to see if their set reflects a balanced meal. If not, they can trade with the others until they have the foods they need.

After several rounds, students can paste their meals on paper plates for an appetizing display.—*Genevieve Bylinowski, Byron, Ill.*

What's in a label?

This project can sharpen your students' awareness about the mystery foods they buy and eat.

1. After students have watched at least two TV commercials promoting food, ask them to use their judgment as to what seems to be the facts of the message and what's most likely irrelevant or exaggerated.

2. Ask each student to bring in an ingredients list from a food package. Be sure all brand-name and food-name identification is removed. Invite several students to read their lists aloud; have the rest of the class guess what the product is. When students have had the opportunity to guess a few, number the lists and mount them on a piece of tagboard with the answer key nearby. Add new lists periodically.

Perceptive students will discover that the ingredients are listed in order of their proportion in the food item. Besides giving a clue to the item's identification, this fact can be an important discussion starter. What vegetables are predominant in mixed vegetables? Is beef the main ingredient of beef stew?

The lists should also spark other questions: What is carrageenan? What does it do? What ingredients are basic in a particular food product and which are additives? Why are preservatives sometimes used? Encourage students to write to manufacturers for explanations of why additives are present in their foods.—*Margaret D. Jones, Valley Springs, Calif.*

INGREDIENTS: CHICKEN BROTH, MUSHROOMS, WATER, CARROTS, ENRICHED BLEACHED FLOUR, POTATO FLOUR, BUTTER, SALT, TOMATO PASTE, ONION POWDER, GARLIC POWDER, SPICE, DEHYDRATE PARSLEY.

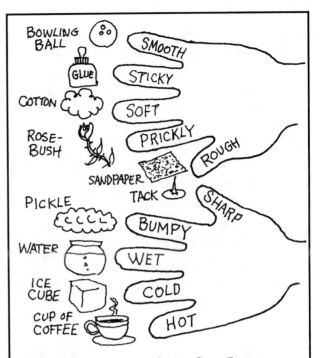

Fingers are for feeling

To encourage young scientists to investigate the world of touch, collect lots of items with various textures: sandpaper, cotton balls, velvet, flour, a thistle, masking tape, pottery, perhaps even an ice cube or a classroom animal. As your students handle the items and describe how they feel, list their words on the chalkboard. They might come up with words such as *sticky, soft, prickly, rough,* and so forth. Then give each student a sheet of plain paper and ask him to follow these steps:

1. Trace both hands with fingers spread.

2. Cut out the pair of hands.

3. On each finger, write a touch word from the list on the chalkboard.

4. Mount the hands on construction paper.

5. Add a "touchable" item (or a drawing of one) for each finger to match the touch word.

For more practice, have your students create a "touchable" bulletin board. Post two sets of hand-pair cutouts labeled with 20 touch words. Encourage your students to discuss their choices as they add to the display.—*Ginger Boese, Flemington, N.J.*

Encouraging inventiveness

To find out the inventiveness quotient of your class—and develop their scientific prowess—invite them to consider the following kinds of inventions:

- a mechanism that blows soap bubbles
- an automatic goldfish-feeding contraption
- an automatic dice thrower
- a silent alarm clock.

After you've filled out the list with about 10 suggestions, ask each student, or small groups of students, to choose one or two of the devices to "invent" and "patent."

When students have finished the inventing process, provide "patent application" sheets on which students record: the name of the invention, a brief description of what it does, how it does it, and the materials required to construct it. (Estimated cost of construction and suggested retail price are optional information.) Also included on the application sheet is a labeled diagram of the invention and how it works. If possible, a working model of the contraption should accompany each patent application.

Following the submission of applications, hold a class discussion and evaluation of the entries. Award patent certificates to all students whose inventions work. Send defective inventions "back to the drawing board," where students collaborate on modifications and improvements of original designs.

On an ongoing basis, encourage your students to come up with their own invention ideas and to create and patent them.— *Jerry Olio, Chico, Calif.*

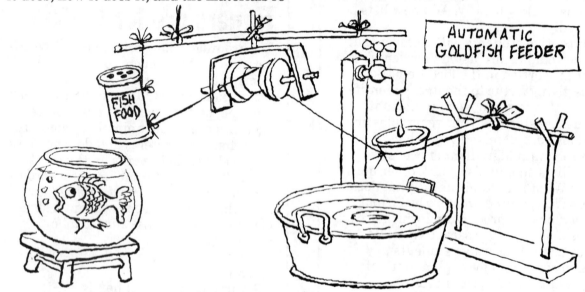

Science stumpers

What science questions stump your students? Even the world's top scientists are still grappling with such questions as:

- Why do newborn babies smile?
- What causes headaches?
- Why do we grow old?
- How do plants sense the arrival of spring?
- Why do herds of whales beach themselves?

- Why does crying make us feel better?

Now ask your students to write one question they'd like clarified. Have teams of two or three students select the question they'd like to research. After a trip to the library, invite groups to share their findings.—*Jean Robbins, Paterson, N.J.*

Track tracers

This tracking activity takes the focus off animals and puts it on people.

Suggest that students look for signs that indicate people and vehicles have passed by. Ask students to describe what they see and to speculate about the track-makers and the conditions when the tracks were made: large feet, ski boots, old tires, snow tires, sled runners; walking, running; deep tracks, blurred tracks; muddy, windy.

Sharpen young children's track-observing skills by playing "How Did I Move?" Establish a GO line and a STOP line. Have all players but one, the trailblazer, turn their backs to the GO/STOP course and close their eyes and cover their ears.

The trailblazer moves—using any sort of footwork he chooses—from GO to STOP. The other students then turn and try to determine if the trailblazer hopped, ran, walked, galloped, and so on. Have the children examine the spacing, depth, and direction of the tracks. After the trail-making method is guessed, choose another trailblazer, and the class keeps on tracking.—*Frank Watson and Christian Watson, Underhill, Vt.*

Future creatures

This imagination-sparking assignment gets your students thinking on a scientific level.

When you teach about how living things survive in diverse environments—through eons of climate changes—suggest that your students imagine adaptations for organisms of a future era.

First, have kids compile a list of common adaptations: protective mechanisms such as claws, shells, camouflage, and quills; food-getting devices such as elongated necks, sticky tongues, and hooked beaks; survival behaviors such as tree climbing and hibernating. Next, encourage students to speculate on the environmental changes that the future might impose on the planet's life forms—such as air and water pollution, increased radiation, habitat displacement, a harsher climate, a move to another planet in the galaxy.

Students then ponder how organisms might survive these environmental changes, and what creatures might emerge through natural selection. How might creatures of the future look? Let fantasy take over and have students sketch their favorite future creatures—keeping their pictures confidential until a later class session. In addition, each futurist writes a detailed account of how the creature looks, where it lives and why, what it eats, how it protects itself, and other pertinent facts. Especially important will be explanations of the creature's special features and how those features add to the creature's survival potential.

Post the portraits to create a futuristic gallery for kids to browse through.— *Katherine Lawder, Ephrata, Pa.*

Filter-like nose for smog

Radiation shield

Flora and fauna, unite

Suppose the Plant and Animal World (PAW) decided to elect a president to cope with problems of biological welfare.

Now, there's a fantasy to get your creative scientists thinking—one that should raise all sorts of questions for discussion. For example: What might be the duties and responsibilities of a PAW president? Which issues might be addressed in the candidates' platforms? Which members of the plant and animal world might be most likely to run for office?

Divide the class into two groups, and have each group elect a PAW presidential candidate and run a campaign that includes drawing up a platform and preparing debates about the issues. (Remind students that a convincing debate depends upon having command of well-researched facts as well as a positive delivery.) Campaigners might be asked such questions as the following to uncover issues:

- What do you feel are the major problems caused by natural forces—droughts, temperature extremes, storms, volcanoes—affecting PAW welfare? What do you think can be done to solve these problems?

- What comments do you have on any of the following areas of interaction between PAW and the human world: extending the national park system, zoo practices, domesticated animal affairs, the use of pesticides?

Encourage students not running for office to get involved by forming lobbies. For example, several students might form a coalition of corn and cotton to promote the use of pesticides.—*Calvernetta Williams, Columbia, S.C.*

Einstein for a day

Get your students excited about doing science reports by having them research and then "become" famous scientists.

You might introduce the assignment by choosing a scientist *you'd* like to be, donning an appropriate costume, and inviting students to ask you questions you've written ahead of time. Next, explain that instead of writing the usual report on a scientist, students will do what you did—choose and research the life and contributions of an important scientist. They'll also write interview questions (and answers) covering what they think their classmates should know and would find most fascinating about the person. Then, using whatever costumes or disguises they like, they'll pretend to *be* the scientist and let the rest of the class "interview" them with the prepared questions.

Students can begin by focusing their research on four areas: how their scientists got started in their work, what contributions they made to science, what scientific procedures they used to conduct their experiments, and what obstacles (if any) hindered their work.

To help prevent students from merely copying and memorizing material from books, require them to write all information in a first-person, conversational style—as if they're the scientist being interviewed.—*Diana Townsend, Spokane, Wash.*

$$E = Mc^2$$

Solid-state transport

During a heat wave, give your students this unlikely assignment: "Please bring in an ice cube tomorrow."

Students probably will begin to plot strategies for completing this strange assignment, but don't let discussion run on too long. A greater variety of cube carriers will result if comments are held to a minimum. Just be sure that the students are aware of the challenge: to devise a method to keep ice from rapidly melting.

The next morning as the cube-carriers arrive, check and compare the effectiveness of their insulation methods and devices. The ice cubes and their containers can serve as starters for a discussion of melting, insulation, and packaging:

- What materials are good insulators? Which are only fair?
- How do various kinds of commercial "cold keepers" work?
- When the cube starts melting, can you stop the process?
- How long does it take for an ice cube to melt in an open plastic foam cup? In a glass jar? In your hand?

Challenge students to devise "the ultimate" in homemade cube carriers and discuss their reasoning.—*Deborah Ferris, Vacaville, Calif.*

Getting to know scientists

For a change of pace, this science project involves the people—instead of the principles—of science.

Have each student choose a scientist from a list of science superstars—Nicolaus Copernicus, Gregor Mendel, Marie Curie, Michael Faraday, Charles Drew, Albert Einstein. You might add a few contemporary scientists as well.

Have students collect material about their chosen scientist's work, family, and education. Then, invite students to cross the barriers of time by arranging a hypothetical discussion between two science superstars (or among several) who worked in the same field, but who were separated from each other by several hundred years.

Other people-in-science projects (written or oral) might be sparked by the following questions or ideas:

- From your research into the lives of scientists, what personality traits would you say science superstars have in common? Why do you think these qualities might be important to that kind of work?

- Scientists have contributed much to the quality of our lives by making discoveries that have led to curing disease and making work easier. If you were a scientist, what contributions would you wish to make? What problems would you work on solving?

- Science involves a wide variety of special fields, such as archaeology, biology, geology, volcanology, and zoology. Investigate several careers in science; look into the training needed, the daily work environment, the occupational problems and advantages.

Learning about the dedication to work and the spirit of creative inquiry that characterize science superstars might just rub off on student scientists.—*Teddy Meister, Orlando, Fla.*

Scientific scavengers

A science scavenger hunt can be more than a simple shopping list of objects to locate. Try investing the listing with a little mystery—some items that require applying some science knowledge or creative thinking. Here are a few for instances:

- an animal that has its own oars
- a forest dining table
- togetherness
- a tree that would be in 6th grade
- an insect apartment
- something invisible
- a predator-prey relationship
- something needed (tell by whom)
- a traveler without feet
- a highway.

With this sort of list, many of the "finds" will require some explanation and justification as the scavengers check in. An idea is considered acceptable as long as the hunter has a reasonable explanation.—*Bebe Sarcia, Glastonbury, Conn.*

Does a leaf remember its tree?

You can encourage students to think about cause-and-effect relationships by borrowing from some whimsy of Carl Sandburg. In "Metamorphosis" (found in *Rainbows are Made: Poems by Carl Sandburg,* selected by Lee Bennett Hopkins; Harcourt Brace Jovanovich, 1984), Sandburg asks:

"When water turns ice does it remember one time it was water?"

Invite your students to write their own before-and-after statements. Here are a few to get them started: When a leaf...When snow...When a pollywog...When a caterpillar...When the sun goes down...When my shadow...—*Shirley Russell, Lincoln, Calif.*

Creating a human fish

Ask students to brainstorm and to bring to class examples of devices invented to help humans "adapt" to the sea (for example, flippers, snorkels, wet suits). Then invite students to design and draw an aquahuman—a human body capable of living most of its life in the water.—*Denise Lee, Springhouse, Pa.*

Rising raisins

To get your students thinking, try this simple experiment: Put some raisins into a glass of soda water and observe. After the raisins sink to the bottom, bubbles begin to collect on them. When enough bubbles are attached to the raisins to float them, the raisins rise. When they reach the surface, the bubbles pop, and the raisins sink again.

Now, encourage your students to ask questions. Here are a few to get them started:

- Do big raisins and small raisins rise and fall at the same rate?
- Do the raisins rise faster if we use more soda water?
- What happens if we punch pin holes in the raisins?
- If we mix soda water with regular water, will the raisins rise and fall as fast?
- Do the raisins ever stop collecting bubbles?
- Will 7-Up or Coke make the raisins rise and fall?
- Does the temperature of the soda water make any difference?
- Will a fresh grape behave the same as a raisin?

Have students formulate predictions about outcomes. Then invite teams of two or three students to investigate the questions. In their work, they might discover the need for keeping track of materials, conditions, and results—or you might want to prepare them for the record-keeping responsibilities.

When all groups have completed their experiments, discuss the results.—*Leon Spreyer, San Leandro, Calif.*

A lesson in direction

When you and your students are ready for an outdoor lesson, try making a shadow compass. First, pound a tall stick into the ground in an area that's open enough to be in sunshine for at least an hour without the encroachment of shadows.

Put a stone at the end of the shadow that's cast by the stick. In 15 minutes, return to the stick and note the change in the position of the shadow. Put another stone where the end of the stick's shadow now falls. Place a third stone after another 15-minute wait. Then draw an arrow from the first stone, over the second stone to the third. The arrow points east. (Check with a compass.) Discuss why this happens. Place the other compass points in relationship to the one direction you now have.

You can also find north using shadows. When the sun is at its highest in the sky (and shadows are at their shortest), return to the stick you've placed in the ground. At that moment, the shadow of the stick will point north.

Try making a shadow compass during different seasons of the year and at various times of the day. In which ways is the experience the same at these varying times and in which ways is it different?—*July Holt, Scottsdale, Ariz.*

Rainbow wrap

Science and art blend effectively in this color-mixing activity. You'll need white tissue paper, food coloring (red, yellow, blue), and shallow containers for colors (jar lids are good).

Introduce the project with a discussion of colors in nature—fruits, vegetables, flowers, animal coverings—and colors in the man-made world. Ask students how many colors they think they'd need to make a true-to-life picture of their classmates.

The first step in the rainbow-wrap process is to prepare the paper. Each student takes a sheet of tissue paper and folds it back and forth to make a fan. The strips should be about 2½ inches wide. Next, have students fold their strips as if folding a flag. All folds should be pressed firmly. The final shape is a triangle.

Provide a number of areas for the coloring phase. It'd be best if each pair of students could have a set of the three colors. To color, students dip each corner of the triangle into one or two colors. Encourage students to try mixing.

When the dipping is done, invite students to carefully unfold the triangles until they're back into long strips. (Don't let them open papers out flat yet.) Have students look carefully at the patterns and color mixtures. Any surprises? Each strip is then placed inside a newspaper sandwich and ironed with a warm iron. Now have students open the strips into flat sheets. What new patterns appear?

Allow the sheets to become almost dry, then iron them again between newspaper. While the first sheets are drying, take students on a "field trip" among the projects to observe, discuss, and share dipping techniques.—*Carol Chesley, Burlington, Vt.*

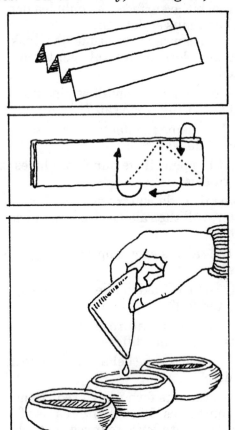

Pop-top magnifiers

Each one of your would-be scientists can have their own magnifier when you have the class make them out of pop-tops. To make a viewer, choose a soft drink or beer can pop top that has a slight indentation where the finger loop is riveted to the tab that seals the can. File off the bottom of the rivet so that the rivet and the tab can be removed, leaving the loop part with a hole in it. The rivet hole is the magnifier.

To use the magnifier, dip the rivet hole into a glass of water. The drop of water that remains in the hole is the magnifying lens. Surface tension will hold the water in the hole as long as you hold the *loop* horizontally; it will magnify nicely if the drop is fairly large. To look through the magnifier, place one eye very near the drop and bring the object being viewed close to the lens.—*George B. Barnes, Pullman, Wash.*

Playground pendulums

You need go no farther than the playground to find a set of pendulums—swings. For this activity, select several students to be part of the equipment (swingers).

First, pendulum vocabulary:

- bob—usually a weight; in this case the swing seat
- cycle—the length of one back-and-forth swing
- period—the time a cycle takes
- amplitude—the arc from the vertical (at rest) position of the pendulum to the high point of the cycle.

Try a number of experiments with bob-riders (students) aboard. (Bobs will have to submit to "hands on" propulsion.) Record results to answer these questions:

- What can you do to vary the way a pendulum swings?
- Does the size, weight, or position of the bob make a difference in the cycle?
- Which swings farther, a heavy or a light bob? Which swings longer?
- Can you predict how far the bob will swing from various release heights?
- Can you get two pendulums to swing together for more than one cycle? What are the most cycles you can achieve with two pendulums? With three pendulums?
- At what point in the cycle do bob-riders feel they're going fastest? Slowest?
- Can you make the bob swing other than just back and forth?

Remove the bob-riders and try further investigations:

- If the pendulum is shortened (wrap swing chains over the pole), how does it affect the swing?
- Does the bob swing longer when there's no rider?

Swings are not long-playing pendulums. Encourage kids to look into the principles behind this problem, setting in motion further pendulum projects.— *Martin Beberman, Champaign, Ill.*

Floodwaters in a jar

What happens when a river goes on a rampage? Help students find out about how the soil settles with a simulation right in your classroom.

Collect four or five different kinds of soil and pebble samples from several sources—a garden, woodland, bog, and shore. Place them in a large jar, filling it to about ⅓ its capacity. Then add water until the jar is about ⅔ full.

Screw the top on firmly and shake the jar vigorously. As the particles swirl and then begin to settle, ask students the following questions:

- How does the water change during the shaking? When the shaking stops?
- What causes the water to clear?
- How would you describe the particles that are falling? How can you tell that not all of them are falling? Which particles settle first?
- Have you noticed the difference in a local river or stream before and after a rainstorm? How is the action in the jar similar? How is it different?

When all the particles have settled, ask students to compare the layers that have formed—perhaps drawing pictures showing the different layers—and to come to some conclusions.— *Jan Owens, Newark, Del.*

Getting in gear

By making a working model of gears, you'll be able to give your students a hands-on lesson in this principle. You'll need lids of various sizes that will nest and corrugated cardboard, fiberboard, or other board to serve as a foundation for mounting gears.

To make your model, follow this procedure:

- Select two pairs of nesting lids. The larger of each pair will be a gear wheel.

- Cut strips of corrugated cardboard in widths to match the heights of the gear wheel sides.

- Test wrap a strip of cardboard around each of the gear wheels. The strips should fit in such a way that the cogs mesh when the two wheels are brought side by side and rotated. If the strips fit well, glue them in place. If they don't, try other pairs of nesting lids until you find a good match.

- After gluing a cardboard strip onto both gear wheels, you're ready to position the gear wheels over their smaller "partner" wheels. Glue or nail one of the small lids onto the foundation board and place its gear wheel over it. Carefully position the second pair of lids—gear wheel on top—so that when the small lid is glued down, the cogs of the two gear wheels will mesh.

- Put a dot or arrow on top of each gear wheel to help you keep track of the revolutions.

Now set the wheels in motion. You might suggest some of the following inquiry activities:

- Turn one gear in a clockwise direction. In which direction does the other wheel turn?

- Turn one gear wheel so that it makes one complete revolution. How many revolutions does the other gear make? Note the number of revolutions the second gear makes when the first gear makes three complete revolutions.

Compare the circumferences of the two gear wheels. Compare the wheels' diameters.

What kinds of gears are involved in our daily lives? Examine a working clock. Try to arrange for a visit by an auto mechanic instructor who can explain about gears in cars. And don't overlook the bicycle for gear exploration.—*Karen E. Reynolds, Oakland, Calif.*

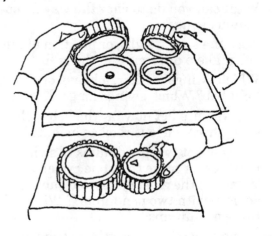

Explaining technology

Here's a simple way to stir up excitement as you help your students understand the impact of technology on society. Just pit four students against each other in a race to whip a bowl of cream, and the principle will illustrate itself.

Supply the contestants with identical bowls and amounts of whipping cream. But give each student a different tool: a wooden spoon, a wire whisk, a hand-held eggbeater, and an electric mixer. Give the signal to begin. While your whippers are working, you can explain the principle of aeration that makes the cream stiffen. Of course, the student with the electric mixer wins. Point out that he's not tired, but the other three students were "beat" even before the cream began to thicken.

You might end the lesson with a discussion on how technology makes many jobs easier.—*Mary Ghisolfo, San Francisco*

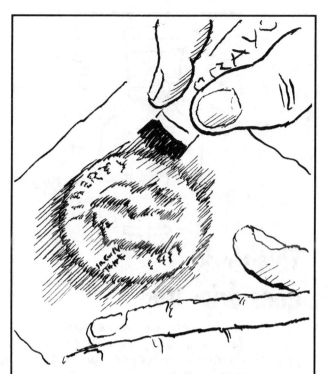

On the texture trail

To introduce textures to your students, cover a coin with paper and rub over it with a blunted crayon until the raised portion of the design becomes clear. Next, give your students crayons and newsprint and invite them to make rubbings of classroom items. Which things make good rubbings? Can you tell whether an object will make a good rubbing by looking at it? By touching it?

Give students wider boundaries—including outdoors, if possible—and invite them to make "mystery" rubbings. See if others can guess what the object is and where it might be found.

For more challenge, give rubbings sets to groups of students and challenge them to find the objects that the textures represent. Provide hunters with equipment to make their own rubbings of the objects as they locate them. You might also want to have the hunters record the names of the objects from which the rubbings were taken.

Later, each group might collaborate to produce a map of the route they took, attaching the rubbings they made at the appropriate spots.—*B. Galin, Burlington, Vt.*

The great dam experiment

If rivers, ponds, and streams fascinate your students, you might suggest a project that promotes inquiry into the design of dams.

Provide groups of four students with metal trays with sides, modeling clay, and water. Challenge each group to construct a clay dam across the tray (dams should be no more than ¼ inch thick), then to add water in back of the dam to see if it can withstand the pressure.

As the experimenting gets underway, invite students to check with other groups to see which dams hold and which don't. Encourage questions relating to the design features that hold back water most efficiently.

Suggest that students search reference books for pictures of famous dams, checking their configurations and noting whether dams usually are straight or curved. (Do curved dams bend toward the contained water or away from it?) This research might suggest new designs for the damming project. Students might also try experimenting with the addition of reinforcing materials.—*Barbara Clary, Columbia, S.C.*

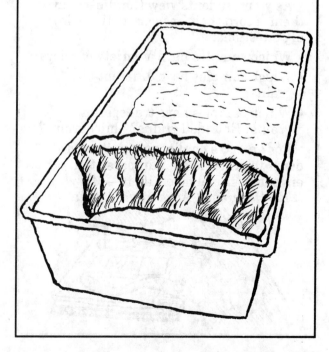

Sand-y studies

This simple project will help your students practice using a microscope—and sharpen their ability to observe, describe, and compare. You'll need five or six microscopes, 3 x 5-inch index cards, clear tape, and samples of several kinds of sand. (Have your students collect sand from as many different places as possible—beaches, rivers, lakes, and desert dunes—so the samples vary in color and composition.) Before you begin, ask your students to rinse each sample and let it dry.

Start your sand studies by talking about how the samples differ in general. Do some seem finer? Lighter in color? And so on. Next, your students can work in small groups to make sand slides that they'll observe more closely under the microscope. Here's how:

1. Cut a window in the center of an index card by folding the card in half, then in half again, and cutting away the corner where the folds meet.

2. Cover the window with clear tape, then turn the card over.

3. Sprinkle sand onto the sticky side of the window. Cover with another strip of tape.

4. Write identifying information on the slide.

As your students view the slides, have them record their answers to the following questions:

• Which samples have a variety of colors?

• Which samples have different-size grains?

• Which samples have transparent grains? Rounded grains? Shiny grains?

For an extra challenge, ask your students to describe one sample so that others can positively identify it.—*Mary Klatt Hoekzema, Anchorage, Alaska*

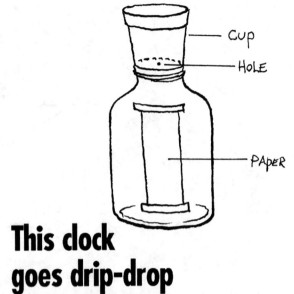

This clock goes drip-drop

In this age of hi-tech electronic clocks, your students might enjoy making this primitive water time-keeper. For each student, you'll need:

• a paper, plastic, or plastic foam cup that holds about 8 ounces

• a plastic or glass jar with a mouth that will hold the cup

• a strip of paper that's as long as the jar and about 1½ inches wide

• clear tape, a straight pin, water, a watch, or a kitchen timer. (Students can share the watch or timer.)

To make the clock, students use the pin to punch a tiny hole in the bottom of the cup. Then, they place the cup so that it sits in the mouth of the jar, and they tape the paper strip to the jar.

Next, students fill the cup with water. As the water drips into the jar, they mark off the water level on the strip of paper once each minute. Have them use a wall clock, kitchen timer, or watch to time the 1-minute intervals.

Invite students to use their Drip-Drip Clocks to time events and activities. How long does it take to walk from the classroom to the nearest water fountain and back again? How long is recess according to the water clock? How many other ways can they use the clock to measure time?—*Denise Lee, Springhouse, Pa.*

Spinning your wheels

With just a few materials and a collection of inquiring minds, you can get a study of ball bearings ready to roll in your science class.

The first step is putting together a ball-bearing assemblage. You'll need a collection of marbles, all the same diameter; an assortment of metal jar lids and clear plastic lids of various diameters; glue that adheres to metal; and a board on which to attach the assemblage.

1. Select a metal jar lid that will accommodate a circle of about 16 marbles just inside its rim. Glue the lid, top side down, to the board.

2. Arrange a ring of marbles around the inside edge of the lid.

3. Find a smaller metal lid—one whose rim is shorter than the diameter of the marbles—that fits within the circle of marbles and allows them to roll around freely.

4. Glue the smaller lid to a larger clear plastic lid. Insert this double-layer lid inside the ring of marbles.

5. Try spinning the plastic lid. Watch the action of the marbles.

Now you're ready to make the following observations:

- What are the moving parts of the ball-bearing model?
- How does each part move?
- Where are the contact points—where does friction occur?

When students have had an opportunity to examine and discuss how the ball-bearing model operates, you might want to extend the project with the following experiments:

- Put sand or sugar in the ball-bearing track and observe results.
- Experiment with lubricants.
- Find out how far a marble rolls with each revolution of the plastic lid. (Tape a paper clip to the edge of the plastic lid as a reference point to determine a full revolution of the lid.)—*Karen Reynolds, Oakland, Calif.*

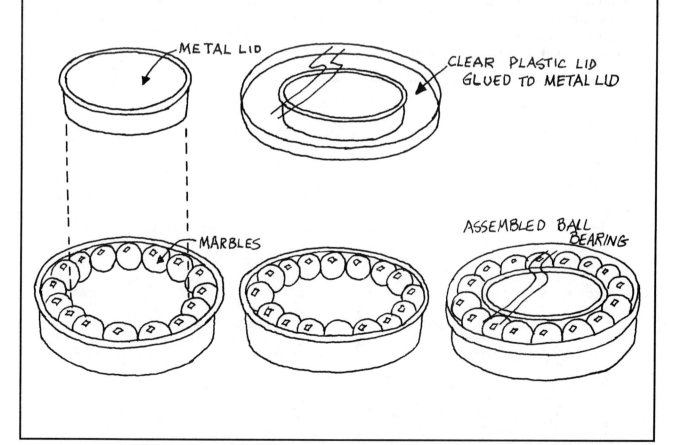

METAL LID

CLEAR PLASTIC LID
GLUED TO METAL LID

MARBLES

ASSEMBLED BALL BEARING

The other side of magnets

A dramatic way to get repulsive discovery started might be called the "no-visible means-of-support" gimmick. To try it, you'll need eight doughnut-shaped magnets (⅜-inch hole size; rubberized magnets are durable and not too expensive) and a couple of pencils fixed upright in wooden (or cardboard or foam) bases.

Start with four magnets in a stack in your hand. (*Note:* Magnets will not lie quietly in a stack unless attracting surfaces—opposite poles—are in contact.) Now slip magnet number one over the pencil and let the doughnut slide down to the base. Then, one at a time, slide the other magnets onto the pencil.

Now go to pencil number two with the other stack of four magnets. Slide the first magnet on as before. But before sliding magnet two on, turn it over. This time, the magnet hangs suspended on the pencil shaft, not touching the magnet below. Slip the third magnet on as is; turn over the last magnet before sliding it on the pencil. You now have a column of "floating" magnets. Let the inquiry begin.

- What happens when you try pushing the magnets together with your fingers?

- What do you observe about the amount of space between the pairs of magnets? (The bottom magnets are closer together than the top ones because cumulative weight is pushing on the lower ones. Even though the magnets don't touch each other, their weight is a factor. If you remove the pencil from the base and hold it as you slide the magnets on one at a time—in an alternative pattern as in the second phase of the experiment—you can feel the weight increasing.)

- What happens to the spacing when you turn the pencil on its side? (With the factor of cumulative weight eliminated, the space should equalize.)

- Take off the top magnet and move it near the suspended ones—up, down, and around the rims—to see if anything happens.

- What about the rim of the magnet—does it seem to have any kind of force?

- If magnets are not already marked, devise a system that will allow you to know ahead of time which surfaces are going to repel each other.—*Philip White, Flushing, N.Y.*

Chapter 7
SOCIAL STUDIES

Hooray—a parade!

State study takes on real excitement when students know they'll use their knowledge of the states to design mini-floats for a class parade.

First, have each student choose a state to research. Encourage students to use many sources—almanacs, atlases, books, magazines, and others—to gather information. Each student will be an "expert" on his state when the whole class studies it.

As parade time nears, let your students start constructing their floats. They can make these of cardboard, clay, or other materials, and mount them on skateboards or other wheelbases. (Use a long rope to tie them together and tow them around the room.)

Your students should make sure their floats display interesting state facts and features—famous landmarks or an important industry, for example. Each designer also should write a short commentary about his float to present on Parade Day.

After the floats have toured your room, you might "take the show on the road" around the school.—*Tamara G. Hild, Canyon Country, Calif.*

Safari adventure

Your students will learn about Africa as they develop their own itineraries. Here's what to do:

- Begin by explaining to your students that they're going on an African safari. They'll travel to Africa, dock at one of Africa's coastal ports, travel through several countries, and depart Africa from a different port. Maps and reference books will be available to them.

- Have your students make their own passports out of blank index cards. One side of the card is for the traveler's name, birthplace, small passport-size photograph, and signature. On the other side of the card, your students can record the countries they visit plus the entry and departure dates.

- When a student enters a country, he completes a descriptive summary, including the country's name, its capital, population, major language, and chief products. Students also draw the country's flag and a picture of some highlights. When a student has shown you his research, sign your name under the departure date on his passport. Then send him off to a bordering country to repeat the steps until he reaches a port of exit.

- Display the passport books around a large map of Africa on a bulletin board. Ask your students to use different felt-tip pens or crayons to trace their travels.—*Lynn E. Nielsen, Janet McClain, Betty Strub, and Joan Duea, Cedar Falls, Iowa*

What's in a name?

For a fun geography lesson, introduce your students to the list of U.S. towns in the back of an atlas. Have them look up humorous names—such as, Two Medicine, Radio, Wonder Lake, Ozona, Deers Ears, Soddy-Daisy, Twitty, Truth or Consequences.

Have each student choose a town and write a fictional story about how it got its unusual name. When students finish their stories, share some of the more amusing ones with the class. Then, have students write to the chambers of commerce of the towns they chose to find out the real stories behind the funny names.—*Denise Lee, Springhouse, Pa.*

State champ game

A word game can add spark to lessons about your own state. You'll need a few state maps and copies of a 5 x 5-block grid, with "STATE CHAMP" as a title. Each box in the grid should have a clue to the name of a city, town, or natural feature in your state. For example, in Nebraska one clue might be "The last name of a U.S. president" (Lincoln). Other clues could be "an animal," "a tree," "a color," "an occupation," and so on. Be sure to leave space below the clue for students to write in their answers.

Give each student (or team of students) a map and announce a contest to correctly complete a row of five blocks horizontally, vertically, or diagonally. Remind your students that each clue could have more than one answer. Once a champ is declared, give all students time to complete the entire grid.—*Sandra J. Frey, Lancaster, Pa.*

Postmark geography

For an interesting geography lesson, collect an assortment of used envelopes with a variety of foreign and domestic postmarks. Give each student or small group of students an envelope, and have them research the postmark city, finding out such things as its location, population, founding date, and so on. Later, display the envelopes, along with interesting research findings.—*Sister Roberta Ann Lesky, Philadelphia*

Earn-a-journey

This activity makes studying geography a privilege rather than a chore.

Post on the bulletin board a large map of the United States—or the world, depending on what your class is studying. Invite students to browse around the map and select individual spots to begin a journey. Mark each student's location with a pin—to which he's attached a flag bearing his name.

When you want to reward a student—for a job well done, a day's good behavior, whatever—surprise him with a "visa." The student then chooses a place on the map to visit—but he may move across only one state line or international boundary. Have the student move his flag to the spot he's visiting; he should keep a list of all journeys he makes.

While visiting, a student investigates his vacation spot and reports his findings to the class, perhaps in a postcard format. As an alternative to the one-boundary move, use a spinner or die to determine how many border crossings travelers may take. Ocean crossings might ride on a certain number.—*David R. Carlisle, Anderson, Ind.*

State in a box

When your social studies curriculum calls for a study of the United States, challenge students to work independently with "state in a box" projects. Allow each child to choose a state. Then have students collect information about their states and put it in appropriately decorated cardboard boxes.

The following are a few ways students might go about locating and presenting information pertaining to their states:

- Write letters to the department of tourism in the capital city and to chambers of commerce in the state's major cities.
- Check with the school and public librarians about fiction and nonfiction books with story settings in particular states. Students may read these and write short reports or design informative book covers to place in state boxes.
- Collect information about and report on famous people strongly identified with a particular state.
- Make small-scale state flags.
- Tape-record songs with reference to the state being studied.
- Make a poster telling about a state's main crops and industrial products.
- Interview a person who has lived in the state under study.
- Make a poster showing the state flower and bird.
- Write a short report about the historic sites in the state and show their locations on a state map.—*Beth Diaz, Memphis*

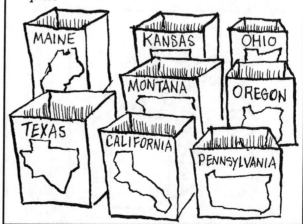

Place-name puzzlers

Give your students practice using an atlas by presenting puzzles based on place names.

Begin with a challenge that matches a list of occupations (such as auto-body worker, doctor, plumber, banker, carpenter) with a list of cities where they'd likely be performed (Fender, Doctortown, Faucett, Deposit, Hammer). When your students have completed the matchups, reveal that the city names refer to real places.

Have them use an atlas index to find a state for each city. Next, have your students copy the grid coordinates listed in the atlas index and locate each city on the appropriate state map. Then, post a map of the United States and have them label the approximate locations of the cities they tracked down.

Invite your students to add more job/city matchups to the original list. Or have them create their own place name puzzlers, such as:

- cities that stock supermarkets (Dairy, Ore.; Fruitville, Fla.)
- cities that evoke the seasons (Snowflake, Ariz.; Summer Shade, Ky.)
- cities that belong in Europe (Paris, Me.; London, Tex.).

Again, ask your puzzle solvers to look up the cities, name the states, list the coordinates, and locate the cities on the map.—*Donald Lankiewicz, Westerville, Ohio*

Welcome to our town

To help your students get to know their community, have them put together a welcome packet and brochure for newcomers.

Brainstorm areas of information that might be included in such a packet: schools, churches, hospitals, stores, libraries, recreational facilities—for starters. Post the list of major topics and allow students time to add other ideas or subtopics. When the list is complete, have students pair off to research specific areas. Provide general guidelines for the kinds of information to be included and the format to be followed.

Besides collecting informational materials, the research process might include making telephone contacts, writing letters, making visits to sites, and taking photos, or doing illustrations of things important to the community. When students have finished their research, discuss the results; call for suggestions about the brochure's final form.

When the welcome booklet is complete, have students send a copy to each person who supplied help or information.
—*Robert Bridges, Strongsville, Ohio*

Traveling blind

A large map of the United States and a blindfold are all that's needed for students to practice their knowledge of U.S. geography.

Ask a volunteer to stand in front of the map and to point to the state in which you live. With the student's finger still on that state, blindfold him and name another state. The student tries to point to that state. As students become more adept at the game, add challenge by having them start from a city and locate such places as the Grand Canyon, the Rocky Mountains, Mount Rushmore, or the Everglades.—*Robert Young, Junction City, Ore.*

Letters from afar

Give your students (and yourself) a break from the traditional end-of-the-unit test with this letter-writing activity.

Invite students to put themselves 15 years into the future. Each has gone to live in the geographic region you're studying and writes you a letter. The letter should tell why the writer decided to move to that country, how he's making a living, and what he misses most about his homeland.

Encourage your students to use reference materials and allow them several days to complete the assignment.

To ensure your students cover all the basics, give them specifics to include, such as the country's weather, economy, physical features, landmarks, education, manufacturing, agriculture, and the health care system. Then, prepare a checklist of the specifics to help with grading.—*Trudy Hathaway, Syracuse, N.Y.*

Touring the world

You can arrange for your students to go on an informational "tour" of countries. Here's how.

Invite students to help choose countries to visit (half as many as the number of students), locate them on the map, and plot a route. After highlighting a few intriguing facts about each country, have pairs of students choose a country to study and compile a list of 10 to 25 facts about it. Then, proceeding in tour order, allow time for one pair a week to present an oral report.

At the end of the class tour, put all the lists together in a booklet. Then have each pair of travelers illustrate its country in a display or diorama. Invite visitors to walk through this "world's fair," while world-wise students describe their displays.—*Alberta Goodine, Websterville, Vt.*

Flags a' flying

Flags are a colorful way to get students hooked on studying countries and their locations. Have each student choose a country, research its flag, and then create a replica of the flag from construction paper.

Post all the flags and have students describe them for the class, explaining why the countries chose their particular colors and symbols, and pointing out the country on a world map.—*Nell Smith, Cedar Grove, N.J.*

What's new?

New York, New Orleans, New Salem. Settlers to this country must have found it comforting to stick with names from their homelands. Ask your students to look at a map of the United States. How many places can they find with the word *New* in their names? On a world map, see if they can find the place the new location was named after.—*Denise Lee, Springhouse, Pa.*

Coordinate-code treasure hunt

Put some fun into latitude and longitude by turning a practice session into a treasure hunt. You'll need several copies of a world map showing latitude and longitude lines; index cards; and treasures, such as candy, peanuts, or raisins.

To find the treasure, students will work in groups of two or three. For each group, do the following:

1. Mark a map with a symbol, such as a star or triangle. Put a matching symbol on a pair of index cards. (One card will tell— in code—where to find the other card, which will tell—in code—where to find the treasure.) Decide where to hide the treasure and the second index card (for example, "behind the fish tank" and "in Ted's hat").

2. Now create a code linked to map coordinates. First determine how many of each letter you need to spell out both locations.

Then write these letters on the map at the intersections of various coordinates (for example, in "behind the fish tank," the *b* might be at latitude 40 degrees N, longitude 120 degrees W; the letter *e*, at latitude 60 degrees N, longitude 60 degrees E). Include a few unused letters at other locations to increase the difficulty a bit.

3. Next, using the coordinate points you've designated for each letter, encode the two locations on the index cards.

Hide the treasures and the second index cards as the messages dictate. Then divide your students into their groups and give each group a map and its appropriate index card. As each group finds its treasure, they share it.

To add more challenge, scramble the letters in each word when you prepare the messages.—*Randolph Lyon, Dubuque, Iowa*

Fly's eye view

Add a new perspective to mapping by having your students pretend they're flies on the ceiling, looking down at the classroom. Ask them how different items would appear. How would a chair look? A table? Someone sitting at a desk? A plant on the teacher's desk? A drinking fountain? Then ask the students to draw the classroom from a fly's perspective. For homework, have your students draw another "fly view"—of an amusement park, airport, aquarium, open car trunk, toolbox, purse, or desk drawer. Post the maps on a bulletin board.—*Mrs. Louis Welsh, Huntington, Ind.*

Search for Sue City

Inject some humor into learning cardinal directions by creating a personalized map. Name the town after you (Smithville or Jonestown) and load it with landmarks named after your students. Your town could include Conti Airport, which is just east of Jackson Zoo on Ronald Road.

To accompany the map, prepare a work sheet with statements such as:

- Morgan Bridge is _____ of Leesville.
- To get from Jordan Junction to David Memorial School, you go _____.

Even older students might enjoy this approach and improve their direction skills without suffering drill doldrums.—*Gail Brown, Eastsound, Wash.*

Jigsaw geography

Take map tracing a step further, and your students end up with jigsaw puzzles that reinforce geographic knowledge.

For each mapmaker, you'll need a map of the area you want students to study, tracing paper, pencils, scissors, glue, crayons or felt-tip pens, and two 11 x 14-inch pieces of oak tag. To begin, ask students to carefully trace the map onto tracing paper. Have them include all interior borders, cities, rivers, and other geographic features. Make sure they leave space for a map title and key.

Then, ask students to cut out the tracing-paper map—following its outer edge—and glue it in the center of one of the pieces of oak tag. Have them carefully cut along the oak tag border of the map, being sure to follow the map outline exactly and to keep the border in one piece. When they've finished, they should have a mounted map tracing and an oaktag perimeter.

Now, have students glue the oak tag perimeter onto the other piece of oak tag, matching the outer edges exactly. This is the frame of the puzzle. Next, invite students to decorate, label, and key their mounted maps. Encourage them to add colors, mark capitals with stars—whatever is necessary to make the map as informative and authentic as possible.

After the decorating, have students cut their maps into puzzle pieces. Advise them to consider the most appropriate ways to cut: along political boundary lines, perhaps, or along borders of counties, states, or countries.

Now the map puzzles are ready for recreational use or small-group study. You might have students quiz one another on map details: One student removes a puzzle piece and asks a question about it; the student who answers correctly gets to remove the next piece and ask a question about it. Play continues until students are thoroughly familiar with the area. Then they select another puzzle and perhaps another way to use it.—*June Getchius, Garfield, N.J.*

Storybook maps

With this creative approach to map drawing, your students will also be practicing reading skills. To begin, have each student choose a favorite storybook whose locale is clearly described. After students have had a chance to review their stories, ask them to list all references to setting, noting the relationships of sites to one another whenever possible. Then have them draw maps of their book's locale on heavy-stock paper, using as much color and detail as they wish. (You might want to show them the map of Pooh's neighborhood in *Winnie-the-Pooh* as an example.)

For more challenge, invite students to choose books without a specific setting. Children can use their imaginations to create a map that fits the story.—*Linda Allanson, Delmar, N.Y.*

Map autobiographies

Your students can tell a lot about themselves with the help of a U.S. map. Distribute outline maps and have your students use different crayons to identify the states where they were born, where they have family and special friends, where they've lived or visited, and the states they'd most like to see. Then find out who was born the farthest from the school, who has the most spread-out family, who has visited the most states, and so forth.—*Donna Michaels, Raleigh, N.C.*

Compass course

Put your students "over the edge" with this game that reinforces directions and compass reading. You'll need a game board, 25 3 x 5 index cards, and player tokens.

Make the game board by dividing a 13 x 13-inch piece of tagboard into 1-inch squares; mark START in the center square. In the bottom right-hand corner of the board, make a compass rose labeled with all cardinal and intercardinal directions. On the index cards write instructions such as "Move NE two squares" and "Move S three squares." To add more interest, build the game around a theme—such as a stormy sea or a haunted forest—by appropriately decorating the board and adding hazards that force players to lose a turn.

The game is open to as many players as can comfortably fit around the board. To start, each player puts his token on the START square. Player One draws an instruction card, reads it aloud, and moves in the designated direction the number of spaces indicated. Play passes to the left. The winner is the first player to move off the game board—sailing out of the storm, walking out of the woods, or whatever.—*Sister Mary Robert, Appleton, Wis.*

States alive!

For the annual tour of the states, combine fact-finding and map-making skills. Your students will create their own state maps—then use them as visual aids for oral reports.

Begin by using the overhead projector to prepare a wall map of the United States on white butcher paper, as large as your space and projector allow. Outline each state very clearly; don't label the states. Have each student select a state (or two) to research, then trace its shape on separate paper.

As the students learn about their states, have them decorate their tracings with facts, pictures, symbols (representing major cities, topographic features, attractions, and industries), labels from state-produced goods, and other materials that depict state history, economy, and allure.

Finally, have each student use his map to report to the class on his state, then attach it to the wall outline. The result is a wonderful class-made map to view and review.—*Susan Nelson, Ramona, Calif.*

Mini-maps and math

Turn your out-of-date road maps into opportunities for your students to combine map and math skills.

First, cut the road maps into 11 x 16-inch sections and glue each section across the inside of a file folder. Around the edges, mark number-and-letter coordinates for locating cities and other features, and paste on a small legend that includes the scale of miles and selected symbols and their meanings. Then, laminate the maps for durability.

For each map, prepare tasks similar to the following:

• If you drive from Riverton (G-3) to Leadville (F-3) and then to Burnt Hills (E-6), about how many miles will you travel? (Use the scale of miles or the map's high-way mileage markers.)

• You live in Lewis (A-9). You commute 5 days a week to Niles (G-2). How many miles do you commute in 3 weeks?

• You rent a car in Ormsby (B-7) for 1 day. You're allowed 75 free miles. Name places you can visit and return from without paying extra.

Place a task card and an answer card in a pocket attached to the outside of each folder, and store the folders at an independent activity area. Encourage students to add their own map-reading tasks when they've completed the ones you've provided.—*Ron Castro, Downey, Calif.*

Where are you?

Teach your students compass directions—and sharpen their listening skills at the same time. Here's how:

• On an 8½ x 11-inch piece of paper, make a grid of blocks and label the center block with compass directions.

• Pass the grid around the class and have each student sketch a different picture or symbol (such as a cat or a star) in two or more different blocks (depending on class size).

• Make copies of the grid and give one to each student.

Now you're ready to begin "giving directions." For example, tell students to start at the center compass design and go 2 blocks north, 1 block west, and 3 blocks south. Then ask, "Where are you?"

When you students are ready for more of a challenge, ask them to move northeast, southwest, and so on.—*Sandy Turner, Philadelphia*

Map happenings

Here's a way to help your students become familiar with the names and locations of cities, states, and foreign countries. Keep a large world map and a map of the United States posted at all times. Whenever you find the name of a particular place while sharing current events, vacation plans, folktales, birthplaces of famous people, and so on, find the location on the map. Then have your students illustrate the fact and write where the event is taking place. Select several pictures and post them around the edge of the map. Then use yarn to connect them to the proper location.—*Gaile Senette, Baton Rouge, La.*

Around the U.S.A.

To help your students learn the names and locations of our 50 states, have them play this game.

Prepare a game board on an unlabeled copy of a U.S. map. First, mark each state with the number representing its order of entry into the Union. Next, draw a follow-the-path game track around the U.S. border. Divide the track into 62 sections: one at the beginning marked "Off We Go!", one for each state number, 10 for "rest areas," and one at the end marked "Home Again!"

Collect a die, a few tokens, and two or three players, and the game is ready to play. Player One rolls the die and moves that number of spaces. If he lands on a "rest area," he stays there until his next turn. If he lands on a number, he locates the number on the map and tries to identify the state. Players immediately check answers on an answer key. If the player is correct, he stays on the space. If not, he must go back to the nearest rest area. The first player to reach "Home Again!" is the winner. The order-of-states' entry adds a historic dimension.—*Shirley Carter, Greenville, Tenn.*

Making mountains

Take the mystery out of topographic maps with a mountain-making project. You'll need thick cardboard, rulers, pencils, glue, paints, and brushes.

Have each of your students draw and cut out a free-form circle or oval about 2 inches in diameter. Then ask them to cut out five more of the same shape, each one about a ½ inch bigger than the previous one.

To construct their topographic mountains, students stack their six shapes with the largest one on the bottom. Because hills and mountains aren't perfect cones, encourage the students to experiment. For example, have them try stacking their layers off center or aligning all of them along one edge to form a cliff.

When your students have found a configuration they like, they can glue the layers in place on poster board and tint the elevations. They might also want to assign an elevation height to each layer and mark this on a key. Some may want to research the elevation color code. You might even go on to create a class mountain range or town.—*Carol Eyster, San Pedro, Calif.*

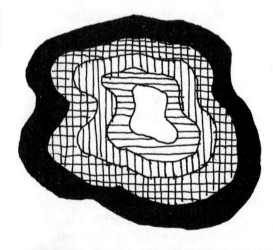

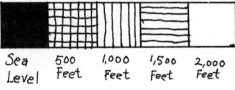

Sea Level   500 Feet   1,000 Feet   1,500 Feet   2,000 Feet

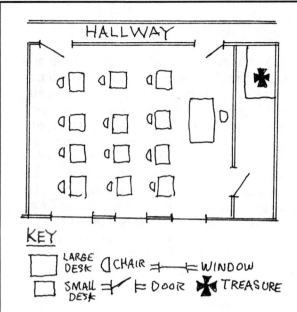

KEY

☐ LARGE DESK ◖ CHAIR ⊨⊨ WINDOW

▢ SMALL DESK ⊬⊨ DOOR ✤ TREASURE

Mapping the classroom

Here's an easy and fun way to introduce mapping to your students. Give each child a sheet of construction paper, along with an assortment of cut-out squares and rectangles to represent classroom furniture. Have students try placing the furniture pieces on the construction paper "floor" according to the present room arrangement. Then, invite students to rearrange the furniture pieces on their own maps; you might recreate some of these new interior designs, moving the real furniture to match the maps.

Take the activity a step further by converting shapes to symbols—such as an *x* for a chair, a box for a table, and an *x* inside a box for a chair-table combination. Or ask students to come up with their own symbols, providing a key to explain what each stands for.

Put students' map-reading skills to work with a treasure hunt. Choose a student to hide an object in the room; have him mark its location on his map with an agreed-upon symbol. It's up to a classmate to find the hidden object by using this treasure map. To add more challenge, help students sketch the layout of the school—in much less detail—and try a treasure hunt within these broader boundaries.—*Clara Greisman, Richmond, Calif.*

Postmark collectors

Here's an ongoing project to help your students reinforce their map-reading skills.

Make a chart listing all 50 states, their conventional abbreviations, and zip codes. Post the chart next to a U.S. map that has states outlined and labeled, but no cities marked. Ask your students to bring in envelopes or postcards with legible postmarks. Then, challenge them to work together to collect at least one postmark from each state. As each new postmark arrives, have the contributor use an atlas to locate the city and label it on the displayed map. What ideas do your students have for getting postmarks from hard-to-collect states? (Write the state tourist bureau, a national park, a popular tourist attraction, and so on.)— *Sandra Frey, Lancaster, Pa.*

Colossal compass

Your students will have an easier time learning about compass points if you create a rose that's big enough for them to stand on.

Invite everyone outside to the playground or other paved area. Draw on the ground a large chalk circle and place a compass in the center (make sure it's level). When the needle is still, slowly turn the compass until the needle lines up with the north axis on the compass face. Draw a line from this point to the edge of the circle and write *north* above it. Complete the compass rose by drawing in the other directional lines and labels; include northeast, northwest, southeast, and southwest if you wish.

Have your students take turns standing at various points on the edge of the circle and moving in the directions you call out. Ask them to face certain visible landmarks and then tell you in which direction they're facing.—*Caroline Arnold, Los Angeles*

States in a flash

If you think flash cards are good only for practicing math facts, you haven't used them for teaching the locations of the states. Here's how.

Make 48 copies of a mini-map of the 48 contiguous states. Mount the maps on separate index cards and on each one color a different state. On the back of each card, name the state indicated and its capital. You might also include other information, such as population, principal products, order of entry into the Union. Laminate the cards, and you're ready to put them to use in a variety of ways.

Have students quiz each other on identifying states by their locations; invite students to devise Go Fish-type card games that call for making up collections of states that form regions, that begin with the same letter, or that produce similar products. Base activities on the alphabetical order of state names and the order of the states' admission to the Union. Distribute the cards among your students and call for groups to form according to criteria you call out: states west of the Mississippi, states bordering the Gulf of Mexico, and so on.—*Tina Bucci, Jamestown, Pa.*

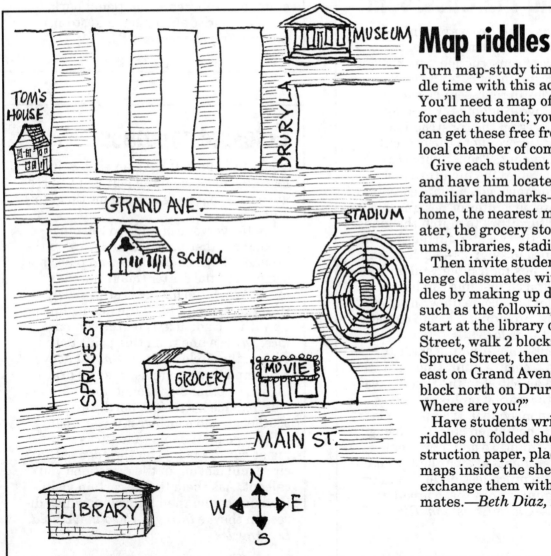

Map riddles

Turn map-study time into riddle time with this activity. You'll need a map of your city for each student; you probably can get these free from your local chamber of commerce.

Give each student a map and have him locate and mark familiar landmarks—school, home, the nearest movie theater, the grocery store, museums, libraries, stadiums.

Then invite students to challenge classmates with map riddles by making up directions such as the following: "You start at the library on Main Street, walk 2 blocks north on Spruce Street, then 3 blocks east on Grand Avenue, and 1 block north on Drury Lane. Where are you?"

Have students write their riddles on folded sheets of construction paper, place their maps inside the sheets, and exchange them with classmates.—*Beth Diaz, Memphis*

Archaeologists in action

Challenge your students with a problem faced by archaeologists who try to translate hieroglyphics and other ancient writings: missing pieces.

First, concoct a code for the alphabet—a simple symbol-for-letter substitution. Use the code to develop a short message about events from the period the class is studying. Make four copies of the coded message, cut all copies into the same size pieces, and discard a few pieces from each set so that each set is missing the same pieces.

Next, introduce the code to your students in a chart showing the symbol/letter matchups—or have students practice solving a sentence that contains all the letters of the alphabet. (You might use the classic, "The quick brown fox jumps over the lazy dog.")

Then divide the class into four decoding teams, giving each a set of the message pieces you copied. Advise the teams that pieces might be missing, so they'll be prepared to make educated guesses to fill in the gaps. When the decoders reveal their findings, ask them to explain how they tackled the problem. Also discuss the possibilities for other interpretations and for error, ambiguity, and misunderstanding.—*Robert Baum, Pitman, N.J.*

Collecting folk culture

Your students can learn about cultural and regional influences on their language by collecting favorite sayings, expressions, and regionalisms, then compiling them into their own commonplace book. Explain that public figures from Cicero to John F. Kennedy have kept such books of favorite sayings to use in speeches.

Encourage your students to listen more carefully to conversation—particularly among older people—for sayings that enrich the language. These may include greetings (such as the desert phrase, "You're as welcome as rain."), advice ("Keep your eye on the ball."), proverbs, taunts, or insults—even chants from children's games. Have each child collect five folk sayings from relatives and neighbors, recording the speaker's identity, age, hometown, and the date. From these, ask each student to choose his favorite to write in the class commonplace book.—*K.C. Benedict, Blanding, Utah*

Culture shock

With a little imagination, you can give your students a first-hand lesson in culture shock. First, discuss how it might feel to be in a foreign land coping with new customs, languages, faces, and rules. Then transform your class into a different place for a day.

Hold a Backward Culture Day: Do everything in reverse. Play games backward. Write backward. Walk backward. Or have a New Manners Day where everyone wears gloves all day. Laughing is allowed only if you cover your face with both hands. No one can answer a question without first being addressed as *Sir* or *Miss*.

Later, encourage your students to express how it felt to follow the new rules. Ask how it would feel if everyone except them knew the rules.—*Denise Lee, Springhouse, Pa.*

Wish you were here

For a social studies activity that combines research and language arts skills, start collecting postcards. Save any you receive in the mail and buy a few extras on your own trips.

Place the colorful postcards in a box or on a learning center table and ask each student to choose one to investigate. Have the students find out as much as they can about the areas or persons the postcards depict and then present their information in oral or written reports. Post the reports along with the postcards that inspired them.—*Frances Leahy, Chicago*

Visitor for a day

Give your students a quick cross-cultural lesson by arranging a student exchange. Have several of your students spend the day in another class in your district, city, even your own building. At a later date, invite students from the other class to share a day with you.

When your students return from their visit, ask them to tell the rest of the class about the experience. How did it feel to be in a different classroom? What did they like best and least about how the other class was run? Would they like to see some changes in their own class? Classroom exchanges can provide insight into the varieties of teaching styles and how other classes work.— *Kay Kimes, New Madrid, Mo.*

Heritage circles

Here's an activity to try when you study immigration and your students' ethnic heritage.

Give each student a 12 x 18-inch sheet of white drawing paper. Ask your students to use a compass to draw three side-by-side circles with a radius of about 2 inches each. Then, have your students write their names under the middle circle, and label the others "Mom" and "Dad." For homework, your students ask their parents to fill in the circles according to their ethnic backgrounds. Back in class, have your students combine this information to make heritage circles for themselves. Display the circles on a bulletin board with fraction questions such as "Whose dad is half Canadian?" or "Jeff's heritage includes ⅛ what?"—*Linda Doane, Old Lyme, Conn.*

Pictures worth a thousand words

Students can better understand nonphonetic languages if they play a game with ideograms and pictographs. When studying ancient or current cultures that use nonphonetic alphabets, show your students samples of cuneiform, hieroglyphics, and Oriental pictographs and ideograms. Have the students break into groups of four or five. Give each group drawing paper, a crayon (color-coded for easy group identification), and a written message, such as "The cow jumped over the moon."

Ask the students to "rewrite" the message using pictographs and ideograms. Invite students to share their messages and compare the different ways students use pictures and symbols to communicate ideas.—*Ellen Peskoff Shelton, Brooklyn, N.Y.*

Digging up school dirt

All schools—even young ones—have an array of stories to tell. Challenge your students to dig up those stories and record them for posterity—and the school library.

To begin, send a team of students to the public library, local newspaper office, board of education office, or historic museum to find out such things as when the school was built, how it got its name, why this location was chosen, and what the area looked like before the school was built. Send another team to interview school neighbors, teachers who've been in the building a number of years (or who were living in the area when the school was built), parents, and former students to find out who the first teachers were and what sort of memories they have about the school.

Encourage students to take cameras and note-taking materials on their research visits. They might consider photographing folks whose reminiscences they're writing about, or perhaps they'd like photos of buildings of the same vintage as your school, or a shot of the new wing to compare with the look of the original building.

Students might also be able to dig up memorabilia such as copies of the school song, team cheers, ancient school newspapers, programs from school events, school calendars, old photos—perhaps some showing the building under construction.

When the research is finished, have both teams write a report on their findings. Display these—along with any photos, diagrams, and memorabilia—on a hallway bulletin board for the whole school to share. Afterward, file the reports in the school library.—*Beverly Kruse, Freeport, Ill.*

Pack the wagon

Many of today's kids—who consider cassette players and tapes to be part of life's necessities—might have a hard time understanding the struggle early pioneers faced. You can help illustrate their dilemmas by posing this problem:

It's the year 1865. You, your spouse, and two children live in Georgia, but you've decided to move to the Great Plains to start a farm. There are 50 things you want to take, but the wagon has room for only 40. (Remember, you can't go to the store when you get there.) What will you need to survive the journey and start your new home and farm? Make sure you have a good reason for taking each item you choose.

Make a list of 50 items, including such supplies as rope, hatchet, water, kegs, clock, lantern, barrel of cornmeal, and so on. After your students have completed their individual lists, have each student read his list and field challenges. Encourage students to discuss the frustrations of decision making.—*Marilyn Dennis, Denver*

"I remember" interviews

You can help students get a real *sense* of history by having them interview people who personally remember important events.

Your students could talk with someone who heard Dr. Martin Luther King, Jr.'s, "I Have a Dream" speech, or recalled his assassination, or took part in a civil-rights demonstration. They could talk with people who remember John F. Kennedy's assassination, the first landing on the moon, or Richard Nixon's resignation. They could talk with someone who served in Viet Nam or someone who participated in peace demonstrations.

To prepare your students for interviewing on such emotion-laden events, you might discuss happenings that have touched them personally, such as the *Challenger* accident or the Kennedy assassination. Ask:

- How did you feel when you first heard the news?

- How did you feel about it after a few days? A few weeks?

- How do you feel about that event today? Have your feelings changed? Has the event become important in your life? In what ways?

When your students are ready, have them set up interviews with parents, older friends, relatives, or neighbors to explore historic events that affected *them* deeply. If possible, arrange to have students tape their interviews.

After students share their interviews, discuss which events seem to be most significant to particular age-groups and which opinions or reactions seem to be most common.—*Rose Reissman, Brooklyn, N.Y.*

Now and then

Whether you're studying colonial America or ancient Rome, the period can become more vivid if students make comparisons between daily life today and that of the period they're studying.

Have students collaborate in preparing a list of 15 common household items of today. They might reconstruct a typical day at home to determine the items or they might picture rooms of their homes—the living room with its TV, electric lights, CD player, and so on; the kitchen with its telephone, refrigerator, sink, and stove. Encourage students to name items that are important to the daily routine, even if they're not distinctly modern. Record the list on the chalkboard.

Have students speculate on what might have been used to fulfill the function of each "now" item during the period being studied. Discuss speculations. Students might be surprised that perhaps one of the heftiest entries in the "then" list will be the substitutes for TV.—*Marilyn Dennis, Denver*

Selling a cruise to the New World

Inject creativity and fun into social studies by inviting students to create ad campaigns promoting passage on the *Mayflower* to the New World. Encourage students to borrow freely from familiar commercial come-ons to entice the Pilgrims to leave hearth, home, and harassment for an early autumn cruise on the North Atlantic. Students practice research skills by including the departure date, embarkation location, and accommodation details. Have them turn their ad into a poster, and you have an art lesson too.—*Tom Tobias, Ypsilanti, Mich.*

Ye olde diary

You can give a here-and-now excitement to a moment in history. Here's how: Invite your students to put their feelings into diary entries for special days in history, giving a personal perspective to historic facts.

If you're studying America's colonial period, have your students imagine themselves standing on a Boston street on March 5, 1770, as British soldiers fire into the crowd. Or they could be listening to Paul Revere shouting his warning on the night of April 18, 1775. Ask your students to reflect on their own feelings and reactions, worries, and concerns about what was happening and how it might have affected them.

To set the mood for this new kind of journal writing, read actual entries from historic diaries. Point out the informal and spontaneous style. Point out, also, the interesting facts addressed or implied, such as the transportation or communications systems of the day.—*Nancy Fleckinger, Highland Falls, N.Y.*

The good old days?

To help your computer-minded, TV-watching students appreciate a pioneer school day, have them experience one.

First, have students research pioneer education, family life, customs, and recreation. On the designated day, ask students to dress appropriately to enter the world of earlier times. Awaiting them will be no electric lights, no running water—unless some sturdy lad takes an oaken bucket down to the nearest stream (water fountain), no heat—the long skirts and heavy shirts had a definite purpose.

Arrange boys and girls in their proper places—at opposite ends of the room—to begin the day's lessons. Instruct the boys in ciphering, Latin, reading, and writing. Teach the girls the finer points of domestic arts and allow them to read from the Scriptures. Remind students about the consequences of unseemly behavior: Smiling or talking out of turn might be punishable by a good switching; talking with someone of the opposite sex could result in a dunking.

If students survive into the afternoon, treat them to entertainment—bobbing for apples, cutting out a jack-o'-lantern, square dancing, and telling tall tales.

At day's end, most students will express respect for our pioneer heritage—and for modern conveniences.—*Ralph Covington, Jr., Concord, N.C.*

The olden days

To give your students a greater understanding of changing times, have them do some comparisons of school life today, in their parents' and grandparents' days, and in the times they're studying.

To find out what school was like for their parents and grandparents, they can develop a take-home questionnaire that asks such things as:

• How far was school from your home?

• How did you get there?

• How many children were in your class? How many were in your school?

• What subjects did you study that aren't taught today? What subjects didn't you study that we study today?

• What games did you play at recess?

• What did you like best about school? What did you like least?

Share the responses. Then, have your students try to find or imagine answers for the historic period they're learning about in class. Finally, they might enjoy writing their own answers to the questions. Compile all the various answers into a booklet for the whole class to read.—*Julie S. Polak, Bucyrus, Ohio*

A constitution is born

To make the dramatic times of the U.S. Constitution's beginnings come alive, focus on the event as though it were a feature film "coming to a theater near you," and on the leaders of the day as popular film stars.

After studying the Constitutional Convention of 1787 (perhaps role-playing some of its colorful debates), encourage your students to name the film by making a play on popular film titles with the Constitution theme in mind. For example: *Who Framed the Constitution? Dirty Debating,* and *Red-Coat Busters.* Talk about how to involve an audience in drama, and ask students to suggest "good story" aspects of this historic happening. Have your students then work in small groups to develop advertising posters

for the film.

As a first step in poster production, your students need to recall effective advertising strategies they've seen. Next, have them list the kinds of information the poster should include: the title, the stars, art depicting a crucial scene, praise from the critics, attention-getting adjectives, and the rating designation.

Have each group present its completed poster to advertise the film. Include these questions as part of the poster presentation: What aspects of the convention provided dramatic appeal for these films? Why did groups select the stars they did?—*Jackie Johnson, Denver*

A monumental task

To spice up your study of American symbols and landmarks, invite your students to create their own patriotic monument.

Discuss the idea of establishing a West Coast counterpart to New York's Statue of Liberty. Someone once suggested the country should have a Statue of Responsibility on the West Coast to complement the East Coast's Statue of Liberty. What reasons might there have been for the suggested pairing of *liberty* and *responsibility*? What other qualities might be appropriate for the partner landmark? What forms could such a landmark take? Where might the West Coast landmark be located?

After raising some of these questions, suggest that your students—working in pairs or individually—create a West Coast landmark. They should decide on its theme and form, explain its symbolism, and provide a rationale for selecting the quality symbolized.

Students may demonstrate their thinking in a number of ways, possibly using illustrations or models along with oral or written reports. Encourage them to include a quoted or original inscription, such as the Statue of Liberty's poem welcoming the "huddled masses yearning to breathe free."—*Sister Mary Philip De Camara, Washington, D.C.*

No law and order

For a social studies lesson that evokes strong images, ask your students to imagine what life would be like without laws or rules. At first, the kids might be elated thinking about the joys of anarchy, but then they'll probably admit to the likelihood of some inconvenience and even disorder.

List the chaotic possibilities students mention according to jurisdiction: school, city, state, nation. Suggest that each student pick from each of the four categories a chaotic situation to illustrate and caption, storyboard style, on a large piece of construction paper. Staple the four-panel pictures together to create a class booklet on no-rules chaos.—*Denise Lee, Springhouse, Pa.*

Getting-out-of-jams jar

You can help students know what to do when they get in a "jam" by inviting them to dip into the Jam Jar.

Decorate the front of a large jar with a strawberry, grape, or other popular jam fruit. Then give each student a corresponding fruit shape made from construction paper. Now discuss different types of jams, such as being home alone and suddenly seeing smoke coming from the kitchen or playing in the park with a friend who has a bad fall.

Ask each student to write an original jam on his fruit cutout. Place all the jams in the Jam Jar and then invite each child to take one. Have students write short stories or solutions that explain how they got out of, or solved, their jams. Invite students to share their solutions with the class.—*T.S. White, Omaha*

All assembled

Help your students understand how the assembly line changed both production processes and products with this simulation.

Arrange most of the class in two semicircular rows with the same number in each, say 10 and 10. These rows will be assembly lines A and B. Each student will assume the role of a worker with a specialized task.

Students will be building a car. Before class, plan a car consisting of 10 parts. Each part will be a job for one of your assembly-line workers. For example, the outline of the body is skill number one; the front fender, skill number two; a window, skill number three, and so on. Draw the car on the chalkboard and label the parts with corresponding numbers.

Assign Assembly lines A and B identical tasks. The first worker in each line gets 25 sheets of paper. This worker draws the outline of the car on a sheet and, before drawing the outline on the second sheet, passes the first sheet to worker two, who draws in a fender. The papers progress down both lines and the cars grow. Students are to draw the parts identically each time—same size, same shape, no spontaneous creativity allowed.

The students not in the assembly lines are craftsmen who build cars from scratch. They begin their work as the assembly lines get started.

When the assembly lines have completed their quotas, collect their cars and the custom-built models. Discuss how and why the products are different and which method was faster. Have workers in both production methods discuss their feelings about their jobs. Discuss also any problems that arose—pile-ups, uneven distribution of work—and possible solutions.—*S.B. Hirni, North Kansas City, Mo.*

Uniformity and diversity

To illustrate the dangers of trying to fit people into molds, invite your students to look for examples of "equalizers": form letters, "one-size-fits-all" labels, ads aimed at "everybody," uniformity in theater seats and other standard equipment. Then have students look for ways in which degrees of diversity are accommodated: variety in foods, sizes of clothing, choices and "adjustables" in other consumer goods, individual health care, provisions for the needs of special groups.

As a follow-up exercise, invite your students to design two cities: the absolute "melting pot"—where everything is built for the "average person" and there are standard procedures for all circumstances; and the ultimate overspecialized society—in which everything must be custom-built to unique specifications and no groupings of any kind are allowed.—*Denise Lee, Springhouse, Pa.*

Supply and demand

Teach your students the concept of supply and demand in a way that hits home—by having them bid on a limited supply of good grades!

Tell your students to prepare for a quiz. While they're clearing their desks, walk around the room with a box of cardboard coins or tokens, each bearing a specific value. Have each student take five or six.

Announce that only those students who write in green pencil will get A's on the quiz and that you happen to have some green pencils. Pull out only five pencils and offer to "rent" them to students who are willing to pay for them with the coins or tokens. Start the bids— "Do I hear a dime?"—and keep the bidding going until you've reached a point where the pencil is overpriced. Repeat the auctioning, until you've rented the five pencils.

Now, suddenly pull out 20 more pencils (or enough for the rest of the class), and wait for the reaction. Ask the students who rented the overpriced pencils to explain their motivation. Ask if they'd have paid the same amount for the pencils if they'd known there were enough to go around.

Write the terms "supply" and "demand" on the board and ask students to define each term in the context of their experience at the pencil auction. Mention examples of other items for which demand might exceed supply, such as popular toys or in-demand concert tickets. Ask your students to come up with their own examples. Then ask them what they think might have happened if you'd given them a day to furnish their own green pencils or if you'd told them that the first five green pencils were the only ones on earth.—*Rosemary Faucette, Fayetteville, Ark.*

PENCILS FOR RENT

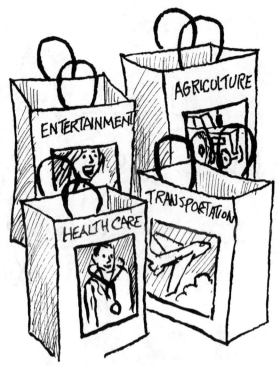

Career kits

To broaden your students' awareness of the diversity of occupations, create career kits for them to browse through.

Clip informational items and pictures from magazines, newspapers, and pamphlets showing people in various kinds of work. To complement these materials, add cassette tapes of interviews with people at work. Parents could add insights through a questionnaire which you and your class draw up and send home. Sample questions: Where do you work? What kinds of things do you do? What do you like best about your job?

Arrange the collection into categories— health care, education, transportation, communication, service occupations, social work, entertainment, agriculture. Then prepare a shopping bag with handles to hold each classification. Label each bag with its appropriate category; add a picture if you like.

Display your kits on a coat tree or pegboard with hooks. In addition to independent browsing, use the kits for resource information for study units and panel discussions, and for story-writing fodder.—*Florence Rives, Selma, Ala.*

A hunger banquet

You can teach your students—and their parents—about world hunger in a direct way when you organize a hunger banquet. Participation is voluntary and might not be appropriate for younger children.

On the day of the banquet, have participants skip breakfast and lunch. At dinnertime, randomly give each person a packet representing a country. The packet contains economic information about the country and tokens for "buying" dinner in the cafeteria. The number of tokens varies from packet to packet, reflecting the economic status of the country: A U.S. packet has enough tokens for two complete dinners; a Mexico packet has enough for a small dish of rice; an Ethiopia packet has no tokens.

Encourage your students to observe patterns emerging among people who have food. Some might become greedy and hoard it; others might offer to share. Before the end of the evening, make sure everyone *does* eat a full meal, then invite them to discuss their feelings and reactions.—*Rosetta Cohen, New York, N.Y.*

Peopling statistics

Here's a dramatic way to emphasize how many people die each week as a result of drunk-driving accidents. Get the current figures from the National Highway Traffic and Safety Administration. Say the number is 326. Don't just state this figure to your students, *show* it to them.

On a piece of paper, draw shapes of men, women, and children. Make enough copies to produce 326 figures. Every morning, without explanation or comment, ask each student to cut out several figures, draw faces and clothing on them, and post them in rows on the board.

Continue this for 1 week—until you've used 326 figures. At that point, introduce the statistic about alcohol-related accidents. Students will have a vivid picture of the average number of people who die every week as a result of drunk driving. Have them figure out the yearly average from this weekly one.—*John A. Slavik, Wheaton, Ill.*

Needs vs. wants

Needs and wants are often confused with each other, and advertisers try to play on this ambiguity. Help kids pinpoint the difference between needs and wants by holding a class discussion on the subject, then assembling a "Needs" folder and a "Wants" or "Wishes" folder.

Invite your students to put into the "Needs" folder magazine or newspaper ads for items that are necessities. In the "Wants" folder, they put pictures of things that they'd like to have but can live without. As a wrap-up, hold a discussion including such questions as, "Was it easier to find ads for needs or wants?" and "What do your findings tell you about products offered in advertisements?"—*Shirley S. Cummings, East Lansing, Mich.*

I read it on a T-shirt

To make sure your students give more than a passing glance to data researched by classmates, have the researchers put that data on "T-shirts."

Suppose your students are researching facts on American states: major cities, products, tourist spots, the land, history, and so on. Each student selects one fact for each state, thinks up a slogan depicting that fact, and writes the slogan on a construction-paper T-shirt. Examples include "South Dakota: Home of Mount Rushmore" and "Idaho: No. 1 in Potatoes." Display the finished T-shirts on a clothesline.

Select a few shirts each day to highlight and discuss. Alert your researchers so they're ready to provide further information for the class.—*Sandra Frey, Lancaster, Pa.*

Say it with comics

Try an offbeat approach to research report writing: the research comic book.

The comic-book format of drawings and dialogue lends itself to many social studies topics. For example, students studying the Middle Ages can use it to present facts about a serf's life or a knight's daily routine in pictures and dialogue.

For the serf topic, you might start your students off by giving these directions: Life as a serf wasn't so great. What can you find out about how serfs lived? After doing your research, plot out a fact-filled story with serfs as the main characters; plan for about 20 comic-book-style frames. Use conversations between characters—in speech balloons—to tell the story and to share what you've learned.

The comic-book report could be done in booklet form or as a continuous panel of paper rolled into a scroll.—*Karen Ehman, San Carlos, Calif.*

Urban renewal

For an out-of-the-ordinary research project, have students redesign America's cities.

Invite each student to choose a state capital. Then announce that the center of each of these cities needs to be redesigned and rebuilt. After researching the city, each student develops a plan for its renewal. Stress that the city's center should reflect the great achievements and noted personalities of its past.

Students decide what will be memorialized and by which means—street names, parks, monuments, schools, museums. When the planning is complete, students map out their renewed city center with labels indicating the commemorative structures. Then students prepare background materials explaining the rationale for their memorials.

As students share their city plans, they might be able to attach history to places for easier recall. They might also discover that some famous people—such as Franklin and Lincoln—pop up in a number of different cities.—*James W. McCoy, Provo, Utah*

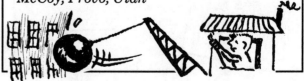

Dressing the part

When it's time for your students to research and report on a state, have them dress as residents—past or present—of that state.

For example, a child who researched Massachusetts might dress as a pilgrim; Oregon, a fur trapper or an Indian; Kentucky, a horseback rider. Or researchers might wear costumes representing noted persons from their states—Kansan Amelia Earhart, New Mexican Kit Carson, or Ohioan John Glenn.

You also can invite your students to make food a part of their reports. Suggest that they find out about foods raised or processed in their chosen states and bring a "state snack" to class. Students are likely to remember reports on Arkansas, Maine, and Washington that include chicken soup, potato salad, and golden delicious apples.
—*Maureen A. Bauer, Traverse City, Mich.*

"Paste-and-post" cards

When you're ready to review your next social studies unit, try this new approach: Have your students create picture postcards illustrating key concepts.

To do this, you'll need stacks of heavily illustrated magazines, 4 x 6-inch cards, scissors, and rubber cement. On one side of a card, students paste one or more pictures. On the other side, leaving room for an address and a message, they write a caption tying the pictures to the study unit.

Students can use the postcards to send messages to friends, relatives, or teachers. The cards are also a good way to keep in touch with a student who's sick or who's moved away.—*Jule Marine, Salt Lake City*

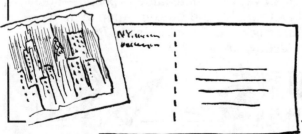

Alma mater investigations

To help spark kids' interest in their school and develop valuable research skills in the process, try posing some trivia questions about the school for students to investigate and answer. For example:

- How many pictures hang in the auditorium?
- In what year was the school dedicated, and where in the building is that information prominently displayed?
- For whom was the school named, and where would you find a portrait of this person?

When students have researched and discussed a few of these kinds of questions, encourage them to make up questions of their own about the school to exchange with classmates and perhaps other classes.—*Mark N. Chester, Brooklyn, N.Y.*

Personality pop-ups

For a memorable lesson on historic figures, invite your students to create pop-up puzzle boxes.

Have each student choose a personality from the past and select five important facts about that person, including one or two that aren't well known. Students then phrase their facts as five single-sentence clues to the identity of their famous persons.

Next, students prepare boxes by covering small milk cartons with paper and replacing the tops with tagboard flaps. Students write their five clues on individual slips of paper and attach each to one face of the box. (Leave the bottoms of the cartons blank.) Now students make drawings of the head and shoulders of their famous people. Drawings should fit inside their boxes upright without being bent.

To make the pop-up feature of their puzzle boxes, students fashion a spring from two paper strips, each 18 inches long and 1 inch wide. Here's how:

1. Place one end of strip A over one end of strip B at a right angle.
2. Fold strip B over strip A at a right angle.
3. Now fold A over B, again at a right angle.
4. Continue to fold the strips in this alternating pattern, maintaining the right angle. Fix the last fold in place with glue.
5. Glue one end of the paper spring to the inside of the box; the other to the famous person's picture.
6. Press the spring down to lower the picture into the box, and lightly fasten the lid with a small piece of tape.

Have your students exchange their puzzle boxes with a friend for a biographic challenge.—*Elizabeth Osga, Stonington, Conn.*

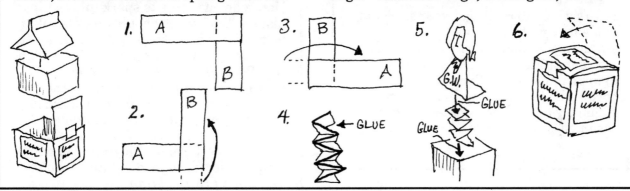

The mystery guest

This activity gives students a chance to research interesting personalities—both past and present—and also challenges them to stump their classmates.

On Friday, secretly tell a student that he's to represent next Friday's "Mystery Guest" and tell him whom he should portray. It could be someone in a unit you're studying, the author of a book currently being read, even a seasonal "guest."

Monday through Thursday of the following week, the student secretly gives you a clue to help the class identify the Mystery Guest. Put the clue on a "Mystery Guest Clue Board" hanging in the room. Throughout the week, students place their guesses of the Mystery Guest's identity in a box near the clue board.

On Friday, the featured student comes to school dressed as the Mystery Guest. Tally the guesses in the box; the student then gives a 5- to 10-minute monologue about the Mystery Guest's life and accomplishments as if he were the famous person.—*Ann Marie Stalteri, Lansdowne, Pa.*

Split personalities

Here's a way to really get your students to identify with the people they're researching. Without warning, start calling your students by their research figure's name. Have them write the report in the first person, then present a summary to their classmates under their assumed identity.—*Matthew Kelley, Meriden, Conn.*

List with a twist

Have your students make a list of famous people who have the same *first* name as they do. (Encourage them to get help from parents, librarians, and friends.) Then ask them to select and research one of those people for a 5-minute oral report. After they summarize the highlights of their subject's life, ask your students to note any similarities between their life and their subject's. Even students who'd be reluctant to talk only about themselves will enjoy pointing out some interesting comparisons.—*Ruth Badal, Oswego, Ill.*

Biographic acrostics

Spark new interest in biography reporting by inviting your students to write their reports in the form of acrostics. Demonstrate the style with this acrostic about inventor Alexander Graham Bell:

Beginning with the telephone,
Experimenter extraordinaire
    Alexander Graham Bell
Launched decades of inventions that
Led to hydrofoils, hang gliders,
    helicopters, and air conditioners.

Challenge students to create longer "reports" by using a person's first *and* last names.—*Sue Nations, Sylva, N.C.*

A moment in history

Here's an easy way to spark interest in history. Each week choose an unfamiliar historic person or event and ask your students to guess the mystery subject's identity. Post daily clues on the bulletin board to help students zero in on the correct name or event. At the end of the designated time period, ask your students to make their guesses. When the puzzle is solved, post a short biography or description for all to read.—*Nanette Johnson, Eden Prairie, Minn.*

Working undercover

By adding some intrigue to your classroom, you can help students discover the excitement of reading about other people.

First, read a biography of a well-known person yourself. When you're finished, tell the class you're a "mystery guest" who's described in a book found in the school library. Give the students a few hints, then have them guess who you are by asking questions that you can answer yes or no to.

After students identify you, invite them to become guests themselves by carrying out an "undercover mission"—reading a biography. Give them these procedures to follow:

- Sneak into the library and choose a biography of someone whose identity you'd like to assume. Maintain a low profile as you read the book; reading at home guarantees maximum security. If you read in school, use a book cover.
- Prepare a data card: Write unusual facts about yourself as the "guest" and clues to your identity.
- When you're ready to be the guest, sign in secretly with the teacher.

Help students prepare for their guest appearances with private warm-up sessions.
—*Mary Wilson, Chandler, Ariz.*

Biography reports—with pictures

Here's a *different* way for your students to learn about historic figures. They'll team up to gather research, share ideas, and create a fascinating bulletin board in the process.

Choose a famous person your class is going to study. Divide your students into groups, and have each group research a different time period in the person's life, including early childhood.

Now cover a bulletin board with drawing paper and divide it to give the groups equal space. Ask the groups to think of a representative scene from their time period and plan a drawing of it for the bulletin board. Then, have the groups take turns drawing the scene on their assigned sections of the board. As a wrap-up, a spokesperson from each group reports their findings.—*Florence Rives, Selma, Ala.*

Reading, writing, and news

Cultivate a current-events tree and improve your students' language skills along with their awareness of the world around them.

First, find a large tree branch with plenty of smaller branches. Then, anchor it in a pot. To fill the tree with current events, have your students help you clip short, interesting news items. Try to get a balance of local, state, national, and international stories. For each item, prepare two questions:

• a content question (either factual or opinion/discussion)

• a language arts question based on recently introduced skills (such as naming synonyms or recognizing main ideas).

Mount each item and its questions on a card, using a different color for each category. Hang the cards on the tree. Keep two folders near the tree: one for blank answer paper and color-coded answer keys, and one for finished work.

Every 2 weeks, make the tree bloom with new stories and tasks that reinforce new lessons.—*Mary Modlin, Tarboro, N.C.*

Focus on what's important

Bolster critical thinking skills by inviting your students to analyze what makes certain news events more important than others.

First, divide your students into several groups. Give each group the day's issue of the same newspaper. Have the groups examine the front-page stories and headlines and ask themselves how newspaper editors decide which stories to put on the front page.

Now have the class discuss the attributes of the events covered in the front-page articles. Here are some points to consider:

• How many people have been and will be affected by the event?

• How will the event affect other parts of the world?

• How often does an event like this happen?

• How unusual is the event?

• Is the issue something new, or about a significant change in something that has been going on for a long time?

• Where did the event happen—someplace local or far away?

• What might be the long-term effects?

• What do people like to read about?

After the discussion, have each group list the day's major stories in order of importance. Collect the lists and newspapers and store them. Three months later, ask your students if they can remember the most important stories in the news 3 months ago. After some discussion, return their lists and ask a few volunteers to retell the stories as best they can.

Is there one story the kids remember more clearly than the others? Is it the same story that appears first on their lists? Would the students rank the original stories in the same order if they reread them today? Discuss how events that transpired during the last 3 months changed or reinforced their priorities and their perspectives. Also discuss how time—even as short an interval as 3 months—affected the significance of the stories.—*Donald Lankiewicz, Columbus, Ohio*

You are there

Inject a sense of immediacy into current events by having your students imagine themselves right into a situation. Bring in intriguing newspaper articles, particularly ones that leave the reader with unanswered questions—for example, an account of explorers discovering a previously unknown tribe, a report on a kidnapped diplomat, or a science article predicting the coming of a new Ice Age.

Read the articles aloud and discuss them with the class. Use a map to pinpoint the setting of each event, and then have students write their own first-person accounts in which they imagine themselves participants. Encourage them to add missing facts and invent outcomes. Ask for volunteers to read their stories to the class.—*Fran Bush, Ogden, Utah*

News makers gallery

This distinctive bulletin board highlights people in the news and doubles as a research and writing resource.

Each Monday post a newsmagazine cover featuring a personality your students will find appealing. Also post a one-sentence caption identifying the person's newsworthy actions. Ask for a volunteer to do further research and prepare a one-paragraph report on a 5 x 7 card to read to the class at the end of the week. Post the paragraph with the picture.

The following week move the picture and its paragraph from the featured spot to a sidelines position in the gallery. The center spot is then ready for a new news maker. Add to the gallery lineup for several months.

Encourage your students to adopt a news maker, keep track of the person's activities, and report to the class periodically. Then file away the portraits and their cards in separate folders. Your students can use the files later for matching activities.

During the school year, periodically stage a news makers-in-review quiz show during which you display several selected portraits for your students to identify and discuss.—*Bonnie Dunbar Egeland, Pittsburgh*

Keeping current

Here's a way to encourage your students to share current-events items they read in newspapers or magazines.

Prepare a reproducible that has a line for the student's name, and space for the student to enter the article headline and date, a brief summary of the main idea followed by important details, and a parent's signature. Ask your students to take the reproducible home and complete it when they've found an article to share.

Having a parent sign the form increases the chance that your students will go over the facts with a parent. That way, they'll feel more confident—and be better prepared to answer questions—when they discuss the item with the entire class.—*Tom Bernagozzi, Bay Shore, N.Y.*

Student's Name

Article Headline and Date

Brief Summary

Important Details

Parent's Signature

Dollar bill history

When your students *really* examine a dollar bill, they'll find there's more there than what meets the eye.

Divide the class into small groups and give each a dollar bill (and a magnifying glass if possible). Allow each group 5 minutes to list all the items they can find that are grouped in sets of 13. If you like, give them the hint that they'll find the items on the back of the bill.

Here are the items they should find: Across the eagle's chest are 13 stripes. In one talon the eagle is holding 13 arrows; in the other, an olive branch with 13 leaves. Above the eagle's head are 13 stars. There are 13 "steps" to the unfinished pyramid.

When students have compiled their lists, discuss their findings. Encourage students to speculate on their symbolism. They'll probably realize that "13" represents the 13 original colonies, but do they know that the eagle's nine tail feathers represent the number of states ratifying the Constitution? That the olive branch and arrows symbolize the desire for peace and the readiness to protect the country? That the eye represents the eye of God? That the unfinished pyramid signifies that more states would be added? Or that the roman numeral at the base of the pyramid is 1776?—*Mary Skavinski, Covina, Calif.*

A priceless lesson

Ask your students to find out whose portrait now appears on each denomination of our paper bills. Then, as a class, discuss why these people might have been selected. Next, invite each student to suggest a public figure—past or present—for a new bill. Have them design the bill, including a picture of their candidate on it. On a separate sheet, have students write a biographic paragraph about their candidate and the reasons for their choice.

As a follow-up, ask your students to imagine that *they* have been chosen to appear on a new bill. Have them write stories of how, when, and why they were honored. Invite them to paste a personal snapshot on play money or to design their own money around their portrait. Display the "money" with their stories.
—*Shirley T. Shratter, Pittsburgh*

Every coin tells a story

Capitalize on children's fascination with money to develop their research and organization skills as well as their knowledge of American history.

With your students' help, make a complete collection of U.S. coins in circulation. Make pencil rubbings of both sides of each coin, and compile the rubbings into a booklet—one page for each coin. Find out the names of all those pictured on our paper currency, and add this information to the booklet as well.

Now have your students work in teams to research the background of each person or event pictured on the money. Have the teams write brief biographic or historic sketches to accompany the various coin rubbings or names. To complete the booklet, add a construction-paper cover and a title such as "Honoring Americans on Money."
—*Ruth Hilterbrand, Ewing, Ky.*

Chapter 8
THINKING SKILLS

Creating rebuses that add up

Picture this: 2 cookies + 3 hungry kids = ? An argument? Crumbs? Unlike most equations students encounter, the answer to this one is open for discussion—and imagination.

Picture/language equations can be tricky to create at first, but a few examples should help get your students started. Display on a bulletin board several picture/language equations. For example:

Ask students to "read" them aloud, then challenge them to create rebus equations of their own. When they get the hang of plus-and-minus equations, challenge them to create equations involving multiplication or division. For example: 1 cake ÷ Jack Sprat + Mrs. Sprat = 1 large piece + 1 tiny piece (no remainder).

Students may work in groups brainstorming equation material and the pictures that might interpret each situation. Encourage them to draw on literature, history, sports, and so on, for ideas. Then have students draw or cut out pictures for their rebuses and add their finished equations to the bulletin board display.—*Bernice Cohan, Riverdale, N.J.*

Super sales talk

Challenge your creative thinkers to come up with some persuasive advertising copy—for posters, TV spots, catchy jingles. The catch is that these ads are for utterly useless products, such as a broken window, a jacket with three sleeves, two right shoes, a glass with no bottom, a dead plant, used staples, and so on.

To get your copywriters on the right track, make sure they include in their ads these points:

1. How could this product be useful?
2. Is there any particular sort of person who might need this product more than others?
3. What modifications or accessories are available?
4. Why would a person be getting his money's worth in buying this product?

Display the ads around the room and invite students to cast their votes for "The Most Persuasive Ad."—*Portia Burke and Ellen Alquist, Rancho Cordova, Calif.*

Creative excuses

This fun—and funny— activity will test your students' creative powers.

Begin by having the class break into groups of five or six. Then tell the groups they're to come up with excuses to "Why I don't have my homework." Choose a way to rotate turns (for example, alphabetically by name, or tallest to shortest).

Here's the twist: The first student must use as many A's in his answer as possible; the second student, as many B's, and so on. For example, Student No. 1 might say, "Because an ape ate it." Student No. 2 might say, "Because my brother beat it with a bat."

When students run out of excuses, change the question to another zany topic, such as why running in the halls isn't allowed (it would make our ankles ache) or what's for lunch (alphabet soup and animal crackers).—*Carmen Ritter Hannah, Corunna, Mich.*

Skill-sheet designers

Get your students *creating* instead of just *doing* by having them make their own skill sheets—from start to finish.

First, ask your students to compare the layouts, main ideas, and types of questions on various skill sheets. Then, using the most interesting traits, make some sample pages together; coach your students on writing clear directions, choosing important information, and stating objectives.

Next, have your students plan skill sheets, based on any textbook or trade book. Advise them to read the material carefully, then reread it, pulling out the most important facts for the project.

Make copies of the best skill sheets for everyone to try. Let the creator of each be the "teacher" and grade the others' work. You can file some away for use with next year's class too.—*Julie Polak, Bucyrus, Ohio*

TV tie-in

Capitalize on children's fascination with TV to help them increase their thinking skills. Here's how.

First, ask students to list their favorite TV programs in order of preference. Next, design a series of activities around the most popular programs. Here are a few examples:

- **Recognizing fact and fantasy.** Choose events from a specific program and ask students to discuss those that could really happen and those that could not.
- **Supporting conclusions.** Ask the class to draw five conclusions about a TV character. Have each student write three details that support those conclusions.
- **Forming comparisons.** Select two similar programs (such as two favorite sitcoms) and ask students which setting they'd prefer to live in and why.

- **Sequencing.** Have students summarize an episode of a program. Guide them by using a format such as: *The story started when _____. After that, _____. Next, _____. Then, _____. The problem was solved when _____*
- **Distinguishing facts from opinions.** Ask students to quote TV ads about well-known products, then to discuss which are based on fact and which on opinion. How do they tell the difference?—*Louise Soper, Elfers, Fla.*

Editorial comparisons

When your students read a news item, do they distinguish fact from opinion? Do they notice when information isn't given? Try using different newspapers and newsmagazines to encourage critical thinking.

Have students collect newspapers and magazines for a few days. From these, each student selects a news story that interests him. He should then cut out articles on that topic from at least three sources and compare them. Does one have more information or a different approach from another? How are the articles similar? What article seems to be the most objective? The most biased?

Invite students to give oral reports or make charts showing the differences among articles.—*Denise Lee, Springhouse, Pa.*

FACT vs. OPINION

On the other hand...

To help students understand that not all questions and answers come in neat pairs, pose a problem of crisis proportions with no clear-cut solution:

You are the chief surgeon at a big hospital. You must make a decision about four patients in need of heart transplants. There is just one donor. Assuming all the patients could receive this heart, which one would you choose? (1) a famous brain surgeon at the height of his career; (2) a 12-year-old musician; (3) a 40-year-old lawyer; (4) an expectant mother.

Divide the class into small groups to discuss the case. After 20 to 25 minutes, bring the class together to share ideas and grounds for decisions.

Such decision-making forums can lead to other activities. Students might want to investigate the difficult decisions involved in such fields as environment, city planning, economics, foreign relations.—*Herb Bacon, Pedricktown, N.J.*

Think pads

You can encourage kids to think before they raise their hands by giving each student a scratch pad. The pads will also ensure that everybody participates, not just those you call on.

Make the pads by stapling together small pieces of blank paper. Younger children can use the pads to answer yes and no questions, to write a number answer, or to copy an answer from a word list on the board. Older children can use the pads to write down key words or phrases they want to use to answer more substantive questions.

This note making lets kids collect and organize their thoughts instead of rushing to prove their knowledge with a quick raise of the hand.—*Elizabeth A. Lowser, Seattle*

Be prepared

Have your students practice thinking cyclically, and they'll see that forewarned is forearmed. Have them brainstorm for cyclical problems they might have noticed—for example, classroom discipline problem every Friday or flu epidemics in February.

Or invite students to invent possible cycles such as:

- an angry mood that seems to afflict parents every September
- world wars every 20 years
- ice ages that occur every 20,000 years and last 1,000 years.

Then they can challenge the class to come up with personal or governmental plans to solve these problems.—*Denise Lee, Springhouse, Pa.*

Statistical scrutiny

Here's a way to give your students first-hand experience in gathering data and drawing conclusions. And it will help them understand the difference between statistical projections and actual facts.

First select a textbook, choose a page at random, and carefully count the number of times the letter *a* appears on that page. Ask students to individually make the same count and submit their tallies to a "statistician," who records the different tallies on the chalkboard. Have students discuss which number is right; then take a recount.

Next have students work in small groups to estimate the number of times the letter *a* appears in the whole book. They'll need to determine an average number of *a*'s per page; they'll also need to decide whether to include the introduction and index in their count.

When the results are in, have your students consider the following:

- Do we have an accurate figure for the total number of *a*'s in the book?
- What can we conclude from the data we have? What kinds of conclusions wouldn't be wise?
- Based on the number of people in your room, estimate the number of people in your building. In what circumstances would this estimate be useful? When would it be unwise to use this figure?
- What if you brought in cupcakes for a class based on the average number of children in a classroom?
- How would you compare the methods we've used in this project with the methods used in conducting the census of the U.S. population? How do you think the number of deer or hawks or coyotes in the state is determined? (You might see if you can find an "outside expert" to come in and help with this point.)—*Karl Engleka, Titusville, Pa.*

a's per page?

Student workbook teams

Get the most from workbook and skill-sheet practice by putting your students in charge of reviewing their own work. Here's how to get the process going:

- Organize your students into teams of two.
- With the daily assignment, give each student a checklist such as the one shown here.

> **Partner Checklist**
>
> 1. Name: _____
>   Partner: _____
>
> 2. Pages assigned: _____
> _____
>
> 3. My partner didn't finish the following pages:
> _____
>
> 4. My answers matched my partner's answers on pages: _____
>
> 5. Some of our answers did *not* match on the following pages: Page   Problem numbers
>
>   _____   _____
>
>   _____   _____

- When most of your students have finished the assignment, have them compare answers with their partners.
- Tell your students to fill in their checklists. Where their answers don't match their partners' answers, ask them to find the reasons for the discrepancies.
- Listen as your students confer over their checklists. Did they get the material wrong because directions were unclear, because they were rushing, or because they needed more practice?
- When your students have finished checking, ask which work sheet they found most helpful and why.

From the beginning, you can get your students off on the right foot: As you discuss the assignments and give directions, ask your students why they think you're assigning a particular page. They'll begin to identify what they already know and what they still need to work on.—*Will Harpest and Ruth E. Badal, Oswego, Ill.*

Comprehension challenges

Supplement your basal reader's end-of-the-selection questions and activities with some real thought-provokers to help your students analyze story characters and their actions. For example:

- Which character is most like you? Why?
- Write to a character in the story and ask questions about what happened after the story.
- What kind of student do you think each character would be? Make a report card for each one.
- What kind of gift would you give each of the characters? Why?
- Which of the characters would you like to have as a friend? Why?
- Pretend you're one of the characters. How

would you change the story?

- Would substituting boys for girls and vice versa affect the story? Explain.
- Change the roles of the characters. Make a hero out of a villain and a villain out of a hero. How will this change the story?— *Mildred J. Sims, Champaign, Ill.*

Inventive adventures

You probably have on hand all you need for an "inventions box": paper clips, strips of paper, pencils, ribbon, pipe cleaners, fabric scraps, buttons, spools, cans, wire, bottle caps. Now it's up to your students to decide what to make of the junk.

Have your students pick partners. Then each student selects an item from your "invention box," and partners collaborate to see what they can invent with their two items.

As they work out their invention, students should keep in mind that they'll need to name the invention; write a short description of it, telling what it's made of and how it works; and make up a commercial to help sell the product to the class.

After partners show off their inventions and air their commercials, compile the written descriptions into a class book of inventions.—*Sharon Ackerman, Leesburg, Va.*

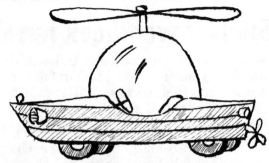

Idea of the decade

To get your students in an inventive frame of mind, ask what new invention they'd like to see in the next 10 years. Is it a better bicycle, skateboard, car, school? Challenge them, working in groups or individually, to dream up an invention that would either improve something, solve a problem, or fill a need. Invite them to draw a picture or make a model of their inventions. Have them describe what it does, how it works, why it's needed, and who'll use it.— *Denise Lee, Springhouse, Pa.*

No-paper-day alternatives

Doing without paper for one school day could be a revealing experience in creative coping. Work with your students to establish alternative ways of handling the usual paper-dependent activities. Play more games, make the chalkboard center stage for more events, hold a spelling bee. Science explorations will likely go on without a hitch, while paperless art projects may take some thought.

Each new task becomes a subject for analysis and cooperative planning as students discover new—and old—ways to do things. At the end of the day, along with reviewing your creative approaches of the day, think about how many trees you saved.—*Phyllis Fox Stump, Richmond, Va.*

Fun and egg-citement

Challenge your students by having them invent games using one or more egg cartons as their basic material. Students must assemble their creations and write out their rules and directions. After exchanging games so that classmates can critique them and help with debugging, invite students to select names and prices, design packaging, and write ads for their products.—*Patricia Harris, Fairborn, Ohio*

Disks, rings, and loopy things

To help your students think inventively, have them explore the artistic possibilities in a single shape, such as a circle.

You'll need different-size circular templates or traceable items, construction paper, felt-tip pens, glue, staplers, scissors, and tape. To start, have your students trace circles on construction paper and cut them out. Then challenge them to think about what a circle could become—a person, an orange, a hole, a wheel, a button, an eye. Then ask them to incorporate their ideas in circle-motif art. They might also modify the basic circular shape by cutting out the centers to make rings or by folding and layering the circles to create three-dimensional pieces.—*Sister Ann Claire Rhoads, Emmitsburg, Md.*

Turning on inventiveness

Turn everyday activities into opportunities for the step-by-step exploratory thinking that warms up inventiveness. Here are a few ideas to get you started:

• Suggest that students think of ways to hold things together without using glue, paste, or any other stickum. Ask them to look around the room, find two things to join, think of a nonsticking way to join them, and share it with the class (tying, pinning, braiding...).

• Invite your students to demonstrate ways—other than walking—of crossing an open space. Have students stand in a circle and ask each in turn to cross the circle without walking and without repeating any mode already used (sliding, scooting, somersaulting...).

• Ask students to imagine that they must leave an important message for someone, but they have no pencils, crayons, pens, or other writing tools. Have them think of ways to leave the message (glue, trails, carvings...).
—*Sharon Crawley and Lee Mountain, Houston*

Observation situation

Sharpen your students' observation skills by staging a prearranged "confrontation" right in your own classroom. Here's the scene:

You're in the middle of a lesson using the overhead projector when Mr. Smith interrupts your period to say he needs the overhead projector; in fact, he signed up for it weeks ago for this time. You say you'll be finished in a few minutes, but he insists he needs it now. *You try reasoning with him. His voice goes up a notch. You stand your ground, and he leaves.*

Immediately ask your students to take out paper and pencils and respond to the following:

1. Does Mr. Smith wear glasses? How was he dressed? What colors was he wearing?

2. Was Mr. Smith carrying anything?

3. What time did Mr. Smith come into the room? How long did he stay?

4. What started the argument?

5. How would you describe the actions and voices of the persons involved?

6. Give some direct quotations from the discussion.

Invite students to read their answers aloud. Most likely, the reports will vary widely. Encourage students to listen for the points of difference and the areas of general agreement. Discuss the reasons for the differences in the answers.

Before the end of the lesson, be sure to exonerate Mr. Smith, lest some students forget the event was staged.—*Ben Neideigh, New Hampton, Iowa*

Picture sorting

To help your students practice listening, following directions, and classifying, collect pictures of everyday items. Paste each to a 4 x 6-inch card, and laminate it if you like. Individually or in small groups, invite students to sort the cards according to your directions. For example:

- Find all the pictures that have something red in them.
- Find all the pictures of tools that are usually used in the kitchen.
- Find all the pictures of things that are alive.—*Lois Ann Dove, Federal Way, Wash.*

Shopping bag sort-out

Help your class explore the sorting possibilities in the contents of the typical shopping bag by focusing on where the various products will be stored at home.

Make a set of product cards and a set of category cards. Use labels, carton panels, and pictures cut from magazines to make product cards, such as freezer foods, refrigerator foods, pantry foods, cleaning products, and drug products. Category cards would consist of a picture of a refrigerator/freezer, large enough to accommodate a stack of product cards on each section; a picture of a kitchen cabinet or pantry shelves; a utility cabinet; and a medicine cabinet.

Have students shuffle the product cards, then sort them onto the appropriate category cards. If students work in pairs, the partners can check and discuss each other's choices.—*Joan Babika, Mentor, Ohio*

Chapter 9
ART

The hole thing

Pencils, scissors, glue, and sheets of construction paper are the only materials your students will need to experiment with this unusual Central American art technique. To make mola-type decorations, have your young artists follow these steps:

1. Select four different-colored sheets of construction paper. Fold the first sheet in half and cut a large, abstract-shaped hole in the center. Open the paper to create layer one.

2. Place layer one on top of your second sheet of paper. Draw on this layer cutting line—slightly inside and similar in shape to the hole in layer one. Cut along the cutting line to make a hole.

3. Place layer two on top of your third sheet of paper. Repeat the procedure described in step 2.

4. Your fourth—and uncut—sheet of paper will be the base for your design. Glue layer three on top of layer four; layer two on top of layer three; and layer one on top of layer two.

Encourage students to experiment with more layers of paper, or to cut out more than one hole in each layer.—*Marj Rife, Encino, Calif.*

"Schoolscapes"

Discover the art possibilities right in your own front yard by organizing a draw-the-school project. Because drawing the whole building can be somewhat daunting for the young student, divvy up the task by assigning only a section of the building to pairs of students.

Take your students outside to study and sketch their assigned sections. Have them include steps, cornerstones, windows, doors, shrubs, and other details in their sketches. When they return to the classroom, your students can transfer their sketches onto large pieces of colored construction paper. Help them standardize sizes so that the various sections will go together properly.

For a final touch, have your students draw, on separate paper, pictures of themselves in characteristic activities, then cut out the figures and place them around the building to add to the "schoolscape." Use the poster to welcome parents and other guests to your classroom.—*Constance B. Reeves, Haddonfield, N.J.*

Pastel surprises

This art activity carries a built-in surprise. It's also a technique on which children will enjoy creating variations.

For each student, you'll need assorted colors of 12 x 18-inch construction paper, 12 x 18-inch newsprint—or other lightweight paper, lots of colored chalk or pastels, and cotton balls. Here's what your students should do:

- Lay a newsprint sheet on top of a construction paper sheet and staple the two together across the top.
- Slip another newsprint sheet between the stapled-together sheets as a protector sheet.
- Raise the stapled newsprint sheet and tear a strip off the bottom. Tear slowly, trying to make an interesting edge with peaks and valleys.
- Apply colored chalk (one color or several) in a thick layer all along the torn edge of newsprint. Be sure the protector sheet is in place.
- Carefully remove the protector sheet. Using a cotton ball, rub chalk firmly downward from the newsprint onto the construction paper. Don't move the newsprint sheet until you've completed rubbing along the entire length of the torn edge; then raise the sheet and see the surprise results.
- Continue the tearing and chalking and rubbing until only a few inches of newsprint remain. Then remove the staples.

Now, students may mount the pastel "painting" or use the chalked paper as a background for an impressionistic drawing—a fantastic castle, an enchanted forest, a dreamlike portrait, even an underwater scene.—*Helen Randall, Oak Park, Ill.*

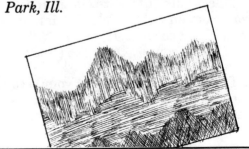

Complete portraits

If your students' self-portraits usually consist of a smiling face and nothing more, challenge them to include the rest of their fronts—and all of their backs too!

Ask each student to draw two portraits: one of the front, the other of the back. Portraits should show heads, toes, and everything in between, including belts, buttons, and zippers. Be sure students use their imaginations—not mirrors—to make their drawings.—*Gloria Gale, Prairie Village, Kan.*

Box puppets

This activity turns fast-food containers into versatile talking puppets.

To create their puppets, have students cover a hamburger container with construction paper. The opening will be the mouth. Students can use crayons, felt-tip pens, paper scraps, yarn, buttons, and the like to add facial features, including bushy brows, teeth, freckles, and scars. Encourage students to add plenty of hair, which will hide the puppeteer's hand.

Next, have students attach a strip of heavy paper (about 1 inch wide and 2½ inches long) to the bottom of the carton. Glue the strip on the ends only so it can serve as a strap into which the puppeteer inserts his thumb. The puppeteer can then manipulate the puppet by cupping his hand around the hinge of the carton—thumb underneath, fingers on the top part of the carton. By gently moving the thumb and fingers, the puppeteer can open and close the puppet's mouth.

The puppets can be made to represent a wide range of characters, from storybook figures to spokespersons for social studies debate issues.—*Diane Ebert, St. Louis*

Milk carton constructions

Turn milk cartons into building blocks and invite your students to create sizable constructions.

Ask students to bring in clean half-gallon cartons from home. To transform the cartons into bricks, open out the spout end, cutting down the four top seams and taping these flaps down to make a hollow rectangle. Next, wrap each carton tightly with old newspapers, taped in place to provide a surface that glue and paint will stick to.

Prepare the floor of your building by cutting butcher paper to the desired shape and size and taping it to the floor. (A simple 6-foot square makes a good size house for 1st graders.)

Help students lay the first row of bricks and glue them along the perimeter of the floor. (Be sure to leave a space for the door.) Erect walls a row at time, with drying time in between. White glue, well diluted with water, makes an excellent "mortar" and can be easily painted on. For greater wall strength, show students how to stagger the bricks. When the structure reaches its desired height, invite students to paint it.

When completed, put your structure to work as a reading room, carrel, stage setting, scenery, playhouse, or room divider.— *Sandra Plaskon, Imperial Beach, Calif.*

Postage-stamp art

For an inexpensive decoupage project, get your colleagues, your students, and their parents collecting used postage stamps—and a variety of containers: juice cans, note-paper boxes, coffee cans. To tackle the project, you'll also need glue, varnish, and brushes.

Give each student a collection of stamps and a container. Students can glue the stamps on their containers according to a color scheme or in a random fashion. However the students position the stamps—straight, slanted, upside down—tell them to be sure the edges overlap.

Allow the finished projects to dry for 24 hours, then have your artists use brushes to apply the varnish (or other sealer). Students can use their artwork for pencil holders, pin boxes, junk collectors, jewelry boxes, or gifts.—*Alan W. Farrant, South Pasadena, Calif.*

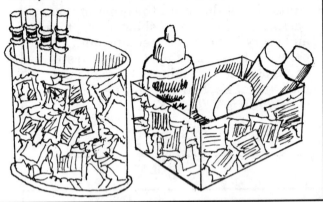

Say it with flowers

For the next gift-giving holiday, have your students make paper corsages. All they'll need are pin-on buttons (such as political buttons), small pieces of colored tissue paper, diluted white glue, a small paintbrush, clear nail polish, scraps of construction paper, pencils, and these directions:

- Pull out the pin at the back of the button *slightly* so that you can hold it as you work. Cover the button with seven or eight layers of tissue paper, using a small paintbrush to apply each coat of diluted glue and tucking the sides of the paper around the curved edge of the button. Let dry and paint with clear nail polish.

- To make the "flower," cut scraps of construction paper into strips about ⅛ inch wide and 1 inch long. Roll each strip around a pencil to make the paper curl. Glue the paper curlicues to the button and coat with nail polish for a glossy finish.

- Present your corsage or boutonniere to a parent, relative, or friend.—*Sister Shirley Reilly, Oak Park, Ill.*

Creative clay

This process focuses on open-ended creativity and thinking about opposites rather than product-oriented activity.

Each student will need a fistful of modeling clay, a few paper towels, newspaper to protect desks, a small dish of water, and tools to impress the clay—bottle caps, pennies, screws, toothpicks, or other small items.

Tell your students that they need not make an animal, a pot, or anything identifiable. They're to follow the directions and use the tools as they see fit. After each instruction, have students destroy what they made; let them know that all the clay will be put back into the pack at the end of the lesson.

Then tell your students to make something small, big; skinny, fat; short, tall; smooth, rough; pretty, ugly; even, uneven; complicated, simple; round, square.

At this point, invite students to create some opposites of their own.—*Diana Hensley, Costa Mesa, Calif.*

Solid-standing sculptures

This project helps solve a difficulty among young clay workers: how to make animals that stand solidly.

For each student, you'll need clay, newspaper, string, a nail about 1½ to 2 inches long, and a rolling pin (students can share this).

Give students these instructions:

• Cut strips of newspaper 5 inches wide. Stack the strips and roll them tightly together to make a compact tube 5 inches long and about ¾ inch thick. Cut clay in a squarish shape about 8 inches on a side. Drape the clay square over the newspaper tube, arranging it so that some extends beyond both ends of the tube.

• Using the nail, draw and cut out an animal. The clay extending beyond the ends becomes the head and tail of the animal. The clay on the sides becomes short, stubby legs and feet. Give imagination full rein when forming your creature: how about a curving tail, horns, hooves, a long snout?

• While the clay is still wet, "comb" in the animal's hair with the nail or tool a design on its back—a turtle shell pattern or fanciful flowery scrolls. Because drying clay shrinks, carefully remove the animal from the tube while the clay is still moist.

After about 2 weeks' drying time, the animal should be ready for firing or painting and for displaying with pride—perhaps in a diorama of mythical beasts.—*Jean Lyon, Cedar Rapids, Iowa*

clay

tightly rolled newspaper

ready to make animal

Nature greeting cards

Your students can share nature's beauty when they make greeting cards from flowers.

Ask your students to collect a few colorful flowers from their gardens. (Perhaps those with gardens can bring a few extras for those without them.) As soon as possible, have them carefully pull the petals off large flowers; they can leave small flowers intact. Next, have them place the petals and flowers between sheets of blank newsprint or white paper and put them under a heavy object, such as a book. After several days, the flowers and petals will be dried.

To make the cards, you'll need glue, half-sheets of 8½ x 11-inch white paper, 12 x 18-inch colored construction paper, felt-tip pens, and clear adhesive paper or access to a laminating machine. Here's what to do:

• Have your students arrange the petals and flowers in the center of the white paper, then glue them in place.

• Laminate the pages for your students or help them cover them with clear adhesive paper.

• Have each student fold a piece of art paper in half twice—first horizontally, then vertically—to make a 6 x 9-inch "card."

• Next, have your students cut an oval, circular, or diamond-shaped window in the front panel of the card, then insert the flower sheet behind the window and glue it in place.

When finished, the cards can carry messages or poems to a special someone.—*Beatrice McLaughlin, Akron, Ohio*

Easy-to-make hand puppets

Young children can make attractive hand puppets from their own drawings using fabric crayons.

Give each student a photocopy outline of a simple puppet. Have him use the crayons to color the puppet any way he likes. When the drawings are finished, iron each drawing facedown onto a piece of cloth (following the directions on crayon package).

Next, cut out the puppets and machine-stitch them to a plain cloth backing.— *Judy E. Hartwig, Omaha*

"V" is for variations

Pine trees, clown hair, porcupines— there's no limit to the things students can create with this activity. And it requires only pieces of cardboard, sheets of white paper, poster paint, and shallow dishes or jar lids.

To begin, give each of your students a piece of cardboard, which they fold into a "V" shape. Pour a little paint into each dish or jar lid. Show your students how to dip the edge of the cardboard into the paint and then press the edge onto the white paper.

Now encourage the kids to use more of the "V" marks to create any shape they please. They can color in by hand any details that can't be created with the "V" (such as a clown's face under a bush of "V" hair or a trunk of a pine tree).
—*Marj Hart, Encino, Calif.*

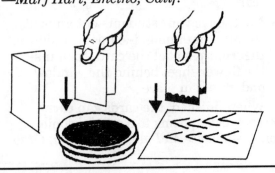

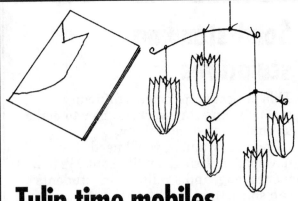

Tulip time mobiles

This group activity will bring one of spring's early arrivals into your classroom. First, divide your students into groups of five. Then give each student two pieces of the same color construction paper, making sure everyone in the group has a different color.

Have your students cut the paper in half width-wise, put one sheet on top of the other, and fold the four papers in half, one inside the other. Then have them draw half a tulip on the fold of the outside paper and cut through all thicknesses. This will give each student four tulips. Next, have your students staple the four tulips together along the fold and spread the petals.

Pass a spool of wire and have one student in each group use a wire cutter to cut off two lengths, one about 7 inches, the other about 9 inches. Have students form each wire into a slight arc and use pliers to bend the ends into hooks. Next, they fasten the wires together by tying a 7-inch piece of colored string from the end of the 9-inch wire to the middle of the 7-inch wire.

Now, each student fastens colored string to the top staple of his flower and suspends it from the wire: three flowers from the 7-inch wire, two from the 9-inch wire. Students might have to experiment with the lengths of string to balance the mobile.

To complete the mobile, each group ties a string on the 9-inch wire, about halfway between the middle tulip and the end that supports the 7-inch wire. Use that string to hang the mobile.— *Karen Hansen, Doylestown, Pa.*

School-supplies tracings

For this appealing art activity, students create trace-around designs, using as their templates scissors, erasers, pens, oversize paper clips, staplers, glue bottles, pencils, hole punchers, protractors.

Have your students sit in small groups so they can share supplies. Suggest that they try some exploratory positioning of items on 12 x 18-inch drawing paper. When they're pleased with the arrangement, they should trace the items lightly and then use crayons, felt-tip pens, or colored pencils to fill in the resulting forms. They can leave the background white or color it with a light tint.—*Gene T. Menicucci, Helena, Mont.*

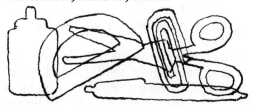

What's in a scribble?

You can fire your young students' imaginations by having them draw the motion of flight. Each student will need a large sheet of blank paper, a pencil, crayons, and a dark felt-tip pen.

Begin by asking your students to imagine a beautiful butterfly flitting around your classroom. Have them put their pencils on one corner of their papers, close their eyes, and draw the butterfly's path. When they're finished, ask them to color in the designs they've created.

Hold up one of the completed drawings. Turn it every which way, and ask students what they see in it. What shapes? Figures? Return the drawing and ask the artist to outline the shape he sees with a dark felt-tip pen. Ask the other students to do the same with their artwork.—*Marilyn Y. Doner, Syracuse, N.Y.*

Snowless snowmen

For a fun project with a winter theme, invite your students to make snowless snowmen.

Ask each student to bring in one adult-size tube sock with a striped top. You'll also need old newspapers, white glue, paintbrushes, odd buttons, felt scraps, strips of fabric, and polyester batting (available at fabric stores). For each snowman, you'll need approximately 15 square inches of batting. To make the snowmen, have your students follow the steps listed below:

1. Turn the sock inside out and stuff it with newspaper, making sure the toe is well stuffed (to give the snowman a firm base).
2. Knot the sock about 1 inch below the bottom stripe on the top.
3. "Paint" the sides and bottom of the sock with white glue and immediately roll it up in the batting, tucking the batting up from the bottom. Clip off any excess.
4. Dry the sock overnight.

5. Tie a fabric strip scarf around the snowman's neck (about ⅔ the distance from the snowman's bottom).
6. Turn down the top of the sock to make a ski cap, then add features (using the felt scraps) and glue buttons down the front.
7. Cut strips of batting into arm shapes and glue them to the sides of the snowman.—*Helen L. Miller, Granite City, Ill.*

Leaf-cluster flowers

With little fuss, your students can turn leaves, seeds, and small berries into flower plaques. Each student will need from 5 to 15 leaves. You'll also need white glue (with applicator), felt-tip pens, construction paper, and poster board (or recyclable scrap cardboard) cut into 8 x 10-inch pieces.

Selection and care of the leaves is important. Small leaves (1 to 3 inches long) with simple shapes work best. Keep the leaves moist so tips and edges don't dry out. Here's how to prepare the plaques:

- Cut a vase shape from colored construction paper.
- Glue the vase on the poster board, then design flowers above it by laying three to five leaves in a star shape with the stems toward the center and the tips radiating out.
- Lightly trace the positions of the leaves, then lift them, one at a time, and thoroughly coat each with glue, especially the tips and edges.
- Slide each leaf back into position and press lightly. (Excess glue will dry clear or can be wiped away.)
- Make flower centers by gluing on seeds or small berries.
- Use a felt-tip pen to draw stems from the blossoms to the rim of the vase.
- Allow 2 or 3 days' drying time, then coat the whole arrangement with plastic spray.
- Attach a picture hanger or tape a paper clip to the back of the plaque; then frame it with poster board, foil, or other trim.—*Barbara Keitt Mabry, Brooklyn, N.Y.*

String-board paintings

Paintings that help paint themselves, are fun for both eager artists and reluctant Rembrandts. Each artist will need a rectangular piece of wood, approximately 8 x 10 inches; sandpaper; a 4-foot length of string or light cord; tempera paints (if possible, put paints in squeezable containers such as empty detergent bottles or catsup dispensers); shellac or varnish; a brush; and a bundle of newspapers to protect the work area.

To make their paintings, have students follow these directions:

1. Sand the front surface and the edges of the board.
2. Paint the front of the board with a thin coat of two or more pale colors in irregular strips. Let the board dry.
3. Wrap string around the board in a crisscrossing, spiderweb design. Tie the string securely at the back of the board. Strings should be taut but in contact with the surface of the board as much as possible. If strings slip and loosen, wrap shorter lengths and tie each in place; you can also tape strings on the back.
4. Squeeze a color (or two) onto the string pattern. Tilt the board and let the paint follow the strings. Changing the tilt controls the flow somewhat, but the final design probably will be a surprise. Let the first color dry a bit before adding another. (*Note*: The paint should run, but not too fast; you might want to test the paint's viscosity.)
5. Squeeze on a few spots of contrasting color. Tilt the board again— if you like—but stop the process before the colors become homogenized.
6. When the paint dries, apply one or two coats of shellac.

If students like, they can frame their paintings and give them as special gifts.—*Judy Dahl, Salt Lake City*

Walking puppets

These mobile puppets will add a festive touch to your next dramatics production. The finished puppet sits on the puppeteer's hand with its clothing spread to conceal all but the finger "feet."

For each puppet, you'll need fabric (enough to cut a circle that's 20 inches in diameter); a 2-inch plastic foam ball; a ribbon, yarn, or felt strip for a neck bow; materials to make facial features; needle and thread or glue; a short strip of narrow elastic; Velcro fastener.

To make the puppets, have students follow these directions:

• Cut a 20-inch diameter circle of fabric. Make a slit from the edge to the center.

• To make the head, enclose the plastic foam ball in the center of the fabric circle. Secure it in place by gathering up the fabric snugly below the ball and tying a bow "collar" around the gathers.

• Before adding the facial features, adjust the puppet so that the slit in the fabric is at the back. Glue or sew features on the head.

• Inside the lower edge (hem) of the fabric, attach the elastic strip (ends only), one end at the front and the other at the back, on one side of the slit. Attach the halves of the Velcro fastener on either side of the slit, toward the bottom, so that the cut edges can be brought together. (You might need to help younger students with this step.)

• To operate the puppet, the student rests the puppet head on his wrist, poking his index and middle fingers downward on either side of the elastic strip. The puppet's clothing can then be held in place around the wrist by closing the Velcro fastener.

The puppet is now ready to walk, hop, tap-dance, or dramatize a scene from a book the child has just read.—*Alma B. Sanderson, Albuquerque, N.M.*

3-D snowman

Here's a project that makes use of all those plastic-foam pieces you might have been saving.

Distribute two 12 x 18 sheets—one oak tag, one white drawing paper—to each student. Have everyone draw a three-ball snowman on the oak tag, cut it out, trace it on the drawing paper, and cut again. Next, have your students glue a layer of plastic-foam "popcorn" pieces to the oak tag, taking care not to glue them too close to the edge.

(A 1½- inch margin is best.) When the glue dries, have your students staple the oaktag and white paper together around the edges, with the plastic-foam pieces inside. Now your students can use construction paper to make facial features, buttons, broom, boots, mittens, and a hat. A colored pipe cleaner makes an engaging grin. For a final touch, use a scrap of material to fashion a scarf.—*Joan Mary Macey, Binghamton, N.Y.*

Artistic angles

This activity illustrates the beauty and simplicity of design.

Have your students place a ruler diagonally across the middle of a piece of art paper and use a pencil to make two dots, about 5 or 6 inches apart. Next, students use their rulers to make lines through each of the dots, extending at different angles to the edges of the paper. The number and angles of lines will vary according to artistic taste.

To add more interest to the geometric patterns, your students may want to paint or color some sections. For the best effect, they should use only two colors.—*Sister Roberta Ann Leskey, Philadelphia*

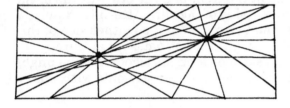

Paper-scrap art

Don't throw away all those paper scraps your art projects generate. Use them to create *more* art. Here are two ideas to try:

• Cut 8½ x 11-inch white drawing paper in half and distribute to your students. Then have your class arrange and glue the scraps on the white paper in a design that challenges the viewer to look at white space in new ways.

• Ask your students to select an 8½ x 11-inch sheet of construction paper plus some paper scraps. Then have each student cut or tear the scraps into various shapes and sizes, arrange them mosaic-style to depict a simple object (apple, rocket, ice-cream cone, and so on), and glue them to the construction paper.—*Shirley Russell, Lincoln, Calif., and Diana Curtis, Albuquerque, N.M.*

Black and white names

Have your students take a new look at themselves by giving their names a positive/negative art treatment. To prepare for the project, cut white and black construction paper in 2-inch squares. You'll need as many black squares as there are letters in the first names of your students. Cut half as many white squares as black; then cut each white square in half to form two rectangles.

Give each student one white rectangle and one black square for each letter in his first name. Then have your students follow this procedure:

• Draw a fat block letter on each white rectangle; each letter must abut the right-hand edge of the paper.

• Cut out the letters, using a continuous cutting line so that the hole left in the white paper is a letter shape. Save centers of closed letters, such as *A, B, D, and O.*

• To prepare one positive/negative letter block, glue a white rectangle—with its letter-shaped hole—over the left side of a black square, matching edges on the left side. The hole will expose a black letter. (Replace the cutout centers of *A*'s, *B*'s, and other closed letters.)

• Flip over the white cutout letter so that it appears backward, and glue it onto the right-hand portion of the black square, facing and making contact with its black mirror image on the left side.

Arrange the names on a "Here's Looking at Us" bulletin board or use them for making name cards.—*Sandra J. Frey, Lancaster, Pa.*

Shadow as substance—for art

If you're looking for an opportunity to take your class outdoors, this is it: a shadow art project.

For several days before the project, have students start looking for shadows, taking note of the shapes various things make. On a bright, sunny day give each student a large sheet of paper and go outside to find interesting shadows to trace. Students interested in large objects can trace small portions of their shadows.

Back inside the classroom, the students retrace their shadows with a firm, clear outline. Now invite students to use the shape as the basis for a piece of art. Some students might fill in the shape solidly and apply a contrasting background. Others might make the shape the center of concentric outlines. In any case, the abstract designs that result will be amazing.—*Neal Baer, Denver*

Twist-tie quilling

To achieve the attractive effect of quilling without the painstaking effort, try putting twist ties to work for you.

Give each student a bunch of twist ties to shape into flower petals, leaves, curlicues, or whatever. Then have students dip their twist ties into a dish of white glue and arrange designs on any flat surface—cardboard, construction paper, plastic lids, pieces of wood. Tell your students that the closer they fit the shapes together, the more their designs will look like quilling.—*Janet Mertrud, Lake Hopatcong, N.J.*

Sew-and-stuff friends

You can double your enrollment without adding to your roster when you invite your students to create stuffed clones.

You'll need a sewing machine and a parent volunteer to help with stitching. Materials consist of one bed sheet per child, scissors, stuffing (shredded foam, crumpled newspaper, cast-off stockings), chalk, and crayons.

Working in pairs, have students make chalk tracings of each other on their sheets. (Fold the sheets so that to get two shapes students have to draw the outline only once; have tracers make "mitten" hands to avoid problems with fingers.) Students then cut out the body shapes, leaving an inch border around the chalk line.

Sew each doll's body inside out along the chalk line, leaving a small opening for stuffing. Turn the doll right side out and have students draw a face on the doll using crayons. Fill the doll with stuffing and slip stitch the opening.

As an alternative to the crayoned face, ask students to study the ways that faces change to express different feelings. Then invite students to make a variety of paper masks to depict alternative moods—excitement, annoyance, sadness, apprehension, happiness, and so on. Staple all the masks to the top of the doll's head so the appropriate expression can be flipped down. To finish the dolls, have each student bring in an old outfit to clothe his clone.

Use the dolls in a variety of ways throughout the year— costume them for drama, arrange them in tableaux relating to social studies units, manipulate them to work out math story problems. They're also patient read-to listeners and intriguing subjects to write about.—*Sheila Marcy, Aldan, Pa.*

Texturing

Children can add a new dimension to their crayon artwork by using the "texturing" technique. Have them place their papers on different kinds of surfaces and color as they do with rubbings. For example, to provide a realistic texture for pictures of houses or trees, they might place their papers on pieces of rough wood. Clothing could be represented by coloring on a piece of corduroy. Another effect can be created by using two or more colors, one over the other.—*Linda Bynum, Metairie, La.*

Creative comb painting

Long ago, Americans used to decorate their houses with comb paintings. Students can make their own comb paintings— to hang or use as gift wrapping paper—by first making cardboard "combs" like the one shown here. When students pull the comb along a sheet of paper covered with thick, wet poster paint, they can create any number of designs.—*Marj Hart, Encino, Calif.*

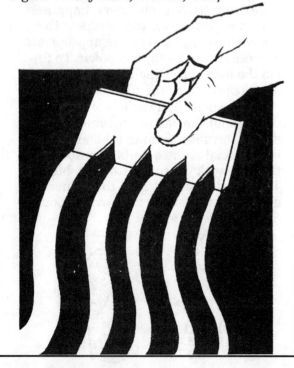

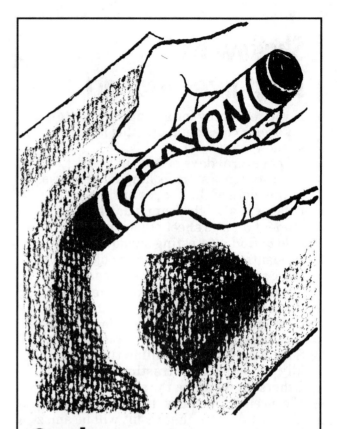

Sandpaper art

For artwork with a lot of texture, have your students make sandpaper pictures. Then you can transfer them with an iron onto drawing paper (or T-shirts).

Begin by having your students make a rough draft of a picture with crayons on plain paper (so they don't waste sandpaper). To include words, they should draw them backward— transferring will make them legible; they can sign their pictures *after* the transfer.

Next, students copy their pictures onto medium-grade sandpaper. They should use old crayons you've collected ahead of time and press hard.

To transfer the sandpaper picture to paper, place it facedown on a piece of white or buff paper. Under this put a piece of clean paper (change it for each drawing) and several sheets of newspaper for padding. On top, put another piece of clean paper to protect the iron. With the heat on high, move the iron slowly, applying firm pressure. Lift a corner to check the transfer.—*Shirley Russell, Lincoln, Calif.*

Bleach painting

In this backward art activity, kids paint the color *off* instead of *on*. You'll need bleach, paint cups or glass jars, cotton swabs, crayons, and dark-colored construction paper.

If possible, take your students outside so the fumes from the bleach won't be so strong, and have them all wear aprons for protection. Give each child a small amount of bleach in a paint cup or glass jar and tell the students to draw an outline picture in crayon on a sheet of construction paper. Drawings should be simple: A sailboat, mushrooms, butterflies, a race car, a fish, or a daisy make good designs.

When students have finished their drawings, they dip a cotton swab in the bleach and "paint" with bold strokes along the lines of their figures. Lay the bleach paintings on papers to dry. (Leave the pictures outside or in a well-ventilated area to dry.)

At first, nothing will happen; then slowly the bleach will take the color from the paper, leaving the drawing lines highlighted in gray or off-white. When the paintings are dry, the artists might want to do some touching up with crayons or felt-tip pens.—*Michael and Libby Robold, Brooklyn, Mich.*

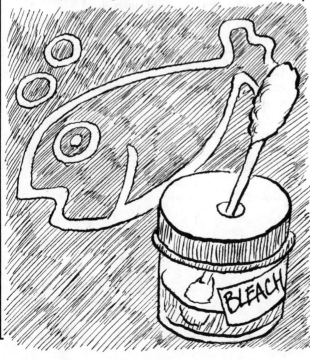

Quick-stroke calligraphy

Chinese calligraphers use stylized images to represent ideas. With this technique, students create similar images to represent visual impressions.

Give students brushes, water, and paper towels. Ask someone to stand in front of the class and assume different poses (each pose should last about 5 seconds). Students represent these poses by making two quick strokes with water on their paper towels.

When students feel comfortable with this activity, switch to paints and manila paper. Now student models should carry out a series of planned quick poses. For example, they could imitate animals, such as monkeys, dogs, or cats. The student painters respond as before. When they've finished their quick-stroke responses, invite each student to pick his favorite painting and enlarge it, using similar strokes and adding detail and color.—*Kathy Gustafson, Kila, Mont.*

Straw painting

Who needs brushes? Your students will be delighted with the range of free-form designs they can create with this uninhibiting painting technique.

Give each student a piece of drawing or construction paper and a drinking straw. Place a spoonful of thinned-out tempera paint on each paper. After demonstrating the process, invite students to blow gently through their straws at one part of the pool of paint. Students continue blowing at the different paint flows until they have formed designs they like.

If students wish, they can add one or more pools of different-colored paint to the paper after the first color has dried and then repeat the blowing activity. When the children have finished their paintings, frame and display them.—*Ruth Etkin, Brooklyn, N.Y.*

Pinhole pictures

Minimal materials (and messes) make these see-through pictures a welcome artistic activity.

On colored construction paper, invite your students to draw a simple outline of a picture or design. Students then place their pictures over newspaper padding and pierce them with pins, making tiny holes as close together as possible. For fancier designs, children can experiment with different size needles and pins, or they can poke holes closer together in some areas than in others to create various shading and tinting effects.

Display the finished pictures on windows or hang them as mobiles.—*Helen Wubbenhorst, Mesa, Ariz.*

Pointillism

This activity introduces impressionist Georges Seurat's late nineteenth century style of painting. The technique uses dots to produce images.

If possible, show your students a few pointillist paintings. Then, pass out sturdy paper patterns of simple objects (a heart, apple, or candle) and have students trace them lightly on plain white paper. The kids then use thin, colored felt-tip pens to fill in the tracings with tiny dots, erase the pencil outline, and mount the finished picture on colored construction paper.

If students prefer, they can draw their own patterns or create their dot art without outlines. Point out some of the finer techniques—for example, how the image can appear darker or shaded when the dots are placed closer together.—*Janice Wagner, Greenbelt, Md.*

Lessons from the masters

To help your students better appreciate composition and detail in famous paintings, take a tack used by professional art schools: Tell them to copy!

Select a painting you think will appeal to your students. (Check your local library for large art prints or have your students work in groups with different art books.) Give your class some background information about the artist. Help them sense the painting's mood, colors, and shapes. Then encourage your students to make their own copies of the masterpiece. (It might be more satisfying for students to work with felt-tip pens, crayons, or pastels rather than paint.) Encourage other classes to take a second look at famous paintings by displaying, in a central location, the print of the original masterpiece along with your students' copies.—*Violet Olson, Davenport, Iowa*

Pinhole dot to dot

Save that background paper from your bulletin board display area. The pinholes it's probably covered with can be the start of a creative art activity.

If you've used sheets of construction paper for backing, give one sheet to each student, plus a ruler and a pencil. Ask the kids to connect the dots (holes), then color the shapes and patterns in any way they like. Each picture will be different and the results so satisfying that the recycled papers might find their way back to the display area.—*Lora Lee Curtiss, Virginia, Minn.*

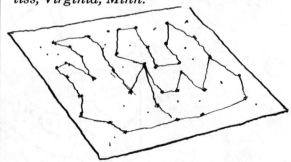

Paper-plate looms. Bright blooms!

This roundabout flower weaving process is basic enough for primary graders, and the preparation procedure gives older students practice with mathematical problem solving. For each flower, you'll need a 9-inch paper plate, a one-hole paper punch, a yarn needle, light string (about 10 feet), tape, and several yards of yarn in various colors.

To prepare to weave, you (or older students) determine the center of the paper plate and punch a hole. Mark 15 dots spaced evenly on the circumference of the plate. Draw a radius "spoke" from each dot to the center hole. Fit the paper punch over the edge of the plate at each spoke as deeply as possible and punch a hole. Now you're ready to thread the loom. (Younger students might need help.) Here's how:

1. Using light string on the needle, poke up through an outer-ring hole and then down through the center hole. Secure the end of the string on the back of the plate.

2. Poke the needle up through the next hole in the outer ring and down through the center hole. Be sure strings lie flat around the center and don't cross.

3. When you've threaded all the holes, secure the end of the string at the back with tape.

Now students are ready to start weaving flowers. Have them:

1. Thread the needle with a 3-foot length of yarn in the color desired for the center of the flower. Poke the needle up through the center hole, and tape the end of the yarn to the back of the plate.

2. Weave over and under the string spoke continuously, around and around, pushing layers of the spiral tightly together.

3. Change colors by attaching new yarn with a tight knot.

4. Finish by tucking the end of the yarn into the outer edges of the design (on the back of the plate), weaving in and out several times.

You can cut the edge of the plate in a scallop design and add painted or crayoned leaves. Use the flower weavings as wall hangings or table mats.—*Judy Dahl, Salt Lake City*

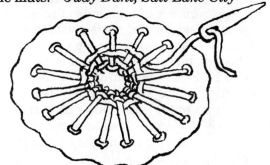

Candle creations

This candle-making method is simple, quick, and appropriate for all ages. You'll need four coffee cans, four jars, old candle wax, crayons, a wick for each student, and a hot plate.

Use the hot plate to heat the wax in the coffee cans, adding a crayon to each for color. Place the cans in the four corners of a square table. In between the cans, place jars of cold water.

Line up your students and have them walk around the table, dipping the wicks alternately into the wax, then into the water.

Students continue walking and dipping until their candles reach a desired size. Caution the students not to let the hot wax touch their fingers. (Have bowls of cold water ready to immerse any hands on which the hot wax drips.)

To make specially shaped candles, pour hot wax into a milk carton, paper cup, or egg carton mold. Tie the wick to a pencil placed horizontally across the top of the mold. When the candle has set, tear away the mold.—*Debra Birnbaum, Yellow Springs, Ohio*

Basic basket weaving

Starting with recycled materials, your students can create beautiful baskets. For each basket, you'll need an empty plastic cottage cheese, sour cream, or margarine container and scads of yarn. Help students follow these directions:

- Measure the circumference of the container. Divide this measurement into an *odd* number of segments of roughly the same width and mark the intervals along the rim with a felt-tip pen. (For a 14-inch circumference, you might have 13 1⅟₁₆-inch sections.) Slice the container sides at the segment markings from top to base, being careful of sharp edges. Push down and out on the sections from inside the carton to help separate the sections for easy weaving.

- For a handle, securely anchor a strip of tagboard or cardboard in several spots down the length of two sections that are approximately opposite each other.

- Tie the end of a hank of yarn around the base of one section, knotting it inside, and weave it in and out of the sections. Push initial rings of yarn all the way down to the base. When you start a new color, tie off the preceding color and knot the new one inside the container as before. Weave the colors until the container is covered. Wrap the handle with yarn.

Now your basket is ready to hold a plant, candy, or trinkets.—*Marlene Rorke, Yakima, Wash.*

New soaps from old

Invite your students to create attractive guest soaps from old soap scraps. You'll need pieces of leftover soap (as students bring in pieces, store them in a covered container, adding a little water to start the softening process); assorted cookie cutters (simple shapes); cookie sheets; an egg turner; a large spoon; a double boiler; a hot plate or stove; food coloring and scents (optional); and newspaper and paper towels. With the assistance of your students (depending on your grade level), proceed as follows:

1. Spread newspaper to cover the work area.
2. Soften soap pieces with a little water in a double boiler.
3. As the soap warms and softens, use the spoon to smooth out any lumps, adding a bit more water if necessary. (Don't let the mixture get thin.) If you like, add food coloring or scents.
4. When the soap has softened to the consistency of thick oatmeal, turn it out on a cookie sheet, smoothing it to about ⅜ inch thick.
5. Allow to cool and harden a few minutes. Then invite your students to cut shapes with cookie cutters.
6. Remove soaps with the egg turner and place them on paper towels to dry.
7. Gather up scraps and resoften or mold into soap balls.
8. Allow soap to harden overnight.

Now your students are ready with attractive and useful presents for the next gift-giving holiday.—*Lillian Cooper, New York City*

A crewel mural

For this class project, you'll need a couple of yards of brightly colored burlap, scrap lumber for building a stretching frame, a staple gun for attaching the burlap to the frame, crewel needles, and a sizable quantity of odd yarn bits.

Hold a class brainstorming session to decide on the picture you'll create—a seasonal picture, a sampler, a proverb or poem. Then introduce your students to the basics—the satin stitch, an outlining stitch, and the backstitch.

Set up the project in a convenient location and have stitchers sign up to work in groups of four or five at a time. As the design comes alive, the work slots should fill up fast. And before long, the finished art piece will be ready for displaying so everyone can take pride in the work they did together.—*Kathleen Emmons, Lewisburg, Pa.*

Patchwork of memories

For a meaningful class memento, have your students create a patchwork "quilt" of the school year's most memorable moments. Give each student an 8 x 8-inch square of felt or other suitable fabric, and on these have the youngsters glue or paint pictures or words that describe their remembrances. Either stitch the squares together or glue them in place on a large sheet of material. Hang the "quilt" on a dowel for an unforgettable display.—*Linda Valentino, Slate Hill, N.Y.*

Touch-me collages

For an art project in an unusual medium, invite your students to create tissue-paper and sawdust collages. You'll need sawdust (check at a lumberyard for a free supply); heavy 9 x 12-inch drawing paper; tissue-paper scraps in a variety of colors and shapes; liquid starch; watercolors, brushes, water; crayons; and glue. To get started, give your artists the above supplies and these directions:

1. On the heavy paper, paint a watercolor background wash.

2. When the background is dry, apply scraps of tissue paper in a random pattern of harmonious colors using the starch as glue.

3. On the tissue-paper base, use a crayon to draw a simple outline design—an abstract shape, a daisy, a mushroom.

4. Spread glue inside the design, making sure the glue is flat and smooth, not bubbly.

5. Sprinkle sawdust over the entire glue-filled area; shake off the excess.

6. Retrace the outline of the design with crayon. Use heavy lines—perhaps a double outline.

7. Cover the remaining tissued background with liquid starch, using fingers as brushes. Let dry.

You might need to flatten the collages under a pile of heavy books before mounting them on contrasting oak tag or construction paper. Students may mount their collages as they are, or cut them into interesting shapes before mounting. Artists may also wish to cut the mounting paper to follow the shape of the contoured art piece.—*Judy Dahl, Salt Lake City*

Spring wind catchers

Originally used as wind direction indicators, wind socks have become popular decorations for doorways and gardens. Your students can make them as gifts or just to decorate their own yards.

To make each wind sock, you'll need a 20 x 8-inch piece of poster board, glue, a paper punch, yarn, crepe-paper streamers, and decorations such as sewing notions, paper scraps, wallpaper samples, crayons, felt-tip pens, and so on.

Have your students begin by decorating their poster board. (They can draw designs on directly, or glue on items. They can use a holiday motif—such as pumpkins or shamrocks—or a generic motif—such as flowers, hearts, or rainbows.) Next, have your students attach streamers along one of the 20-inch sides. Then, roll the poster board into a cylinder and staple. Punch four holes, evenly spaced, around the top, about ½ inch from the edge. Finally, insert yarn through these holes to form a hanger. Now the wind sock is ready to bob and flutter in the breeze.—*Doris Neff and Marilyn Plasket, Glassboro, N.J.*

"Stained glass" candle holders

These make great gifts or decorations. And they're quick to make. You'll need small baby food jars; scraps of colored tissue paper (cut into small, straight-sided pieces and separated according to color); white glue, slightly thinned; brushes; black felt-tip pens; candles—about ¾ inch in diameter, to be cut into short lengths; and string.

Give your students these instructions:

1. Coat the outside of the jar with a thin layer of glue.
2. Apply a tissue piece and recoat the area with glue—for shine and to keep the paper smooth.
3. Keep applying pieces of tissue paper (you may overlap some pieces) until the jar is covered.
4. To make a neat rim, wind string around the neck of the jar, fixing the ends in place with tape.
5. Allow the jar to dry. Then trace each colored shape with a black felt-tip pen to give the stained-glass effect.
6. Cut candles to a length that's no longer than half the height of the jar. Fix the candle upright in the jar by setting it into soft wax drippings.

Light the candles for a remarkable effect.—*Patricia Mays, Folsom, Pa.*

Family ties surprise

Invite your students to introduce their families through art, and they'll also have a head start on learning how families vary. In advance, you'll need a small photo of each child.

Begin by giving each student a sheet of paper. Have students draw a 2 x 3-inch box in the upper right-hand corner, but tell them to leave the box empty for a surprise. Then ask them to draw portraits of their families, including any pets.

Now, collect the family portraits and tape or glue each student's photo in the box. Staple a flap of construction paper over each photo. Display the portraits on a bulletin board titled, "Can You Guess Whose Family This Is?" Your students will enjoy checking their guesses. Finally, ask your students to show their portraits and describe their families and the activities they enjoy doing together.—*Cynthia Nardiello, Rockford, Ill.*

Thumbprint characters

Students' thumbprints can become small creatures, which then become the subjects of this paragraph-writing activity.

Provide ink pads so that each student can place his thumbprint on a piece of paper. Then challenge your students to incorporate their prints into drawings of animals or imaginary creatures.

Under the finished drawings, have students list the following: the name of the creature, its habitat, eating habits, and behavior. Then ask the kids to use the information they've listed to write a paragaph describing their creatures.— *Nina Hilsenbeck, Daytona Beach, Fla.*

Alphabet picture pockets

This activity requires advance preparation, but the outcome is well worth the effort.

First, using calico, felt, or other fabric, cut out 26 squares, each about 3 x 3 inches. Next, cut a "window" in each square, then glue acetate or another clear material over it. Sew or glue the squares to a heavy piece of fabric, leaving the tops unfastened to create a pocket. Make construction-paper letters and label the pockets from A to Z. Hang the display in a prominent spot in the room, then let your students' imaginations take over.

Write a letter of the alphabet on each of 26 papers. (If you have more than 26 students, duplicate enough letters so there's one for each student.) Have your students each pick a letter (or two) without looking.

Next, fill a box with scraps of cloth, felt pieces, construction paper, yarn, and similar materials. Invite your students to use these materials to make an item that corresponds with their letter. The only rule is that items must be less than 3 inches wide so they'll fit in the pockets; it's okay if some items peek out over the tops. Tell your students to slip their creations into the proper pocket when they're finished.—*Lee Farnsworth, Troy, N.Y.*

History hats—1776

When you're studying Early American history, have your students get "in the mood" by making their own three-cornered hats.

Each student will need a bowl that exactly fits his head; newspapers—some for protection, some cut in strips 1 to 1½ inches wide and the length of the page; petroleum jelly or cold cream; wheat paste, water, and a large mixing container; black poster paint and brushes; thumbtacks; and shellac. When you're ready for students to begin, give them these instructions:

1. Stack two or three newspapers opened out to full double size and place the bowl—upside down—in the center.
2. Coat the outside of the bowl with petroleum jelly or cold cream.
3. Mix wheat paste and water to a consistency of thin pancake batter, pressing out any lumps with your fingers.
4. Dip a newspaper strip into the paste; remove excess paste by drawing the strip through nearly closed fingers. Place the strip across the bowl and smooth down onto the newspaper on both sides.
5. Prepare and place another strip at right angles to the first so that the bowl will be anchored to the paper. Continue to smooth on strips until the entire bowl and about 10 inches surrounding it are covered. Dry overnight.

6. Apply one more layer of strips over the same area. Let dry. Apply two more layers to the bowl part only (in all, four layers on the crown, two on the brim). Let dry several days.
7. Turn the whole construction over and cut away the paper that covers the opening of the bowl. The bowl should slip out.
8. Measure the height of the crown. Trim away the brim to a depth matching this measurement.
9. Paint the outside of the crown (not the brim) with black poster paint. Let dry. Put your name inside the crown.
10. To shape the brim (an adult should do this), dip it in and out of water carefully, watching closely until it's just soft enough to bend easily without cracking. Fold up one-third of the brim at a time, securing each section against the crown in turn with a thumbtack. Keep sections as equal as possible.
11. Wait 1 day and remove tacks. Finish painting the outside. Let dry, then coat with shellac so dampness won't affect the paint.

When the hats are finished, propose a school-wide fashion show so your young patriots can show off their work.—*Esther Murray McConnon, Pittsburgh*

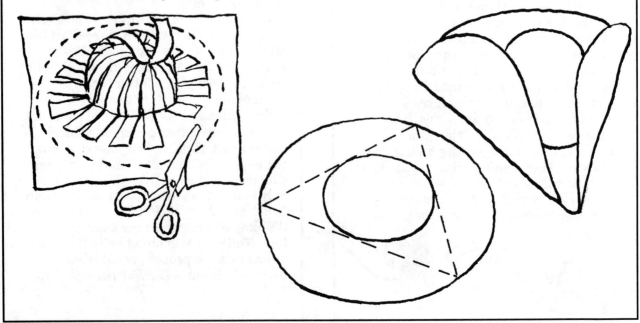

Breakfast table art

For a project that combines art and social studies, commission your students to design packages for new breakfast cereals. Their job is to create cartons that will shout at shoppers from the shelves, persuading them to buy.

First, put out a call for cereal boxes. Have kids study the boxes, taking note of design elements such as the use of color, letter size and style, photos and art.

Now that your students have studied the competition, challenge them to beat it by creating their own boxes. Remind them to keep in mind their target market. Are they targeting fantasy-loving children or calorie-conscious adults? Or are they going after an offbeat market such as household robots or weight-lifting mice?

After students decide on a name and package design, they move into constructing the carton, following these steps:

- Use a small carton (not a single-serving size) as a pattern.
- Flatten the carton by carefully cutting along the seams, retaining all flaps.
- Trace the edges of the pattern—including all flaps—on poster board.
- Cut along the traced lines.
- Reposition the pattern on the cutout; fold up each pattern flap and trace the location of each fold line on the cutout. Lightly score fold lines with a mat knife.

Before assembling the carton, students should apply art and lettering. Then they fold the flaps in place and secure them with glue or tape. Invite students to introduce their new products; display them, grocery-store style.—*Jo Ann Wray, Tulsa, Okla.*

Store-and-review boxes

Have students make personal treasure boxes that double as memory aids. You'll need an assortment of containers— chip canisters, ice cream cartons, oatmeal boxes; construction paper (sheets and odd bits); scissors; glue; and felt-tip pens and crayons.

Give each student a container, and ask him to cover it with construction paper. Then invite students to decorate their boxes with items to be remembered in a specific subject area—pesky points of punctuation or grammar, difficult vocabulary, metric data, math facts or symbols, homonyms, spelling oddities. Students write their memory aids on bits of construction paper and paste them to their boxes. Or encourage students to use their imaginations to create the memory aids, employing fancy lettering, doodle borders, cartoon characters, and the like.

Now the containers are ready to store crayons, erasers, string, baseball cards— and be a constant reinforcement of study facts.—*Ann M. Hamminga, Olcott, N.Y.*

Mother Nature preserves

One way to save those souvenirs from field and forest trips is to put them under glass.

Before your scheduled nature walk, ask each student to bring in a medium-size clear glass jar with a screw-on top. During your walk, encourage students to collect a variety of dried plants, seeds, pods, nuts, burrs, twigs, bits of bark, and the like. After investigating these items in science class, have each student select a "bouquet" of the field-trip goodies for preserving. Here's how:

    1. Put a lump of clay on the inside of the jar lid, deep enough to support the stems of the dried plants. Don't apply the clay all the way to the edges; leave room for the jar to fit back inside.

    2. Arrange the plants and other items in the clay base, keeping the jar's dimensions in mind.

    3. Place the jar carefully over the arrangement and screw it into the lid.

To add color, you might want to offer a bunch of tiny straw flowers for students to share. Students can keep their "preserves" or give them as gifts.—*Sue Morrow, Old Hickory, Tenn.*

Musical pitch pictures

Deciding whether a musical note is above, below, or the same as a note previously heard is usually an aural exercise. But this activity turns pitch practice into a paper-and-pencil lesson.

Give your students large-gauge graph paper. Have them mark the number 9 at a point near the upper left corner of the paper. On the points directly below, they should write 8, 7, and so on down to 1. Now play a low note on a piano, recorder, or other instrument. Tell the children that it's the note for number 1 and that they should put a dot at point 1 on their papers.

Next, play a note a step higher and ask your students to listen carefully and decide whether it's a step above, a step below, or the same as the first note. Because it's higher, students should move their pencils to the right and up one box. If it were the same, they'd move their pencils to the right on the same line. Continue up the scale as students mark their graphs. By the time you play the ninth note, students will have drawn an upward staircase on their papers. Then repeat the process going down the staircase, from 9 to 1.

Now that everyone is comfortable with the procedure, play all kinds of patterns for your students to draw. As their ears grow more acute, you can skip notes, going from 1 to 3 or from 8 to 5. Try symmetrical patterns: Follow a musical line that starts at 5 and goes up to 9 and back to 5. You could even work out a series of notes that, when translated onto paper, result in a recognizable shape.—*Deborah A. Kutchman, Jerome, Pa.*

Apple-head dolls

Amaze your students by demonstrating how a simple apple can transform itself into a human face. The technique for making apple-head dolls is rather basic, but as students bring their imaginations to the task, each doll will become a unique work of art.

For each doll, you'll need a hard cooking-type apple; a knife or sharp tool; paint or lemon juice; needle and thread; straight pins; glue; flannel, cotton, old stockings, fabric scraps (for body); beads, seeds, sequins (for eyes); and cotton, yarn, doll wigs (for hair); and shellac or clear nail polish. Students should follow these instructions:

1. Peel the apple. Leave the stem—and a bit of peel around it—for a "handle."
2. Use a knife or sharp tool to carve the facial features. These should be exaggerated, allowing for shrinkage.
3. Hang up the apple in a well-ventilated place to dry. Allow 2 to 4 weeks. (The apple will turn a caramel brown as it dries. For a darker shade, paint it after it's dry. For a lighter tone, soak it in lemon juice for 45 minutes before the drying.)
4. Fashion a rag-doll-style body from flannel cut to a simple outline, stitched, and stuffed with cotton, old stockings, or fabric scraps.
5. After the apple head is dry, decorate it. If the facial features closed during the drying process, gently pry them open. Add beads, seeds, or sequins for eyes. Emphasize features with pens or paint. Apply hair with glue or pins.

6. Apply shellac or clear nail polish to add sheen and help preserve the face. When dry, use straight pins to attach the head to the body.

Now your students are ready to clothe their dolls. Inspire them to create elaborate outfits by offering a rich variety of fabric scraps, trims, buttons, feathers, and so on. When all is said and done, arrange for a doll parade.—*Denise Lee, Springhouse, Pa.*

Musical montages

Combine music and art by having your students create montages of their favorite songs.

Write down the lyrics of some songs. Make copies and let each student choose a song. Then, with a pile of magazines nearby, hand out construction paper and invite students to cut out pictures that describe the song or the feeling it gives them. They could also cut out key words and incorporate them into the montage. For lengthy songs, students can choose a few favorite lines to depict.

Display the montages alongside copies of the lyrics that inspired them.—*Mary Costello, Rolling Hills Estates, Calif.*

Commemorative plates

Have your students honor famous people, places, and events by making commemorative plates. Provide students with paper plates and crayons and let them create their own designs for the occasion.

The idea is a natural for historic events but also works well for current events—the safe landing of astronauts, birthdays of famous people, and the like. As an alternative to standard book reports, students could make plates to honor books and their authors.—*Sally Gordon, Dallas*

Brand-name art

To help your students discover the art of lettering, have them collect logos (and trademarks) from magazines and packages.

When you have a good collection of logos, invite students to use them to create a colorful bulletin board display for study. Discuss how letter styles reflect the product's purpose. For example, a luxury automobile logo might exude elegance, or a soft-drink label might explode with energy. Talk about design elements in each logo—the use of space and color, lettering styles, balance, and symmetry.

Extend your study by asking students to make an enlargement of a favorite logo. They'll get practice in measuring, centering, and drawing guidelines. The enlarged logos make colorful "pop art" for decorating the classroom.

For a follow-up activity, challenge students to design original logos for favorite products (or for products they'd like to invent).—*David A. Peterson, Salt Lake City*

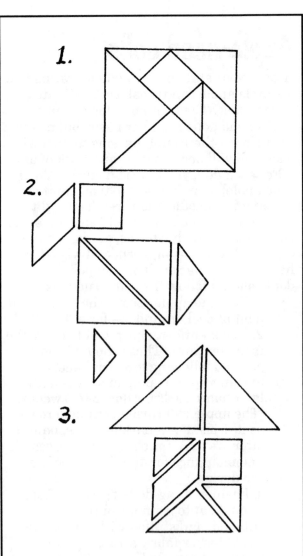

Tangram shapes

For an art and math lesson have your students make their own tangrams.

To make tangrams, students will need: a ruler, a pencil, scissors, and a square piece of oak tag or cardboard with sides 4 inches or longer.

On the oaktag square, have students draw the pattern shown in Figure 1 and cut out the pieces. Challenge them to put the pieces back into a square, without looking at the original pattern. Then see if they can duplicate the puzzles in Figures 2 and 3, using all the pieces. Now they're ready to create puzzles of their own, using all or a few of the pieces.— *Denise Lee, Springhouse, Pa.*

Manageable art

If you've come across a great art project only to be disillusioned by the long list of materials needed for each child, this idea is for you.

Have students work on a variety of different projects, each requiring smaller numbers of specific items. Put all the materials and equipment required for each project in a large numbered bag or box. Place in the container a laminated card with directions for the activity; a sample of the finished project is helpful too.

At the beginning of the art period, have each student select a number that corresponds to one of the numbered bags. All you'll have to do is monitor the activities, see that unused materials are returned to their proper bags, and replenish supplies that run low.—*Anita Nolan, Bethel, Conn.*

Creative junk

Set up a trash renewal center and challenge your students to invent crafty uses for recyclables.

Have your students bring in some clean throwaways: egg cartons, plastic tubs, bottles, tubes, cans, aluminum pans, and so on. And have available string, tape, glue, staplers, paint, brushes, and other such fastening and decorating items.

At your center, post suggestions for putting trash to creative use. With each idea, include a list of materials needed and illustrations or models if possible. Here are a few suggestions:

Egg cartons

- Seedling planters. Use the pulp cartons so that seedlings can be planted outside right in the container.
- Artificial flowers. Cut slits in separate cups to form petals and attach the cups to pipe cleaners.
- Caterpillar toys. String cups together and decorate.

Milk cartons

- Bird feeders. Cut out one side and insert Popsicle sticks for perches.

- Desk organizers. Cut tops off cartons and staple several together, side by side or stacked.
- Pencil organizers. Cut off tops, invert, punch holes of appropriate sizes for pencils (or scissors).

Cans

- Hanging planters
- Pencil holders
- Kitchen containers

Newspapers

- Fireplace logs. Roll newspapers tightly and secure with string.

Provide plenty of space for your inventors to use while creating. Encourage them to set up displays and to post directions for their craft ideas. Reserve a bulletin board devoted to construction instructions as an incentive for polishing clean, step-by-step descriptive writing. When you've collected a good supply of ideas, you might have students compile a *Creative Trashcraft* booklet to share with other classes.—*Jane Sammis, New London, Conn.*

Dripless painting

To cut down on drips and spills, put paint in fast-food beverage containers. With the fitted lid on top, you'll have a built-in hole for brushes. Paintbrushes will bend slightly on the way in, but they come out neat and clean—free from excess paint. Store the cups upright and reuse.—*Beverly Maffei, East Boston, Mass.*

Quick tips

These two ideas for classroom art management will help prevent sticky, discolored display surfaces and rejuvenate worn-out supplies.

- Dabs of toothpaste can hold children's art to walls and windows. The paste won't damage either surface, unlike tape, which leaves a sticky residue. As a bonus, the paste acts as a window polish when it's scrubbed off.
- To restore a dried-out felt-tip pen, dip it in water and use it as a brush with water colors.—*Jeannine Perez, Bloomington, Ill.*

Six-pack organizers

Cardboard carriers that hold beverage bottles make excellent personal organizers for your youngsters' everyday art supplies.

Have students help you collect six-pack carriers and clean, empty juice cans until you have a carrier and six cans for each child in the class. Invite students to paint and decorate their cartons. When the cartons are dry, have students insert a can in each compartment.

Give each student a personal supply of crayons, felt-tip pens, pencils, paste, a ruler, and scissors to put in the cans. Have the children print their names on their organizers and place them on a shelf, ready for the next art project. —*Sandra Noble, Durango, Colo.*

Frames for artwork

Display student artwork richly framed, without the bother of measuring or cutting. Save—and have your students bring in—collapsible gift boxes in a variety of sizes. Each student can then pick a suitably sized box half, position his picture inside, fold the sides down over the picture edges, then staple or tape the corners of the box in place for a professional-looking frame.—*Joyce K. McShara, Putnam Valley, N.Y.*

Art fair for parents

Instead of just inviting parents to see the art projects their children have done, give them a chance to do some creating of their own at an art fair.

After deciding which art projects to display, divide your students into small groups. Each group will choose an art process to teach parents. Then the teaching groups draw up lists of needed materials and work out the steps they'll teach. They might want to rehearse the steps aloud.

Two weeks before the fair, have students design, and take home, invitations. Then set up the exhibits of children's art in the classroom. Plan for numbered worktables where the student art teachers will be stationed. As parents arrive, provide name tags with numbers to indicate initial art project stops. Encourage parents to participate in several workshops.

The following day, invite students to recall and write about parents' experiences and comments during the fair. Post the comments and display parents' artwork in the hall for all to admire.
—*Jeane Thompson, Kenyon, Minn.*

Paint cups by the dozen

The next time you're passing out tempera paint, keep things tidy by giving each student a foam egg carton to use as a paint tray. Students then carry their paint trays to their desks without spills. And they can mix colors right in the empty egg holes. Cleanup is a breeze. Simply rinse, stack, and save the cartons for the next art project.—*Katherine Butala, Palmdale, Calif.*

Paper-cutting tip

The next time you demonstrate a specific way to cut paper, try this. As you show the students each step, draw the cut mark with chalk on a piece of dark construction paper. If different steps are involved, number each sample as you go. Tape the samples to the chalkboard or bulletin board to help your students remember.—*Diana Curtis, Albuquerque, N.M.*

Easy-to-make smocks

Those large (26-gallon) plastic trash bags make ideal artists' smocks for the young painters and sculptors in your class. Simply cut out one hole for the head and two for the arms, and the trash bag is ready to serve as the perfect clothing protector.—*Patricia A. Denmon, Minersville, Pa.*

Fresh materials

Use margarine tubs to keep paste and clay soft. The tubs are easy to move among desks, and they stack for easy storage. They're also good for holding tacks, paper clips, and so on.—*Beverly Maffei, East Boston, Mass.*

Classroom catchalls

Have students glue pictures—either those they've colored or cut out of magazines—onto large sheets of construction paper. After students put their names on the sheets, laminate them or cover them with clear self-sticking paper. Students can use these as catchalls for drips and spills during craft time or as placemats for classtime parties.—*Rhonda Thurman-Rice, Tulsa, Okla.*

Chapter 10
HOLIDAYS

The 12 days of Halloween

Challenge your students to create a spook-tacular parody of the song, "The Twelve Days of Christmas." The spirit(s) of Hallow-een should inspire kids to come up with a collection of offbeat "gifts."

First, ask your students to brainstorm as many Halloween symbols as they can—from bats and cats to tricks and witches. Write their suggestions on the board. Then, have students draw from the list to compose indi-vidual songs in the style of the popular Christmas tune. For example, students might offer a screech owl in a dead tree, two witches' brooms, three black cats, four gob-lins, five flying bats, six skeletons a-rattling, and so on.

When the songs are finished, invite each student to illustrate his favorite line; stu-dents who enjoy a math challenge might want to compute the grand total of gifts while others will appreciate a chance to act out their songs.—*Suzy Zeiser, Cincinnati*

Haunted high rise

Get all the season's ghosts, bats, and goblins off the streets—and into your classroom—by inviting your students to build a spooky diorama mansion for them.

Bring in a collection of shoe boxes and stack them with their open sides to the front. Staple the boxes together to build a house as wide and as tall as you wish. Each box becomes a room in the haunted mansion. If you like, add a cardboard piece for a peaked roof.

When you've constructed the house, invite your students to scare up a collection of spooky dwellers, such as ghosts (coming through walls), bats (in the belfry), skeletons (in the closets or just hanging around). Students also should decorate the mansion with such items as cob-webbed furniture; dramatic doorways; dark, heavy draperies; scary portraits; massive fireplaces; jack-o'-lanterns; and the like.

When the haunted high rise is complete, invite your students to share stories about what might be going on inside its ghastly walls.—*Linda L. Wangerin, Pompano Beach, Fla.*

Creature cookout

Stir your students' imaginations by challenging them to create recipes for wretched entrées, such as Boogeyman Burgers, Ghastly Ghoul-lash, Bat Broth, and the like.

Provide cookbooks for students to browse through to help them add the humor of authentic vocabulary to their recipe parodies. Such standard descriptions as "finely diced" and "well beaten" take on new meaning when applied to ingredients such as lizard gizzards.

Encourage students to illustrate their recipes. Then post them on a bulletin board featuring a witch and various creepy characters standing over a bubbling cauldron. Label the display "What's Cooking?"—*Kathy Lowe, Fayetteville, N.C.*

Halloween high jinks

Help your students let off steam by inviting them to act out silly or spooky Halloween scenes.

Prepare a collection of acting-out ideas and mount them on Halloween symbol shapes. Deposit the shapes in a plastic jack-o'-lantern, and ask for a volunteer to draw a shape, read the message aloud, and act it out. Or have the student keep the message a secret, challenging the rest of the class to guess the action.

Here are some acting-out ideas to get you started:

- Be the ghost of Miss Piggy (or Big Bird or a Teenage Mutant Ninja Turtle).
- Be Frankenstein's monster coming to life.
- Be a witch who's trying to decide on something *different* to wear this Halloween.
- Be a trick-or-treater on the day after Halloween.
- Be a ghost who gets caught on a bush while trying to scare someone.
- Be a clumsy Halloween cat who's trying to walk along a fence.
- Be a trick-or-treater who discovers something surprising (valuable, frightening, magical) among the treats.
- Be a ghost trying out scary sounds to make in a haunted house on Halloween.

The week *after* Halloween, why not ask your young actors to help supply you with fresh new act-outs for next year.—*Rebecca Webster Graves, Burlington, N.C.*

Halloween h(a)unt

Capture the spooky spirit of Halloween by sending small groups of children around the school in quest of unusual treasures. Prepare a list, with some of the following suggestions in mind:

- Find one cat's whisker; it looks like a broom straw.
- Find 6 inches of mummy wrapping; it looks like toilet tissue.
- Find two dragon eyes; they look like marbles.
- Find a lizard's tail; it looks like string.
- Go to the gym teacher and ask for a warrior's head; it looks like a helmet.
- Go to the cafeteria and ask for the secret potion; it looks like a packet of sugar.—*Sylvia Foust, Long Beach, Calif.*

Make Halloween history

Inject real life into your Halloween parties by having students resurrect historic personalities. Invite each student to select and research a well-known figure from the past; he should find out about the character's life, personal traits, and the style of dress for that period. Then students create costumes (from material brought from home along with your contributions) based on their research. Encourage students to use props to further identify their characters.

During your class party, invite students to talk about their chosen characters, or hold talk-show-type interviews with the various personalities. To add more challenge, have students arrange themselves in a "living time line," according to the dates their characters lived.—*Doug Siebert, Connersville, Ind.*

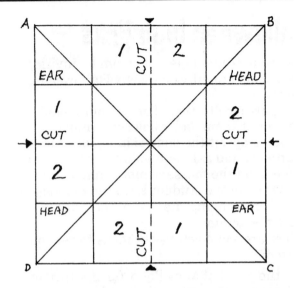

Cats on the prowl

For a Halloween project that's the cat's meow, invite your students to make fierce feline faces. You'll need black construction paper cut into 9 x 9-inch squares; scraps of green, red, and black paper; scissors; and glue. Have your students follow this procedure:

- Divide the paper into 16 sections by folding it in half four times, vertically and horizontally. Firmly crease all folds. Open flat.
- Make two diagonal folds by bringing corner C to corner A and corner D to corner B (see diagram).
- Number and label squares as shown on diagram.
- Cut between sections 1 and 2 on all sides.

- Working on one side at a time, spread glue on section 2. Glue the bottom of section 1 over the top of section 2. Repeat on the remaining sides, pushing outward on the center section of the square.
- Hold the "cat" with pushed-out center section down, corner points up.
- Again, crease folds in "ear" points, then pull them to the sides.
- Pull one "head" point over the other and secure with glue.
- Cut green eyes, red nose and tongue, and black whiskers for face. Glue in place.

Suspend the cat faces from the ceiling with black and orange paper chains.—*Alma B. Sanderson, Albuquerque, N.M.*

Monstrous messages

When spook season takes over your class, capture the mood with this creative writing project.

Arrange for a collection of mysterious letters to arrive, signed by a variety of scary characters: Frankenstein, Count Dracula, the Wicked Witch of the West, Marley's Ghost. You can send an individual letter to each student or a few letters to the whole class. Either way, the letters should contain a problem or question that needs an answer. Here's an example:

Dear Jennifer:
Halloween is getting closer. But I have a terrible problem, which you MUST help me solve. Each day I'm getting weaker. My batteries are running low. How can I get recharged. Please write back quickly with your ideas.

Monstrously yours,
Frankenstein

Provide a monster motif mailbox in which students can deposit their replies.—*Judy Hatfield, Romney, W.Va.*

The pumpkin curriculum

Plan now to make the most of your toothy Halloween jack-o'-lantern, beginning with a scientific scooping-out ceremony.

Encourage your students to investigate and discuss what comes out of the pumpkin as you prepare it for carving. Ask them to suggest different uses for the seeds and pulp (both can be used for food; seeds can be used in games and art projects).

Light a candle in the pumpkin, replace the lid, and demonstrate the fruit's use as a lantern. Discuss the candle's need for air, and point out how air gets in through the eyes, nose, and mouth openings.

Before the pumpkin passes its peak, help students measure its girth and weigh it, recording the statistics. Then place it on a pie tin or dish and put it in a sunny spot. Have students predict what will happen to its size, shape, and weight in 2 weeks. Have them record their predictions.

Compile a list of vocabulary words—such as *disintegrate, compost, deteriorate,* and *recycle*—that students can use to describe the pumpkin's organic breakdown. Provide magnifying glasses for observing mold.

After 2 weeks, measure and weigh the pumpkin's remains. Have students record the measurements and compare them with the original ones. Recycle the pumpkin by chopping it up, mashing it, and burying it to make compost. Mark the spot. In the spring, dig up the composted soil and use it for a planting mix for some pumpkin seeds. —*Jean Stangl, Carmarillo, Calif.*

Ghostly graveyard

As part of your Halloween activities, try this framed paragraph project.

Ask everyone to think of a favorite inanimate object—such as a toy, game, or doll—that's been broken or destroyed. Then have them complete a framed paragraph about the object (note the useful phrases italicized in the example below).

Here lies the remains of my portable radio. *Born on* Easter, *died on* September 30, 1987. *Whenever we were together,* I would listen to songs, news, and weather reports. *The last time we were together,* we were on a boat *when suddenly* it got splashed with an unexpected wave and gurgled its final sound. *The next thing I knew,* it *was dead. I will miss* my radio *because* it always gave me good music and entertainment. *Farewell old friend.*

Mount the paragraphs and appropriate illustrations on cut-out tombstones, and post them on a bulletin board.—*Tom Bernagozzi, Bay Shore, N.Y.*

Halloween costumes

Here's an activity you can try in early October when many kids are starting to plan their Halloween costumes. Ask your students to think of the ideal Halloween costume and then write a poem about it. For example:

I want to be a big fat witch
'Cause all the rest are skinny,
And wear my daddy's big black
boots And scare the pants off Jimmy.

Next, have your students illustrate their costumes on large white drawing paper. After they print their poems under their illustrations, display the finished pieces in the hallway so everyone can get into the Halloween spirit.— *Glenn Coats, Flemington, N.J.*

Going batty

These origami bats are easy to make, and they'll be quite at home hanging around your room this time of year. For each bat, you'll need a 6-inch square of black paper. Then follow these steps:

- Fold the square in half, corner-to-corner, to form a triangle. Press the crease firmly. (Figure 1)

- Open the square. Then fold it in half, this time putting the already-creased corners together to form a triangle. (Figures 2 and 3)

- Open the square and see how the fold lines cross at the center (E). (Figure 4)

- Pinch at E, pushing triangles AEC and BED inward as you flatten triangles CED and AEB against each other. (Figures 5 and 6)

- Fold the flap with point D toward the center so that there's a vertical line from E to D. (Figure 7)

- Fold the flap with point C toward the center so that there's a vertical line from E to C. Lines EC and ED meet in the center of triangle AEB. (Figure 8)

- Fold point E down ½ inch over the flaps to make the bat's head. (Figure 9)

- Hang the bat from points C and D. Attach the bat to a branch or a perch made out of a rolled paper cylinder.—*Barbara New, Pittsburgh*

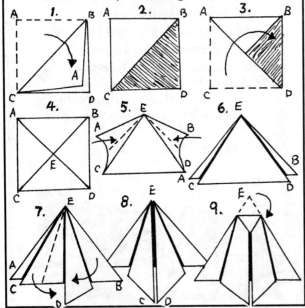

Boo!-tiful stories

To give your students practice with prepositional phrases, challenge them to trace a ghost's travels around a haunted house.

Have each student draw or paint a haunted house, preferably a cutaway view showing the house's interior. When the illustrations are complete, have students describe on paper the wanderings of their own personal ghosts. Every sentence should begin "My ghost..." and include a verb and prepositional phrase: "My ghost flew up the chimney." "My ghost slithered behind the dresser." "My ghost sulked beneath the sofa." Challenge students to see how many sentences they can think of without using the same preposition twice.

After a reasonable time, have your students make ghosts out of tissue and place them in one of the spots mentioned in their sentences. Then invite students to share their stories, complete with dark, dramatic readings and sound effects.—*Bettie Weber, Houston*

Harvest wreaths

You and your students can celebrate nature with these harvest wreaths. You'll need a large collection of seeds and grains; good choices are pumpkin seeds, sunflower seeds, rice, acorns, and dried corn kernels. You'll also need a paper plate for each student and liquid glue.

To make the wreaths, have each student cut a circle out of the middle of a paper plate. Next, the students put a small puddle of glue on one section of their plates and place an assortment of seeds in the glue. They finish the wreaths by working around the plate, section by section.

When the wreaths are dry, add a bow made from construction paper or yarn. Hang them in your room for a harvest display.—*Marilyn Doner, Syracuse, N.Y.*

Countdown to turkey

Giving your students a set of countdown activities will make the pre-holiday period fly. Here's how.

On your bulletin board post a large turkey—with eight removable tail feathers. Number the feathers one to eight and key them to special activities, such as:

    1. Put a list of Thanksgiving dinner foods in alphabetical order.

    2. Read a Thanksgiving story.

    3. Write a thank-you note.

    4. Decode a Thanksgiving message.

    5. Write a story about a surprising Thanksgiving visitor.

    6. Make table decorations.

Each day, starting 8 days before the holiday, invite a student to pluck the appropriate feather to choose the day's activity. Then all students follow the instructions. For Day 8, cook up something really special—such as a cupcake treat or favorite game—to end the holiday countdown.—*Donna Milanovich, Coraopolis, Pa.*

TURKEY NOTES

Talking turkey

Have your students celebrate Thanksgiving by sending each other turkey notes—a custom that originated in Davenport, Iowa, in the 1890s. What are turkey notes? Here are some examples:

> *Turkey red, turkey blue,*
> *Don't end up*
> *In a stew.*

> *Turkey green, turkey yellow*
> *Turkey says*
> *You're a fine fellow.*

To make turkey notes, ask your students to write a verse (following the pattern above) on a 3 x 5-inch card. (They can sign the verse if they wish, but turkey notes traditionally are anonymous.) Each student then rolls up his card in a colorful tissue or construction-paper wrapper that extends beyond the card at both ends and then secures the wrapper with tape.

Students can finish off their turkey notes by cutting the ends of the wrapper to make fringes. Use ribbon, yarn, or string to tie the ends and attach a name tag for the receiver. Students can store the notes in a specially made classroom mailbox until the day before Thanksgiving, when they're distributed.—*Evelyn Witter, Milan, Ill.*

Ring in the holidays

Have your students follow these steps to make napkin rings for a special in-school holiday meal or as gifts:

    1. Gather felt in assorted harvest colors.

    2. Cut some of the felt into 6 x 1-inch strips.

    3. Make a loop with each strip by overlapping the ends about one inch and gluing together.

    4. Use other pieces of felt to make designs, such as pilgrim hats, Indian feathers, or turkeys.

    5. Glue one design to each ring.

—*Marilyn Doner, Syracuse, N.Y.*

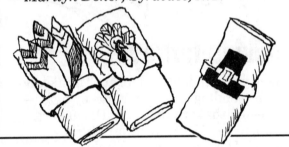

Thinking about Thanksgiving

Keep your students on their toes with Thanksgiving brain teasers:

- Describe 10 ways to catch a turkey.
- How many ways can you use a wishbone?
- Which fictional or real-life characters would you like to see as balloons in the Thanksgiving Day parade? Why?
- Suppose the *Mayflower* had landed in Florida rather than in Massachusetts. What would the Pilgrims' lives have been like? Write a journal entry describing a typical day.

Write one brain teaser on the board every day, and your students can make the most of those few extra minutes between lessons or when they've finished an assignment.—*Sylvia J. Foust, Long Beach, N.C.*

Turkeys in disguise

Spark your students' imaginations with this holiday activity.

Copy on the chalkboard these lines from "If Turkeys Thought," a poem by Jack Prelutsky: "If turkeys thought, they'd run away/A week before Thanksgiving Day."

Next, ask your students to pretend that turkeys *can* think. Have them draw a turkey, then create a disguise that will keep it hidden from hungry humans on Thanksgiving.

Finally, have your students select the most original, funniest, most effective, and best disguises. Display the poem and all the disguised turkeys in your classroom.— *Marilyn Borden, Bomoseen, Vt.*

A thankful tree

Help your students appreciate the true meaning of Thanksgiving with this project. Give each student a colored construction-paper leaf. Then invite everyone to write on his leaf one or two "I'm thankful for" ideas. Attach all the leaves to a giant paper tree displayed on your bulletin board.—*Wendy Vogt, Claysville, Pa.*

DAY	1	2	3	4
1 PARTRIDGE	1	1	1	1
2 DOVES		2	2	2
3 HENS			3	3
4 BIRDS				4

40 maids a-milking

Inject holiday fun into charting and calculating by using that song of gift-giving gone overboard, "The Twelve Days of Christmas."

First, post the words to the song, then have your students chart the number of each gift given day by day, with totals for each day and a grand total for the 12-day period. You might work out a chart as a class—or allow your students to work independently.

Then, use the chart to pose further problems:

- What's the total number of all gifts given on day 1, 2, 3, and so on?
- What's the total number of gifts given over the 12 days? (364)
- Which gift boasts the largest total? (Six geese on 7 days ties with seven swans on 6 days.)

Encourage students to go further and design graphs—perhaps pictographs—showing all the gifts received on each day. Invite them to devise their own puzzlers for each other, such as: If every goose lays two eggs a day, how many eggs would pile up by the end of the 12th day? (336)

Some students might even be interested in researching and calculating the cost of the effusive gift-giving.—*Craig Dickinson, Orono, Me.*

Holiday letter exchange

The holiday season is a fine time to introduce letter-writing skills. After describing the parts of a letter, ask the kids to write to a parent, Santa, or anyone else they choose. Then explain the proper way of writing an address and have the kids make an address book that includes each child's address.

Several days before winter vacation, invite each student to pick a classmate's name out of a box. Then each child composes a letter to the person he's chosen. Letters might include plans for the upcoming vacation or hopes for the New Year.

After the letters are composed, each child looks up his recipient's address and writes it on the envelope. Then you check the envelopes and award each letter writer a stamp. Mail the letters as soon as school is out for the holidays.—*Donna Anderson, Spencerport, N.Y.*

Santa work bags

Just before the holidays, when kids are so hard to steer toward any kind of work, get them to steer each other.

During the week before vacation, invite each student to prepare a Santa "work bag" for a secret pal—whose identity won't be known until the last morning of school. Into the bag go things to do: review questions (for which "Santa" must also prepare an answer key), puzzles, cartoons, original dot-to-dot pictures, and the like.

Post guidelines so that the work bags will have similar contents. For example, you might have each student create five math computation problems, five math word problems, five dictionary questions, five sentences to finish and punctuate, five map questions, and so on.

On the big day, hold a name drawing and distribute the Santa work bags.—*Janet A. Lundquist, Burlingame, Calif.*

The gift of giving

Here's a holiday activity your students are sure to enjoy. Ask your class to think of a present they'd like to give someone special.

Then have them turn their gift idea into a story that starts, "If I were a gift...." Include in the story who gets the gift and how the person would enjoy it. For example:

> If I were a gift, I'd be a shiny blue-and-white bowling ball with big finger holes. My dad would roll me down the lane, and I'd get strikes for him every time.—Chris

Have your class illustrate their stories, then display them in the hall for other classes to read and enjoy.—*Tom Bernagozzi, Bay Shore, N.Y.*

Gifts for the world

Guide your students to think creatively about those less fortunate—and fill a bulletin board with their warm holiday wishes for the world.

As you talk with your students about their holiday plans, steer them toward considering people in their neighborhood, town, country, and the world who won't enjoy as happy a holiday. For example, they might think about those who are ill, homeless, hungry, or at war. Ask each child to decide on a specific group he'd help if he had unlimited resources, and the gift he'd give that group. Perhaps he'd give parks and playgrounds to inner-city children or a cure to AIDS patients.

Then, invite your students to design construction-paper "package" cards for their imaginary gifts. On the inside of the cards, they should write their gift-giving messages. They can decorate the covers to resemble gift-wrapped packages tied with bows. Gift tags or glued-on stickers should name the intended recipient and the gift giver.

With the bulletin board display complete, your students can enjoy opening the "packages" and reading each other's gift ideas.—*Mary E. Modlin, Tarboro, N.C.*

Floating messages

Looking for an easy holiday gift your students can make? Have them follow these simple directions for a message mobile:

- On a piece of cardboard, draw and cut out a holiday symbol, such as a Christmas tree, an ornament, a Star of David.

- Use your cardboard as a pattern to trace several of the shapes on holiday wrapping paper and an equal number on construction paper. Cut these out.

- Paste each construction-paper shape to a wrapping-paper shape, with a piece of yarn running between them and holding the mobile together (as shown). Tie a loop at the top.

Students can write a special message on the construction-paper side (one word to a symbol), such as "I love you, Grandma." They could put a picture of themselves on one symbol.—*Marcia Schmidt, Green Bay, Wis.*

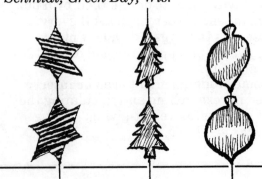

Happy holiday traditions

After sharing a personal holiday tradition with your class, invite your students to talk about some of their holiday traditions. Then, ask them to write a paragraph about one thing their family does every year. Let them do the assignment at home, and encourage them to discuss it with family members. Along with the assignment, ask them to bring a special keepsake that represents their tradition to class (for example, a picture of their grandparents, a favorite Christmas ornament, a Chanukah menorah).

Finally, have your students read their traditions aloud.—*Carolyn Wilmot, Northford, Conn.*

Holiday parts of speech

Parts of speech take on an air of festivity when students use them to describe a collection of holiday pictures.

Cut out from calendars and magazines pictures showing seasonal or holiday scenes, and display them on a bulletin board. Ask your students to list all the nouns they find in the pictures, including proper nouns. Then have the kids describe the nouns with appropriate adjectives. Their lists will now include phrases such as, "burning candles," "glittery ornaments," "frosty windows."

For work on prepositions, have students each choose a picture in which to "hide a gift." They'll have to describe where the gift is hidden, using a prepositional phrase: "under the table," "next to the fireplace," "in the sleigh." Next, have students incorporate their prepositional phrases (and noun phrases, too, if they like) in sentences or rhyming verses that celebrate the holiday season. Display the pictures with their accompanying texts, or let the kids take them home to show.—*Mary Tynan, Marlboro, Mass.*

Gift ideas for parents

Besieged by their children's requests for trendy gifts, parents might appreciate suggestions for gifts that would be suitable to each child's skills and interests. With a little research, you can compile a list and then choose five or six ideas for each student.

The possibilities for gift ideas might include some of the following:

- Fine motor coordination: mazes, jigsaw puzzles, children's carpentry tools, art materials (drawing pads, felt-tip pens, clay), craft kits, building sets
- Language arts: books or story records (suggest titles or themes for particular children), word-building games, magazine subscription, diary or blank book for journal writing, children's cookbook
- Math and science: inexpensive calculator, compass, protractor, calendar, indoor/outdoor thermometer, planting kit.

Send the gift ideas home with each student (in a plain sealed envelope to discourage curious eyes) or mail them. Be sure to enclose a brief cover letter assuring parents that the ideas are meant to be helpful suggestions, not mandatory purchases.—*Pixie Holbrook, Middlefield, Conn.*

Presidential sentiments

This activity will add a presidential flair to your Valentine's Day celebration.

First, have students research U.S. presidents, including their families, hobbies, physical appearance, and so on. Then, ask each student to pick a president and create a valentine for that president to give to someone special—or vice versa. Messages may be serious or funny but should provide clues to the president's identity. Clues may also be "hidden" in the artwork of the valentine or on the envelope.

Collect the valentines and plan a guess-the-president session.—*Shirley T. Shratter, Pittsburgh*

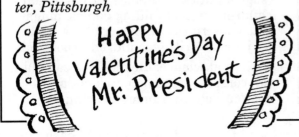

Dear John...

This project combines Valentine's Day romance with creative thinking to reinforce your students' letter-writing skills.

Invite each of your students to choose a famous couple from history or literature. Then, writing as one of the sweethearts, the student composes a letter breaking off the relationship. For instance, students may choose to be Romeo writing to Juliet (or vice versa), John Smith writing to Pocahontas, Marie Curie writing to Pierre, Victoria writing to Albert, Tom Sawyer writing to Becky.

To add authenticity, students should research the quarreling couples—their period in history, significant events in their lives, or in the case of literary pairs, other characters in their stories.

As a follow-up activity, have students respond to the "Dear John" letters in the recipient's voice.—*Trudy Whitman, Brooklyn, N.Y.*

Valentine word hunt

Valentine greetings, sight-word review, and a treasure hunt—this activity combines all three.

First, prepare a list of sight vocabulary words that need review, enough words for one per child. Then, for each of your students, make two construction paper hearts, one large and one small. Choose a word from your list and write it on both hearts.

On the backs of the large hearts, write a valentine greeting to each student, including in your message the vocabulary word that's printed on the face of the heart. Hide the large hearts around the room; give the small hearts to your students, and explain that each student has a special valentine message hidden somewhere in the room. To get his message, each child must check the word on the small heart and go out looking for the large heart that has the matching word.

When students find their valentines, they may read the messages to you and may choose to share them with others.—*Susan Doyle, Weippe, Idaho*

Valentine verses

Your students are sure to enjoy sending these valentines to special adults.

In *A Bunch of Poems and Verses* (Clarion/Seabury Press, 1976), poet Beatrice Schenk de Regniers claims that she likes her valentine more than "pork chops, potato chips, or chocolate candy." Ask your students to follow her example by writing what they like their own valentine "more than." Have them design cards for their sayings, then encourage them to give the finished cards to a school staff member (the nurse, custodian, aide, building secretary, crossing guard), a new neighbor, or someone at the local fire or police station.—*Bonnie Douglas, Norfolk, Va.*

Pulling on heart strings

This project will provide dozens of dancing hearts for your Valentine's Day party—and your students do all the "work." You'll need red construction paper, white drawing paper, felt-tip pens or crayons, glue, a paper punch, and string cut into 8-inch lengths.

For every letter in his name, give each student one piece of red paper (about 4 x 5 inches), one piece of white paper (slightly smaller), and one 8-inch piece of string. Then, have your students follow these instructions:

• Cut out a heart from each piece of red paper.

• Cut out a smaller heart from each piece of white paper.

• Write the letters of your name on the white hearts, one letter on each.

• Glue each white heart onto a red one.

• Punch a hole in the center top of the mounted letter heart and another hole in the center bottom.

• Use the string to link the letter hearts in their proper order so they hang in a vertical chain.

When students finish their name strings, divide the class into groups and give each group several wire hangers. Challenge each group to create a balanced mobile using their name strings. Encourage students to experiment with sliding the string back and forth to accommodate the different weights of longer and shorter names. They may add blank hearts of various sizes to balance the mobile.

Suspend the mobiles from the ceiling, and your room is decorated for the big day.—*Connie Connely, Catoosa, Okla.*

Heart-y calculations

Don't miss a beat during Valentine week. Circulate the following heart facts and sample problems to your students as special math challenges:

• A child's heart beats about 90 times each minute. How many times will it beat during math class? While you sleep? In 1 day?

• During periods of exercise, the heart pumps 35 quarts of blood each minute. How many cups, pints, gallons are pumped during the time you're in gym class?

• Every minute, the heart pumps blood through 60,000 miles of blood vessels. Calculate the distance for 1 second, 10 seconds, 45 seconds, 2 hours.

• A blue whale's heart beats about 6 times each minute; an adult human's heart beats about 70 times each minute. Compare the number of beats after 5 minutes. After 1 hour.

• The human heart is about $\frac{1}{200}$ of the total body weight. Calculate the weight in ounces of the hearts of an 8-pound newborn baby; a 236-pound professional football player; a 429-pound sumo wrestler; and the world's heaviest man, who weighs 1,300 pounds.

Encourage your students to make up their own problems based on facts of the heart.—*Karen Hansen, Doylestown, Pa.*

Mending broken hearts

For a break in the Valentine's Day bedlam, try an activity that involves challenge, cooperation—and absolute quiet.

You'll need one construction paper heart for each of your students. The backs of the hearts must be different from the fronts; an easy way to accomplish this is by making two-layer hearts—white on one side, red on the other.

Divide the class into groups of nearly equal size. For each group, prepare an envelope containing the same number of hearts as members in the group. Before distributing the envelopes, cut each heart into five pieces, using different cutting patterns for each.

Give each child five heart pieces from his group's envelope. Challenge each student to put together a complete heart. Group members may give pieces to others in their group, but no one may take or ask out loud for a needed piece. *Oral communication is off limits.*

If you like, declare as the "winner" the group that gets its hearts together first.
—*Alison Wilbur, West Caldwell, N.J.*

Valentine similes

Introduce similes and metaphors on an occasion when kids are likely to use them—Valentine's Day.

Propose that the class make homemade valentines for display rather than personal giving. First, discuss how traditional valentines often make comparisons—sweet as sugar, pretty as a picture, eyes that shine like stars. Encourage students to point out that all these comparisons contain the word *like* or *as*.

Next, talk about valentines that make more implicit comparisons—without the use of *like* or *as*. For example, "You hold the key to my heart" (the key is probably love) or "My heart soars when I think of you" (heart is compared to a bird).

Ask your students to each think of several similes and at least one metaphor—original ones, if possible—to write on homemade valentines. Provide construction paper, lace or paper doilies, glitter, ribbon, and other decorative materials for making the valentines. When the cards are finished and the similes and metaphors printed inside or out, mount them on a bulletin board.—*Paula K. Holdren, Louisville*

Hearts for sale

When your students create valentines to sell to the whole school, they'll get a lesson in economics as well as in art.

The first step is to advertise. Students need to let the rest of the school know about their plan before the local shopping mall sews up the business. A few large, colorful posters strategically placed should do the trick. Then students go into production. The valentines should be somewhat standardized. Perhaps offer three sizes of hearts, which students can trace from templates. Students can be creative in decorating the cards, writing verses on the inside of some, leaving others blank. Sell each size for a different price (15¢, 20¢, and 25¢).

A few days before the sale, have students help you set up a display. When the selling begins, students get practice in making and counting change—and also get a boost in self-esteem knowing that their project involves the whole school. You might plan to use the proceeds for a class Valentine's party.
—*Sunny Dixon, Suffolk, Va.*

Cupcake calendar

Try this easy idea to help keep track of students' birthdays.

Cut out 12 cardboard cupcakes, each about 3 inches high and 4 inches wide. Label the "frosting" of each cupcake with a month, and color each with a different-colored felt-tip pen. On each "cake," write the names and birth dates of your students born in that month.

Post the cupcakes on a wall or bulletin board. Create a tagboard candle that you can move from month to month to tell you at a glance whose birthdays are coming up.—*Carole J. Hefflinger, Yakima, Wash.*

Birthday booklets

For a quick-and-easy birthday celebration, invite each child to write a letter to (or draw a picture for) the birthday boy or girl. Collect the messages, create a construction-paper cover, and assemble the pages into a booklet. Present the birthday child with his take-home memento.—*Susan Terrill, Cuba City, Wis.*

A real gift

Looking for a different way to celebrate birthdays? Give the birthday child a "gift certificate" entitling him to one night free from homework. Tell him he can cash the certificate in anytime during the school year. Periodically, pick a child with a summer birthday and surprise him with the gift.—*Diane B. Misko, Abington, Pa.*

Meet our birthday mates

Make student birthdays even more special by including famous visitors.

Create a "Happy Birthday to You...and Who Else?" bulletin board that features a large birthday cake. Beneath the cake, write the date of the current month's student birthdays. Beside each date, write the celebrant's name and the name of a noted person who shares the same birthday. (Get these from almanacs or day-by-day references such as *Chase's Annual Events.*)

Have students research their birthday mates, and when their birthdays arrive, introduce their famous birthday partners to the class. Observe vacation-time birthdays when no other birthdays occur.—*Sandra J. Frey, Lancaster, Pa.*

Books for birthdays

Make birthdays special with books instead of—or along with—cupcakes. Encourage parents to donate to the class library a copy of one of their child's favorite books and inscribe it in honor of his birthday. Or allow the birthday child to select a book of the day, and when you read it to the class, dedicate the reading to him.—*Lee Farnsworth, Troy, N.Y.*

News of their day

This activity will motivate your class to read and analyze front-page news—and will foster interest in historic and current events.

On each student's birthday, present him with a copy of the front page of the newspaper that came out on the day he was born. (You can copy these from a library's microfiche file.) Also give the student a copy of the front page from the current day's paper. Invite him to read both front pages to the class. Discuss the events of both years. What was happening on the earlier date? Are similar things happening now?—*Tom Collette, El Granada, Calif.*

Birthday twins

For a birthday activity with a math focus, challenge your students to find as many birthday twins as they can. First, explain to your students that birthday twins are people who share the same birthday. Then, have them take a poll to find out how common this phenomenon is. Here's what students should do:

1. Ask several people when their birthdays are.
2. Count how many people you asked before you got a birthday twin.
3. Record that number on a class chart.
4. Compare your results with what others found. What's the average number of people asked?

There's more than a 50-50 chance that students will find birthday twins in a group of 30 people. How do the class results agree with this? Are there any birthday twins in your class?—*Denise Lee, Springhouse, Pa.*

Happy birthday to all!

Children with summer birthdays miss out on the fun of being classroom king or queen for a day. So plan a birthday party at the end of the school year to honor them.

First, decorate the room with a special bulletin board. Make large birthday candles from construction paper, each inscribed with a student's name and birth date. (Include everyone in the class—even those whose birthdays you've already celebrated.) Group the candles by months and title the display "Happy Birthday to Us!"

At the birthday party, give the students with summer birthdays the royal treatment with crowns, stickers, special privileges, or whatever is traditional in your room.—*Betsy Youngblood, Scranton, Pa.*

Chapter 11
POTPOURRI

Monster menu

Here's a grrrreat way to introduce new material, review lessons, and reinforce skills. Just invite your students to "feed" their work to a monster.

Make a monster from a large (the bigger the better) piece of tagboard. Then, using drapery hooks, attach under the monster a lunch basket or pouch with a "Feed Me!" sign on it. Each day, place a note next to the monster stating what he'd like to gobble up that day. For younger students, the message might read, "I'm hungry for foods that grow on trees." For older students, a menu mandate could be "Look through the dictionary and feed me three words you think no one in the class knows."

Students feed the monster by putting their assignments in the lunch basket. You might want to keep magazines, catalogs, picture dictionaries, and other helpful resources nearby.— *Penny Moldofsky, Media, Pa.*

All-purpose activity table

Try this novel idea for an activity table to get maximum use from puzzles, workbooks, and activity sheets.

Cover a classroom table with a sheet of clear plastic. Insert puzzles and worksheets under the plastic. Then, invite students to work directly on the plastic, using water-soluble felt-tip pens. For erasing, keep a small bottle of water and toilet tissue nearby. Make a handy container for the toilet tissue by decorating a 2-pound coffee can, cutting a hole in the center of the plastic lid, and pulling the paper through the hole.—*Mary Elliott, Laurel, Miss.*

Chalk it up

Don't overlook the abundant teaching possibilities of one of your more obvious tools—the chalkboard.

- **Study board.** Encourage students to use one section of the board to write out spelling words or math problems for review. Provide a yardstick so that students can rule an area of the study board to practice penmanship.

- **Game center.** Chalkboard games can range from a coded message greeting students as they arrive in the morning to a goalpost and football decorating the "scoreboard" for a review game involving any subject.

- **Message board.** Encourage your students to use a designated area of the chalkboard to leave personal messages and make general announcements. Older children might want to share a joke or comment on something of interest to all students. One rule: Students cannot write messages that would hurt or embarrass a classmate.—*Peggy Egan, Bridgeport, N.Y.*

Play ball!

Capitalize on the popularity of baseball cards by using them as the basis for a variety of learning station activities. Here are a few ideas to get you started:

- Put the cards in alphabetical order using the players' last names.
- Make a chart of the teams to which the players on the cards belong. List the name of each player under the correct team.
- Locate on a map the home states of the players. How many players come from the same state?
- Look at the batting records of the players on the cards. Which player has the most home runs for the past season? Which player has the greatest number of RBIs?
- Make a graph to show the heights of the players. Which player is the tallest? Which player is the shortest?
- After reading the cards, list three interesting baseball facts you've learned.
- Put the names of all the baseball teams in alphabetical order. In which cities do these clubs play their home games? (You might have to use references to find this information.)

Encourage students to suggest additions to the activity list.—*Cloe Giampaola, Baltimore*

Pick a project

All you'll need to keep early finishers busy are a shoe box covered with wrapping paper and one envelope for each subject area.

Label the envelopes, and in each one put several cards with directions for simple projects to be done by individuals, pairs, or groups. A card in the science envelope, for example, could contain directions for an experiment proving that a plant absorbs water through its roots and carries it to its leaves. An art card might instruct a student to draw a seasonal picture or illustrate a story read in class.

Change the cards in the envelopes every 3 or 4 weeks so that you can gear projects toward the current studies or season. Design a sign-up sheet that students can use to reserve a time to share their projects with the class. As time goes on, they might want to add project ideas of their own to the box.—*Wanda Mikkelson, Minot, N.D.*

Portable study carrels

Students who would benefit from a private work area can create their own study carrels. Start by bringing large, sturdy cardboard boxes to class. Then help students cut "U" shapes that remove one corner and most of two sides of their boxes.

The result is a stable, portable divider that can turn any desk top into a study carrel. Encourage students to decorate their carrels using pieces of colored self-stick vinyl.— *David B. Hakan, Ft. Scott, Kan.*

Sharpen your wits

You can turn sharpening a pencil into a learning experience by posting interesting facts and unusual bits of information just above the sharpener. Include newspaper and magazine clippings, provocative quotations, uncommon words with their definitions, cartoons—anything and everything that will entertain and enlighten. Change the clippings weekly and provide time to discuss entries. Invite students to submit items too.— *Susan J. Kreibich, Winona, Minn.*

"I want to know" place

This learning center gets kids asking— and answering— questions.

Place a large note pad or sheets of paper on a table and label the learning center "Things I Want to Know." Then stand back and watch your students cover the paper with every imaginable question. Encourage students to help each other answer their questions.

You might want to set up a procedure for the center, perhaps matching a questioner with a child interested in helping to answer the question. Encourage the two students to investigate solutions or find information using available resources. They might want to write up their findings or share them with the rest of the class.

Students might also wish to select some questions for an all-class search for information. Kids can bring in material from home or ask parents and siblings to contribute data.—*Robert N. Clegg, Darby, Pa.*

A use-your-senses center

Invite your students to investigate their five senses—one at a time—by designing a hands-on (eyes-on, ears-on) learning center. Each day, focus on a single sense and collect an intriguing array of items for your students to explore with that sense. Label the collection with the appropriate sense.

When students are familiar with the look-listen-touch vocabulary, open the senses center to a wider assortment of items—each labeled to indicate the mode of investigation. For example, you could label a butterfly, look; a flower, smell; and so on.—*Carole A. Kurtines, Miami*

Crowd control

You can easily control the number of students using book nooks and other learning centers by creating student tags for each center.

Use 2 x 3-inch pieces of ¼-inch Masonite to make the tags. On each one, print a letter that stands for the area—B for book corner, L for listening center, and so on. Drill a hole in the top of each tag, and thread a cord through the hole, tying it in a loop large enough to fit over a child's head.

For each area, make only enough tags for a manageable number of students. Establish the rule that only a student wearing a tag may use a special area. —*David B. Hakan, Ft. Scott, Kan.*

F.Y.I. collection

All you need is an imagination—and a tape recorder—to share with your students valuable bits of offbeat information.

First, gather background materials— magazine articles, booklets, pictures, souvenirs, postcards—about a particular item of interest, then prepare a tape that explains or describes the subject (the St. Louis Arch, Norman Rockwell, Laplanders, schooners).

Next, assemble your collection of tapes and accompanying visual materials. Catalog and sort the information packets in a specially set up "information center." Now, invite your students to hear about your experiences and "fact finds." If possible, provide a headset for private listening.—*Sandra J. Frey, Lancaster, Pa.*

3-D box displays

You can double your bulletin board space by transforming discarded appliance cartons into additional wall space. As a bonus, you'll pick up extra storage space, too.

Place a large carton (free from appliance dealers) in a convenient spot in your classroom, preferably so all four sides are accessible. Then, display newspaper clippings, student work, posters, or class projects on the four outside "walls"; use the inside for storage.—*Marilyn Doner, Syracuse, N.Y.*

Photographic memory

Before disassembling a favorite bulletin board, snap a picture of it and store the photo along with the pieces of your display. When you're ready to reuse the display, refer to the photo so you'll know exactly how it went together.—*Mary Ghisolfo, San Francisco*

Starched letters

Brighten your bulletin boards with fabric letters that won't fade or fray around the edges. Buy cotton fabric remnants (⅛ yard is enough to make a fair-size alphabet). Soak the fabric in full-strength liquid starch until it's well saturated; then hang it on a clothesline. When the remnant is dry and stiff, trace the letters onto the fabric and cut them out.
—*Pamela A. Kuchaj, Chicago*

Laying it on thick

Changing bulletin board displays is quick and easy when you mount all the paper backings at once, layering one on top of the other. Then when it's time to take down one display and put up another, simply remove the old display and its backing; the new backing is ready for decorating.—*Myron Flindt, Paradise, Calif.*

Is your b-board bare?

Keep two easy-to-make posters on hand and avoid "bare-board" embarrassment between bulletin board displays. You can use these again and again:

1. A simple TV shape with the message "Stay tuned for an important announcement" on the screen. Add a curly antenna made of aluminum foil for a bright finishing touch.
2. A "road sign" that says "Under construction."—*Joyce K. McShara, Putnam Valley, N.Y.*

Borders by kids

Involve your students in bulletin board production by inviting them to create the borders that frame your displays.

Give the kids squares of paper to use for drawing, coloring, or cutting out pictures related to a specific theme—perhaps a seasonal or topical one. Suggest a subject or let the students decide on one of their own. Working independently or in groups, students design and create borders for entire sections of the bulletin board.

When the pictures are ready, staple them along the sides of the bulletin board in a pattern. The result is a colorful, attention-getting border that kids will be proud to call their own.—*Karen Malin, Owatonna, Minn.*

Double duty

Don't just use your bulletin board for a display area, put it to good use by turning it into an "interactive" learning center.

Display maps, charts, posters, students' reports, or anything else that's packed with information. Tell students they'll be using the bulletin board to play a question-and-answer game in their free time. Have them make up questions from the posted material, write the questions on separate index cards, sign the cards, then post them on the bulletin board for their classmates to answer.

To answer a question, a student writes his name and the answer on a separate index card and takes it to the student who wrote the question. If the answer is correct, the questioner signs the card. Students can answer as many questions as they like.

Appoint a "secretary" to post scores on the bulletin board and keep them up-to-date. Students get one point for each question they write or correctly answer.—*Laurie Todd, Spring Valley, Calif.*

Write-on bulletin boards

Bulletin board displays won't lose their attraction as soon as students look at them if you invite your students to add input to the displays. Write-on bulletin boards can feature questions and riddles for students to answer; present pictures, quotations, or short articles for them to comment on; or call for suggestions about any topic.—*Sharon Fredman, Baltimore*

A sharing center

Turn your bulletin board—or a section of it—into a place where students can share ideas, knowledge, and goodwill.

Title the board "I Want to Share This with You" or something similar. Then invite kids to fill the space with favorite comic strips, original drawings, pictures of admired athletes and movie stars, birthday cards to classmates, favorite short stories, and the like. You might want to have a few guidelines, such as certain kinds of material be screened by you before going up on the board. Give students the option of signing or not signing their contributions.—*Cory D. Spears, Cypress, Calif.*

Class-ified ads

When you turn your bulletin board into a trading post for your students, classified ads take on a whole new meaning.

Invite students to post ads for items they'd like to trade— rabbits, baseball cards, toys, books. Encourage the kids to be imaginative in creating their ads—to say a lot in a few words and to include zany illustrations—and the trading post will be educational as well as useful.—*Ann Edmonds, Morrison, Ill.*

Tips on trips

Save time choosing and setting up field trips by creating a central file of tips for you and your co-workers.

Ask teachers to contribute information on successful field trips. Then, organize each trip's data in a separate envelope and categorize the envelopes according to subjects, such as colonial period, conservation, and so on. In addition to specific visitor information, the file could include local restaurants and other helpful hints.

If you'd like to expand the file, select a committee to track down information about new attractions.—*Suzanne Harrington, Spinnerstown, Pa.*

"Lookout Bingo"

This game is a quick and easy way to help organize a field trip and to lend a sense of productivity without spoiling the fun.

Set up bingo cards (five rows of five cells each) with content that will encourage students to use several senses as they explore. Or design the game to concentrate on only one sense. The cells describe (with pictures or words) objects, places, processes, even people for the explorers to find during their visit. Sample items might be a spider web, rough bark, a seed, a sign of erosion.

All cards may be alike, or you may list items and let students fill in their own cards randomly. To play, students mark their individual cards as they discover the various items. "Finds" in a straight line score a "Lookout Bingo."—*Charlie Rathbone, Burlington, Vt.*

Mark those landmarks

Traveling to your field trip destination can be as productive as the destination if you prepare a travel work sheet featuring landmarks along the way.

Find out the exact route the bus driver will take on your field trip. Before the trip, take the drive yourself, noting highly visible landmarks—a gas station, a store, a street sign, a billboard, an unusual house.

Write the various landmarks in spaces blocked along the perimeter of a worksheet. Add a few items students might see by chance—a certain number of people walking on the street, a person pumping gas, a friendly passerby who waves to them, a red light.

Before your departure, pass out copies of the work sheet and explain how the game is played. As the students locate the sights listed, they make a small tear in the appropriate box. The object is to find as many as possible of the people, places, and things listed on the work sheet before arriving at the field trip site. Children may work independently or as seatmates.—*Janet Diaz, Miami*

Surprise circle

To make time spent on show-and-tell more effective, have your students sit in a circle and keep their treasures behind their backs. This way, they won't play with what they've brought in, and since no one sees ahead of time what each child has, you add an element of surprise.—*Sandra Huth, Frederic, Pa.*

Tell-and-show

What happens when you turn show-and-tell inside out? You get tell-and-show, a game that will keep your primary students guessing.

Send small paper sacks home with your students, telling them to hide something inside that they'd like to share with the class. (You might want to enclose a note to parents.) Have the children prepare clues that tell about the hidden object.

At tell-and-show time, the class tries to guess from the clues what's inside each sack. When someone guesses the object—or when a predetermined number of incorrect guesses has been made—it's time to show.—*Lucy Stamper, Wever, Iowa*

Share and speak

If your students have outgrown show-and-tell but still enjoy bringing in things to share and talk about, why not upgrade the format to an "in-class experts" program?

Suggest that prospective speakers check in with you a day ahead to discuss their "guest lecture." Ask them to brief you on important points they want to make. Speculate together about what types of questions might be asked and how much time might be needed. At times, you could suggest topics for "guest lectures," and ask a team of two or three students to do some supplementary research and report to the class.— *Daniel Geery, Shelley, Idaho*

Pre-selected themes

By scheduling themes for show-and-tell time, you'll avoid the typical "bring-and-brag" shows. You can select themes that reinforce topics you're studying or promote personal growth. Here are some examples: a sign of winter, something from the ocean, a favorite book, my family, "I made it myself," a holiday tradition at my house.

Let your students know in advance when these are scheduled by posting a show-and-tell calendar. Get parents involved, too, by sending home a list of themes and dates every few weeks.— *Wanda Thurmond, Johnson City, Tex.*

Follow the golden rule

Substitutes can do a better job for you (and your students!) if you help them feel like professional members of your staff. Here's how:

1. Introduce yourself to subs and ask them who *they* are before you ask who they're standing in for. Offer help with school and district rules and procedures.

2. Suggest that your professional association include subs in workshops, seminars, and contracts. Encourage your administrators to provide substitutes with incentives and opportunities to improve their professionalism.

3. Leave complete and specific lesson plans. For example, if you're giving a reading assignment, note whether you want the material read aloud or silently. Leave an assignment for students to finish in class, so everyone feels productive.

4. Leave clear instructions about classroom behavior rules. List typical punishments and rewards.

5. Teach your students to respect substitutes as an important part of the school. Let students know that you expect them to perform well while you're away.

6. Let good substitutes know that you appreciate the job they do.—*Joyce Maloley, Kent County, Mich.*

Care package

Make things easier for substitute teachers by setting up a file now and adding to it during the year. You might include the following:

- daily school schedule and your classroom procedures
- names of teachers who come into the class to teach and students who leave the class to attend special classes
- seating chart and bus list, with notes on students with particular needs
- short lessons or activities that can be presented at any time
- names of aides and their schedules
- names of a few students who can be trusted to give accurate information to a substitute teacher
- a note to the substitute, asking how things went and what other materials should be added to the file.—*Denise Lee, Springhouse, Pa.*

Photo seating chart

You can easily provide substitutes (other classroom visitors too) with an up-to-date seating chart. Simply obtain a photo of each of your students and arrange the pictures in proper order—identified with names—on a piece of white paper.—*C.C. Dunmore, Wilmington, Ill.*

The parent place

You can help parents who visit your class by setting up a "Parent Information Center" inside the entrance to your classroom.

Post a list of classroom and school rules and your daily class schedule. As the school year progresses, add other items, including:

- copies of current notices and letters being sent home
- a calendar of meetings, events, and holidays
- descriptions of special projects your students have been working on
- class newsletters
- special awards students have received.—*Gloria Kilpatrick, San Bernardino, Calif.*

Yearly outline

Involve parents in their child's learning right from the start by sending home an outline of the year's curriculum. You might also send along related activity sheets in each subject area. Follow up on your yearly outline by sending out a weekly newsletter that explains learning objectives, upcoming assignments and tests, and special projects.—*Rosalind Wiley, Detroit*

Communication

To ensure that all your messages get home to parents, give each student a copy book for you and his parents to use. Students are responsible for bringing their books to class and taking them home every day, every week, or whatever. You write in the books brief messages to parents about their children's progress or about upcoming school events. Parents can use the books to respond to your notes.—*Terry Hallman, Sussex, N.J.*

Rolling along

Keep a Rolodex card file with a card for each student. As the year progresses, jot down positive and negative comments about each student's performance and behavior. Refer to the file whenever you need a quick update, such as during parent-teacher conferences.—*Peggy Bookey, North Pole, Alaska*

The daily news

You can keep parents well-informed by giving your students a hand in passing along each day's news.

Begin by inviting each child to design his own format for a daily newsletter to parents. The format might include sections headed "Special Events," "Humorous Happenings," "Something I Learned"— or whatever categories kids dream. Encourage students to design a decorative logo as well.

When the designs are completed, make several weeks' supply of copies. Then each day, students take a copy of one of the designs and write about some of what happened that day.—*Jeannine Underwood, Grand Rapids, Mich.*

Bake a batch of projects

For your next school bazaar, instead of baking brownies, collaborate with other teachers to create packets of do-at-home projects to sell to parents. Each teacher might provide a couple of pages relating to a specific area:

- **Art.** Projects using household recyclables: tubes, cans, foil; recipes for modeling clay, finger paint, dough sculpture; activity sheets designed for paper-folding constructions.

- **Math.** Ideas for number experiences in daily routine—counting, sorting, one-to-one relationships, measuring; activity sheets for construction of metric measures, geometric shapes; number games, puzzles, tricks.

- **Language arts.** Word hunts using the phone book, newspapers, magazines, catalogs; word games for family members to play together.

- **Social studies.** Ideas for family field trips— places and events of historic, economic, geographic, or career interest; map activities.

- **Science.** Discovery investigations with foods; making an electric answer board; tips about plants, feeding birds.

Coordinate the project to avoid duplicating activities and to achieve a good mix of subjects. You can compile separate packets for each subject area, or you might want to make some packets geared toward young children, others for older students.—*Loretta L. See, Belleville, Ill.*

Teacher-child conference

When you schedule a parent-teacher conference, also schedule a teacher-child conference. Such a conference can be reassuring to students who are worried about what you're going to tell their parents.

While the rest of your students are doing independent seat work, meet with individual children in a private corner or just outside the classroom. Discuss with each child what you plan to say to his parents, explaining grades as well as your comments.—*Florence Garnet, North Merrick, N.Y.*

Class video library

The next time you're planning a class play or other special program, ask the school media specialist or librarian to videotape the event. Then parents who couldn't attend can borrow the tape overnight.—*Myrna Ellison, San Antonio, Tex.*

Helpful "homework"

Many parents would like to help in the classroom, but just don't have the time. Here's a way to involve them. Send a letter asking parents if they'd like to participate—without leaving home. Describe the kind of help they can give: making games, cutting out letters, drawing banners or posters.

Then when you need help with a project, send a "Home-Aide Goodie Bag" home with the volunteer's child. Inside the bag, place project directions and all needed supplies, such as scissors, felt-tip pens, paper, and tape.—*Margie Rusnak, Menomonee Falls, Wis.*

Test paper tactics

Here's a quick and easy way to sent test papers home for parents' signatures. Prepare a folder for each student. On the front, put a sheet of paper with at least 20 horizontal lines. Divide the lines into four columns, and label them "Week Ending," "Number of Papers," "Student's Conduct," and "Parent's Signature."

Each Monday, send home the updated folders with the previous week's tests. Parents can check that the number of test papers inside is the same as what's marked on the folder. If a child gets a poor conduct grade, include an explanatory note inside the folder.—*Anthony Danile, Brooklyn, N.Y.*

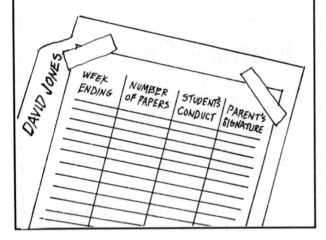

Conference openers

To start parent conferences on the right foot, begin each with a taped student interview.

When you've scheduled a parent conference, interview the student involved. Be sure to explain the format and style of the interview before you begin taping. You might also provide several sample questions for the student to consider ahead of time.

Start by introducing the student and giving a brief explanation of the interview to follow. Then begin the questions: "What do you like best about the school year so far?" "Which subject do you think is going to be hardest for you?" "Why do you think that subject is difficult?"

In preparing the questions and conducting the interview, avoid threatening questions or putting the student on the spot. To ensure a relaxed, easy session, develop a good mix of light and serious discussion topics.

The tapes can provide a point of reference for discussion. And because they can be entertaining as well as enlightening, they serve to open the lines of communication between parents and teacher.—*Pam Engel, Wabash, Ind.*

Chapter 12
END OF YEAR

Mind/body Olympics

This review—spread over several days—gives kids a chance to work off extra energy while they get ready for final tests and exams.

Prepare for two sets of Olympics by having your students help choose 10 mental and 10 physical activities in which they'll all compete.

The "Mind Olympics" could include a spelling bee, oral and written math computation, logic puzzles, and library skills. You might also try a "Curriculum Trivia Championship"—each student submits a question on a topic studied during the year. The winner is chosen in a round-robin question-and-answer session.

Intersperse these "games" with a "Fitness Olympics," held outdoors. Events might include short- and long-distance races, a baseball toss, a Frisbee throw, long jump, high jump, an obstacle course, rope jumping, and a basketball throw.

Plan an awards ceremony after the Olympics, and invite parents. Class artists can design posters announcing the celebration and ribbons for the winners. Don't forget good sportsmanship awards!—*Pamela Amick Klawitter, Mt. Nebo, W.Va.*

Student tutors

Add a pinch of the unexpected to the final weeks of school by "hiring" tutors from other classrooms.

First, discuss the plan with colleagues whose students might enjoy the challenge of becoming junior teachers. You could even post "Help Wanted" signs to attract attention. Then, arrange interviews to explain the task and determine the applicants' willingness to take on the responsibility. Hold an orientation meeting for tutors to explain the program and introduce the materials. These might include workbooks, flash cards, games, puzzles, and other supplies that junior teachers will be able to use after a little preparation.

When you have a list of tutors, make a folder for each recruit, naming his "students," the times of the sessions, and the subject areas needing attention. Keep a form in the folder for the tutor to record each meeting date and what was done. Be sure to recognize tutors with praise and other signs of commendation.—*Jo Ludwig, Knoxville, Tenn.*

Metric decathlon

To review metrics, measuring, and estimating skills, challenge your students in a metric decathlon.

First, students will estimate their performance before each event. Then, they'll perform the event and compare their results with their estimates. Award one point for each centimeter, gram, or milliliter difference involved. The person with the fewest points wins. Here are several events to get you started:

- **Potato jump.** Place a potato on a teaspoon and, with both feet together, jump forward as many times as you can until the potato falls. Measure the distance traveled.
- **Paper plane race.** Using a 10 x 20-cm piece of construction paper, create and fly a paper airplane. Measure the distance from takeoff to landing.
- **Paper-on-straw run.** Hold a 10 x 10-cm piece of paper at the end of a straw by sucking; walk until the paper drops. Measure the distance traveled.
- **Eyedropper exchange.** Using an eyedropper, move water from one container to another. Measure the amount of water moved in 2 minutes.
- **Popcorn throw.** Kneel on a line and toss popcorn into a bowl 2 meters away. Measure the weight of the popcorn in the bowl after 2 minutes.
- **Dried bean blow.** Place a dried bean at a starting line and blow it three times. Measure the distance the bean moved.
- **Blindfolded backward hop.** While blindfolded, hop backward three times. Measure the total distance traveled.— *Karen McGillivray, Salem, Ore.*

Looking ahead to next year

As your class approaches the end of the stay in your room, have them take a look at themselves—experts in coping at their grade level. Then ask them to fantasize about the next grade and try to picture the ideal "next-grader."

Finally, challenge students to translate their perfect student into a poster caricature of that ideal next-grader. Encourage your students to use their imaginations and senses of humor. They may want to follow the format that has arrows pointing to distinctive features. A student poster might feature a character sporting a trendy T-shirt, wearing big running shoes for winning recess races, and equipped with long fingers for passing notes.

Have students work individually or in small groups to create their posters. When the posters are finished, set up an exhibit and invite the real next-graders and their teachers.—*Jean Nietupski, Torrington, Conn.*

Big running shoes for winning recess races.

SUPER STUDENT

Long fingers for passing notes.

A word of advice

For an end-of-the-year letter-writing project, have your students share with the incoming class their expertise about the grade from which they're "graduating."

To begin, contact the class one year below yours and invite those students to write letters asking questions about the upcoming year. Pair each of your students with a younger correspondent, then have them respond to the letters—answering questions, giving information, and sharing insights and advice. Next, your students can write notes inviting the younger children to visit your room for a special event, such as a shared art activity.—*Merrill Watrous, San Francisco*

Keeping in touch

In the end-of-the-year excitement, it's easy to miss chances to speak individually with your students. Here's a way to prevent that.

Turn a corner of your chalkboard or bulletin board into a "Please See Me Sometime Today" board. Explain to the class that you'll want to talk briefly with those students whose names appear on the board. When the students come to see you, provide a compliment on recent behavior, a special certificate for improved spelling tests, a positive letter to take home, a newspaper article you thought they'd enjoy, an extra copy of a book you thought they'd like to read over the summer, and so on. Your students will enjoy the positive attention and will eagerly await their next message.—*Jule Marine, Salt Lake City*

Quick and easy yearbook

For an end-of-the-year activity that's sure to make a lasting impression, have your students create a bulletin board "yearbook."

First, ask each student to plan a personal yearbook "page" that will include four categories:

- Identification—the student's name, perhaps written in calligraphy or other fancy writing, and a photo or self-portrait

- Hobbies and interests—favorite TV shows, foods, music, rock stars, books, and so on

- Class memories—favorite (and not so favorite) subjects, outstanding moments, and so on

- The future—funny or serious thoughts or predictions; things students want to learn or do; illustrations of possible scenarios for coming years.

Explain to your students that they can use different colored pens, felt-tip pens, and crayons as well as magazine clippings, photos, memorabilia—anything that strikes their fancy.

When they have some ideas ready, have them divide a sheet of blank paper into four sections of varying shapes and sizes, then design their pages. Frame each page with construction paper and hang them on the bulletin board for an instant yearbook.—*Cathy Carroll, San Francisco*

Summer boredom beaters

Prompt your students to keep busy all summer by having them create a projects box full of ideas and activities.

Ask each student to search out a good-size sturdy cardboard box. Then have them organize it using cardboard dividers, file folders, even shoe boxes to keep projects separate.

Hold a brainstorming session to generate ideas for the contents of the boxes. Divide the class into groups and suggest to each a general topic to explore for summer project ideas. For example:

- **Food.** Choose a recipe and make something from scratch; set up a restaurant for a limited clientele—make menus, serve your customers.

- **Sports/games.** Organize a Summer Olympics in your neighborhood; set up a makeshift bowling alley in your backyard using milk cartons for pins and a large rubber ball; set up a file on your favorite sports star.

- **Garden/nature.** Plant and care for a vegetable or flower garden, keeping records of plant growth; make a study of insects—what and how they eat, what they look like; press wildflowers to use for art projects.

- **Woods/lake/beach.** Make sketches of various kinds of boats; collect shells and devise your own classification system for them.

- **Trips/vacations.** Conduct research to find places in your area that would make good family trips; make a file of on-the-road (or in-the-air) games and activities; collect maps, brochures, and postcards from your travels and file them in your box.

After each group has presented its ideas, call for additional contributions from the class. Then, have students compile "Summer Project Ideas" booklets to take home along with their project boxes.—*Patricia Budde, Douglas, Mass.*

End-of-the-year(book) tradition

Tempt your students to leave an indelible mark in your room by having them create a class yearbook.

Assign each student a page in the yearbook (a three-ring binder, perhaps). The page should reflect—through design, illustrations, and ideas expressed—what's important to that student. Students may include bits of memorabilia, such as student snapshots, baby pictures, names and perhaps photos of family members and pets, zodiac signs, hobbies, likes and dislikes. Encourage students to incorporate a favorite quotation or poem, a philosophical thought, or a statement of goals and aspirations.

Store the yearbook in your classroom for present and future classes to enjoy—and for next year's students to use as inspiration when they continue the tradition.—*Ann Elizabeth Edmonds, Sterling, Ill.*

Posters for next year

Entice your students into creating welcome posters for next fall's class by having them think back to how it felt to be starting the year in a new room, with a new teacher, new subjects, and new rules. Some poster topics might include: "How to Survive in Room 10"; "Holidays, Vacations, and Parties"; "Favorite Field Trips"; "Things I Learned."

After sharing and enjoying the posters—perhaps with a few nostalgic recountings of adventures past—put the posters away to become part of your opening-day icebreakers in September.—*Mary Alice Anglen, Columbia, Mo.*

The year that was

Your students will vividly recall their activity-packed school year when you ask them to choose and illustrate the events that were most important to them.

Ask each child to think of an activity or occasion from the last 9 months—humorous or serious, special or ordinary—that had significance for him. Then have each student write a headline that describes his chosen event—"The Day We Made a Tepee," or "Engine Company No. 9 Visits Our Classroom"—and below it draw a picture that brings the event to life. Display the illustrations on a bulletin board so everyone will remember at a glance what a wonderful year it was.—*Sandra J. Frey, Lancaster, Pa.*

Idea-a-day summer calendar

Encourage your students to be productive all summer long by helping them create a calendar of activities.

Hold a brainstorming session to collect summer activities. Encourage students to go beyond run-of-the-mill ideas (going to the movies or playing miniature golf). Here are a few suggestions to get them thinking in the right direction:

- Make a sandwich. Cut it in fourths.
- Pull 15 weeds in the garden. Count the leaves on each stem.
- Guess how many windows your house or apartment has. Count the windows. How good was your guess?
- Keep a list of things you see today that George Washington would have been surprised to encounter.
- Look for metric labeling. Give yourself 10 points for every metric marking you find today.
- Estimate what percentage of cars passing a certain spot during a set time will have only one person inside. Check your estimate.

Allow several days for collecting ideas. Provide a box for depositing students' suggestions. Make calendar grids for July and August, marking an activity in each box. Distribute a copy to each student. Or post the suggestions on the bulletin board and let students create their own calendars.— *Loretta See, Belleville, Ill.*